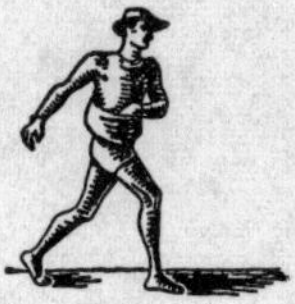

Supreme Court

A NOVEL BY

ANDREW TULLY

SIMON AND SCHUSTER • NEW YORK

THIS IS DON CONGDON'S BOOK

Although certain of this book's fictional conflicts may reflect actual issues involving the Supreme Court, none of the fictional justices has been patterned in any way after a real justice of the Supreme Court. In fact, all the characters in this novel are fictitious.

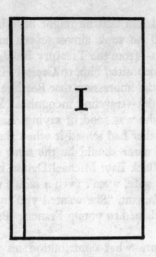

I

Mr. Justice Francis Copley Dalton of the Supreme Court of the United States had once merited a box on the first page of the Washington *Post*'s society section when he remarked at a Georgetown cocktail party that the Supreme Court building would have been a thing of joy to the ancient Romans—"at their decadent worst." He grinned at the passing recollection now as he walked briskly up the broad flight of marble steps to the double row of Corinthian columns which with icy solemnity guarded entry to the neo-classic temple. Well, he also had managed to become known as the Associate Justice who referred to this temple as "the old salt mine," and periodically some columnist would make passing reference to him as the only member of the Court who regularly used the public entrance to the building. It had honestly not occurred to him on that first day, two years ago, that walking up the steps would start a legend in the Washington press; now that the legend was whole, he rather enjoyed it and saw no point in dissolving it. "Anyway, it's good exercise," he had told Beatrice, and Beatrice had winked her saucy backstage wink and accused him of trying to set himself up as a tourist attraction in competition with the Washington Monument.

She did not remind him that he might have been satisfied with the mile-long stroll he took almost every morning while the Court was in session—from the Treasury Building, where the cab from Georgetown deposited him, to Capitol Hill. Sometimes Mr. Justice Dalton got the impression that Beatrice looked on him as a kind of matinee idol—traveling incognito. "You do have presence, you know," she was fond of saying. And Beatrice always insisted that his mother had sensed it when she ordered that her infant son's middle name should be the same as the fashionable square in Boston's Back Bay. Michael Dalton had been appalled; Copley, he told his wife, wasn't even a saint's name. But Bridget Dalton had been adamant. "She wanted you to be an aristocrat," Michael Dalton explained to young Francis. "Parnell wasn't good enough."

Francis wasn't sure what contribution his middle name had made to his career, but being an Irishman who could get along with the Italians was no hindrance in his swift emergence as the youngest governor in the long history of Massachusetts. Yet, knowing Bridget Dalton, he was sure that had she lived long enough to see her son go on to become Attorney General of the United States, and then the youngest member of the Supreme Court, she would not have hesitated to claim credit for her insistence at the baptismal font.

He was late; he'd barely have time to drop his hat and coat in his office before going on to the robing room. As he walked through the cathedral-like lobby of dead-white marble, he threw a wave and a brisk hello to Mac and Horace, the two Court policemen standing on each side of the red velvet rope athwart the entrance to the Court chamber. "A nice morning, Mr. Justice Dalton," Mac threw back at him, and he smiled, as he always did, and said, "Just fine," automatically. It was a fine morning, especially for January, but he was thinking not so much of the brave, thin sunlight as of how he could have used another hour in bed. It had been a good dinner at the Pratts' and he had been home only a little after midnight, but at forty-two Francis was still young enough never to be pleased with the hour of waking. He also was still young enough to be impatiently perplexed by the habits of the Court's oldest member, the cranky Angus Whitfield, who proudly arose at five o'clock every morning. Mornings, thought Justice Dalton, must have been more leisurely in the days when the Court convened at noon instead of ten o'clock.

He turned right, past the first half-dozen or so tourists—who'd have recognized his red hair had he not carefully kept on his hat —and in precarious anonymity hurried down the corridor to the private door of his suite.

Jake was standing in front of his desk, fiddling with some briefs. Jake was always standing in front of his desk when the justice arrived in the morning. Jake Moriarty knew how to save the boss's time.

"Hello, Jake," Francis said.

"Good morning, Mr. Justice." Jake Moriarty was in a hurry for his boss; Francis Dalton could tell that by the way Jake was using his hand nervously to try to smooth the unruly black hair that was always falling down over his eyes. Although a fat man, Jake liked to keep things moving; if you knew him, it did not seem incongruous that he had been a running guard on a pretty good Harvard football team.

"Well—I suppose you're suggesting that it's getting late, Jake," Francis said. He grinned as he took off his gray felt hat with the turned-up brim—a poor man's Homburg, Beatrice called it— and threw the hat and his black chesterfield on the brown leather sofa.

Jake's face stayed earnest. "Yes, sir, you've only got about five minutes, and I had kind of hoped you'd have time to look over some of the research I did on the Banks opinion."

"I know, Jake—it'll have to wait until this afternoon. But, Jake, we're on schedule, aren't we?" Francis Dalton was proud of the way he kept abreast of the heavy work load that had come to the Court with the Hughes administration.

"Oh, sure, Mr. Justice," Jake said. He could return the grin now, and he did. "You know me—I like to get a little ahead."

"I know you, all right, Jake," Francis said. "It's you married men who keep us bachelors hustling—no matter how late we've been out the night before. But you're not perfect, Jake—Sally tells me she has a hell of a time getting you up in the morning."

9

"Yes, sir, I guess that's right," Jake said. He was looking a little sheepish now. "But that's one of the advantages of married life. You don't need an alarm clock."

"I suppose I'll have to try it one of these days—if I ever get the time." Francis was moving toward the door. "But right now I'd better get going or Bacon will be giving me a black look."

"Right, sir." Jake Moriarty hurried over to open the door. "Good luck, Mr. Justice," Jake said, as he always said. "See you later, Jake," Francis said, as he always said, and he marched out the door and down the hall. He'd make the robing room with a minute or two to spare and that was good. Robert McNair Bacon, Chief Justice of the United States, was not only a crusty, narrow-minded old fool; he was also a stickler for punctuality. Another early riser, Francis reflected.

Everybody was there but Angus Whitfield when Francis reached the robing room and started down the line of oak-paneled lockers with their silver nameplates to pay obeisance to the tradition started by old Melville Fuller in the Gay Nineties. It was that Chief Justice's premise that if the justices shook hands with each other before every session of the Court, they might somehow manage to remain on speaking terms. Optimist, thought Francis, as he went down the line with his hand out—to tall, spare Hume, and roly-poly Gillette, Chief Justice Bacon with his white hair flowing back in waves and the cold blue eyes behind the pince-nez, the tiny, bald-headed and pink-cheeked Robson of Florida, Baker with the Rotary pin in the lapel of his blue serge suit, Mitchell, the cowboy from Nevada with the bourbon breath, and Feldman, from the sidewalks of New York, Wall Street division.

"Reckon I saw you at LaSalle du Bois the other night, Mr. Justice." It was the cowboy, Frank Mitchell, hearty and gregarious, a man who enjoyed what passed for fleshpots in provincial Washington.

"Ah there, Frank, nobody can hide from you." Francis' smile was real. You couldn't help liking Mitchell, despite his professional air of the barefoot boy. Mitchell was worth at least fifty million good oil dollars, and he had never ceased to enjoy his wealth.

"About time to get stirring," Bacon muttered grudgingly.

"Good morning, Mr. Justice," Hume said with the correctness that yet was always overlaid with grace.

"How are you, Mr. Justice?" the Rotarian Baker said in the boom practiced at innumerable back-slapping luncheons.

"Ah, Dalton," said little Robson, in intellectual absent-mindedness: "Hello, boy," said Gillette, his voice a puffing effort. "Morning," said the banker Feldman, frugally.

Jones, the Negro attendant, was standing ready at the locker whose open door bore the name Justice Dalton, and Francis turned his back and Jones slipped the robe on, adjusting it about his shoulders and giving it the three final little pats.

"Good morning, Jones," Francis said.

"Good morning, Mr. Justice," Jones said. Francis had never heard Jones say anything else. Jones was a man of dignity, and he wore his dignity aloofly, as though forbidding intimacy. "Jones doesn't approve of ol' Frank," Mitchell had told Dalton once. Francis could understand that.

Bacon was fretful. His enormous gold watch was in his hand and his lips were moving crankily.

"Where's Whitfield?" Bacon growled. He held up one finger to Jones, and Jones hustled over.

"Jones, get me a page," Bacon said.

Jones all but loped out the door, to return within a few seconds with a little boy in the traditional blue knickerbockers, blue jacket and black lisle stockings. It was Sammy Heller, and he had the habitual frightened look that went with a summons from the Chief Justice.

"Page, go to Mr. Justice Whitfield's suite and deliver a message for me," Chief Justice Bacon told him. "Tell Mr. Justice Whitfield the Court is about to convene and his presence is required."

"Yes, sir, Mr. Chief Justice," Sammy said—and fled.

This should be good, Francis thought, and he looked over at Frank Mitchell and was met by one of Mitchell's outlandish, exaggerated winks.

"Maybe he's got a date with a girl," Mitchell suggested with awesome irreverence.

Bacon turned to Mitchell. His icy blue eyes started at the top of Mitchell's head with its crew-cut frieze of salt-and-pepper hair and descended slowly to the cowboy boots with the high heels that Mitchell wore even with white tie and tails. Then, silently, Bacon turned away.

When the knock came on the door, Jones opened it immediately and little Sammy Heller blew in as though shot from a gun. He stopped about ten feet in front of Chief Justice Bacon.

"Well, boy?" Bacon's glare was like a punch on the jaw.

"Mr. Chief Justice, sir, Mr. Justice Whitfield—sir, he says to tell Mr. Chief Justice Bacon that Mr. Justice Whitfield doesn't work for him."

For a moment the silence was so complete it seemed to have substance, as though an immense hulk had suddenly shouldered its way into the room. Then it was broken by Frank Mitchell's voice.

"Jesus Christ!" Mitchell said.

Bacon seemed not to hear the explosive words. He was staring down at Sammy Heller like an avenging angel, his eyes frigid with rage, one arm half raised in furious reflex. My God, he's going to strike the boy, Francis thought, and in that split second's reflection he felt rather than saw Mitchell's slight movement next to him.

But as Sammy stood there, eyes wide and whole body trembling, Bacon merely glared his fury. And then, pointing to the door, he uttered two words. "Get out!" Bacon said, the words slapping across the boy like a whip. Sammy's mouth opened and his head bobbed crazily—and he fled through the door suddenly held open by Jones.

"Poor little cuss." It was Mitchell's voice again, and this time Bacon turned to the Nevadan, his upper lip curled back to show his big square teeth, his glare now heightened by a crimsoning at the cheekbones.

"Well, sir?" Bacon's voice was like the cut of an ax. "Do you wish to comment, Mr. Justice Mitchell?"

Mitchell's eyes turned with lazy casualness to the Chief Justice and for a moment the two men stood there, appraising each other in icy hatred. Finally Mitchell spoke, his tone soft even while his eyes stayed hard. "No," Mitchell said. "No—I don't think so, sir. I think perhaps I had better not." He turned to Francis. "I wonder if we can get this show on the road."

"Heavens, yes—let's get moving." The angry whine of a voice

belonged to David Benjamin Feldman, across the room. "This Court is getting to be worse than a grammar-school debating society!"

There was a general movement in the room, and Francis saw Hume, his face lined with concern, put out an arm and touch Bacon's shoulder lightly with a friendly hand. Bacon seemed suddenly to slump, to lose an inch or two of his height. He turned to Hume and suddenly his eyes had a sadness to them.

"Yes, let us go in, brethren," Bacon said.

And that was all. Robed and silent, the justices filed across the private corridor, Mitchell's hand touching Francis' arm lightly, Bacon looking straight ahead, Feldman mumbling to himself. They marched into the end of the courtroom curtained off with the huge maroon velours drapery, and Bacon immediately and mechanically gave the signal. They stood there, then, as the buzzer sounded from the marshal's desk beyond the drapery at one end of the bench, and the crier's voice came loud and clear as usual: "The Honorable, the Chief Justice and the Associate Justices of the Supreme Court of the United States!"

After what had happened, Francis half expected the curtain would refuse to operate, but automation proved unaffected by the robing room crisis. Unhesitatingly, the heavy drapery parted in three places and the solemn justices entered the courtroom in threes, by seniority. Or rather, in two groups of three and one of two, since Whitfield was still back in his suite, probably chortling horribly over his declaration of independence. As the spectators rose and the justices strode with determined majesty to their big chairs, the return to an air of normalcy was strengthened by the crier's austerely comforting announcement: "Oyez! Oyez! Oyez! All persons having business before the Honorable, the Supreme Court of the United States, are admonished to draw near and give their attention, for the Court is now sitting! God save the United States and this honorable Court!" Francis couldn't help wondering, as Bridget Dalton's son, whether the Deity was interested in preserving such a quarrelsome body.

Francis sat down, his eyes taking in the audience without seeing it. That had been a precious moment when little Sammy Heller had delivered Angus Whitfield's message to the Chief Justice. Francis held a hand to his face to conceal an intruding grin.

Whitfield, of course, had been well within his rights, if somewhat aggressive in his assertion of them. After all, a justice of the Supreme Court was a kind of sovereign state, an autonomous little one-man principality who was in no way beholden to the Chief Justice. The Chief Justice was merely a presiding officer, not a warden or an office manager. Moreover, Whitfield was acutely conscious of his prerogatives as the oldest member of the Court— all self-assigned, of course—and he had always shown his independence of Bacon. When Whitfield wanted to go fishing of a weekend, he always skipped town early, frequently stalking out in the middle of the Friday morning conference. There was nothing Bacon could do about it; as Whitfield had informed him through Sammy Heller, Mr. Justice Whitfield did not work for the Chief Justice.

Francis' mind continued to wander as Bacon, irritability coloring his face, spent willful moments going over some papers in front of him. Francis surveyed the huge marble courtroom with its high ceiling—forty-four towering feet above the mortals below it—and its two dozen practically genuine Ionic columns of Siena marble. And he recalled now, as he so often did, Beatrice's remark when she first had stood before this judicial temple with its great bronze doors and its look of a cut-rate Taj Mahal.

"Really, Francis," Beatrice said, "I think you justices should ride to work on elephants." The remark was honestly original with Beatrice; Francis knew she would not knowingly pilfer from the late Justice Harlan Fiske Stone, who had uttered the identical comment when that dignitary caught his first look at the building before its dedication in 1935.

His attempts to shake off the waywardness of his thoughts were helped by the traditional first business before the Court, which the books called "the admission of qualified lawyers to practice before the Supreme Court of the United States" but which Frank Mitchell referred to as "looking over the human sacrifices." There was young Tom Nelson, junior, stiff and solemn despite his blond, almost whitish, cowlick, and Francis succeeded in catching his eye as he stepped forward and by an eyelid flicker wished him well. It was Tom Nelson, senior, who had come to young Francis Copley Dalton's rescue during his last year at Holy Cross with a loan and the promise of a job that saw him through Harvard Law School, and if Mr. Justice Dalton could manage it he would in turn smooth young Tom's path. Not that young Tom needed much help; he had stepped into a junior partnership in a million-dollar corporation law business in Boston, and that tribe of Back Bay Brahmins named Nelson was about as self-sufficient as Boston's First National Bank, and considerably more genteel. Francis had never before been so warmed by the Chief Justice's practice of calling each new admitted lawyer by name and bidding him gracious welcome to the club.

But—it was Monday, and therefore opinion day, and suddenly Francis found Bacon looking down the bench at him, that habitual half-snarl twisting his lips. Francis' dreaming had carried him cozily right up to the moment when the stage was his for his delivery of the majority opinion in the case of the State of Alabama versus Adam Lockett. The case was cut and dried; the Court had voted seven to two to uphold the state in its insistence that the Negro Lockett had indeed incited his audience to riot by his obscene and profane demands that they arm themselves with clubs and march on the state Capitol in Montgomery to protest a new segregated housing project. There had been incidents at Lockett's trial, but none that had impaired the fairness of his trial. Of course, Bacon and Hume had dissented—in their maddening way—but their dissents were mild, almost apologetic.

Francis saw no point in reading the majority opinion, although usually he preferred to subject himself to the ordeal in order to place the emphasis where it was needed. But after handing down the opinion, he looked over at Bacon for the Chief Justice's nod, and added what he felt was a necessary postscript.

Looking down from the bench and past the rows of spectators to the marble pillars at the rear of the courtroom, he summed up, keeping his voice low. "This case involves the so-called Bill of Rights," he said. "Or it is alleged to involve the Bill of Rights. But the majority has found that nowhere in the state's prosecution of the case or in its confinement of the defendant was any basic right infringed. Indeed, there was such care taken by the state of Alabama in its conduct of the prosecution that it seems presumptuous for the defendant to suggest that any infringement of his civil rights was involved. With all the facts before the Court, the conclusion is inescapable that defendant's counsel has depended throughout on arguments that are tendentious and frivolous."

Francis looked down at young Tom Nelson and then looked away swiftly lest he smile at young Tom's open-mouthed attentiveness. That would do; there was no point in saying more. He had wanted to be sure the word frivolous was given the prominence it might not seem to have been given in a printed opinion which was the work of seven nit-picking justices, and he had done so with those few words. He would not make any speeches; it wasn't necessary.

He sat there, then, as the Court ponderously labored to hand down the other opinions, in other cases, that were the result of haggling sessions in the Friday conference room and long nights of brain-burning toil in office and home. Little Robson, of course, had to read every opinion he had a hand in, and his dissents as usual were sharp and sneering with sarcasm. And Baker, who loved the sound of his Chautauqua lecture-platform tones, would never miss a chance to orate.

But Francis was surprised when Hume did not read the majority opinion in the Highland case, still another of the civil rights matters that were clogging the Court's calendar. The vote was by the five-to-four margin with which the Court had legally heckled President Hughes almost from the moment he took office, and Francis, who had written a biting dissent, had expected a full-dress performance from the liberal Hoosier. In conference, Hume's arguments for the little labor leader had been long and unusually forceful, and Francis was sure he had carried the wavering Feldman with him to eke out the majority opinion that the state of Mississippi had violated Highland's right of free speech.

Now, however, with the spectators leaning forward eagerly, Hume disappointed them. Taking the whole courtroom in with a slow smile, the tall Hoosier moved his head in a slight bow and when he spoke his tone was mild. "The majority opinion speaks for itself," he said. "It would be pointless to try to decry its substance. But I should like to remind my brethren that this case concerns the Bill of Rights, not—as one of my brothers has remarked—the *so-called* Bill of Rights."

Hume turned slowly and looked at Francis, the little smile still on his face. Francis found himself smiling back, even as the old impatience surged within him. Oh, all right, Hume, Francis thought, go ahead and wave your precious Bill of Rights while anarchy runs amok in the streets. And yet once again Francis found the irritation Hume planted in him tinged with an honest respect and admiration for the Hoosier's calm appraisal of the law. He could not dislike such a man, even while vehemently disagreeing with him; he could only wish that he could get through to Hume's blind spot, to his weakness in arguing for what he called the "absolutes" in the Bill of Rights even when the invoking of them was a clear danger to the community. To Francis, those earliest congressmen were practical men who would be appalled at the frivolous invoking of the Bill of Rights against the interests of the state. While acknowledging that the Bill of Rights set forth certain freedoms, Francis considered it juvenile to assume that the founding fathers intended those rights to be used to tear down the community and the Constitution itself. Hume, he felt, refused to recognize that there were times of danger or times when the nation cried for action, when the community's welfare had to come before the rights of the individual.

Now, Francis noticed, Hume had leaned back in his chair with eyes closed as the plump Gillette settled into the droning tones of his concurring opinion in the Highland case. Francis knew Hume was listening intently, but his own mind continued to wander. In recent months he had found it harder to concentrate on matters immediately at hand, especially at such times as Gillette was pontificating in public, indecently exposing his Southern California mentality. His thoughts returned to his continuing disagreement with Hume, a man of whom he thought so highly. He could not believe that their disagreement was based merely on the fact that Hume was a liberal while he was a conservative. The labels didn't mean that much to either of them—despite the fact that he, Francis Dalton, had been carried to one political success after another by the conservative tide that had swept the country. It was more that Francis agreed with the President that, for the present at least, the times cried for drastic action and for the creation of a kind of national discipline to combat the mounting crises. He had had his doubts about the Walsh Act because he was uncomfortable with legislation that banned strikes and imposed compulsory governmental arbitration, but he had felt it was a necessary abridgment of rights under the circumstances—circumstances that constituted a national emergency without being formally called by that name. It had required considerable soul-searching before he had cast his vote with the minority when the Court invalidated the act, but he felt he had been correct in upholding a President's right to take measures in a critical moment of history to protect the whole community. With the Soviet Union threatening war if the President armed the German military machine with atomic warheads, the means of production had to be guarded against both irresponsible stoppages and the throwing of subversive monkey wrenches.

Well, Gillette was through, thank God, and that was that. The opinions hadn't taken so very long, after all. Francis leaned forward with his usual expectation as the Court shifted gears to begin the chore he always found exciting—hearing the oral arguments of the lawyers pleading their cases. Even when their performances were routine, Francis usually enjoyed them; they brought the Court out of its isolation and exposed it to the strident legalisms of the world of law outside its neo-Grecian palace.

Francis felt sorry almost at once for Sam Hyde as he opened the Williams case. It was an antitrust action against the little steel companies, and the raw materials were dull to start with, no help to a plodding lawyer like Hyde. Francis winced for Hyde as he stood there, his pot belly straining on the buttons of his blue suit coat, his fingers fiddling with the edge of the lectern, and sweat already gathering on his red face. And—my God! Sam *must* be in a funk—he was reading from his brief, although even the callowest law student knew the Court always scanned the briefs before hearing oral arguments. Francis looked over at Bacon as the Chief Justice's mouth opened, trap fashion.

"We can read, sir!" The trap snapped angrily at Hyde. "May we expect that you have an oral argument to present?"

Crimson stained Hyde's face as he looked down from Bacon's glare and hurriedly closed the folder on the lectern. A giggle rose from the spectators, stilled immediately by Bacon's glare, and in the new hush Hyde plunged into his presentation. Francis was relieved to find that he was fairly well prepared, after all, until suddenly the steel lawyer interposed a lucid line of argument Francis knew was not in the brief.

This time, little Henry Clay Robson pounced on him, his thin lips prim. "Yes, yes," Clay told him in his caustic squeak, "we admire your thought, sir, but your thought unfortunately is not in your brief."

Francis glanced over at Hume. As usual, the Hoosier's face was sad with the sympathy he felt for the lawyer, the human being showing beneath the judicial dignity. Francis knew Hume was waiting for a chance to make Hyde feel more comfortable, and it came immediately as Hyde stumbled on with a valid point about price-fixing that Francis could approve but which Hyde managed to state badly.

"Ah—excuse me." Hume's soft voice interrupted the lawyer. Hyde looked up at Hume, already grateful because he had been noticed by the gentle, courteous jurist.

"As I understand your argument, sir, you are making the point that this particular price was not fixed, in an unlawful sense, because it was provided for in a previous contract," Hume said.

Hyde sighed happily. "Yes, Mr. Justice. That is my point."

From that juncture, things went better for Hyde as his voice took on a more relaxed tone, but Francis noticed he was being carried away by the new force of his arguments. He would have given anything to signal the lawyer when it became obvious that Hyde was paying no attention to the little red light on the lectern, which warned him that his time was up.

"Sir!" Bacon's voice broke in. "Do you suffer from color blindness?"

Hyde looked up at Bacon, his eyes wide. He was incapable at this point of saying anything lucid, but somehow he managed a mumbled "Yes—ah—thank you, Mr. Justices." Then he picked up his brief and, almost literally, fled the lectern.

Francis felt Mitchell's hand on his arm and bent an ear to the Nevadan's whisper. "If I know Hyde," said Mitchell, "he'll never come in here again without a couple of stiff hookers of bourbon."

That case finally disposed of, Francis poked Mitchell. "Now it's Bob Dodge's turn," he said. "And look at him, will you!"

Dodge, an Assistant Solicitor General, for the first time had come to the Court in the cutaway coat traditionally worn by the Solicitor General and his staff. Francis regarded Dodge as a hard-working but uninspired lawyer, and he expected Mitchell's comment.

"By God, his backside's better dressed than his mind," Mitchell whispered.

Francis looked over at Hume and found him regarding Dodge with an affectionate if apprehensive eye. Hume had once delivered a series of invitational lectures at Columbia Law School, and Bob Dodge was one of the students who had listened to his distilled wisdom. A year ago Dodge had made his first appearance before the Supreme Court and had delivered a series of arguments very near the worst ever heard in the chamber. Hume sought out Francis after the case had been heard and reported that Dodge had approached him to renew old acquaintance and had asked how Hume liked his presentation. "I was somewhat embarrassed," Hume said, "but I told him I had found it interesting. He thanked me and said he'd hoped I'd liked it because he'd argued it just the way I'd taught him."

Now Henry Clay Robson was already giving poor Dodge a hard time, peppering him with questions overlaid with judicial irritability. Dodge's case was a good one, but as usual he was presenting it poorly, and Robson could not tolerate legal incompetence. As Francis kept a furtive glance on Hume, he was rewarded; Hume interrupted to put a kindly question to Dodge and then a second and then still a third. Characteristically, Hume was attempting to bring out the facts that obviously were there and should be brought out in fairness to the government, but Robson was annoyed.

"I thought *you* were arguing this case." Robson's remark to Dodge was like a dagger thrust.

Dodge's face reddened, then he managed a smile. "I am, Mr. Justice," he replied, "but I sure can use all the help I can get." Even Hume had to smile at that, and Bacon's swift glare failed immediately to quell the tittering that ran through the spectators' section and overflowed into the one hundred seats in the press area. Francis saw Mrs. Richard McKnight Evans sitting in the reserved box with dainty handkerchief to her smiling mouth and reflected that despite the Olympian façade the Court presented to the public, it was most human in matters pertaining to its social opportunities. Not only had the grim, austere Bacon seen fit to give Molly Evans her own box in the chamber, but the celebrated hostess's limousine was parked regularly in a reserved space in the justices' private garage and she was a member of that exclusive club eligible to use the justices' private elevator. Sometimes it seemed to Francis that the justices performed with considerably more floridness when Molly was in the house. At such times, Bacon was even more the stern patriarch-jurist and little Robson's wit was sharper.

The case was another in the long series involving the refusal of officials of the militant Sons of Slaves to answer questions about their political affiliations before the House Un-American Activities Committee. Franklin, a minor Michigan functionary of the Negro organization, had been charged with contempt by the committee after standing mute before charges that he was a Communist. Dodge was awful; Francis might agree with his argument but he was appalled by his presentation. Yet it was Hume, who surely would vote for the defendant, who kept intervening to help Dodge out of his confusion. Ironically, too, Francis found himself impressed by the argument of defense counsel, the perceptive, penetrating Sam Sharfman, who brought into the chamber the same ability to sweep aside the inconsequentials that had gained him fame in his appearances for murder defendants.

Sharfman was talking now in his low yet penetrating tone, pleading his case and yet also demanding the justices' favor. "If the Court please," he was saying, "is it to be the case in this country from now on that a person may not take a public position contrary to that being urged by the House Un-American Activities Committee? If he does so, must he understand that he will be subpoenaed to appear at a committee hearing where he will be questioned with regard to every minute detail of his past life, where he will be asked to repeat all the gossip he may have heard about any of his friends and acquaintances, where he will be accused of membership in the Communist party, where he will be held up to the public as a subversive and a traitor?"

There was a pause, and then Sharfman continued, almost sadly, "I should note here that the charge linking the defendant Franklin was made by a paid informant and, according to committee practice, the defendant was not permitted to examine the informant. And yet almost everyone in public life—including members of the Supreme Court—have been accused of being Communists." Another pause, for a muted titter from the spectators. And then, "If the Court please, I suggest that this means that government by consent will disappear and will be replaced by government by intimidation—merely because some people fear this country cannot survive unless Congress has the power to set aside the Bill of Rights at will."

Sharfman was good, Francis was thinking—good, but wrong. Sharfman insisted on missing the point. The point was not a question of human liberty but of the Communist party's efforts to manipulate and infiltrate organizations in the United States with the purpose of overthrowing the government. Sharfman refused to face the fact that no government can tolerate revolution, and certainly the Constitution did not preclude the Congress from halting preliminary steps toward that revolution and punishing those responsible. Besides, a Constitution which only a court can save can no longer be saved. Francis was proud of his calling, but he believed deeply that judges were too far removed from the emerging forces of society to overrule them on matters of grave national interest.

He *did* enjoy listening to Sharfman's finely honed legal phrases, and yet as the justices filed through the curtain's openings for lunch, Francis felt himself welcoming the break. Sharfman *was* wrong, but it was depressing to acknowledge the telling power of his points—and to realize that the Court almost surely would throw out the contempt conviction by another of those maddening five-to-four majorities. It was the kind of case in which both Bacon and Hume would cite their Bill of Rights "absolutes," and although Feldman and Baker and Gillette would argue with less force, they would go along. And Francis was just as sure that Mitchell and Whitfield and Robson would join him in holding for the government.

In the justices' private dining room, hardly acknowledging Baker's booming "Sit down, Francis, sit down," Francis slumped into a seat and waited for his lamb chops. He was only faintly conscious of the usual hearty conversation going on between Baker and Gillette, seated across the table. When his food came, he discovered he was not hungry, and after a couple of bites of chop he found himself sitting there staring at his plate.

"What's the matter, Mr. Justice?" Francis was suddenly aware of Baker's locker-room bellow in his ear. "You look as if you just swallowed your lamb chop the wrong way."

Francis managed a small grin, hoping that Baker wouldn't pound him on the back.

"I guess I'll live, Mr. Justice, " he said. Casually, he fabricated an excuse. "I just remembered I forgot to pay the maid last Friday."

Baker was irrelevantly chatty, waving the sports page of the *Post.* "I see where the Senators picked up that pitcher, Lawson, from the Yankees. That should give us another fifteen wins this year. I tell you, this may be the year."

"Right," said Gillette across the table. He was having chocolate cream pie for dessert again. Where did the man put it? He paused to swallow a chunk of the pie, then continued. "We've got Lawson and we've got that new shortstop, Miller. Now if we can just do something about that fellow Rogers who falls all over his big feet in right field."

Francis glanced down to the end of the table where the ascetic little Robson was toying with a small plate of fresh fruit and cottage cheese. He saw Robson's thin, pointed nose wrinkle and could almost hear the sniff. "Baseball!" whispered Robson, disgust framing his pursed mouth. He put down his fork, dabbed at his lips with his napkin and got up to go.

"Take you to a game sometime, Henry," Baker shouted in a half-chortle. "Be good for your blood pressure. Put apples in your cheeks." But the door was closing on Robson's back.

Francis managed to swallow another piece of lamb chop and put down his fork. Sitting for two hours in the courtroom had made him restless; he would go in and look over Jake Moriarty's research on the Banks opinion and then take a little walk.

"Bad for your digestion to rush like that," Baker was saying as Francis got up. Francis smiled and waved a hand and walked out.

Jake walked in from the outer office just as Francis was sitting down at his desk.

"I was just going out to find you, Mr. Justice," Jake said.

"Harry Weiss just called from the White House. He'd like you to call him back as soon as you can."

"Harry Weiss," Francis said, his tone absent-minded. "I wonder what he wants."

"Yes, sir," Jake said. "That is, he didn't say what he wanted. Shall I get him for you?" Like most law clerks, Jake Moriarty was impressed with nothing that was not concerned with the Supreme Court, but he knew of Francis' close relationship with the President and therefore he tendered Harry Weiss his proper importance.

"Yes, get Weiss," Francis said. He stood up and let his eyes mechanically sort out the papers on his desk. Weiss was often a difficult man to talk to, because he was always so fretful about the state of the country. Well, it was a worrisome job being a faceless, highly intellectual assistant to a President of the United States as intellectual and volatile and dynamic—and as adored—as John Alden Hughes. The whopping majority in November had meant only one thing to the Philadelphia aristocrat in the White House—that the people wanted him to go ahead with his program, and devil take Congress and the Supreme Court of the United States. Even in the excited affection that always suffused him when he thought of John Alden Hughes, Francis reminded himself that that would take some doing.

"He's on the line." Jake held out the phone to him, and Francis took it, still standing.

"Harry, how are you?" Francis said. "Don't tell me you want me for that damned Bankers' Association again?"

"Francis, I'm glad I caught you." As usual, Harry Weiss's voice sounded gloomily ominous, as though he had the unpleasant duty of announcing a national catastrophe to an irresponsible populace. Harry Weiss would not have time to be amused by the gag about the bankers, whom Mr. Justice Dalton had turned livid with his casual innuendoes. Harry Weiss had seven children and he was a skier. He also ate yogurt.

Weiss hurried on, as though determined to stave off any further attempt at frivolity. "The Boss would like to see you after work tonight. Can you be here at seven? At the Mansion, not the West Wing."

"Yes, sure," Francis said. Did Weiss expect him to say no, he had tickets to a striptease show? "Uh, Harry . . . any idea what's on the fire?" For Weiss's sake, he managed what he hoped was a judicial clearing of the throat before putting the question.

"Nope. The Boss didn't say. Just told me to call and ask you to come around with some other people. A bull session, he said." Weiss's voice was that of a man who wanted to get back to his work.

"Oh. Oh, fine, Harry." Francis supposed he should be thankful that for once Harry Weiss didn't want to prolong the conversation with a long discussion about the miseries of the migrant workers in Texas. Weiss sounded almost—nervous. "Good enough, Harry," Dalton said. "I'll be there."

"Fine," Weiss said. "G'bye, Francis." And he hung up.

Francis felt a prick of excitement at Weiss's call. Despite Harry's seeming impatience and gloomy tone, it was evident that whatever was on the fire at the White House had the quality of urgency; for once, Weiss had not encouraged Francis to inquire about his troubles with Congress. Either Weiss knew what was up and was himself too excited about it to risk confiding it prematurely, or he didn't know and was bursting to get on with the business of finding out.

If Harry Weiss didn't know now, he would have to be let in on the secret soon; the President would be foolish to tackle any important project without Weiss's assistance. Francis supposed that Harry Weiss was the best lawyer he had ever encountered, or worked with, and he had emerged as much more than that since slipping quietly into his purposefully faceless role at the White House. Weiss was faceless as far as the general public was concerned, but his features by now were well known to the gentlemen on the Hill, with whom he had earned the reputation as the shrewdest negotiator—and manipulator—to represent a President since Harry Hopkins.

Francis often wondered how much of the glory should be passed along to Harry Weiss for the coup engineered by the young Attorney General from Massachusetts at The Hague. Francis had been only three months in the Cabinet when he earned the title of "The Man Who Made the Reds Pay Up," and he knew he could not have managed without Harry Weiss's help. Nobody had expected Francis to succeed in the assignment given him so casually by John Alden Hughes, the assignment to force the Soviet Union to pay its United Nations dues, and Francis himself would have settled for a propaganda victory. But with Harry Weiss maneuvering behind closed doors and confronting the Russians with a kind of polite blackmail, they had pulled it off. In such ways, Francis reflected, do young Irishmen from Massachusetts achieve sudden fame.

Francis had supposed the President had been too busy lately with the business of giving nuclear warheads to Germany to be concerned about any matter on which a Supreme Court justice's counsel might be sought. Hughes was going to have a sticky time with Congress on that one. And on the civil rights mess. And on the White House's efforts to push through an industry-wide shiftover to automation to catch up with the Russians' war production.

Well, there was one way he might find out what was in the wind. He had to call Charlie Mayborn anyway about that Omaha dinner, and perhaps the Attorney General would know something. When Hughes had something up his sleeve, his old campaign manager usually knew about it. Francis wished the President wouldn't call them bull sessions. It made him sound like an insurance salesman.

Francis sat down and dialed Mayborn's private number, and as the number rang, he leaned back in his chair and put his feet up on the desk. Mayborn answered the phone himself, as he often did, in order, he explained, "to find out what's going on around town."

Francis managed to sound casual as he put some questions to Mayborn about the Omaha dinner, but the Attorney General's voice seemed amused. Suddenly, Mayborn tackled him.

"Francis, you didn't call me just to talk about Phillips and Adams," he cut in. "I know you pretty well. I suppose you've heard from the White House."

Francis grinned into the phone. "Well, yes, I have. If you know me so well, Charlie, tell me what it's all about. You know how curious I am."

Mayborn's flat, Midwestern laugh cackled on the line.

"Good. I finally got you pinned down." The Attorney General paused, a man who was enjoying the conversation. "Well, Francis,

I don't know for sure a helluva lot more than you do, but I can tell you this: It wouldn't surprise me a bit if the Boss came up with a plan to take care of those senile old fools who sit on the bench with you."

WELL, BY GOD, it *is* a jack-o'-lantern. In January. Mr. Justice Dalton was sure now as he turned in from Pennsylvania Avenue and nosed the Corvette up against the iron gate of the northwest entrance to the White House grounds.

It was the McCoy, too—a huge orange pumpkin with buckteeth and gleaming eyes—and it was hoisted on one of the iron spikes at the top of the gate. The White House policeman in his trim blue overcoat was grinning widely as he came out of the little white booth, and when he opened the gate he did so carefully, to maintain the pumpkin on its high perch.

As Francis started to pull into the driveway, a small figure detached itself from the shadows around the guard booth, a figure that in the fuzzy gloom had the appearance of some kind of woodsy animal on its hind legs.

"Stick 'em up!" Suddenly the small figure had a silvery pistol in one hand, or paw, and was moving with the mincingly menacing steps of a television gunman toward the Corvette. Francis' laugh was a small explosion as he braked the slowly moving car to a stop and leaned over to stick his head out of the window on the passenger side.

"Don't shoot! Don't shoot!" Francis hoped his tone was an authentic whimper. He saw now that the small figure was dressed in what appeared to be a dog costume, with a silver star on its chest and the dog-face mask slightly awry.

Through the mask came a giggle and a thin voice. "It's all right. Don't be really scared, Mr. Justice. It's me—I mean it's I —Bounce."

Francis opened the passenger door and John Alden Hughes III, four years old, slid in onto the seat beside him.

Francis took the small tendered hand and grinned at the mask. "Well, Bounce, you really scared me. I thought it was a holdup."

"Well." Bounce seemed uncertain. "Well, I guess you did at first—at the very first. Even if it isn't Halloween. I guess you didn't expect to be held up—here."

"I certainly didn't." Francis reached over and plucked at the badge on the small chest. "What's this, Bounce? Are you a policeman?"

The boy's voice was tinged with disgust. "A policeman? Of course not. Can't you see—I'm Deputy Dog!"

"Deputy Dog?" That's what comes of being a bachelor, Francis thought swiftly; it must be some television cartoon character. "Oh, of course, Bounce. I didn't really mean policeman. Anybody can see that you're a deputy."

"That's right." Bounce was instantly mollified. "Deputy Dog. He's tough—I mean, I'm tough."

"You certainly are, Bounce. I'm glad you turned out to be a friend of mine."

"Well, I am, I guess. At least, I know you and you know Dad. I guess that makes it all right. Say, can I ride with you to the house? I never rode in a Corvette."

Francis leaned over and patted Deputy Dog's head. "Sure you can, Bounce. Hold on, now."

They made it to the North Portico in one short, gunned-up spurt, and as the car jolted to a halt with screeching brakes, Bounce was shrieking his delight. Then he settled back in the seat as Francis edged the car into a parking space along the driveway.

Bounce was out of the car before Dalton had turned out the lights. "Thanks, Mr. Justice," he yelled. "Thanks very much. I've gotta go and scare Martha." And by the time Francis got out of the car, John Alden Hughes III had—literally—bounced up the broad marble steps and into the Mansion.

That is a pretty good boy, Francis thought as he followed Bounce up the steps under the huge brass-trimmed lantern which hung gracefully from the high ceiling of the portico. He's going to be all right because his father and mother are letting him and the two girls use the White House as a home. His sister Sheila had written Francis that she had seen a picture of Bounce, eleven-year-old Barbara and seven-year-old Martha "playing in the yard," and that is what the White House grounds had become since the Hugheses moved in four years ago—a children's play yard. He wouldn't mind having a boy like Bounce and a couple of girls like Barbara and Martha someday. He knew Beatrice would go along; she was always saying she had the hips for it. It had pleased him when Beatrice told him she had never wanted children with either of her two husbands. Or, as she put it, "My dear, they just didn't seem adequate to the job." Well, *he* was adequate; he was sure of that. At least, in the bed. You had to start there. He was glad Beatrice's show was finally closing tomorrow; now she could come down to Washington for a while.

"Good evening, Mr. Justice." Adams was holding the door open with one hand and reaching for Francis' hat with the other. "The President is downstairs, in the library."

"Thanks, Adams." Francis let the elegant Negro butler help him off with his coat. "I've just been playing cowboy with Bounce."

"Yes, sir, he just raced through here looking to frighten Martha." Adams shook his head, happy but properly dignified as befitted a fond servant.

President John Alden Hughes was sitting in an armchair in one of the far corners of the knotty pine library, with his long legs stretched out on the magazine-strewn coffee table. He was a man who would always be comfortable, Dalton thought as he paused at the door. Hughes's shock of thick, black hair was combed on the side, but here and there were the usual unmanageable little tufts. He was wearing black horn-rimmed glasses— the kind with half lenses for reading—his red-and-blue rep tie was loosened at the collar and his gray flannel suit was rippled with wrinkles. The book in his hand looked like one of those beige-bound volumes from a law library.

"Good evening, Mr. President." Francis was walking into the room as he spoke.

Hughes looked up over the half lenses and let the book drop to the floor, as he swung his legs off the table and got to his feet.

"Mr. Justice Francis Copley Dalton, I'm glad to see you, sir." The big-toothed smile was there now as Hughes strode forward and grasped Francis' hand. "I *am* glad to see you, Francis. You look fine. Red-cheeked and vigorous, sir." The charm was on.

"Thank you, Mr. President," Francis said. "I feel pretty vigorous. It's the atmosphere around here, I guess."

Hughes's grin took over his whole face. "Atmosphere is right. You should get hazard pay for coming here. I tripped over Bounce's tricycle coming down the hall a few minutes ago. Did you happen to run across Deputy Dog on your perilous route?"

Francis laughed. "Yes, he held me up at the gate. I paid him off with a ride up the driveway in the Corvette. He keeps Halloween late, doesn't he?"

"Yes. You know how it is—there was this big pumpkin in the kitchen and he and Barbara requisitioned it and carved it up. But come over and sit down, Francis."

They walked over together to the chairs in the corner, with the books untidy on their shelves on the wall to the left, and Francis sat down in a chair on the other side of the coffee table.

"I haven't been in this room for a long time," Francis said. "The books look as if they're getting read."

"Yes. Oh, this is a reading family. Better at reading than doing chores. I'm usually in the upstairs study at this time of night, but Liz has a flock of artist types in the house and they're all over the family quarters."

"She's done wonders in the last four years," Francis said. He meant it. Mary Elizabeth Hughes had given the White House a new warmth and gaiety.

"Yes. Yes, she has. Liz knows her business. She's done a good job on the kids since we moved in, too. Francis, how is life on the highest court in the land these days?"

31

"Pretty quiet lately, Mr. President. Mostly routine cases." Francis smiled a small smile. "Not as exciting as it was with some of that legislation you were interested in."

"No, damn them." Hughes was not smiling. But then this mouth relaxed. "Those old codgers really gave me quite a beating. I heard that at one point Mr. Chief Justice Bacon referred to me as 'that young squirt.' No, don't get nervous, Francis, I'm not trying to pump you." He grinned again. "Liz was horrified. She said to me, 'Why, you're an old man—you're forty-seven.' "

"That gives you five years on me—one of the old codgers."

"I could use some more *young* codgers like you on that bench." The President was thoughtful now. "Francis, I've about convinced myself that there's not much the administration can do with that five-to-four setup against us on the Court. We've had four acts ruled unconstitutional now, and the lineup has always been the same. That bunch seems determined to deliver us all to the Kremlin. They don't seem to understand that in a country as big and as strong as ours we have to keep pushing ahead with strong measures or we'll become undisciplined and weak."

"I'm afraid you're right, Mr. President. It's no fun agreeing with you, because until recently I kept thinking the Bacon group would see the light. But I'm convinced, too, that they're inflexible."

Hughes sighed, and then grinned. "I'm afraid the Court doesn't have many friends across the country these days. We're getting hundreds of letters a week demanding that something be done about it."

Francis grinned back. "I'm not sure that even you would be significantly successful in brainwashing people like Bacon and Hume."

"No." The President was solemn again. "I don't communicate very well with that liberal bloc."

Francis kept his tone light. "There's always the alternative suggested by those far-right organizations—impeach old Bacon."

"Damned fanatics!" Hughes's voice was irritable. "Those people are becoming an absolute menace to the solid conservative movement. All they want is newspaper headlines—and more dues-paying members. I'm trying to ignore them, in the hope they'll fade away, but their voices seem to be getting louder."

"That kind is always with us, Mr. President. On either side of center and sometimes—as is the situation today—on both sides. But I don't think you have to worry too much about them. And although I can never agree with Robert Bacon, it's nice to know that he's secure against that kind of attack."

The President waved a hand, as though dismissing the subject. "We won't waste time on them, anyway. Francis, I wanted you to come here tonight so we could discuss the situation. Mayborn will be along later, but I wanted a chance to talk to you first. But let's have a drink before we don our hair shirts. My throat is beginning to creak."

Hughes stood up and walked to the table against the book-shelves. "Dry Manhattans?" he asked. The President was proud of his dry Manhattans. "Fine, sir," Francis said. He could drink martinis anywhere.

The President brought the drinks over, one in each hand. "Consternation to the enemies of the republic," he said, and Francis said, "Right," and they drank.

"Francis, we agree that the five-to-four setup is a tough one to crack," Hughes said. "But can it be cracked? Or is it hopeless? I wanted to talk to you about it before I did anything else."

Francis took another sip of his bittersweet drink. "Well, of course, nothing's impossible. But for practical purposes I think you'll have to accept the fact that those five are immovable."

He held up one hand and started counting on his fingers. "Let's see—there's Bacon. I think we've got to mark him as hope-less. He's made of granite. He's not only impatient of opposing opinions; he's a hater, the kind of unrestrained hater whose hate is inflamed by continued opposition."

"Yes, he won't do," the President said. "And I tried, too. About three years ago I had him over here and I suggested, very diplomatically, that it might be a good idea, in these times, if we got together periodically so I could discuss my plans with him and find out how the Court felt about them before I went ahead."

"You did!" Francis' amazement was such that he momentarily forgot one did not interrupt the President of the United States.

Hughes was impatient. "Yes, of course I did. The damned old fool. And do you know what he said to me? He said the Chief Justice of the United States would not tolerate such a suggestion.

He said the only possible relationship between the executive and the judiciary was one of complete separation. You see, Francis, he wouldn't cooperate."

"Yes, I see," Francis said. My God! he thought.

"Well, that takes care of Bacon," Hughes said. "How about the rest?"

"There's Baker," Francis said. "He's so damned genial and hearty, he gives the impression of reasonableness. But he's just as tough as Bacon. He's one of those Rotarians, a railroad lawyer, a jovial country-club locker-room type, and yet he's always bellowing about police-state methods. I don't think you can reason with him, even if you flatter him, because his mind is too narrow."

"He's an ass," Hughes said, his manner glum. "He thinks he discovered the real liberalism late in life."

"There's David Benjamin Feldman," Francis said. "He seems determined to prove the premise that all Jews are liberals. Oh, he's wealthy and an authentic Wall Streeter and he worries about profits, but he seems to have a social conscience. I think the man is insecure. He's afraid of strong measures because he isn't sure how they will affect the kind of country that made him possible—not as a Jew, but as a big financier who's been able to feel that he was really running the show. You recall he wrote that the Walsh Act was as bad as the NRA, that it was a step toward setting up a Fascist state."

"Too bad," Hughes said. "Mother was awfully pleased when Feldman made the bench. Feldman was never a bleeding heart. I suppose he's afraid of me because of that rightist label people have pinned on me. Would he rather I were a leftist? Go ahead, Francis."

"Well, we can dismiss George W. Gillette. He's a kindly enough man, but he's just a party hack. He watches for the party line and then votes it. Too bad he's from the wrong party."

"Forget Gillette," the President said.

"Then that leaves Hume," Francis said. He took another sip of his Manhattan. "He has one of the finest minds I've ever encountered. His integrity is absolutely impeccable. His belief is firm that the Constitution was intended as a piece of working, and workable, machinery whose provisions could be adapted to the times. His political and economic predilections are pretty much yours, Mr. President—after all, he was a fairly conservative Senator from Indiana. Not that a man like Hume would permit his theories to affect his interpretation of the Constitution, but at least he has never closed his mind to new ideas merely because they're new."

"And yet Hume is one of the five," Hughes said.

"Yes, and likely to remain so when it comes to passing on most of your must legislation, Mr. President. And we both know why—it's his insistence on what he calls the absolutes in the Bill of Rights. He will not, ever, I am sure, put his stamp of approval on any act of Congress which he believes infringes on those absolute rights."

"But my God, Francis, I'm not trying to infringe on any rights —not on any absolutes, anywhere. I'm just trying to make this country stronger so that it will be better able to take care of the individual, to give him the things he needs, the protection he needs against exploitation by both labor unions and employers and from anarchic violence by subversives. In any government in these times the needs of the government have to be weighed against individual interests—yes, and rights—in every case."

"I know, Mr. President. But that is just where Hume disagrees most violently with you. Hume contends that the Bill of Rights directs that the government protect the rights of the individual, not make the individual subject to the requirements of a well-ordered state. Hume may believe a piece of legislation is good for the country as a whole, but if it violates his interpretation of the Bill of Rights, he will vote against it. I think he's wrong; I believe the men who wrote the Constitution were deeply concerned with the dangers inherent in a weak government, in a poorly run community. I'm not sure the individual can survive in these times without entrusting some of his rights to his government."

The President sighed. He put down his drink and plucked a cigarette out of a pack on the table and held it between his teeth, unlighted. "Yes, Francis, unfortunately that's the way it is. I won't yield to any man, including Hume, on the question of the defense of human rights. I will always defend them. But how far should we go to defend the rights of the Sons of Slaves, who

35

represent only a small minority of the Negroes and yet range about the country purposely inciting riots? We've got to be firm, Francis. We've got to take strong measures, both politically and economically. We don't have much time." He lit the cigarette with one sweeping gesture of the silver table lighter. "Well, I suppose the others are still all right."

"Oh, I think so, Mr. President. You know Robson, the scholar, the ascetic. He's an awesomely unworldly man, delicate, inclined to be old-maidish, but he's unswerving. He believes, simply, that the government must give direction to the citizen. Mitchell, of course, is the complete antithesis of Robson, but despite his cowboy airs and his professional roughness, he feels strongly about order in government, about the government's preserving order. And old Angus Whitfield is an authentic Old Testament type, a firm believer in the patriarchal system of the wise and strong leading the way and, between times, smiting the enemy hip and thigh."

"Yes, and yet old Whitfield—and Robson and Mitchell and you, Francis—you're all twentieth-century men. Whitfield—my grandfather was a lot like him." The President paused and looked toward the door at the sound of a cough. "Here's Mayborn now. Come in, Charlie—welcome to the corner saloon!"

Attorney General Charles P. Mayborn was striding into the room with the easy, confident air he had acquired during four years as the party's national chairman. He had survived some rough-and-tumble years as the emissary of the Illinois Governor to the Chicago bosses, and this mere survival had given his short, stocky figure a youthful buoyancy. Journalistic pundits had been shocked by his appointment to replace Dalton as the President's chief law officer, but Mayborn had ignored the gibes of "party hack" and gone on to whip his subordinates into a new fever of activity that resulted in a record number of antitrust convictions. Because he was on intimate terms with both men and the law, Mayborn was the nearly perfect political adviser to the President.

"Evenin', Boss." Mayborn's tone was just the right blend of respect and palship, and his handshake was the swift, vigorous gesture of the man who had come on business and planned to get right down to it. He knew John Alden Hughes liked him, respected him—and depended on him. He turned to Francis, hand out. "How are you, Francis? Nice to see you in good company, for a change."

"Hello, Charlie," Francis said. He liked Charlie Mayborn, a practical politician with decent instincts.

Hughes was moving toward the bottles on the table. "The same, Charlie?"

"Yes, sir, Mr. President, if you mean by that a little bourbon and branch water. I'm too young for your fancy drinks."

Hughes laughed. "Charlie, I'm beginning to think you drink bourbon and branch just to pose as one of the folks." He poured some bourbon over two ice cubes in a huge old-fashioned glass and tipped in a little water from a silver pitcher.

Hughes handed the glass to Mayborn, and Mayborn nodded to the President. "Cheers," he said, and gulped half of it.

"Well, let's sit down," the President said. "I know you want to get down to business, Charlie."

"Yes, sir, may as well, if it's all right with you."

The President turned to Dalton. "Francis, I asked you over to-night to discuss a little plan of ours. We've already decided on it, so we're not asking you to assume any responsibility for it. But we want you to know about it, and, of course, we'd like your private opinion on it. Mostly, though, you're here because I hope you'll find it possible to give us a little help in those quarters where you have considerable influence. Charlie Mayborn has been working on this for a long time now, ever since the Court threw out our Wagner Act amendment. We decided then we'd have to move vigorously to meet an impossible situation."

He turned to Mayborn. "Charlie?"

Mayborn stood up and cleared his throat. Momentarily a look almost of self-consciousness passed over his broad face; he seemed to exert himself to wipe it off. "Francis, it's very simple. The President plans to enlarge the Supreme Court."

"Enlarge . . . ?" Francis was conscious that his voice sounded bewildered.

The President's voice cut in. "Enlarge—Charlie's being polite, Francis." Now his tone was gravelly. "I'm going to *pack* the Court, Francis. Since everybody else will call it that, we may as well. Besides, that's the way I look at it."

37

Francis was aware that both the President and Mayborn were looking at him closely. He said, "You certainly caught me by surprise, Mr. President—Charlie."

Hughes's laugh was small. "I don't doubt it, Francis. We caught ourselves by surprise when we first thought of it. Francis, before Charlie continues, what is your first reaction? Aside from surprise, of course."

Francis found that he was not thinking of the two men in the room. He was thinking of a man named Franklin Delano Roosevelt. Roosevelt tried it, Francis thought, and they clobbered him although he was a tough nut. He smiled.

"I'm afraid I was thinking about Franklin Roosevelt," he said.

"I know." The President's voice was matter-of-fact. "Roosevelt couldn't manage it. I haven't forgotten that, Francis. But we think we can put it over, this time. But, Francis—again without your knowing the details and without going into our chances of managing it—what do you think of the idea? That is, do you think it is reasonable, in our time?"

Francis found himself clearing his throat, too, and rebuked himself for stage-managing. "If you mean, do I think it is reasonable to increase the membership of the Supreme Court, then my answer is yes. That is, I don't think there is anything wrong in that, per se. At this time, of course, it has political implications, but that doesn't deny its logic. There are some perfectly legitimate reasons why the membership of the Court should be increased. I can cite them almost offhand."

The President cut in. "Good, Francis, but not right now. First I wanted to know if the idea was reasonable, politics aside. Now I want Charlie Mayborn to tell you more about our plan."

Mayborn was still standing, rocking up and down on his heels.

"It's pretty simple, Francis—not as complicated as F.D.R.'s scheme. We want to increase the size of the Court. Just that. No gimmicks. Roosevelt, as you know, wanted to appoint an extra justice for every justice who reached retirement age and refused to retire. He also wanted to reorganize and increase the membership of the lower courts. We just want to add two new justices to the Supreme Court because there's too much work for nine men to handle. It's as simple as that."

Francis suddenly wanted to be on his feet, too. He was beginning to feel an itchy kind of excitement. When the President looked at him, Francis said in what he thought was a calm voice, "Well, of course, you don't have to worry about what the Supreme Court thinks about it—except that some of the members will do their usual lobbying. After all, it's up to Congress to fix the number of justices on the Court. But some of these gentlemen up on the Hill are going to be pretty troublesome. I can hear the outraged howls now."

Mayborn was ready for this; it was clear the President had yielded the floor for the time being to his Attorney General.

"Troublesome!" Mayborn was impatient. "Who's going to be troublesome except the same old gang that's been troublesome for the last few years and never managed to scrape up more than a handful of votes? The rest of them have done what they were told, because they knew it was good for them—and it's paid off for them. There's only one politician the voters give a damn about these days, and that's the President, and the Congress knows it. Half of those boys on the Hill, including the troublesome ones, rode back into office on the President's coattails. The President led the ticket in every one of the forty-six states he carried in November. As for the other party, how many votes do they have? There's never been a tamer Congress—even when Roosevelt was running things."

Mayborn was right, of course, Francis acknowledged. For four years a docile Congress had obeyed without protest every directive of the President the masses worshiped. And the election returns had proved how well this course had buttered the bread of the party's Congressional candidates. Without Hughes on the ticket, they'd have been mere faceless names. Yet Francis was stirred with a vague unease. History had shown that Congress could always be depended on to be—undependable, unpredictable. Trained seals on the Hill had been known to turn on their trainer before. But how could he rebut Mayborn's logical premise? As of now, Mayborn was so right.

"Of course, I have to agree with you, Charlie," Francis said. "After all, aside from the fact that you know more about politics than I do, it's obvious that Congress is beholden to the President

—and more, that the gentlemen on the Hill have a genuine affection for him. It's just that it's such a radical step. It will cause such a sensation. You've considered the alternatives, I suppose."

"Yup," Mayborn said. His tone was terse. "We've agreed that it's the Court, not the Constitution, we've got to get around, and we've gone over all the alternatives and this is the best. There are three other ways it might be done—*might* be done. We could draw up an amendment to the Constitution specifically enlarging the powers of the executive, we could submit a bill to Congress limiting the Court's jurisdiction by taking away its appellate powers over certain legislation, or we could send up a bill that would require more than a mere majority of the Supreme Court to invalidate an act of Congress."

Mayborn took an impatient sip of his drink. "None of 'em is any good. We'd have a hell of a time jockeying an amendment through a majority of the states in time to do us any good. Besides, an amendment always causes a big fuss; it gives those state legislators a chance to make speeches and pose as saviors of the Constitution. Senator McAdam already has a bill written requiring more than a mere Court majority to invalidate an act of Congress; I don't think it would work—I think the Court would strike it down as unconstitutional. As for the third, we've got precedents for taking away the Supreme Court's appellate jurisdiction in certain cases—Jefferson, for instance, exempted the repealer of the Federalist midnight judges law from review by the Court. But, dammit, the lower courts might prove to be just as recalcitrant as the Supreme Court. Besides, the Constitution specifically gives the Supreme Court jurisdiction in certain types of cases, especially those involving the states.

"No, packing the Court is the best bet. It's constitutional and it doesn't involve changing procedures or judicial structures. Sure there'll be howls, but the President gave the howlers the trouncing of their lives last November. We've got the votes, and I think we can make enough of a case for it so that there won't have to be a prolonged debate on the bill."

Francis said, "Well, of course, there is an alternative of a sort. At least, something that might alter the situation."

"Yes?" the President said.

"It could make quite a difference," Francis said. "You know,

Bacon has talked about retiring. Well, a couple of weeks ago one of my clerks told me Bacon's wife was pressuring him to quit right after the inauguration. That would give you the one vote you need, Mr. President."

"Yes," the President said. "Yes, I'd heard that Bacon was thinking of leaving the bench. It would give me that vote." He didn't seem pleased at the thought; it was as if someone had intruded a fact he had been careful not to notice up to then. "I don't know, Francis. I know the kind of Court I want . . . I just wonder if Bacon is really serious."

"It's worth thinking about," Francis said.

"Yes, I suppose so." The President seemed suddenly uneasy, as though he didn't want to discuss the matter. "We'll see, Francis."

Mayborn sat down; he had finished his exposition. Francis looked over at the President, who had his feet up on the coffee table again. It was the President's turn, now, to justify his plan, to explain the reasons he would offer the public for remaking the Court in his political image.

The President took plenty of time to light a cigarette. Then, "Francis, I think you've recognized where you would come in. Both Charlie and I believe there is a case for our plan; I'd like very much if you could help us make it."

Francis had slowed down a little. "I suppose you mean overload of work," he said. "The Court's backlog of cases."

"Precisely," the President said. "It seems to me that it's obvious the Court can't handle its job—that it needs more help."

Francis ran his hand through his short curly red hair; it was not that simple. "Well, Mr. President, I think there are members of the Court who would be outraged at such a suggestion—Bacon, of course, and Feldman and probably Angus Whitfield. But the Court is overworked; there's no doubt of that. Ever since I joined the Court two years ago, we've been turning down a record number of writs of certiorari; so far this year we've accepted only something like eight per cent of the cases submitted to the Court for review."

"Then the Court does need help?"

"Yes—that is, it needs some kind of help. But, Mr. President, I'm afraid I'm not as confident as you are that the addition of

41

two more members would provide that help. You have to remember that every member of the Court considers and decides upon every question before the Court. Each member passes on each writ of certiorari, each member hears the oral arguments, each member may speak on each case in the justices' regular Friday conferences, each member may write a separate opinion of each case. It's bad enough with nine justices having their hand in; I don't know what would happen if there were eleven."

The President was patient. "Yes, Francis, but when I say the Court needs help, I mean something different than you think. What the Court needs to bring it up to date is a greater diversification of views, and since the justices serve for life there are always too many old men on the bench. Nine men are not enough, under those circumstances, to provide the assortment of legal points of view that the country needs. I'm confident the Court would be more efficient and would be able to speed up its work if it had some new blood."

"Well, possibly." Francis could already hear the vigorous arguments on the other side. "But I'm afraid most of the opposition would find your arguments specious, Mr. President. It's basic that fewer men are more decisive than a large committee." He paused, making certain of his stand. "I suppose I approve of what you want to do, Mr. President. The Court could use streamlining, some new blood. I just want to suggest that your arguments about efficiency may not go down very well."

"Oh, yes, yes. I know all that, Francis. The fact is—I'll be frank with you—what I want is those extra two votes, now. I'm not so damned sure two additional justices will make the Court more efficient or cause it to hear more cases, but they might—they could, Francis. It's a point I intend to make most vigorously, anyway. After all, I can't come right out and say I want two additional justices so I can have my way with legislation."

"No, you can't." Francis grinned. "And I see your point about explaining for your plan. It's an honest case of the end justifying the means. And, of course, some of the justices are getting quite old. They're not as fast, not as alert, as they used to be. Perhaps with two more justices on the bench some of them might not be so insistent on writing individual opinions."

"Let's see, I suppose I can name the slow justices," the President said. "But suppose you tick them off, Francis."

"Whitfield. He has to top the list. He still has a fine mind, but he's a little slower than he used to be in getting at the point of a case. After all, he's eighty years old. Bacon is seventy-seven; he's the type that confuses dawdling with sober deliberation. Robson is seventy-seven, too, but I believe he has the quickest mind on the Court. Feldman is seventy-six and slow; moreover, unless a case happens to involve his pet theories about either economics or civil rights, he hates to make up his mind. Gillette moves like a turtle because he's lazy."

"All right," the President said. "We won't stress age because I'd hate to hurt Whitfield's feelings, or Robson's. We need those two. But the fact is the Court is falling behind in its work, and whatever my opponents say, they won't be able to excuse that. Perhaps my plan won't make the Court more efficient, but, by God, I'm going to stress that word efficiency every time I discuss the plan. People like Frank Hoar are always standing up in the Senate and demanding more efficiency in government. Well, I'll cram efficiency down Hoar's throat in this Supreme Court thing, and even if he takes your tack that eleven justices will be more inefficient than nine, I'll have come out for efficiency first. People remember who used a word first."

"It's a good point," Francis said. "I learned a little bit about that kind of thing when I was running against your second cousin for governor."

"Francis," said Mayborn, "how about that business of law clerks writing opinions? It seems to me we can use that, too."

"Well, there's a lot of it," Francis said. The subject always made him uncomfortable. "Baker, for instance, seldom touches an opinion; I sometimes wonder if he even reads them when his law clerk puts them on his desk. And Frank Mitchell is almost as bad. But I hope you wouldn't have to go into that, Charlie. It's sort of like invading a man's living room."

The President cut in. "Oh, I don't think we have to carry out prying quite that far, gentlemen. I think we've got a good case as it is." He went over and mixed two more dry Manhattans and poured another drink for Mayborn. He came back with the drinks and remained standing after Francis and Mayborn had taken the glasses from him.

"Now then, Francis, I hope you can help us," the President said. "Forget about that efficiency business for a while. I don't expect you to go around making political speeches—although you've done pretty well with the bar associations—but I think you can make your weight felt. You have a lot of good friends on the Hill; some of those people owe you favors, and you're well liked up there for the careful reorganization job you did as Attorney General. You can talk to a lot of those gentlemen socially. You've got some good contacts in business and industry as a result of your friendship with people like Tom Nelson. You're in demand as an after-dinner speaker; it seems to me you have a perfect right to discuss the Court's problems in speeches like that. And, of course, I'd like you to be my discreet advocate among members of the Court. I'd hope you could soften up Hume and Whitfield."

Francis looked up from his drink to find the President regarding him with an intentness that was almost a hard stare. This was the young President who *got things done*, the campaigner Francis had seen so many times in the rough-and-tumble of the hustings. At that moment, Hughes was tendering the promissory note for payment; the realization of this gave Francis a slight tremor. He wished he could smile to break the tension, but he couldn't. Embarrassment made him feel gauche.

"Well, sir, of course I want to help if I can." To satisfy himself, Francis had to put emphasis on the *want* and the *if*. He knew what was being asked of him, and it made him uncomfortable, even when it was asked by an old friend and political mentor. He pushed ahead, but carefully. "You know, Mr. President, we've always seen eye to eye from a purely constitutional viewpoint." Francis paused again; if only he wouldn't keep hearing Sharfman's arguments in behalf of that Sons of Slaves agitator. "And, of course, I believe you can make a valid point for reorganizing the Court."

Hughes's smile was thin. "Yes, I think I can, Francis. I think I've already made it. But—of course, I'd like you to make it, too."

"Yes, sir." I *am* being stuffy, Francis told himself. "Yes, of course I hope I can, too." Sure, he told himself, just put away the robe for a while and hit the sawdust trail. Or keep the robe on—to impress people. Francis felt a small sigh escaping him. "I'll do what I can, Mr. President. You know that. But, of course, as a member of the Court I'll have to be—discreet."

"Of course, Francis." Now Hughes's smile was large again, his voice hearty. "I'm not asking you to debate with Frank Hoar publicly, with your robe flying in the breeze. I think we can see eye to eye on your part in this."

Francis smiled back, but he was not comfortable. Damn Sharfman. "I think we can, Mr. President," he said, discovering that his voice was embarrassingly small. "I'll certainly explore every avenue to see where I can help."

"Good, Francis. I'll need your help. I'm pretty confident, but I realize it's not going to be a picnic."

"Well, you've got good men on the Hill. What do the Congressional leaders think about it?"

From his chair, Mayborn coughed dryly. The President looked over at Mayborn, then turned back to Francis.

"I'd have to guess, Francis. I haven't told them about it yet."

Francis sat up straight. "You haven't told them?" He couldn't keep the startled surprise out of his tone.

"No, I haven't. The only people who know about it are you and Mayborn and, to some extent, Harry Weiss. Now, just a minute, Francis. I can see you're about to ask me why I haven't consulted my Congressional leaders. The answer is simple. There's no point getting them all worked up until I have to. I don't want to be bogged down in a lot of discussion."

"But—I suppose they'll have to know, in advance?"

"Of course, Francis. But not too much in advance. The Court plan will be the theme of my inaugural address next Tuesday. I'll have a little chat a day or so before then with Chet McAdam and Henry Smith—just give them a general idea of what I have in mind without divulging any of the details. Then I'll have the rest of the Congressional leaders in to breakfast the morning of inauguration, with the Cabinet, and I'll tell them about it at that time. I don't anticipate any trouble."

Mayborn's grunt was out of a smoke-filled room. "I hope not, Mr. President. If I had my way, though, I'd keep McAdam and Smith in the dark, too, until Tuesday."

The President smiled. "I know you would, Charlie. Perhaps you're right, too. But I don't feel I can be quite that cavalier with the Senate Majority Leader and the Speaker of the House. I hope the good Senator McAdam and the good Speaker Smith will appreciate they're getting special treatment."

Francis' unease caused him to loose an artificial cough. "Yes," he said, dryly, "I hope they will. That is, I hope they will consider it special treatment—at that late date."

The President's tone was easy. "Oh, I shouldn't think we have much to worry about in that direction, Francis. I've always been able to work through Chet and Henry in the past."

Francis suppressed the shrug he felt was about to lift his shoulders in doubt and resignation. "Of course," he said. "Chet and Henry always go along."

"Right," the President said, "and now back to work."

Later Francis noticed with surprise that his watch said only eight-thirty as he walked down the marble steps on the North Portico with Charlie Mayborn. It seemed to Francis Dalton that he had spent a month in that library with the confident, prowling, restless President of the United States. They had gone over all the groundwork, all their plans; Hughes and Mayborn had even attempted a timetable for the Supreme Court bill. Clearly, the die was cast.

Mayborn grunted at his side. "Hope you can keep a secret, Mr. Justice Dalton."

Francis Dalton looked at Mayborn's corner-of-the-mouth grin. "I guess I can, Charlie," he said. Then, soberly, "Charlie—what do you think?"

Mayborn took his time biting the end off a long black cigar. "I'll tell you what I think, honestly, Francis. I don't think anybody could pull this off—except John Alden Hughes."

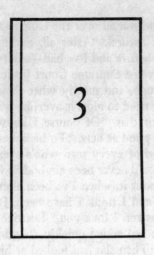

3

H E LOOKED AT HIS WATCH. Still another hour before Beatrice's plane would be in. He should just glance over the Webster brief, but he didn't feel like it. It pleased Francis to know that he was seeing Beatrice again, and to think of touching her and hearing her voice in the same room. He was very much in love with a lovely and charming actress named Beatrice Hart, and the knowledge warmed him. And yet—what was it that always made him hesitate, a moment after he had acknowledged his love? Why did there always have to be a *but*, an *and yet*? It was a small thing, a fleeting feeling of unease, of discomfort. He knew himself well enough to sense that the feeling was unworthy of him; he could know that honestly, with no false modesty. It was not an enormous complication; sometimes, indeed, it seemed minuscule, so inconsequential as to be vapid when he was with Beatrice and her mere presence was filling him with pleasure. And surely he wanted her; he always wanted her, even when that little *but* intruded.

"You know, Francis, my dear, we mustn't gloss things over just to be polite," Beatrice had told him after a week of seeing each other and talking to each other had convinced them they

47

were in love. She had leaned over the table to touch his arm, and her smile had been natural. "After all, darling, you know I've been married twice before and I've had—affairs. I suppose everybody knows that, even a Supreme Court justice. I've been in the gossip columns enough, and mostly what they've said about me is true." He had not tried to gloss it over; he was too proud of his adult intelligence for that. "Of course I know, Bea," he'd said, and his smile was as good as hers. "To be honest about it, I'd like to chop off the head of every man who's ever so much as held your hand. I wish you'd never been anybody's wife—or anything. And I've thought about it, when I've been alone. I've tried to be cold and objective, and I think I have been. But I always come up with the same answer. I love you." Beatrice had said nothing, immediately, and he had added quickly, "And now let's not talk about it any more." Then she had looked at him with eyes very bright and said, "It's all right, anyway, Francis. I've never been anyone's wife—or anything. Not really. Not until now." She had smiled her wry smile that wrinkled her nose. "I do so wish I didn't sound so theatrically trite, darling. But it's true. I have to say it."

He had been truthful when he told her it didn't mean anything to him, so far as his love went. It didn't; she could have been one of the more adept of the murderous Borgias and he would still have loved her. The little *but*, the nagging *and yet*, were not concerned with how he felt about himself. It was hard to explain why they kept creeping into his mind; when he tried to explain to himself it always sounded stuffy—corn wrapped in the American flag. It was not Francis Copley Dalton, individual, who was involved, but Associate Justice Francis Copley Dalton of the Supreme Court. Did Mr. Justice Dalton have the *right* to marry a woman like Beatrice Hart? Did a member of the highest court in the land have a right to indulge himself without regard for the position he held? Francis Dalton had always insisted to himself that his government—the government he served—came first, before any individual consideration. And since he had met Beatrice, he had forced himself to consider his position and its place in the eyes of his fellow citizens. He had never been stuffy, but he had always had an icy contempt for public officials who failed in their respect for their positions, who carried their titles with them into saloon society, who permitted those titles to be linked with people of careless and flamboyant habits. Francis Dalton, son of Michael and Bridget Dalton, would have sacked Secretary Lothrop forthwith for going on that yachting trip with that Italian prince and his friends, even if one of the friends was a former British Foreign Secretary. Francis Dalton had flinched when, upon his elevation to the Supreme Court, a newspaper biography had described him as "dedicated"; he thought of himself as merely a highly competent public official who enjoyed serving in the government and had an honest affection for the system he served. But as such, he believed it should be instinctive in every public official to guard his private life, out of respect for the state. Otherwise, government of the people was weakened. Why did it have to sound so—mawkish?

Well, he was not going to nag himself about it every time he thought of Beatrice. She was coming tonight and he was meeting her at the airport, and he was damned if he was going to think ahead to the headlines when they got married. Yes, *when* they got married. He got up and stretched and walked through the dining room into the kitchen to get a bottle of Löwenbräu. Beatrice would be in at nine, and they would go and eat somewhere, but he was hungry right now. He got a bottle of beer from the refrigerator and sliced himself a couple of pieces of Cheddar. YOUNG JUSTICE ENJOYS ELEGANT SNACK IN BACHELOR QUARTERS, he thought. Washington, with its hordes of fiendishly conscientious journalists, got a man into the habit of thinking in headlines. That neo Dorothy Thompson, the fat girl reporter from Chicago, would give his beer-and-cheese the psychological treatment, would have him harking back to his childhood environment. And she would be right.

He plumped down on the beige sofa and swung both legs up onto the cane seat of the side chair his sister Sheila had bought him at Jordan Marsh's. He drank deeply from the bottle and then, still keeping it in his hand, he bit a chunk off one of the pieces of Cheddar. All right, he was harking back to his childhood environment, but it was pretty comfortable and nobody could see him and start worrying about the dignity of the Supreme Court. He liked his little house on N Street with its long living room and the two good-sized bedrooms upstairs and the little brick-paved patio out back. Michael Dalton had stood on the sidewalk and appraised it with the critical eye of a man who had done all his own repairs on the Dutch colonial house he had finally been able to buy on Maplewood Avenue when Francis was a freshman at Holy Cross.

"The damned thing is out of plumb," he had said. "Is this what Sheila calls 'picturesque'?" Then he had made a muttering, inch-by-inch inspection of the interior and offered the conclusion that "even those skinflints at Bell Worsted wouldn't have their workers living in such a place."

Francis had laughed and made no attempt to explain to Michael Dalton that a house which in Evans, Massachusetts, would be only one of a dreary row of mill houses on Union Street was a fashionable prize with an impeccable Federal background in Georgetown. Throughout Francis' boyhood, the Daltons had lived in just such a mill house while Michael saved what he could from his boss weaver's wages against the day when a down payment could be made on one of Maplewood's Dutch colonials—with two tiled baths. In Evans, living in a mill house confined the Daltons to the same social status as the Poles and Italians who surrounded them on all sides; in Georgetown it was a symbol of one who had arrived, imparting to the occupant not only a hefty measure of success in government and its allied witchcrafts but a touch of intellectualism as well.

Michael Dalton was appalled when Francis told him that he paid three hundred and twenty-five dollars a month rent for his N Street house, and that his landlord had bought the house for fifty thousand dollars. "Jesus, Mary and Joseph," Michael Dalton said, his syllables bursting forth in little explosions. "No wonder the government is bankrupt. Why, your mother and I never paid a cent more than twelve dollars a week for the Union Street place, and it had two more bedrooms than this moldy thing. I could have bought it for six thousand dollars." He shook his head sadly. "Francis, I thought judges were supposed to be smart."

Sheila had stuck up for him. "Now, Pa," she said, "you don't understand. These places are just like those houses on Louisburg Square and Beacon Street. They're antiques."

"Antiques!" Michael Dalton's answer was a snort. "A body will catch his death of cold in a drafty old shed like this one.

Francis, I want a drink and I don't want any of that fancy Scotch of yours. I want a good shot of rye with a glass of beer for a chaser. I don't suppose you've got any Narragansett in this woebegone town?"

Francis laughed happily to himself as he stretched his legs and sipped his Löwenbräu. He did have some Narragansett ale in the house now, because his father had brought him a case on his last visit—"so I'll have something decent to drink." He was sure that Michael Dalton honestly believed his youngest offspring was indulging himself in a kind of genteel slumming, and that he often compared the N Street house unfavorably with the conventionally comfortable homes of his other children in Evans. Mike had an ultramodern establishment on Manchester Hill, paradoxically described as a "ranch house," and his automobile agency was doing well enough that Mike could belong to the Country Club. Kathy Dalton and her husband had remodeled the old Grant place on Elm Street, complete with an old mahogany bar from Durocher's Tavern in the basement recreation room. And Sheila, happily unmarried, presided over the spotless Dutch colonial for her father and often continued to sleep in the sunroom even when the calendar was well into December.

It was odd how his thoughts were going back to Evans and his family; he should be thinking about last night's conference at the White House and the President's spectacular plan to pack the Court. It had been in his thoughts most of the day as he absentmindedly tried to follow the arguments in the Court, but now he seemed to have exhausted his thinking on the subject. The President's plan was one larded with precarious complications, and Francis Dalton knew there was a good chance that John Alden Hughes would fall flat on his handsome face. Francis stood up and walked over and pushed Volume XVI of Balzac back into place on the bookshelf and then stood there for a moment, gazing abstractedly at the bookcases that flanked both sides of the fireplace. Flat on his face was the word for it, all right; the testy gentlemen on the Hill would scream, and their screams would be heard from Maine to California. And, although the President's project fascinated him, it had worried him ever since he heard about it in that quiet White House room. It made him feel self-conscious to be in on it—on the inside of a project emanating from the executive branch. God knows he found it difficult to work with that inflexible majority on the Court, but he was sure their opinions were sincere—if, in the cases of people like Gillette and Baker, not always profound. And whenever he determinedly put down the thought that the President's plan might be dangerous, he was left with a feeling of unease. The feeling was stronger even than his embarrassed reflections on the propriety of a Supreme Court justice's lowering himself from the time-honored isolation of his role to the brawling controversy of the cloakroom. He walked back and sat down again on the sofa and put his feet back on the cane chair.

Yet he did feel that the President's plan, or something like it, was badly needed to keep the Supreme Court in pace with its responsibilities and labors and in tune with the needs of the times. Francis Dalton had a proper respect, even reverence, for the Supreme Court, but he was too practical a lawyer, and politician, not to acknowledge its old-fashioned inadequacies. As for John Alden Hughes, he had the same faith in him he had had since their first meeting, when Francis Dalton had joined the little mixture of idealistic amateurs and hard-nosed politicians dedicated to the elevation of Hughes to the Presidency.

He supposed now he had been preparing for that first meeting with Hughes ever since he emerged from boyhood and plunged into the world of Jesuit logic at Holy Cross—a rangy youth with red hair and freckled forehead, still clinging to some of the innocent piety of the conscientious but merry-hearted altar boy. It was at the feet of the Jesuits that he had first discovered his fascination for the law, for its intricate byways and for its fascinating convolutions that seemed paradoxical until you successfully maneuvered the last of the alleys and detours and came suddenly upon the meat of the matter. He always thought his interest in the law had helped make him a competent enough pitcher so that he could have signed with the Red Sox for a small bonus upon his departure from Worcester. But he realized that his competence depended almost entirely on outthinking the college opposition; he didn't have the speed and the other physical talents to make a major league. Baseball had helped mightily, though; it was through Johnny Broderick of the Red Sox that he had met Tom Nelson, senior, in his junior year at the Cross and, in addition to seeing that young Francis Dalton had the right job offers while in school, Tom Nelson had pressed Francis to go to Harvard Law and thus open the door to a proper career, which was launched when the young law graduate was given a desk in Nelson's office.

Tom Nelson, senior, apparently had had nothing to do with Francis' going into politics; that was instinct. "You're an Irishman and a lawyer, Francis," Nelson had told him when Francis joined the Young Citizens outfit. "You're just doing what comes naturally. It won't do you any harm, and it might do you some good."

The good it did him, eventually, was the opportunity it gave him to meet John Alden Hughes, because it was that meeting that persuaded young Francis Dalton it was reasonable for him to dare to run for public office. Hughes was a little-known and spectacularly youthful Congressman from Pennsylvania when he came to Boston to make a speech, and, although Francis Dalton didn't know it, to appraise the possibilities of national support among the party's straw bosses. Hughes conferred respectfully with the graybeards during that session in his suitably smoke-filled suite at the Parker House, but he had also invited the young amateurs to sample his Scotch and his opinions, and nobody was more surprised than Francis Dalton to find himself holding the midnight floor on the need for diversification of candidates. Francis supposed it was because he felt at home with Hughes from the start; after all, although Francis was only twenty-six, Hughes was barely thirty-one, even if he had stirred the House of Representatives to unusual excitement with his Social Security proposals.

Only a few of the Young Citizens were left in the suite when Hughes, striding restlessly up and down the room, had urged Francis Dalton to practice what he preached. "You, Dalton, I'd like to see you do something besides talk about politics," Hughes said, an index finger waggling in Francis' face. "Third man in your class at Harvard Law, making a good start in a good law office, unmarried and full of beans—what are you doing on the sidelines? Stop holding other people's coats and c'mon in—the water's fine."

The upshot was that Francis Dalton, a little dazed but suffused with a new eagerness, had almost literally walked out of the suite and into public office. He started running the next day for the state Senate from his home district and was surprised to find that he had made enough political friends by playing baseball at Holy Cross, and enough financial friends by being Michael Dalton's son, that he won the seat from drunken old Pierre Boucher in a junior landslide. He still had the telegram Hughes had sent him on that morning of his first political victory: CONGRATULATIONS SENATOR BUT REMEMBER YOU'RE NOT JUST TAKING A QUICK DIP. By that time, Francis had decided on his own to stay in the political swim, and he had found his campaign chores increasingly easy as he went on to the post of Attorney General of Massachusetts and two terms as the youngest Governor in the state's history. From the very first, too, he had been a member of Hughes's secret little cadre of political leaders as Hughes went on to the Senate and to Pennsylvania's State House. He had expected something when Hughes moved into the White House, and he had been very well satisfied with the Attorney General appointment, but he was resting his ambitions when Hughes telephoned him from the White House on that bright morning in May and said, simply, "Francis, I'm going to appoint you to the vacancy on the Supreme Court." Francis had been stunned. He found himself stammering a bewildered "Why?" And Hughes had laughed and said, "Francis, I knew you'd ask that. I've got a lot of good reasons, so don't worry. But for now, let's just say that I like your idea that laws were made to serve men, not vice versa." After hanging up and thinking it over, Francis Dalton had liked that. Hughes had talked law to him; he hadn't mentioned that spectacular UN victory.

The victory at The Hague had helped, of course; it came at a time when the Russians' refusal to pay their share of the United Nations' upkeep had become a last straw with the American people. Francis had collected from them—that sort of thing could not help but impress a country whose people had an instinctive loathing for a welsher. But Francis realized that his rise and his eventual appointment to the Supreme Court had come from something deeper—from the ingrained Puritanism which had been his by birth and background. It was curious that so many people lumped Irish politicians together as liberals; actually the average Irishman was by nature conservative, and this conservatism was bolstered if he happened to come from Massachusetts. The Irish not only replaced the English aristocracy as the political bosses of the state they once shared so acrimoniously, but in the process they took over as their own these latter-day Puritans' stern and literal belief in the concepts of good and evil. Michael Dalton had always been as much of a Puritan as the Saltonstalls and the Lodges—more so as the Back Bay aristocrats expanded into alien fields by marriages outside their immediate circles. Undoubtedly, the Church helped; but the Dalton children had not needed the counsel of their parish priest to influence them for good—they got their rectitude at home.

Alice O'Sullivan had put it correctly, and a trifle bitterly, when he ran into her on Fifth Avenue a year or so ago. Alice, the nearest thing to a best girl Francis had ever had back in Evans, had finally broken away from her slatternly family to wind up as a literary agent in Rockefeller Plaza.

"Oh, Francis," she had told him over a three-martini lunch, "you are such a goddamned Puritan for a handsome Irish boy! You and your Irish pals, Francis, you not only licked the Yankees but you appropriated their stiff-necked righteousness."

"Why, Alice, where did you get that idea?" Francis had said, smiling. "It seems to me I've bought you a very immoral lunch, and I told you before we even sat down that you still had good legs."

Alice grinned and pushed a lock of hair out of her eyes. "I appreciate that, Francis. I was glad to discover you hadn't forgotten about girls."

"I hadn't forgotten about some girls," Francis said. "I remember quite a bit about you, Allie."

"Yes—I suppose it seems like quite a bit to you, Francis." Alice reached out and put her hand on his. "But at the risk of shocking the youngest member of the Supreme Court, darling, I have to remind you that you only laid me once."

"Alice!" Francis said, and then he grinned quickly. "Allie, you're wonderful. Come out from behind that literary-agent bush—I know you. I ought to give you a good spanking."

"I should wink lewdly at you now, Francis, and suggest that you tackle that little job in the privacy of my apartment, but I suppose it would be hopeless." Alice measured her smile, now. "Oh, Francis, you are all right, and sweet and so goddamned intelligent, but I hope you won't let all this Puritanism stand in your way when you meet the authentic, bottled-in-bond Somebody. Please, Francis, don't be stuffy with her or you'll screw it all up."

If he didn't stop dreaming, he'd miss Beatrice's plane. He had less than twenty-five minutes to make it, he noticed, as he swung his legs off the sofa and tightened his necktie. He put the empty beer bottle on the coffee table and dismissed the thought of the cheese on the kitchen counter. No time for tidying up, he thought, knowing he'd forget to put the cheese back when he returned in the morning hours and Mrs. Robinson would chide him about it at breakfast.

When he steered the Corvette into one of the metered parking places at the airport, he still had five minutes to spare, which proved again that Georgetown was convenient, too. Still trying to persuade myself that I belong there, he thought. Beatrice's plane was on time, and after hurrying down the steps of Gate 17 he had to wait only a couple of minutes before the ship was in sight, taxiing toward the gate. He found himself wishing again that there was some way to get rid of those freckles on his forehead. Thinking of Beatrice always made him conscious of his appearance; before he met her he had had only a vague idea of what he looked like, and he was still careless about regular visits to the barbershop. Well, he couldn't change his Irish face now, with the raw-red cheeks that looked as if they had been scrubbed too hard by Bridget Dalton and the thick, curly red hair that swarmed over the tentative parting on the side like jungle growth.

Beatrice was the first off the plane; people always managed such things for her. He enjoyed his look at her before she could see him in the open doorway—at the slenderness of her figure, which made her look taller than her five feet four inches, at her longish golden-brown hair, parted on the side and softly loose about her head, at the way she threw her head back as she peered through the murky light to try to pick him out at the gate. She is lovely and I am in love with her, thought Francis Dalton, and he started to walk toward the ramp and she saw him and he saw her lips part as she called, "Francis." Then she was hurrying down the steps of the ramp, her deep-brown mink coat threatening to slip from her shoulders, and he was there at the bottom of the steps to take her hand, discreetly, and kiss her cheek, discreetly, and to whisper his private welcome in her ear: "My very dearest."

After that, they were together, no matter how many people were around. They were together, alone, as he got her luggage for her—the usual three huge bags—and walking together to the parking space with the porter behind them, and alone among the scores of cars clogging the road into town, in the Carlton lobby as she registered and in the crowded elevator. It wasn't until the bellboy had departed with his dollar and the door had closed and he had Beatrice in his arms that he realized that until that moment he had shared her with others—and felt a wave of exultation that his feeling for her and hers for him had made him until now unconscious of the fact.

"Darling." Beatrice's voice was a murmur against his lips. "Oh, darling, I'm so glad to be here—with you." Their lips met again, gently stopping her words but saying everything, and for minutes they were content merely to be with each other and meltingly against each other. And then they were walking slowly, hand in hand, to the sofa and sitting down together and looking at each other as if newly interested in each other's appearance.

"Francis, your hair is rather properly combed," Beatrice said. She touched a finger to the parting.

"I believe it's getting trained," he said. "Yesterday it stayed that way for almost an hour. I'm beginning to feel like a matinee idol."

"Well—" Beatrice's voice was full of indignation. "You certainly don't look like one, thank God. If you ever did, my good man, I'd send you packing forthwith."

"Oh, I don't know, I thought I looked rather pretty tonight."

"Pretty! Listen to the man! My very own Francis, you are the least pretty man I've ever met—again, thank the good Lord. You're a handsome devil, yes, in a kind of ugly way. But the first time I saw that Irish face it carried a guarantee it would never be pretty."

"All right. You can be the pretty one in the family. I won't compete."

"Good." Beatrice held her head to one side and half closed her eyes. "Now I'll look sultry. You know, darling, I could really be glamorous if I worked at it more. Don't you think I'm a reasonably attractive middle-aged woman?"

"Yes, I do."

"Oh . . . middle-aged?"

"Well, you *are* thirty-six."

"Don't be a devil, Francis. Let's away with that damned judicial objectivity."

"All right." Francis took her face in his hands and kissed her. "That better?"

"Oh, darling, much, much better. Kiss me again. . . . There! Now I am middle-aged and I don't care. I rather like it. It makes me just right for you. You couldn't stand those young things, darling. They're awfully dumb, and kind of hyperthyroid. Keep me. I'm restful."

"All right, I'll keep you. Will you be a comfort to me in my old age?"

"Yes, yes. I'll bring you your pipe and slippers and your heroin."

"Fine, and always be sure the needle is sharp. Dear, you don't look it, but are you tired?"

"No. No, I don't think so. Oh, yes, Francis, I am tired. I'm just kind of depressed-tired." She lifted his arm and put it around her shoulders and burrowed against him.

"Well, you should be, Bea. After two years in the same show. It'll take you some time to unwind."

"Oh, it isn't that, Francis. Oh, sure, I'm wound up, and that nice juicy part was making me almost scream the last few months. But that's normal. No, the trouble lately is that Freddie has been at his worst."

"Freddie? I thought he was over and done with. After all, the divorce became final six months ago."

"I know, Francis, but Freddie is the type that lingers on. He's been on poor old Bill Stone's neck like a leech—or like a vampire bat."

"Bill Stone? But what does Freddie want with your lawyer?"

58

"I won't make you guess, darling—it's too easy. He wants money, of course."

"Money?" Francis sat up straight on the sofa. "Beatrice, I'm sorry, all I seem to do is repeat everything you say. But I'm confused. What right has Freddie to ask you for money? From what you've told me, I gather you made a rather generous settlement on him. I'll be damned if I'd have given him a penny. What kind of a little toad is he, anyway?"

"A rather monstrous kind, darling. There's nothing worse than an actor who is pretty and lazy. Freddie is really not a bad actor in a kind of tired, romantic way, but he won't work."

"Well, that's too bad. But is that any reason why you should support him?"

"Darling, of course not. But there's something else. Something I forgot to tell you at the time I was burdening you with all my domestic complications. No, I don't think I forgot. It just didn't occur to me. It didn't seem important at all, just a rather silly clause in our settlement papers."

"What was the clause, Bea, for heaven's sake?"

"Well, darling, Freddie was being obnoxious. He was always whimpering that I was treating him shabbily. So his lawyer suggested this clause, which said that I'd help him out if he needed help—something like that."

"Help him out? You mean, in addition to the settlement?"

"Yes, I don't really remember what it said. Something about me agreeing to be congenial to giving him some more money, up to so much, if he could prove financial distress."

Francis couldn't believe his ears. "My God, Beatrice! What kind of clause is that to sign? Where was Bill Stone all this time?"

"Oh, he was standing around wringing his hands and telling me I'd lost my mind. He said it was the damnedest fool thing he'd ever heard of, that he ought to have somebody appointed as by guardian. But Freddie was fussing and holding up the divorce. He threatened to be terribly messy about it unless I approved the clause. So I signed on the dotted line."

"My God, darling, how could you be so foolish?" Beatrice, the most intelligent woman he'd ever met, doing something like that. The lawyer in Francis was revolted.

59

"But, Francis, what could I do? I wanted to get rid of the man, and, after all, I do have quite a lot of money—more than even I can ever spend."

"But don't you realize that he can keep coming back to you— he will keep coming back to you, blackmailing you for more money?"

"Yes, that worried me. But Bill Stone talked to Freddie's lawyer, one of those real creepy Broadway types, and he says he thinks Freddie will settle for a lump sum and then the clause will be revoked or made invalid, or something. Anyway, I wouldn't have to pay anything else."

"How much does Stone think Freddie will settle for?"

"Well, that's the rub." Beatrice looked up at Francis, her face asking him not to be angry, or impatient. "Please don't growl, darling. Bill says he thinks Freddie will want a hundred and fifty thousand."

Francis slumped back on the sofa and exhaled in a furious burst. "A hundred and fifty thousand! The greedy, slimy little chiseler!" He took Beatrice's hand and kissed it gently. "Dear, dear Beatrice. You poor little, silly little thing."

"Oh, I know, Francis. Sometimes I'm so brainless, and you're so sweet not to clout me. Only, I did know it was silly, but I just wanted to get rid of Freddie because I'd met you and I was walking on clouds. I hadn't lived with Freddie for three years, and after I met you I didn't want him in the way at all."

"Well, you signed it, so that's that. What does Bill Stone suggest?"

"He wants me to fight it. He says the court probably would uphold the clause but wouldn't make me give up my right arm, as he put it. He says any court would take into consideration the original settlement and would make Freddie be reasonable."

Good for Bill Stone, Francis thought. It had been on the tip of his tongue to advise Beatrice to fight, but he had wanted to be reassured that Stone was thinking the same way. "Stone is right," he said. "You've committed yourself by signing the paper, but the court is sure to take into consideration the original settlement and, probably, the kind of sleazy loafer Freddie is. Judges are human, darling, and inclined to be rather gallant toward the female sex, sometimes too much so."

"Yes, it sounds good." Beatrice seemed unconvinced. "And I can bat my eyelashes with the best of the girls if it suits my purpose, darling. But—oh, there are complications, as usual."

"Not any more secret agreements, I hope? Beatrice, you don't have some private understanding with Freddie that Bill Stone doesn't know about?"

"Oh, no, Francis. Honestly, no. But I'm worried. Freddie's lawyer phoned me and he was terrible in a polite, cozy kind of way. He said something about he hoped for my sake we wouldn't fight it because Freddie was so—indiscreet—and he was always gossiping with those Broadway columnists. I said I didn't know what he meant, and he said—well, darling, he said it would be terrible if a lot of horrid little items about me and 'a certain Supreme Court justice' got into print."

"Why, the goddamned monster!" Francis was up on his feet now, his cheeks reddening under his eyes, his mouth thin. "The indescribably loathsome little toad! What's that lawyer's name? He ought to be disbarred." He went on, furiously, "I never heard of such damned dirty blackmailing tactics. Why, I'll go up to New York and personally wring that man's neck."

"Darling." Beatrice was up on her feet, too, her arms around his taut body. "Oh, darling, we mustn't do anything. We mustn't do anything that might be a risk for you. I don't care a bit about the money. I'll pay Freddie anything he wants. I just won't let that little monster drag you through those dirty little gossip columns."

Francis was in a rage, but he knew he would have to subdue it. When Beatrice had told him about the threat, he had been surprised to discover that he hadn't been thinking about himself but about her. He had been furious at the idea of a conspiracy to hurt Beatrice. And Beatrice was thinking about him, not of herself. Well, they would both have to think about what it meant to both of them. He didn't want to think about the headlines that would come of this. He felt ashamed in anticipation of the mud that might be slung at the high office he held; he was cringing inside. He couldn't let this happen to the Court, to John Alden Hughes, to his government. It mustn't happen. He would feel like a traitor if it did. And then, in tender warmth, he found himself insisting just as fiercely: It mustn't happen to her, either.

He held Beatrice close, not saying anything for a long time, but trying to tell her by his insistent closeness that it was all right, that they were safe—that she was safe. At this point he couldn't bear the thought that she was blaming herself, that she was prepared to do anything to save him—to save Mr. Justice Dalton.

She stayed close to him, fleeing from the sordidness of her problem, but it remained with her. "Oh, darling, I've been such a fool," she said into his cheek, as though trying to hide her words. "I've been such a senseless wanderer. I've spent all my life trying to persuade myself I was in love with somebody—anybody. Just to have someone for myself. And it was all fakery, all self-deceit, until I met you. All those other people—all the Freddies—I persuaded myself they were what I wanted them to be instead of facing up to what they were."

He held her away from him, but not too far away, and his fingers pressed into her arms, reassuring fingers seeking to give her the safety of knowing that he wanted her. "We won't discuss it any more tonight," he said. "No, darling . . ." as she started to speak. "There's no point in talking about it now. We'll think, both of us, about it, and then we'll talk about it and decide what to do. We'll do something that will make it all right. And, Beatrice—I love you very much."

It was three-thirty when he got home, belatedly stirred with absent-minded apprehensions over the dangers of walking through a Washington hotel lobby at such a late hour. He was wide-awake after the drive home in the heavy chill of the January gloom and sleep would be impossible. I'll just think about it for a little while before I go to bed, he told himself. But an hour later he was still trying to keep himself from acknowledging the thought he desperately didn't want to admit—that he had always been afraid of something like this.

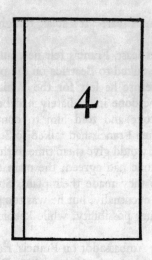

4

I T WAS TYPICAL OF THE MAN, of his cheerful self-confidence,
Francis Dalton was thinking as he started on the hot sole
mousse. The President had scheduled the dinner and Epstein
concert for this January week because it seemed like a fitting
prelude to the usual inaugural events, and it had not appeared
unreasonable to John Alden Hughes that he should have set
the date last October—two weeks before he could have official
reassurance of another term in the White House. "Besides, Liz set
the date and she's the one who really handles these things," the
President had explained to Francis.

Mary Elizabeth Hughes, as usual, had made things glittering.
Instead of the long, stiffly formal dining table, smaller tables
for eight had been set up in the State Dining Room. He noted that
the tablecloths were yellow, and the flowers were white and
yellow carnations and white daisies; Sheila would demand a fill-
in. Michael Dalton would be pleased to learn that the main course
was filet of beef; he complained regularly that the First Lady
"served too much of that French stuff." Francis had once carried
this complaint jestingly to Liz Hughes, and tonight, with the
cocktails in the East Room, she had furnished the private

intelligence for Francis' ear: "It's steak tonight—be sure to tell Papa."

For the present, at least, Francis felt he could relax and enjoy the evening. He had talked to Beatrice on the phone twice, in the morning and just before he left for the White House, and the things that had to be done immediately had been done. Beatrice had phoned Bill Stone and told him to continue negotiations with Freddie, and then Francis had talked to Stone and suggested that the negotiations would give them time to think about whether to fight the case. Stone had agreed; the main thing was to keep Freddie quiet while they made their plans. Stone believed they would have to fight eventually, but he was too good a lawyer not to explore every other possibility, while keeping Freddie Adams immobilized.

"Sir?" The Soviet Ambassador on Francis' right had said something, and as he turned questioningly to him, Francis chided himself for his furtive excursion into private thoughts.

"I was saying, Mr. Justice, that your First Lady looks especially lovely tonight."

"Oh, yes." Francis looked over to the table where Liz Hughes was pampering the social prerogatives of the Secretary of State. She did look fetching; light blue went beautifully with her honey-colored hair. Francis smiled at Volsikov. "She's one of our international assets, don't you think, Mr. Ambassador?"

"Oh, very much." Volsikov was honestly admiring. Then, the cautious Soviet servant: "Both of our countries are very fortunate. The wife of our Premier is equally charming, don't you agree?"

"Most heartily," Francis said, trying to conjure up a mental picture of all two hundred pounds of Madame Shishkin. "The Premier's wife is very active among the workers, I understand."

"Yes." Volsikov was on safely ponderous grounds now. "Irina Shishkin has done much to increase the production of maternity kits by her inspirational speeches. She is a poet, you know, and she also spends several hours every week reading her verse to patients in the maternity wards of our great hospitals."

Poor captive things, Francis thought. "Is that so?" he said. "That must be—inspirational." He bowed across the table to Mrs. Volsikov, and her answering smile was a triumph of the stainless-steel tooth industry.

Volsikov gestured with his pudgy body at the center table where the President's chair paid homage to the guest of honor, Inaugural Chairman Dennis J. Flaherty. "There is a sight, that," Volsikov said, his little purselike mouth splitting in a tentative smile. "The President is paying most gracious attention to—an enemy, shall we say? Is that not Chief Justice Bacon on his left?"

Francis grinned despite himself. That was one table whose seating Liz Hughes had not arranged; it was a quirk of the President's sometimes perverse sense of humor to indulge himself in such elegant gags. As he glanced at the center table, he noticed that Hughes wore a wide grin. Bacon, upright in his chair, seemed to be staring fixedly at the President's white tie. At that moment, the President burst into one of his famous, deep-throated peals of laughter. Bacon looked startled and appeared to shrink away from his host.

"I think perhaps the Chief Justice is not happy to be here," Volsikov suggested. Francis wondered why the Soviet Ambassador, who prided himself on being a modern Bolshevik and spoke fluent English, should always retreat into stilted phrases straight out of the Congress of Vienna.

Francis shrugged it off. "Oh, the Chief Justice is not the smiling type," he said. "But he's really quite a sociable man."

"Yes." Volsikov seemed to be trying out his words to himself. "Of course, there is all that dissension in your government about whether the President's laws are constitutional. It is too bad. It puts much pressure on everyone and causes many ill feelings."

Francis gave the Ambassador what he hoped was the stern look of a Supreme Court justice who does not discuss the Court's business. Nervy bastard. "Oh, it's not quite that bad, Mr. Ambassador," he said. "It's all in the family, you know."

"Yes, I see. But, of course, in the Soviet Union the courts express the will of the people. They are not permitted to interfere with the best interests of the people."

Francis couldn't resist it. "The best interests of what people?" he asked, putting extra politeness into his tone. "The people in the Kremlin?"

Volsikov's mouth closed like a trap and his look was almost

a glare. Then he lifted one corner of his mouth in a crooked smile. "So, you must always joke about things of importance over here. But we, we in the Soviet Union, must take things more seriously." He picked up his knife and fork and put them to work on the filet; that conversation was closed for the time being.

Francis tried the filet himself before looking up to check on what his other table companions were doing. On his left, Jack Smalley, the UPI reporter, stopped chewing for a moment to flash him a broad wink. Governor Horatio W. Summers of Indiana was bending the ear of Secretary of Commerce Roy Nelson Smith; Francis caught the typical phrase ". . . ought to erect a statue to Joe McCarthy for his heroic efforts to awaken the people to their danger." Poor Smith was doomed. Summers was taking seriously his role, assigned by the *Chicago Tribune*, as "the voice of the honest, American reactionary." He had reached his zenith, or nadir, in a Cleveland speech with his denunciation of Herbert Hoover as a "left-winger." Mrs. Smith, oblivious to her husband's distress, was chatting cozily with Mrs. Richard McKnight Evans, whose ruby necklace and skyscraper coiffure were suitable badges of office for a lady invariably described in the society sections as "the well-known hostess."

Smalley's low voice was in Francis' ear. "How come the entire Court is here tonight, Mr. Justice? Isn't the President overdoing the turn-the-other-cheek bit?"

Francis grinned. He liked Smalley, who, as a White House correspondent, did his best to be a statesman but couldn't resist reverting to ingrained Ozarkian reactions.

"I don't think so, Jack. It's protocol, I guess. It must be, because they even squeezed me in."

Smalley grinned back. "Excuse me, Mr. Justice Dalton, but quit your kidding. You're on the right side. Bacon up there looks as if he's going to eat Hughes whole. Say, Mr. Justice, a little bird told me you and the Attorney General were closeted with the President the other night. Is it all right if I ask what was going on?"

"Sure, it's all right," Francis said, his voice amiable. "But you know you won't believe me when I tell you it was just a social chat. After all, I've been lucky enough to know the President for a long time. I'm glad he still enjoys having me over for a quick one at the end of the day."

"Yes, sir, Mr. Justice." Smalley's voice was elaborately contrite. "I'll stop being nosy and go back to my steak."

Yes, he'll go back to his steak, Francis thought, but he is too good a reporter to stop being nosy. I hope the time is too short for anything to leak out before Hughes pops it. But there's no use worrying. I'm going to relax.

He did relax, too, because the food was good, especially the galantine and the green salad, and as the meal progressed, the conversation was marked by a tone of subdued good feeling. A tribute to Liz Hughes's new French chef, Francis concluded. Anyway, by the time the guests had moved into the East Room to hear Epstein and his violin, even Summers was reduced to complimenting Mrs. Evans on her hairdo and Ambassador Volsikov was engaged in an amiable discussion with Bill McDowell, the third-richest man in the world, on the relative merits of sturgeon and Rocky Mountain trout.

Epstein was good. Francis had always preferred either a full symphony orchestra or a piano, but he discovered he could lose himself in the little man's genius. There was even a magnificence about Epstein's tiny figure, so stiffly straight, and there was a gallant touch in the black patch replacing the eye he had lost in that long-ago Nazi concentration camp.

As he finished, the entire assemblage was up on its feet applauding, while the President strode from his seat to shake Epstein's hand and then stand there with one arm thrown lightly over the violinist's slight shoulders. Hughes held up his hand for a while and the applause died down.

"I'm not going to make a speech," Hughes said. "It would embarrass Mr. Epstein, and I am aware of my responsibilities as a host." He turned to the little man with the forehead moist with sweat. "But on behalf of people all over the world, I must thank you, sir. I must thank you for two things. First, for the magic you have given to the world. And second, for surviving through all those dark years and thus giving the world a triumph over the forces of evil." Then he took Epstein's arm and gently led him over to the front row of gilt chairs to present him to the First Lady.

Stretching his legs as he stood up, Francis found himself sharing a part of the aisle with Horatio Summers. "Quite an experience, wasn't it, Governor?" Francis suggested to Summers's red face. Summers's cheeks puffed in a growl-like clearing of his throat. "Yes, dammit, I suppose so," he said. "I can't understand fiddle playing, though. Dammit, I can't understand these refugees, either—why they would have let people walk over 'em."

"Well, I don't suppose Epstein had much choice," Francis said. "After all, he was trapped in Germany."

"Yes, yes, I know. But, dammit, he looks like the kind people step all over. Weak. That's the trouble with those long-haired musicians. He should've gone underground. Can't understand people like that."

Francis started to reply, but Summers was looking past him and growling an amiable "Evenin', Allen. Been wondering where you were hiding."

Mr. Justice William Allen Hume bowed slightly. "Good evening, Horatio. Good evening, Mr. Justice."

"Hello, Mr. Justice," Francis said, strangely warmed as always when he encountered the spare Hoosier. "We're just recovering from Epstein."

Hume's smile was directed at Summers. "Yes, he was superb. Superb. Didn't you think so, Horatio?"

Summers was impatient. "Oh, hell, yes. I suppose so. Don't know much about it. You know that, Allen. Dammit, Allen, I didn't understand your opinion in that Highland case."

Francis cringed. He would never get used to people who wanted to discuss cases with members of the Supreme Court; it was an outgrowth, he supposed, of the celebrity—or notoriety —achieved by the Court in its well-publicized battles with John Alden Hughes. The headlines had tended to haul the Court out of its ivory tower.

Hume didn't seem to mind, however. After all, he and Summers had been college roommates, and they had maintained a strangely affectionate relationship through all the vicissitudes of Hoosier politics and despite their spectacular philosophical differences.

"Didn't understand it?" Hume asked, letting the gentle smile play about his lips. "I had hoped my opinion had a certain awkward clarity, Horatio."

"Oh, hell, you know what I mean, Allen." Summers's impatience was sputtering now. "I don't understand how a good American like you can let a Commie like Highland bamboozle you."

Hume seemed genuinely amused, and yet Francis had seen the Hoosier cut others dead when they tried to steer the conversation into the Court's business. "I'm afraid you have the advantage over me, Horatio," he said. "You seem to know that Highland is a Communist whereas I do not."

"Now, Allen, you know what I mean. Don't split hairs. I know there isn't any *legal* proof that he's a Commie, but everybody knows he is."

"Oh, I see." Hume's manner was bland. "But, Horatio, you realize that a judge is constantly bedeviled by inconsequential things like the laws of evidence. I suppose it makes us rather—difficult."

"Well, never mind all that. That wasn't the isssue, anyway, and you know that better than I do. Highland was convicted of disturbing the peace, and you know it. He was standing up there inciting the citizenry to riot. Are we supposed to put up with that kind of Commie tactic?"

"I'm afraid I have to say yes, Horatio—or rather, the Constitution says yes. I admit that Highland was making a highly offensive and inflammatory speech, and the crowd was getting ugly. But instead of taking action to control the crowd, the police claimed to have concluded that there was danger of trouble if Highland continued, and ordered him to stop. When he didn't stop, they arrested him."

"Well, I should think so." Summers's mouth was working and little drops of saliva gathered on his lips. "The blackguard was insulting every decent public official in the government."

"Yes. Of course he was. But, Horatio—however much we deplore such ugly talk and even the twisted ideology of the speaker, the Bill of Rights says Highland had a right to do so. We can't qualify the rights granted by the Constitution. If a man can be put in jail because his audience doesn't like his speech, and because the police have chosen to shut him up rather than to enforce order on the crowd, all our talk about free speech is nonsense."

"Oh, Allen, Allen, dammit to hell. I'm damned if I know what's happened to you since the old days. Here we're facing the greatest threat to democracy in our history, and you still go around mumbling about freedom of speech. Dammit, if we don't crack down on those Commies, we won't have any freedom left at all."

Hume's low laugh was genuinely affectionate. "Horatio, you haven't changed a bit. Still the direct activist. But I can't fight with you, because I don't think you really believe that liberties are preserved by infringing on them. Let's call a truce, Horatio; we're supposed to be enjoying ourselves in this grand house, and our host and hostess are too gracious and charming for us to impose acrimony on their splendid evening."

Horatio managed a laugh now, too; Francis was impressed again at how Hume's grace and dignified good humor made it impossible for anyone to quarrel with him. "Oh, all right, Allen," Summers said. "Can't get anything through that thick head of yours, anyway. But, by golly, I'm still proud of my old roommate. Now I'm going to leave you two big domes and go talk to some politicians."

Hume watched Summers lumber away, his bald head shining in the bright lights. "I'm very fond of Horatio Summers," he said to Francis. "He is a very decent man. In his way, he's terribly worried about his country and he thinks he's doing all he can to save it from destruction."

Dalton's voice was dry. "If he's confused, I'm afraid he has a great deal of company these days." He had joined in the dissent and he felt that his opinion had shot holes in Hume's majority argument, but Summers's bull-mouthed comments had left him uneasy, had given him a sense of prickly irritation. It was bad enough to have that obnoxiously hearty jurist, Baker, sharing his opinion—but now Summers, too. Damn the man.

"Yes, I gathered you were worried, too." Was there a soothing note in Hume's gentle tone? "It's a difficult matter. It's a difficult time for honest men confronted with the kind of dishonesty that emanates from so many quarters these days."

Francis managed to keep the irritation out of his voice. "I don't suppose I would put it that way, Mr. Justice. I agree that it is a perplexing problem to try to find a way out of the conflict between free speech and other interests that bear on the whole community. We have to be practical, and I believe we have the assistance of the Constitution, which does not insist anywhere that so-called free speech is an inalienable right to be placed above all other considerations. After all, there are times when vital interests such as public order must be held paramount." What he wanted to say was that Hume's viewpoint was all too nice and pat, that there was no place for beautiful rhetoric about freedom which became license in times of clear and present danger.

Hume seemed to read his mind, and his smile held its warmth. "I don't like to make you impatient with me, Mr. Justice. I realize that sometimes I must sound—obstructive, in an old-maid kind of way. I know that things are happening, and that the country must act, almost every day, that it must try to get things done quickly, and I try to accept the theory of balancing all considerations to come up with a reasonable answer. I suppose I'll just never be any good at it, though; somehow I can't believe the Constitution meant for us to be entrusted with such powers."

"We are supposed to attack our work as reasonable men," Francis said. He let the acid seep into his words now. "We are not supposed to shut out the outside world when we sit down to consider a case. After all, Mr. Justice, yours was one of the votes that upheld the breakup of that Nazi community in upper New York State during the war."

"*Touché.*" Hume bowed gravely. "Yes, I voted to uphold, after considerable wrestling with myself. I don't know whether I would vote that way again—and yet, I'm afraid I would. It was a time of national emergency; the Court could not usurp powers which belonged to the military."

Francis had to laugh; suddenly the irritation, the impatience with Hume's nice patness, had gone. "Mr. Justice, I can never really stay angry when I'm arguing with you. You always manage to convince me that you're immensely human, that you aren't always inflexibly sure of yourself. You could never play God."

"I hope not." Hume had never lost his mildness, but now he seemed glad he had persuaded Francis to relax, too. "I should think it would be a very demanding—and tiresome—responsibility. Mr. Justice, I purposely abstained from wine at the table so

I could have a glass of champagne before I left. Will you join me?"

"I will indeed, sir. Even if I did drain every glass in sight at dinner." We'll never agree, Francis was thinking as they walked over to the long cloth-covered bar, but it is a pleasure to know this man.

Talking with Hume, it had seemed to Francis they were alone in the room; now he was aware again of the polite, low-keyed confusion of voices about him. Here came Mrs. Richard McKnight Evans, bustling by with young Senator Bill Martin in tow, stopping just long enough to give Francis an arch look and to report in a conspiratorial tone, "I saw Beatrice today; you both must come to see me." Here was the young Ivy Leaguer from *The New York Times*, Bradford, coolly enjoying his tennis palship with the President. Here was the Speaker of the House, Henry Adam Smith, his ear held close to the whispered words of the intent and nearsighted Vice-President Thomas Morgan. They are all here like courtiers, Francis thought, ready to amuse their king and to do his bidding. All the party lacked was a dozen or so of the opposition in chains, trailing the victor's chariot. Some of them hated Hughes, like young Martin and old Frank Hoar, who totted up his frustrations in daily fits of stridency on the Senate floor and now was making sour comment to the Senate Minority Leader, Cliff Sampson, whose face was lumpy with bourbon and whose mouth twitched with impatience to get out of this room and go home to his bottle. Some of them hated John Alden Hughes, that was certain, but none had the political wherewithal to obstruct him.

"Here you are, Mr. Justice." Francis took two glasses of champagne from a footman's tray and handed one to Hume. "Long live the honorable Court."

Hume nodded and sipped his glass. "Yes—I hope it's all right to drink, so to speak, to ourselves, since others are included. Good champagne is one of my few vices, now that the calendar is catching up with me."

Behind him, the voice had the clipped, yet casually offhand syllables of the English public school. "And do those few other vices, Mr. Justice, come equipped complete with telephone numbers?"

72

Hume turned slightly; his movement carried just the hint of a fastidious impatience. "Good evening, Mr. Hughes," he said to the President's brother. "No, I'm afraid not. The ladies have never favored me with such confidence."

"Hello, Jimmy," Francis said. He supposed that James Truitt Hughes, at forty, was the handsomest man in Washington. His black hair was streaked with premature gray and he wore it long and thick and brushed back at the sides. His face was just bony enough to sharpen its angles, and shadows were beginning to show in the slightly puffed circles under his green eyes. He was tall enough, at about six feet, and aged whiskey had not yet begun to thicken his waist. He looked like the kind of movie extra who would be hired for a scene in the White House East Room. Francis thought it was unfair of him that he so often lectured Jimmy Hughes. Jimmy had charm.

Jimmy Hughes said "Hello, Francis," carelessly, and bowed slightly to Hume. "I can't believe you, Mr. Justice," he said to Hume. "The ladies who favor me with their confidences are all mad for you."

Hume was not smiling, but his expression was serenely bland. "Thank you," he said. "I appreciate your soothing courtesy to an old man."

Jimmy laughed in his soft way, the laugh that never committed itself. "I'll bet you feel younger than I do tonight, Mr. Justice." His voice changed so that it no longer matched the smile on his lips. "The truth is, I feel a little depressed. I suppose it was those damned pickets outside who did it."

"Ah, yes." Hume's voice seemed a trifle sad. "The Gleason pickets. They were still there when I arrived. It's not the sort of thing that makes one feel—festive."

Francis said nothing; the pickets had depressed him, too. Those men and women, some shabby and some well dressed, were continuing their protests over the sentencing to death of the convicted Soviet spy, despite the fact that the evidence against the man had been overwhelming. Their cause seemed so pathetic, so futile, that their persistence angered him. After all, Gleason's case had gone the route—he had been given all the justice at the disposal of the people. Finally, the Supreme Court had rejected his plea. Yet Francis had found his anger tinged with something

73

very close to pity; he had no use for the professional protestants who organized such demonstrations, but he was sorry for the poor soul who had been misled into joining the cause by something he supposed was a quality of mercy.

Jimmy Hughes said, "Those signs are pretty awful, you know. There's one in particular that says, 'President Hughes, Don't Murder This Human Being.' I know that sort of thing has been going on for centuries, but it does give you a start when they're talking about your brother."

"It's sad," Hume said. "Even when the people are forced to prescribe it, capital punishment is never pretty. And, of course, Gleason's was rather a sensational case."

"Sensational—and expensive," Francis said. "I saw the figures the other day. In the last five years, contributions to his defense from all over the world have amounted to more than a quarter of a million dollars. That, of course, is what happens when political ideologies are involved."

"Yes, I suppose that's what bothers me," Jimmy said. "All those outcries from all over the world. Protest meetings in Bangkok and New Delhi and London and Cairo. I don't *feel* guilty—I'm sure Gleason was given the opportunity to exhaust every legal means in his behalf. But there you are—it's an uncomfortable feeling to realize that all over the world people are massing in public squares determined to *make* you feel guilty."

"That's it, of course," Hume said. "We can keep telling ourselves that perhaps ninety per cent of those demonstrations are the cynical inspiration of the Communist hierarchy. But that doesn't make it any more pleasant to endure."

That *was* it, Francis thought. We Americans generally mean so damned well, and we so seldom get credit for it. He said, "I certainly agree with both of you. The man was fairly tried, on the evidence, and his appeals were fairly heard, on the evidence. Yet something like those pickets outside tonight makes me uneasy."

"Oh, hell!" Jimmy Hughes's voice sounded embarrassedly impatient. "I seem to have plunged the assemblage into the darkest gloom. I'm sorry, gentlemen. The world is beyond our ministrations, I'm afraid. Francis, I wouldn't drink too much of that champagne. Liz takes care of the table wines, but John runs the champagne department, and he's inclined to be economical about such things. It's this new, folksy *noblesse oblige* in reverse, I suppose. You know, don't be too chic or they won't like it in the boondocks."

"It tastes all right to me," Francis said. "Of course, I'm a Scotch type myself."

"Good. In this house, it's better to stick to Scotch. John is too much the professional horny-handed son of the soil to be a really good host. Anyway, I shall leave shortly and try to cure my hangover at home, where I can trust the hooch. Like right now, because I see my brother coming."

The President was at Francis' elbow now, stopping off in his accustomed prowling about among the guests. Jimmy had turned to go and John Alden Hughes grinned at his retreating figure. "You'd better run, you ingrate. Giving my champagne a bad name." Francis noted the grin; it was meager.

"Good evening, Mr. President," Hume and Francis said together. There was no doubt Hume was glad to see his host, and not only because he had chased Jimmy away.

"Gentlemen," said the President, "pay no attention to Jimmy. The champagne is perfectly good, if not exactly the best vintage. Have you two been cooking up more trouble for me?"

"I hope not, Mr. President," Hume said. "Unless you suggest that listening to Governor Summers is subversive."

"Horatio!" The President laughed shortly. "No, I should think it would be impossible *not* to listen to the Governor. He and I agree about a lot of things, but sometimes I wish he could be a little less basic, and a little less explosive."

"He was picking on Justice Hume," Francis said. "But I suspect the justice outtalked him."

"That's a feat," the President said. His smile was for Hume. "But then, I've learned not to underrate you, Mr. Justice."

Hume was not uneasy. He returned the President's smile and inclined his head in a deprecating gesture. "Now I am embarrassed, sir," he said. "First your brother proclaims my attractions as a ladies' man and now you pay tribute to my logic."

The President threw up both his hands. "All right, all right, Mr. Justice. I surrender. I wouldn't think, now, of giving it any other name but logic."

75

"Thank you, sir," Hume said gravely.

It was not tense at all. Hume was merely a man the President couldn't charm into anything, and the President knew it and amiably stopped trying. They chatted for a while about the inaugural and the chances for good weather, and both the President and Hume were not only at ease but warmly cordial with each other by the time Hughes strolled off to visit with more guests.

Hume finished his glass of champagne and departed shortly thereafter and a few minutes later Francis saw the President and Liz take their leave. He was about to leave himself when the Attorney General came up to him and motioned him to one side, with that conspiratorial gesture so dear to politicians.

"The Boss would like to see you upstairs for a minute, Francis," Mayborn said, all but putting a hand to the side of his mouth. "Can you come up with me now?"

They found Hughes in his study-office on the second floor, stretched out on the green sofa in front of the big desk, a cigarette dangling from his mouth.

"Sit down, sit down, gentlemen," Hughes said, looking up. "I'm going to stay here because I'm too damned tired to get up. Francis, this won't take a minute, but I thought you'd be interested in a little conversation I had at dinner."

Francis and Mayborn were sitting down and Francis looked over at the President.

"I've already told Charlie," the President said. "As you may have noticed, Bacon and I had quite a chat tonight over the meat course. It started with the usual chaff, but eventually I got him around to the Court and I mentioned rather pointedly that it was a shame the Court had such a heavy backlog. I sympathized with him for the burden it imposed on the justices and especially on himself as Chief Justice. He didn't say much, just an occasional mumble, until I rather baldly remarked that of course I was always ready to help out."

Hughes took the cigarette out of his mouth and leaned over and threw it into the large ashtray on the coffee table.

"I didn't really know what I meant myself; I was just trying to sound him out. And do you know what he said to me? He said, 'Mr. President, I do not want to be impertinent or to violate the role of a guest, but it is obvious to me you are trying to find out when I will retire. I will tell you, Mr. President, that I will not retire at this time—I will not retire for at least another four years.' "

Francis was fascinated and amazed—so much so that all he could manage was a murmured "Hm."

The President's face was split by his huge toothy smile. "How is that for getting told off in your own house, Francis? He won't retire for four years. In other words, he won't retire while I'm in the White House."

"I'm amazed," Francis said. "No, I guess I'm not. Bacon has always been outspoken."

"Well, he didn't leave me any doubts, Francis," the President said. "And that's the point, of course. I didn't really have any doubts about my course the other night when you suggested that Bacon's retirement might solve our problem for us. The shift of one justice is not enough for my purposes. But now, Francis, you can see that we have no alternative but to go ahead full steam with our plans. There's no other way."

"I guess not," Francis said. "No, there's no other way."

Later, after refusing a nightcap, he was digesting it all as he walked out onto the North Portico. It wasn't a matter of guessing; there was no other way. And this, Francis thought, is the way the President wanted it anyway. Even if Bacon had told him he was going to resign tomorrow, the President would have insisted on going ahead. The President was relieved to have been able to tell Francis that Francis' suggestion had not worked out, but only as an added bit of persuasion. Once Hughes had mapped out his campaign, he had been determined to carry it out regardless of circumstances. The President wanted his kind of Supreme Court, a Supreme Court that was safely his, not his by the narrow margin of one precarious vote. Francis believed now that the President was glad Bacon had decided to stay on. It kept things uncomplicated. It sustained the critical nature of the situation, and thus sustained the President in his belief that action was imperative.

77

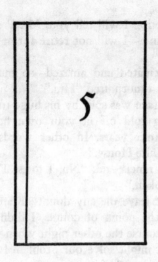

5

JOHN, SPEAK UP—I CAN'T HEAR A THING!" The President of the United States had no trouble at all hearing his mother's voice from Palm Springs; Julia Hughes, he reflected, would be just as audible if she merely poked her head out of the window of her seven-room suite and pointed her voice in the general direction of Washington.

"I'm right here, Mother," the President said, a little louder than usual. "I'm speaking right into the phone." As you've been telling me to do for forty-seven years, he said to himself.

"There, dear, that's better." The voice from Palm Springs had shifted so that it had the hearty quality Julia Hughes employed to congratulate a horse after a particularly difficult jump. "What I was saying, John, is that I haven't received your inaugural address yet. Didn't you send it by courier plane?"

The President glanced idly at the portrait of George Washington across the green rug in his oval West Wing office. It needed straightening. "No, Mother, I didn't," he said. "I haven't finished it yet."

"What *are* you saying, John?" His mother's voice now carried that high-pitched tone of incredulity which was a trademark of her generation at Bryn Mawr. "Really, this line is terrible. Did you *possibly* say you haven't finished your speech yet?"

The President sighed. "The line is all right, Mother. You heard me correctly. I haven't finished it yet. We've still got a few things to get in it, and some smoothing out to do."

"Well." It seemed to John Alden Hughes that he could hear his mother's silence almost as well as her voice. "Well—John dear." The President could almost see his mother reminding herself sternly that her son was the President of the United States and that by acquiring that title he had moved out from under the stern matriarchal—and political—control of his mother. Julia Hughes had managed somehow, for four years, not to meddle—too much. Usually, she carefully refrained from offering an opinion until asked. But the President realized this had been hard for a woman of strong mind and will who had inherited a half-billion dollars and had used some of it and all of her energy to become Pennsylvania's first woman Governor, and then to go on to sit for two terms in the United States Senate in a futile one-woman attempt to balance the national budget. Julia Hughes was a woman accustomed to offering advice to Presidents, whether it was solicited or not.

Now his mother essayed a mild protest. "But it's getting late, isn't it, John? Really, dear, it's the *day* before the inauguration."

"Oh, we'll get it done, Mother. We haven't far to go now. It's just that I want this one to be especially right. It doesn't hurt to take all the time we can." The President knew his mother that well, at least.

"Of course." Julia Hughes had always urged thoroughness upon her two sons—and, with less vigor, on her daughter. "Of course you *want* it to be right, John. It's just that I'd hoped to see it before now." Julia Hughes long ago had forced herself to refrain from suggesting at any time that she might be able to help with the drafting of important White House messages.

"Yes, I know, Mother." The President was genuinely contrite. His mother was a good guy. A very good guy. "I suppose I'm being too much of a perfectionist. But I hope it'll be ready so you can read it tomorrow morning before we go up to the Hill."

"Of course, John." Now Julia Hughes seemed impatient with

herself, and it was inevitable that the stables should intrude on her speech. "Oh, hell, John—it doesn't really matter. I'm just *interested*, that's all." Her voice dropped to a new low. "Your father and I will be in about ten o'clock tonight, as you know."

"Yes, the Secret Service will be out to take care of you, Mother. I've got to go to the concert, you know."

"Yes. I suppose we could have made it, but both your father and I would rather get to bed early." John Alden Hughes I would, the President thought, but not his mother. Julia Hughes would give her right arm—or her best hunter—to be in the box with her son at Constitution Hall, but she was too rigidly proper to intrude on her son's show—her son's show, and her son's wife's show. It was a testament to the rocklike integrity of a woman who for nearly fifty years had been the family's dominant personality . . . with, the President reflected, the complete and often enthusiastic approval of the naturalist who had absent-mindedly fathered Julia Hughes's children. His father, the President told himself, would as soon skip the whole affair to indulge in an orgy of bird-watching.

"The rest of the family is organized, I suppose," his mother said.

"Yes—Jimmy has been in town for the past week, and Pauline and Geoffrey arrived yesterday. We've had quite a family reunion."

"Yes." His mother's tone seemed unconvinced. "How is Jimmy behaving, John?"

"Oh, fine." Except, the President thought, for that monumental drunk he hung on at the Governors' Reception. "Jimmy looks very well—from skiing, I suppose."

"He always looks good." His mother's voice was short and there was emphasis on the *looks*. "I just hope to God he doesn't show up tomorrow morning with some striptease girl from the Inferno. That boy has never learned discretion. You know, I never minded a little healthy playing around by either of you, but Jimmy seems to want everybody to know he's having a good time."

"Oh, he'll be all right," the President said. I hope, he thought. "You know, he always looks very well in public."

"I suppose. Well, Pauline will hold up her end. Just so long as that long-haired professor husband of hers doesn't decide to re-but your inaugural address. I still can't understand where a sensible girl like your sister found that little Communist."

The President laughed, genuinely. He was very fond of his sister Pauline, his saucy little kid sister, and he could forgive her anything, including her marriage to Dr. Geoffrey Parker Osborne of Swarthmore and the little magazines. No point in telling his mother that Geoffrey had monopolized the floor at dinner the other night with a long monologue on the benefits of artificial insemination.

"Geoff is all right, Mother," he said. "You know, he lives in a world of considerable talk. He's really pretty stimulating at times."

"Hah! He stimulates me right into the bathroom. The human laxative."

After he had hung up, the President didn't ring for Harry Weiss immediately. It seemed to him he had been surrounded by people for months; he just wanted to sit and rest for a while. It always did him good to talk to his mother despite the tendency of Julia Hughes to utter her sentences in little explosions. It was like going back to your old neighborhood and finding nothing changed. His mother was a constant in the shifting world which was a President's abiding companion. When he talked to his mother he never had any doubts about where his mother stood. "Don't equivocate," his mother used to tell him during those long chats in the library of the big house in Germantown. "Take your stand and then stick by it. You can alter your course when circumstances dictate, but never change your principles." Julia Hughes had never altered her principles, which were based on a sound system of capitalism, responsible and unintimidated unionism and the responsibility of the wealthy to employ part of their wealth for the benefit of mankind. And his mother had always been the boss, wherever she was: in her own investment bank, on the boards where she sat like a stern Diana, at home. The children were all good swimmers by the time they were four years old, because Julia Hughes decreed it. They were all experts on a horse, on the tennis court, at the helm of a sailboat, on the dance floor, because his mother decreed it. His father was the only non-athlete in the family, but he never interfered in what

Jimmy called "our combat training"; his father was too much in love with his wife, too respectful of her principles, to question her judgment on anything. The family's life was the way Julia Hughes wanted it to be, and John Alden Hughes I wanted it that way, too, because he never had any doubts that his wife was right.

The President reflected now that even Jimmy's rebellion had been late a-borning. Although Jimmy hated football, he had followed his older brother on the Princeton team and had played an adequate if often perfunctory blocking back. "It's curious about Jimmy," his mother had remarked. "He was never interested in being a ball carrier; he always seems to want to play a secondary role. I'm not sure I like that. My son should want to carry the ball." John himself had been a passing quarterback who could run with the ball; he was a good blocker, too, but he had never had any interest in being a member of anyone's supporting cast. Yet it was a small thing to pick on Jimmy for; he had been a fairly good student at Princeton and the scrapes he got into were no more serious than those of most of his mates. It wasn't until he'd been out of school for two years and, presumably, safely ensconced in the investment house, that Jimmy's rebellion flowered. He didn't want to be an investment banker, which was all right, if somewhat disappointing, to his mother. The trouble was, he didn't know what he wanted to be. And so he had become what the headlines described as PLAYBOY SON OF SOCIALITE FINANCIER, and thereby arranged the family's first encounter with a flamboyant world that included Hollywood actresses, jockeys, nightclub owners and an abstract painter named Tom Yastrovic, who lived with a fat Negro woman.

The President supposed that Pauline was a mixture of Jimmy and himself, with something of his father's soft gentility added. Once he had finished Princeton and rushed through Harvard Law in near-record time, there was no doubt where he was going. Politics was his only interest and his mother encouraged him both morally and financially. It was pretty much the same with Pauline. She was more than a very good-looking girl with a healthy body and a high IQ who wanted to be a wife and a mother. She wanted to get away from the kind of socially routine husbands available on the Main Line and among the Ivy

League Good Joes. Her mind was set, inflexibly, on diversifying her life through a husband who lived and worked in the houses of intellectualism. She didn't want a banker or a stockbroker or a lawyer; she wanted a man with whom she could think as well as go to bed, and to the Tennis Club, and to Bimini. She found him in Geoffrey Osborne, who was her political science professor at Swarthmore, ten years her senior and intense in a carefully off-hand way. They were married in Pauline's last year at the school her mother called the "talking factory," and Pauline was happy in the midst of her husband's books and with her two bright children. And Osborne was not merely a theorist when he talked; he was a tough-minded man with a valid point of view, a stubby little man with straggly mustache and uncombed hair, who seemed indolent and who had the stamina of three men. Pauline Hughes and John Alden Hughes II had kept their eyes on the ball.

It looked as if it was going to snow. The President got up from his brown leather swivel chair with its high back and walked over to the French doors that looked out on the Rose Garden. The Weather Bureau had promised it would be crisp and cold for the inauguration, with no mention of snow, but that wasn't what the sky said. It was sullen and gray, and the air, as the President walked over from the Mansion this morning, seemed almost as if it were about to crystallize. He had mentioned it to the Secret Service agent, Sam Fellows, and Sam had said, "Yes, sir, you can almost feel the snow."

Well, snow or not, the die was cast for tomorrow. The speech was ready; but it was not going to be shown around, even to his mother. The only two copies were locked in his desk drawer, and there they would stay until early tomorrow morning, when he would give one copy to Mike Blair to have mimeographed by the girls in his Press Office, and stow the other one in his pocket. The speech made him feel good. It was an excellent one. It was a candid exposition of what was wrong and what he intended to do to make it right. There was no mincing of words. He would tell the country that he was going to enlarge the Supreme Court and explain, in simple language, why this was necessary. He liked the speech because it was an honest speech; he would be honest with the country and he believed he could depend on the country to applaud both his honesty and his intentions. The country had *wanted* the Walsh Act banning strikes, because it also restrained management's tendency to say an automatic no to all of labor's demands; there had been a torrent of indignation when the Supreme Court ruled the act invalid.

He had put into practice his theory that not only the government, but the blocs of selfish interests too, should be prevented from harming the welfare of the community as a whole. His enemies shrieked that he had overdone it, that he was trying to substitute for the republican form of government the autocratic system of pure majority rule, with no consideration for the minorities, but the voters had answered these protests. Things needed to be done, and it was the government that had to determine what those things were. John Alden Hughes was in sympathy with the objectives of the Supreme Court in its move to impose integration in the schools; he believed there was a final wisdom in having white and Negro children attend the same schools to eliminate the trouble-brewing implications of racial inferiority. But he had done his best to slow down integration because he was not prepared to impose his personal will on the South. It was the South's business to change local conditions in accordance with the atmosphere of the time and the place, and he could not permit Negro agitators to whip up violence on the pretext of seeking their civil rights. He had sent in United States marshals to clap those agitators into jail, just as he would have arrested white agitators. His enemies cried out against his "attacks" on the Constitution, and the Supreme Court clearly was in a mood to strike down his actions, but he believed he was on solid ground. The Fourteenth Amendment never suggested outlawing segregated schools; in fact, even as the amendment was being ratified, Congress had established Washington schools for the sole use of Negro children. Moreover, jurisdiction over the entire field of education had been reserved to the states by the Tenth Amendment. John Alden Hughes a dictator? Better apply that label to the nine men in their ivory tower.

Curiously, most of the protests against his farm and labor legislation had come from the Congress and from self-appointed guardians of the farmer and the worker. When he removed most of the controls over agriculture, the uproar had shaken the country, but the fact remained that under the Constitution no branch of the national government had any power to control agriculture—quite aside from the fact, of course, that those attempts to control not only had failed to solve the farm problem but had made it worse. His policies were working. They were persuading the farmer to go into other employment because the government had stopped paying inefficient farmers for produce that merely swelled the surplus. Hughes saw no reason why the natural laws of economics should not apply to farmers as well as to bankers and shoe clerks, and if those laws decreed that there were too many farmers, then the government's wisest policy was to reduce their number. His labor policies had come under fire—but only in Congress and among the less secure labor leaders, those who weren't rich enough to relax. The more mature—and, he reflected wryly, the richer—labor leaders had gone along with him, and so had the workers. The fact was that strikes had become a burden not only to management but to the individual worker and his labor hierarchy as well. The laws on the books were fundamentally sound, but they had resulted in excesses; they had upset the balance of power between labor and management. He was having trouble with his right-to-work program, but he wasn't worried. After all, a right-to-work law was nothing more or less than a civil right which gave an employee the right not to join a union. The bellowing continued, but the voters took note that it was balanced by a bellowing on the other side against the administration's vigorous antitrust campaign. In such ways had he built up, with perfect sincerity, the people's trust in him.

He could trust the country, because the country had backed him to the hilt so far. Not the pressure groups, not the minority blocs, but the country as a whole—the individual citizens who wanted action and reassurance, and security from predators both within and without. The country had backed him when he threw Jake Santelli out on his ear and installed his Undersecretary of Labor as caretaker of the nation's largest union. The country had backed him, and so had the rank and file of Jake Santelli's so-called "captive" union. The Supreme Court had thrown it out, with its mutterings about the corporate state, but the country had wanted it and it had told him so in the thousands of letters and telegrams that poured into the White House.

The Supreme Court had thrown out his antitrust amendment to help the big mining companies, too, but again the country had stood by him and bellowed its protest against the Court's meddling. He had always had the citizen behind him when he insisted that the Constitution was not what the Court said it was, but what its authors intended it to be. The Court might pretend to be a defender of the Constitution, but the people knew better —they knew what he meant when he explained the phrase "to promote the general welfare"; they knew that the Constitution was being defended in the White House, not in that marble palace of the judiciary.

The cigarette in his mouth was still unlit; he held his lighter to it and inhaled a mouth-filling cloud of smoke. It seemed to him he had a right to a portion of the country's gratitude, too, in the field of national security. He had made good on his campaign pledge to take positive action against the dictator, to abandon the old policy of containment, of parrying the dictator's blows. He had taken the first steps toward his announced goal of making the Communist world free when he had gone into Albania. When the Albanian uprising erupted, there had been those who had cautioned him to go slowly, to stand by and watch for developments. He had presented the Kremlin with a blunt ultimatum forbidding Soviet intervention, and when the ultimatum went unnoticed he had electrified—and gladdened—the nation by moving paratroopers into the chaotic country. It had worked. The American troops had the necessary nuclear weapons, and the Kremlin knew it, knew that it was confronted with a superior force ready to fight. There had been some anxious hours, but the Soviet had backed down, finally, admittedly harassed by threatening gestures from Yugoslavia, and today Albania was as free as two years of experimentation with democracy could make it.

He had turned a deaf ear to the alarmists in the Chinese emergency, too, in order to take advantage of the situation. When the revolt came, he had acted quickly. American planes had landed guerrillas from Formosa on the Communist mainland and for the last year now they had made life miserable for the Reds.

Risks had been taken, but he had been tough. When the pleaders came to him, he had firmly resisted; he was damned if he was going to invite Shishkin over here, not under the circumstances. He could not believe that national survival depended upon "accommodating" the Soviet Union. He was tired of seeking settlements while the Kremlin went after victories and world domination. He was tired of the word "negotiate," and he would not admit that there was "no harm in talking." There *was* harm in talking, because the Communists did not look upon negotiations, as the United States did, as an effort to reach an agreement. With them, negotiations were a form of political warfare; they had no intention of compromising, of reaching a *modus vivendi* with capitalism. John Alden Hughes was not intent on achieving victory by force of arms, but he told himself again that the country could not make the avoidance of a shooting war its main objective. War was not unthinkable to the Kremlin; Shishkin was prepared to risk it as a last resort, and the country could not back down merely because of America's greater fear of war.

He found himself staring again at the portrait of Washington across the room, and it brought him to. He looked at his watch and at the same time pressed a buzzer on his desk. Weiss and Mayborn would be biting their nails.

Both of them seemed calm when they came through the door, however. "Good morning, gentlemen," the President said. "I'm sorry to keep you waiting. Just sit right down and we'll get to work."

Mayborn slumped into an armchair and Harry Weiss perched his tall angular frame on the edge of the sofa and fiddled with his horn-rimmed glasses. Weiss looked pale in the same room with the broad red face of the Attorney General.

"First I think I'd better get Mike Blair in here," the President said. "He's going out of his mind about the speech." He pressed a buzzer and the three were silent, waiting for the Press Secretary to come in.

When Mike Blair arrived he seemed to have been running, and his hand was pushing back a lock of his silver hair. But he managed the broad smile that went so well with his hulking body.

"Yes, sir, Mr. President," Mike said. "I'm sure glad to see you at last."

The President laughed in a kind of burst. "I'll bet you are,

Mike. Okay, I've got the word for you. We've still got some work to do on the speech, but I want you to have the girls come in at about six-thirty tomorrow morning to get it mimeographed. We won't need it that fast, but we've got to allow for possible corrections."

"Six-thirty?" The tone was politely questioning. Mike wouldn't protest if his boss asked him to have his girls render the speech into Sanskrit. "Yes, sir, sure. What's the release time?"

"The release time is when I utter the first word of the address," the President said. He looked at Mike carefully above the rims of his half-glasses.

"Not until you start speaking?" Now Mike would have to say something. "Holy Cow! The boys are going to be awful sore. They're expecting it first thing in the morning."

"It can't be helped, Mike." The President was smiling, but his tone was firm. "I don't want this to get out in advance. I'm sorry to inconvenience my friends in the press, but that's the way it has to be."

Mike shifted from one foot to the other. "Yes, sir. I understand. I may have to wear a suit of armor when I tell 'em, though." He laughed, or rather he gave vent to a hideous giggle. "I can just see their faces—they'll have to work like hell up at the Capitol. I can just see Peter Underwood, the impeccable pundit."

"I'm sure you can handle them, Mike—including Pete. O.K.?"

"O.K., sir." Mike turned to go, then looked back. "Give 'em hell, sir."

"I'll do my best, Mike. So long for now."

"Well, Charlie—Harry?" The President lifted an eyebrow at his two aides. "Everything set?"

Charlie looked toward Harry Weiss, and Weiss took off his glasses. "All set, sir," Weiss said. "We finished up with that last-minute research last night, and the bill is ready to go with the speech. It sure took me by surprise when the Attorney General finally let me in on it."

"I suppose it did," the President said. "You don't see any obstacles?" It was not really a question; at this point John Alden Hughes wanted no further discussion.

"No, sir. It's—sticky, but we're used to that. It's an excellent bill."

"It sure is," Mayborn said. "I drove my boys nuts, though, getting the research done. I kept farming out stuff, telling each one only as much as he needed to know about the specific point he was looking for. I asked them for data out of the blue; they must have wondered why they were set to work compiling statistics on the ages of Federal judges and the refusals of writs of certiorari. Nobody's the wiser, though."

"Good," the President said. "You know, Charlie, what pleases me is that in a sense old Robert McNair Bacon is one of the co-authors of our little surprise."

The sound Mayborn made was an authentic chuckle. "You know, I was sure there had been some agitation concerning judges' retirement. I knew I'd read it before somewhere. And, sure enough, there it was, in old Bacon's words, in a recommendation to the Justice Department." He struck a recitative pose. "Bacon said it, all right: 'Whenever a Federal judge fails to avail himself of the privilege of retiring at the age provided by law, the President shall have the power to appoint another judge who shall have precedence over the older one.' Of course, Bacon was younger then. And, of course, they never did anything about it."

"No, and we're going him one better," the President said. "We're going to add two judges anyway."

"Schedule still the same on letting the second-line Congressional leaders in on it?" Weiss put in. That worried Weiss.

"Yes, I'm having them in to breakfast tomorrow morning, with the Cabinet. I'll tell them about it then, but I won't give them a copy of either the speech or the bill."

"They're going to be very unhappy," Weiss said. He was unhappy, now, for them. Weiss was orderly. He had no brief for the Congressional VIPs, who were inclined to regard him as a dangerous radical who had the President's ear, but he liked things neat.

"Well, it can't be helped." The President was determined not to go into that again. "They'll get over it; they always have. We don't have to worry about the opposition; the election settled their hash. And our own boys on the Hill have an almost unblemished record of going down the line for us. They'll do it again. Besides, they've got an inconvenient habit of offering advice when their advice is asked. Any advice at this point would be annoying, and there's always a possibility of a leak."

"That's for sure," Mayborn's voice cut in brusquely. "Those boys can't keep anything to themselves. They're so goddamn anxious to play big shot to their home state correspondents. I just hope we can trust Chet McAdam and Henry Smith."

"So do I." The President's voice stayed grim. "But I had to tell both of them, Charlie. We couldn't go into this with the Majority Leader of the Senate and the Speaker of the House in the dark. You know how Henry Smith is—he's more than Speaker of the House; he's a kind of benevolent proprietor of that institution. As for Chet McAdam, he's terribly sensitive about the dignity of the Senate—I don't have to tell you that after the hassle you had with him about that Jones case down in Georgia."

"Yeah. A couple of prima donnas." Mayborn was grudgingly in agreement.

"Besides, Charlie, I'm not going to make the same mistake Roosevelt made." Hughes slapped fist into hand. "F.D.R. didn't take *any* of the Congressional leaders into his confidence beforehand. As a result, he was handicapped by resentment on the part of the very men he needed to lead his fight. We have to be practical; we need McAdam and Smith, and it's only common sense to tip them off in advance. Besides, they've both done a damn good job for me; I'm grateful to both of them."

"Yes, sir, I go along with you there," Mayborn said. "There was no other way out, as you say. And besides, you didn't give them the whole rundown."

"No, I didn't, as you know. I merely told them I had a plan that was a little different from Chet's plan—for increasing the size of the Court. Frankly, as I told you two, I was pleased with their reaction. I wouldn't say they were enthusiastic, but they both saw my point. I think they'll go down the line for us, Charlie." The President's voice was quiet with the confidence that came from previous victories.

Weiss's worried voice made one of its wonted fact-of-life intrusions. "We'll need 'em to go down the line on more than this, Mr. President. That nuclear warheads for West Germany thing will be a tough one, if we ever get it straightened out. We're going to need more than Chet McAdam and Henry Smith on our side if it develops you have to go through with it."

"Yes, Harry, we will." The President spoke in a low, barely audible voice. "I'm afraid we'll need the Almighty, if that happens. Mere members of Congress don't have enough power to help us on that." He paused and looked down at the rug. "I suppose no one on earth can help, really, if it comes down to that. But if it has to be done, it will have to be done." Suddenly, the President looked all alone in the room's silence—and then, just as suddenly, he was back at work.

"Meanwhile, we've got to handle the business at hand, gentlemen." Hughes's face broke into his wide, campaigning smile. "First things first, whatever Mr. Shishkin may be up to in Moscow. Our job at the moment is to mobilize the troops behind our little Court plan. We've got to see to it that everybody goes along with us. I think we can—persuade them."

"Yes." Weiss did not look any happier. "But what about the labor boys and the NAM and the farmers—that bunch? We're going to need their help, and they're not going to like not being tipped, either."

"Perhaps not, Harry, but they'll go along, too," the President said. "After all, the Court has offended every one of those groups, in one way or another. It seems strange that both labor and management should have grudges against the Court, but you know that's the way it is. One day Bacon and his men will throw out a labor case, the next they'll put their foot down on something the NAM wants. And the farmers are furious. Each one of these groups knows I've tried to help them and the Court has foiled me."

"That's so, sir." Weiss's tone was polite, but he was staying in there. A good man. "But we need their active help in pushing through the Court bill. Will they put out if they feel they've been neglected?"

"They haven't been neglected, Harry. I've got enough bills before the Congress to keep it busy for two sessions, and there's one or more for each one of our pressure groups. They're each going to want their own bills passed. Well, we'll set Congress to work on the Court bill first—the Speaker and Vice-President will see to that—and the word will go out that there'll be no action on anything else until the Court bill is passed. Those people are going to be terribly anxious to get that Court bill out of the way. Self-interest is a great thing, Harry."

"I hope so, sir," Harry Weiss said. "Only—well, you know the farmers are the damnedest greediest bunch that ever infested the capital. They're afraid of new ideas, too, like this Court plan. They think the country owes them a living; they're never grateful. And those labor leaders are fighting among themselves like a pack of alley cats; they'll be hard to handle. And management is in a tizzy most of the time over the budget. I don't trust any of them, by God."

The President laughed a short, unpleasant laugh. "Neither do I, Harry. I don't trust the men at the top. But I trust the men in the ranks, and they've shown the country that they trust me. The tycoons in labor and management and agriculture know what I'll do if they get too balky—I'll take the case to the people. They damn well don't want that, not again. Television is a great thing too, Harry." He picked up some papers from the desk and cleared his throat to put an end to the discussion. "Now, boys, let's get to work. We've got a lot to do before tomorrow morning."

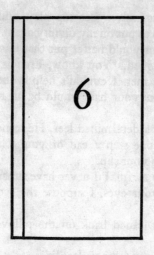

6

H<small>E LOOKS WELL IN BED</small>, Beatrice Hart was thinking—his hair gets all mussed up, the way it's supposed to. She said, "Francis, this is just a little shameless for a Supreme Court justice —hopping off the bench in midmorning to make love to a rather well-known actress."

Francis Dalton reached out to touch her bare shoulder with a gentle hand. "My dear, I believe that in these circumstances it's called a roll in the hay."

"Francis! I *am* a bad influence on you; you're talking more and more like show people. Want your mouth washed out with soap?"

"Nope." Francis kept his hand on her shoulder, lightly. "I hope, though, you'll give me a martini before that lunch you're going to buy me."

"*Two* martinis, darling. I'm a recklessly big spender. And we'd better get up almost immediately because I've got to order. The Carlton does its best, but with the hotel crawling with inauguration visitors, I'm afraid we'll have to wait. And you do have to go back to work this afternoon."

"In a minute or two, Bea." Francis stretched and leaned back on the pillow caressingly. "Let me play human being a little longer before I have to put on my dignity again."

"All right, pet, but you'd better put that dignity on very carefully." Beatrice laughed. "You know, Francis, I was really terrible that night we met. I couldn't help wondering how you'd look in bed—I *knew* your hair would be all tousled, the way it is now."

Francis' grin was a determined leer. He leaned over and kissed her cheek. "I was one step ahead of you. I had your dress off and was working on your slip."

"Francis, you *are* awful. I'd never have dreamed you were undressing me with your eyes. I suppose the red hair should have warned me."

"Mmm." Francis leaned back on the pillow again and closed his eyes.

"Francis—you're *not* falling asleep!"

"Mmm. Nope—just let me close my eyes a minute, Bea."

How it always warmed her to remember the night they met. Beatrice stretched happily, and nuzzled her pillow cozily.

She had met him at—of all places—Molly Evans's annual reception for the Supreme Court. Beatrice had been in Washington for a pre-Broadway run in *Happy Marriage*, and Jimmy Hughes had asked her to go with him to what he called "one of the spectacles of decadent Washington," and she had gone because she liked Jimmy Hughes for both his sardonic candor and his good manners. Jimmy was a part of the so-called theatrical crowd, a sometime show angel on a small scale and a regular at the after-opening parties where he was always so charmingly aggressive in his determination *not* to behave like the brother of the President. At the moment, he had been interested in producing an *avant-garde* thing with Ian Kerr, who wore kilts and did embroidery, and Beatrice had enjoyed his comments on his collaborator.

It had not been quite so dreadful a party as Jimmy Hughes had predicted. Since the Hugheses had moved into the White House, they had set an example of chic little dinner parties, and even Molly Evans, frantically trying to dispose of her late husband's oil millions, had cut back her guest lists a little. The entire

Court was there, except for Angus Whitfield, which still was a considerable triumph for Molly since Whitfield never went out at night.

"And of course, I've got the Soviet Ambassador, too," Molly had confided to her. "I knew he wouldn't be able to resist when I let it be known that I had invited that awful little general from Ecuador."

Jimmy had wangled an invitation for Ian Kerr on the promise that Ian would not wear his kilts, and Ian showed up with an ingenue from off-Broadway whom he introduced as Wednesday Walsh. Beatrice tried not to look startled as she smiled at the tiny child with extremely red hair, but Ian had pounced triumphantly. "How is that!" he gloated in his chortling fashion, his black goatee wiggling hideously. "How is that for a name! By God! Wednesday Walsh! Some goddamned idiot producer out on the Coast thought up that one. I'm reconstructing her. I'm making an actress out of her. You know what her real name is? It's Bernice Goodykoontz. It figures."

Beatrice had said yes, rather dazedly, and accepted a martini from Jimmy Hughes. "He's crazy," Jimmy said mildly, and then had gulped down his own martini and turned to the waiter for another.

Happily, there had been so many people she knew at the party that Beatrice had been spared further exposure to Ian Kerr and Miss Wednesday Walsh, nee Goodykoontz. And Jimmy, of course, was too busy numbing his sensitivities with martinis to be more than casually attentive, at least for a while. She had stood there chatting with first one guest and then another as the crowd surged about, and finally had decided to move out of the path to the bar for safety's sake. She managed to wriggle her way into a corner of the Louis Seize drawing room, and she was lighting a cigarette when all of a sudden there was Francis.

"Francis, I knew you at once, you know." She poked a finger into his naked side.

Francis opened his eyes and closed them again. "Of course you did. You recognized Mr. Justice Dalton by the green dinner jacket he always wears."

"Clown!" Beatrice said. "I knew you because of your red hair,

95

dolt. You had drawn free of the crowd, too, and you were wiping your brow with your handkerchief, not just dabbing at it but scrubbing it. You had freckles on your forehead and under your eyes and across the ridge of your nose, and you had a beleaguered look. You didn't know I was standing there until you put your handkerchief back in your pocket and were looking about you."

"I said something clever, as I recall," Francis said in a sleepy voice.

"Not too clever, darling. You said, 'Oh—another refugee from the mob. May I share your sanctuary, Miss Hart?' Not too bad, though. But then you were great, Francis. I was smiling at you, and before I could say anything, you said, 'My name is Dalton. I know you; you're a beautiful actress named Beatrice Hart.' I may have fallen in love with you then and there, pet."

"You smiled very nicely," Francis said. "I rather liked you."

"I was silly—I couldn't stop smiling. I said, 'Thank you, Mr. Justice—girls like to hear things like that.' And I held out my hand and you took it and held it for a moment, but very firmly."

"Mmm." Francis managed a grunt, eyes still closed.

From then until now, it had been just as she had always wanted it. They had stood there in the corner talking, and he went to get her a second martini and a third, and for the first time she had found herself enjoying the sensation of drinking. The martinis did not affect her except to sustain the lighthearted mood that had come to her at the moment Francis Dalton spoke to her. Even today she could remember almost everything they had said to one another, but at the time she had thought merely: *This is fun. I like this man. I like to talk to him and to listen to him talk to me.* They had discussed everything from the Supreme Court to the Washington Redskins football team, and she was sure that neither she nor Francis had said anything that would be considered clever in the circles where she moved. It was easy, and natural, and nice.

She had been glad to see that Francis shared her annoyance when Molly Evans descended on them with Jimmy Hughes by the hand. She wanted Francis to want to be with her alone, as she wanted to be with him alone. Not romantically, just together and talking. But then they were smiling at Molly Evans and Jimmy Hughes and listening to Molly's report that "Jimmy has just about persuaded me to have my portrait done by that new man, Lavelle." She turned to Jimmy. "He says Lavelle is fantastic—don't you, Jimmy?"

And Jimmy had grinned and bowed and said, "Absolutely, Molly. I promise you, when Lavelle gets done with you, you won't recognize yourself."

She couldn't feel any annoyance at Jimmy because he was taking her back to her hotel instead of Justice Francis Copley Dalton. Jimmy was too nice, if a little drunk. But she had wanted to be with Francis a little longer, and she was glad when Jimmy escorted her to the elevator and left for one of his nightclubs, because if she couldn't be with Francis, she wanted to be alone so she could think about him. She was drawing the water for her bath when Francis phoned and asked her to have lunch the next day and then go with him to the Gaithersburg Fair; he had promised the son of an old friend he'd look in on the cattle judging. It all made her feel so warm and happy. It had been so very good, from the start, and now *Happy Marriage* had closed, and there would be time for Francis and her to talk about a real happy marriage, and think about it, and make wonderful plans, and be together.

"Francis—my lion." She reached over and tweaked his nose—anything to touch him. "Darling, we must get organized. I have to feed you."

Francis opened his eyes and sat up. "Yes, sir, yes, sir, Mr. Chief Justice. Just working on an opinion, sir."

"Oh, Francis, I hate to disturb you—but it is getting late." She kissed his cheek. "And you seem so tired lately. Are they working you too hard?"

She thought Francis suddenly appeared solemn, before he shook off the look and smiled. Then the smile was broken by a yawn.

"No, it's not that, Bea. Some other business—a project."

She waited. He seemed to be pondering whether to go further, but when he didn't say anything more, she grinned and made her own voice gaily casual.

97

"And you can't tell me about it because it's top-secret. I understand, Mr. Justice."

Francis' look was very tender. "Bea—I love you. And no, I can't tell you about it—not now."

"Of course not, darling. All I'd want to do, anyway, is cosset you. You know I never pry, Francis. And you do look tired and I'm sorry I have to hurry you."

"So am I, dear." Francis reached out and took both her hands in his. "I won't be satisfied until we're together, finally—always. For the first two years, let's just lock ourselves up and refuse to answer the doorbell."

"Yes, let's—or maybe for the first three years. Darling, I am in such a hurry to marry you—as soon as I get straightened out with Freddie. I'm sorry it's such a mess."

"It's all right, Bea. Stone is a good man and he'll work something out. Damn Freddie, though. If only he weren't such a toad with all his dirty little innuendoes about gossip columnists."

"I know, Francis. But I'm afraid we can't change him. I just don't want it to change us. I just don't want it to hurt you."

"It won't, Bea." He bent to kiss both her hands and then looked up at her. "We will have to be careful—because of where I work. And so we will be careful. I know we can manage it, dear, dear Bea." His smile was gentle. "We have to—because I love you." They moved toward each other at once, and they were in each other's arms for a long time before Francis released her and put one hand under her chin and said, "And now, woman, feed me!"

She was still thinking about it hours after Francis had gone. She just would not let it become complicated, Beatrice Hart was thinking. It was useless to harass herself about Freddie. If she had to pay him off, then she'd pay him off. It was as simple as that. She had the money, and if that was all it took to be rid of Freddie —well, good. She could give him twice what he was asking and still not suffer. She would not permit Francis to worry about it. He had a right to be outraged, but she would not have him worrying because she had been such a fool. There was only one thing that mattered and that was to protect Francis, to keep his name out of those messy conversations that nourished saloon society. It was a quite straightforward thing, after all. Bill Stone would haggle with Freddie's lawyer for a while and, perhaps, get Freddie to accept a little less. Then she would pay Freddie off. She would do anything that was necessary to save Francis—to save him for herself. Dear, dear Francis, she thought, I love him so very much and it is wonderful to know that not only did I never love anyone else, but that with Francis I am so proud of my love for him. It is what happens, she thought wryly, when you meet someone who is a better man than you are.

She found herself smiling idiotically at her image in the mirror of her dressing table. Beatrice Krasnov of Columbus, Ohio, she said to herself, you're one up on that girl in the sailor suit in *South Pacific*. She threw both arms into the air and sang, "I'm in love, I'm in love, I'm in love, I'm in love—I'm in love with a wonderful *goy!*" She grinned into the mirror again and decided that her nose *did* turn up a little. A little. In one happy, whirling movement she got up and half danced across the bedroom and through the door into the living room of the suite. She got a cigarette from a box on one of the end tables and lit it and then dropped into the green easy chair. They had never discussed religion with any considerable seriousness, because neither was self-conscious about things like that. Francis had laughed uproariously when he asked her what she did on Yom Kippur and she replied why, of course, she drank the blood of Gentile babies. And he had delighted her with his stories of the fashionable Monsignor who always checked the Social Register before accepting sponsorship of any would-be convert.

There wouldn't be any trouble about that, Beatrice thought. She would become a Catholic, if that was permitted, and she'd agree to bring up the children as Catholics, and if Francis wanted to turn Rosicrucian or Mohammedan she would join up along with him. She was neither unfeeling nor irreverent about religion; she merely felt that that was the husband's affair. She had gone to the synagogue regularly all through high school and even during her one year at Ohio State; she had done so dutifully, to please Jacob and Esther Krasnov, but it had been a warm and pleasant duty. It was also, of course, a duty she easily dropped once she was away from home, not in any spirit of renunciation but merely because there were other things that took up her time. It was during that period she discovered that to be a Jew was supposedly to be somewhat different from other people, but it made no deep impression on her. Later she became more acutely aware of the apartness, but it was a thing she accepted without either pride or embarrassment. She regarded the anti-Semites as idiotic, in the same class with other bigots whose warped tastes ran to the lynching of Negroes; she could not regard them as important, for the simple reason that their theories and actions were so illogical, so unintelligent. Anyway, such people never intruded on her little world, which was part of the bigger, but still small, world of the theater. In that world, she was able to sustain her easy good opinion of people generally even when she suffered honest pain and anger over the victims of Nazi and Soviet persecutions. She saw no reason to be proud she was a Jew, any more than it would occur to her to be ashamed of it, because she honestly didn't feel different.

She didn't know whether Francis was what was considered a good Catholic. She knew he went to Mass every Sunday at that rather fashionable church in Georgetown, but he always seemed rather casual about it. He never talked about things like confession and she supposed she shouldn't ask him about them; Francis didn't seem to be the type that liked to talk about his religion; he never wore it on his sleeve. He told her about his days at Holy Cross and about the logic of the Jesuits and about his escapades as an altar boy back home in Evans, but there was nothing devout in his conversation. It seemed to Beatrice that Francis was particularly offhand about a religion that so many people took with terrible seriousness; he was more like an Italian than an Irishman. Anyway, she would do what Francis asked her to do; she would make that clear to him. He'd know about what kind of a wedding they could have, too. Her first two marriages were both civil ceremonies and she knew the Catholic Church didn't recognize them. Smart church, she thought; neither do I. Perhaps because of that she could take those instructions, or whatever they called them, and she and Francis could be married by a priest. It didn't matter, but she would rather like that. This time she wanted it to be as right, and as binding, as it could be. She'd be a good Catholic, if they'd let her. But perhaps she'd better remind them, occasionally, that it was the Krasnovs who had the Chairman of the Board.

Francis was very understanding about the life she had led during all the years before they met. Francis was honestly respectable and decent, but he was not stuffy. She knew him well enough by now to appreciate that he was not merely tolerant; he genuinely believed that a person's private life was his own business. Once he had said, "After all, Bea, you might not have been you if you had spent your life in a convent." Bless him. Nevertheless, she was aware of the depth of his feeling of responsibility toward his government. He had put it bluntly the night she had told him so frankly about that part of her life of which the columnists were her historians.

"Of course it doesn't matter, Bea," he had said. "That's all past now." And then he had added, so quietly, and yet in a voice insistent in its candor, "It has to be all over with. Otherwise, there couldn't be you and me, dear. We couldn't be together—not unless I left the bench." It was not anything remotely resembling a warning; Francis was incapable of such a thing. It was Francis being honest, as he had to be in everything, and merely reminding her that he had another obligation, a public obligation that was apart from—and, because he was Francis Copley Dalton, *above*—any personal consideration. He would not do anything, or permit anyone close to him to do anything, that might soil the robes of the Supreme Court of the United States. The thought exalted her; she had always fought against admitting that it also frightened her. But—she understood him, and she loved him. She was sure she could keep them safe.

She always had difficulty thinking of herself as a woman with a past. The term amused her; she just wasn't the type. She was pleased that in public she exuded a certain amount of authentic glamour; after all, she had a good face and the golden hair was natural, thanks to Esther Krasnov and her fair-haired Polish Jew ancestors, and her legs had always been good. She was no Bernhardt, but she was very good at her trade; she had never had any doubts about that because it all had come so naturally and easily and it had always been fun. England might challenge her rank, but here in the United States she could accept without self-consciousness her designation by the critics as Number One. And when the public was looking, she could play the part to the hilt. But it always made her smile, because basically she was so old-shoe, still the slightly tomboyish Bea Krasnov who had helped Pa in the candy store and played baseball in bare feet. It was horrible, and she'd kill anybody else who used the word, but she supposed she was terribly *wholesome*. She just did not enjoy those after-theater champagne parties with men and women who spoke in four-letter words, and homosexuals who were such *professional* homosexuals, and famous playwrights who got drunk and piddled on the floor.

That's fine, she thought, but you cannot pose as Jane Eyre in a gingham gown to people who live in Sioux Falls and Kansas City—and Washington, D. C. You've been married twice, and both the divorces were rather messy, and there have been the others, the little boys posing as men, and fancy beds from coast to coast. No, she couldn't ever be Beatrice Krasnov, Girl Guide, to those people, because they'd think she was trying to kid them. And yet, she wouldn't be kidding; it was all so true. They would never believe that, if anything, she had been too innocent, too natural and ingenuous. She had given herself to those little boys because she had believed, each time, that she was in love and that that was what they wanted. That was what they wanted, all right, she thought; I was half right. That was all they wanted, a roll in the hay and, usually, a paycheck. It had taken her a long time to pull herself out of that rut, not because she was a blackened sinner, not because she enjoyed the sexual pulling and hauling, but because she didn't know any better, because she kept her trust too long, because she had faith that if she kept searching—and kept giving—she would find a *man*. It had taken her so long, almost too long, to discover that a bed was useless unless you could share it with someone who loved you, too, someone who was giving as well as taking.

She realized now that, to a great extent, it had been the fault of her upbringing, although fault was not quite the graceful word. There had been love in the Krasnov household, so much that at times it seemed to overflow the little house where Jacob Krasnov presided as a benevolent monarch. Her mother and father had been deeply, demonstratively, in love, two people who used loving words like caresses and who deferred to each other with grace and affection. The nicest thing that had ever happened to young Beatrice Krasnov was on the day she burst into the kitchen and caught her father in the act of pinching her mother's behind. Jacob Krasnov had explained blandly—while Esther Krasnov turned her blushing, smiling face away—"Could a man do otherwise, when his wife has such a beautiful behind?" Jacob and Esther Krasnov, by example, had taught their three children to love one another, to share with one another and to be unselfishly delighted with one another's small triumphs. The children had protected each other and read books together and studied together, and when their small tempers erupted into violence, the aftermath had always been a genuinely repentant and tear-stained reconciliation. For Beatrice, time hadn't changed anything; she still loved her younger sister, Rebecca, and her older brother, Benjamin, with something that approached desperation.

She would not have had her home any other way, and yet because she was sensitive and believed in the generosity of others, it had not prepared Beatrice for the life she entered into after her one casually scholastic year at Ohio State. Bill Stone had told her in discussing Freddie the other day, "You know, Bea, until only recently you had always been ripe for the plucking." She supposed it was true. She thought of the theater not only as a world of glamour and exalting artistic triumph, but as a tight little community of mutual affection and mutual assistance as well. It was the world she loved, the world she had loved since she was a scrawny child with freckles, and because the other world she had loved—the world of Jacob and Esther Krasnov—had loved her back, she was sure the theater would reciprocate, too.

It didn't, of course, work out that way, because it couldn't. No part of any world could be like Jacob and Esther Krasnov's world, and Beatrice should have realized it. Shortly she had been made to understand that she would have to fight for her place in her new world, and she did so. She fought hard and relentlessly, to the point of sheer exhaustion. She did not fight unfairly, because she could not; the sly little maneuverings and vicious professional gouging always filled her with revulsion. Happily, she discovered there were people who were big enough and rich enough and talented enough that they could afford to be interested only in talent. It was to these people that she tied her career, and because she had the talent and worked hard, she was rewarded first with opportunity and then with the really good roles that carried her to success.

But she had not been as careful, as discriminating, with the people she admitted into her private life. It was almost as if that part of her existence were a rebellion against the Spartan, mind-numbing toil of her professional day. She had always been innately merry; in her after hours she found release in the carefree and worldly wit and partying of those on the fringes of the theater. She had married Robert, with his little-lost-boy air and underneath it the icy calculation that had made him editor of a metropolitan newspaper at twenty-eight. She had married Freddie, the bit player with so much untapped talent, and too much charm to waste on the drudgery of rehearsals. Both marriages had been hopeless—the sudden realization of the real, nastily conniving parvenu that was behind Robert's youthful pout, and the belated discovery not only that Freddie was congenitally lazy and a nagging financial drain but that he expected her to be tolerant of his harem as well. Between the two marriages and after them, she had fled to others, seemingly numberless others, always seeking, always trusting, wearing herself out in her campaign to be *needed*. It had all been so senseless, so stupid, and yet she acknowledged now that she could not have escaped it. It was the way she was, and almost until she met Francis she had had to keep trying, rendered defenseless by the love she had known as a child, which she was so sure she could find again, around that next corner.

She had managed, for nearly a year before she met Francis, to discipline herself against further seeking. She had forced herself into a kind of solitary confinement while she took stock. It had been a somber period of loneliness and long hours of self-searching, and she had been filled with suspicion of herself. But she had managed it. She had stepped out of the past and across the threshold into a world of self-sufficiency. She had looked into herself and known that she must abandon her search, and there had been serenity in the knowledge that if she was to have the thing for which she had searched so long, it would come to her without further door-to-door peddling.

The little china clock Francis had won for her at the Gaithersburg Fair chimed the time into her consciousness from the end table. She looked over at it fondly: his first gift to her and the one thing she carried with her everywhere, despite its tinny, $5.95 gaudiness. Francis had won it by knocking down three of the wooden milk bottles in a row, and he had been pleased—"How is that for control?"

Six-thirty. She would have to hurry; the inaugural concert was at eight and Francis had said he'd pick her up early because of the snow. It was still coming down, softly pelting the window in the teeth of the brisk wind, and from the rush-hour confusion of Sixteenth and K Streets seven floors below she could hear the cacophony of automobile horns as frustrated drivers struggled in the traffic. If the storm didn't subside soon, she thought, people attending President John Alden Hughes's second inauguration tomorrow would need dogsleds.

She would have to hurry, even with her casually simple makeup chores, or she would keep Francis waiting. She got up and started for the bedroom. Then the telephone rang and she walked back to the desk to pick it up.

"Beatrice, dear," said Francis' voice over the wire.

"Francis, darling, it's not seven yet. Am I late? Did I misunderstand?"

"No, darling, I said seven-thirty." Francis sounded excited. "But the storm has created a hell of a mess. Traffic is snarled all over town and the streets are full of stalled cars. I couldn't make it home to change into black tie; I'll have to go as I am. Could I come up and wash my face?"

"Darling, of course. Come right up. You can wash your face and I'll skulk behind doors and put on my makeup. Come right up."

"Good. I'll be there in a minute. Bea, wait till you see it. It's fantastic. Luckily, Jack Williams in the office here has got us a friendly cab driver for the evening. With chains on his tires. He said he was afraid you might need it, Miss VIP."

"Oh, wonderful, Francis. Wasn't he sweet?" She felt like giggling. "Francis?"

"Yes, Miss Krasnov."

"Francis, don't you think all this snow—don't you think the Supreme Court has gone too far this time?"

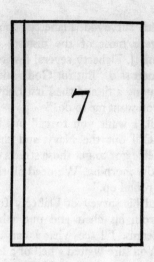

7

BY EIGHT-THIRTY, enough members of the National Symphony had fought their way through the blizzard to Constitution Hall that Conductor Henri Renault could lift his baton and get the inaugural concert under way—half an hour late. At precisely that moment, Inaugural Chairman Dennis J. Flaherty, a wealthy Philadelphia contractor, made his flustered, red-necked way to the box occupied by Secretary of Defense William Otis Bennett, next to the box in which sat Chief Justice Robert McNair Bacon and Mrs. Bacon, Attorney General Charles P. Mayborn and Mrs. Mayborn, Associate Justice Francis Copley Dalton and Miss Beatrice Hart, and Harry Weiss, assistant to the President. Mrs. Weiss was at home nursing eleven-year-old Penelope, who had the measles.

Flaherty was choking with mixed anxiety and impatience, and his voice, starting out as a whisper, broke into a hoarse growl that was not quite drowned out by the music of Rossini. "Bill, goddammit!" Flaherty announced, half angrily, half pleading. "Bill, you've got to do something. This goddamned snow has screwed up the whole town and as usual the silly Highway Department is caught with its pants down."

Secretary Bennett surveyed Flaherty coolly, managing to keep out of his gaze most of the distaste he felt. Secretary Bennett owed Dennis J. Flaherty several favors. "All right, Dennis," Secretary Bennett said. "But for God's sake, keep your voice down. Renault is having a fit and the First Lady is giving you the bad eye. What do you want me to do?"

"Goddammit, Bill, I want you to call out the Army and get rid of this snow. Call out the Navy and the Marines, too, if you have to. But we've got to get those streets cleared by inauguration time tomorrow morning. We need all the men and all the equipment you can round up."

Bennett continued his survey of Flaherty for a long moment. Then he got up from his chair and put a hand on Flaherty's arm. "All right, Dennis. I'll see what I can do. I'll get on the phone right away. You sure waited a hell of a long time, though." But I should have thought of it myself, Bennett was thinking.

Secretary Bennett had made a phone call from a booth in the lobby of Constitution Hall at eight thirty-five. Within an hour, the first detachment of Army troops in fatigues appeared on Pennsylvania Avenue. They came in trucks with snowplows attached, in half-tracks and in jeeps. They brought shovels, pickaxes, rock salt and flamethrowers. They worked until five o'clock in the morning, helped somewhat by the fact that the blizzard blew itself out shortly after midnight.

Now, on inaugural morning, President John Alden Hughes, in blue pajamas, sat on the edge of his bed and inspected some photographs handed him by Dennis Flaherty, who perched uneasily on the edge of a red velvet armchair. The photographs showed long stretches of Pennsylvania and Constitution Avenues, the part of Fifteenth Street along the east side of the Treasury Building which connects the interrupted sections of Pennsylvania Avenue, and the East Plaza of the Capitol building. All these areas had been cleared of snow down to the black asphalt.

"Marvelous, Dennis," the President said. "It's absolutely amazing. The streets are as bare as they were in June. How on earth did you accomplish this miracle?"

Dennis Flaherty's red face beamed. He had not been to bed

for thirty-six hours, but nothing else mattered in this hour of triumph.

"I took—you might say—the law into my own hands, Mr. President," he reported happily. "I got ahold of Secretary Bennett last night and told him we had to get those streets cleared. We decided to call out the troops."

The President's laugh bounced off the walls of the big room with its blue walls that were darker than usual in the gray of early daylight. "Dennis, you're wonderful! What a marvelous idea! I was so busy, I couldn't give it much thought other than to wonder if Joe Morin had chains for my Cadillac. Dennis, you've done a great job. I'm very grateful to you. And thanks for thinking of these photos to reassure me."

Dennis's pleasure at the President's praise was aggressive. "Well, I just busted in on Bennett at the concert. It was no time to wait on formality, you might say. After I explained things, he moved fast."

"He certainly did, Dennis. But you moved fast first. I wondered what was going on in Bennett's box. Renault's back looked as if he was having a coronary." The President took a sip of coffee from the gold-rimmed cup on the mahogany end table. "Thank you again, Dennis. Now I've got to get going. I've got some people coming in for breakfast in half an hour."

"Yes, sir." Dennis Flaherty got to his feet, in the same motion already beginning to back out. "I'll be downstairs when you come out, to make sure everything goes right."

After Dennis left, it took the President less than twenty minutes to shave with his old-fashioned straight razor, shower and—with the assistance of his valet Billy Hanford—get into his cutaway coat and striped gray trousers. Tory, he thought. English High Church clothes. Still, eminently suitable for an inauguration because a Presidential oath-taking was not an ordinary affair, not a business-suit affair. He had time, before going down to the State Dining Room, to make three telephone calls and to sign forty-one papers left on his bureau the night before for tending to in odd moments.

One of the documents bore the endorsement of Clay Stebbins, president of the National Association for the Advancement of

Colored People. It was a minor matter, concerned with a claim against the government by the widow of a truck driver, but it distracted the President's thoughts from his Court-packing plan and the imminent meeting with his party leaders. Stebbins had come around, just as they all had come around. Stebbins had accepted the conservative approach to the integration problem because the times and the national atmosphere, with John Alden Hughes as an expert catalyst, had convinced Stebbins there was no other path . . . just as others had been convinced—by confusion and portents of peril. AFL-CIO, the National Association of Manufacturers, the teachers' lobby, the farmers—they had all had to come around to the philosophies of John Alden Hughes, who had bluntly proclaimed that if the voters put him in the White House, he was determined to be known as Mr. Conservative as well as Mr. President.

He had put it over, he knew, because he had used every trick of politics and of modern promotion. But he could not have put it over had he not believed so fiercely in its logic and its strength and its basic appeal to the ordinary citizen. He had taken the big gamble four years ago. He had proclaimed his independence of all blocs—the Negro, labor, big business, the farmer—and he had sworn allegiance to "just one bloc—the people." And he had proved it could be done. He had won without catering to the blocs. He admitted now that this had been possible partly because poor old President Finlay had been thoroughly discredited by a series of bitter diplomatic defeats at the hands of the Soviet Union. The opposition had had nowhere else to go; it had to renominate Finlay, but he was dead even before his pathetic acceptance speech. Labor had been forced to fall into line for the fresh new candidate, because it had nowhere else to go, either. The Negro, big business, the farmer, the more practical liberals, went along for the same reason.

The first four years had been bone-wearying and tough, but he had insisted on boldness, on maintaining his independence, on disciplining the blocs. And in November his personal bloc, the ordinary citizens, had returned him to office in a sensational landslide. He had lost New York, Illinois and Michigan because of his go-slow policies on integration, and he still had buried his opponent, poor Jim Clayton, because he had dedicated his first term to persuading the voters that if they stuck together they could prevail over any and all minority groups. And now . . . time to go downstairs, he thought. And he swept out of the room and through the hall and raced two steps at a time down the marble staircase.

It should go well, the President was thinking, as he stood just inside the dining room door, greeting his guests. They were all his men. They had gone down the line for him for four years, and they had been rewarded by the cordiality of the electorate. Even as he greeted each one with a special, custom-tailored pleasantry —"Hello, Tom, Virginia sausages this morning"—he was ticking them off mentally.

Vice-President Thomas P. Morgan of Montana—amiable, dull and completely loyal. President pro Tempore of the Senate, Frederick C. Pilney of Nevada—shrewd, rich, dyspeptic. Speaker of the House Henry Adam Smith of Kentucky—a solid party man dedicated exclusively to keeping his men in line. Senate Majority Leader Chester W. McAdam of New York—highly intelligent and with the usual complementing independence, but dependable. House Majority Leader William C. Ball of Pennsylvania (It was always "Welcome, neighbor" with Bill Ball)— twenty years in the House, another strong believer in party regularity. And the two Judiciary Committee chairmen—was he chancing a leak, having them in? Probably, but it couldn't be helped. Paul Anderson of Minnesota, the House Judiciary chairman, was a tough Populist; he could not be sure that Anderson could be controlled. But the Senate chairman, Alpheus P. Ward of Illinois—though irascible, a veteran operator, jealous of his prerogatives—was predictably loyal.

They seemed to fill the dining room at first, as they stood around chatting, but when they were all seated, the big room resumed its air of spaciousness. It didn't matter particularly, but the entire Cabinet was on hand in their seats of privilege on each side of the President's chair. State's Douglas C. Wilson, the hardbitten and yet strangely pious Ivy Leaguer from Connecticut. Lawrence B. Sprague of Treasury and New York, introspective, calculating, about whom it was said he had given a pint of ice water to the Red Cross. Secretary of Defense William Otis Bennett of Texas, of the steely eye and the bad liver and the choleric impatience with ADA. Attorney General Charlie Mayborn, the best politician in the room, including John Alden Hughes. Amiable Postmaster General Tom Dugan of Massachusetts, the epitome of caretaker government. Interior's John W. Eccleston of Colorado, perpetually aghast at the President's careless effrontery toward certain public power enthusiasts. Agriculture's August Brandt, the former Iowa governor, a patriarchal, unimaginative Dutchman. Commerce's Roy Nelson Smith of Pennsylvania, a friend of Julia Hughes and not much more. Labor's Allen W. Lehman, scholar and disciple of Gaitskell and the Fabians. Health, Education and Welfare's Grace Butler, friend of Julia Hughes, broad of beam, motherly yet virginal, a crusader with a budget that could never be large enough for her maternal theories.

They were all here, the President reflected, a small army of specialists come to hear its marching orders over sausages and scrambled eggs.

He got up to speak the moment everybody had been served his second cup of coffee. Everybody's plate was empty except the belching Pilney's, and Tom Dugan was surreptitiously picking his teeth with a match folder. The President explained that he had very little time this morning "because of an event I must attend on the Hill," and they all smiled dutifully and Tom Morgan offered a tentative "Hear! Hear!" Anyway, he told them, his tones soothing, they would know all about it in a couple of hours because he would cover it in complete detail in his inaugural address. But, as "the leaders of this administration," he said, he felt they should know about it in broad outline before he made it public.

The faces were regarding him with polite attentiveness, but showed no sign of excitement or apprehension. They were used to him by now, and he could almost feel them thinking that he was going to ask for new sacrifices, more taxes perhaps, but that his proposals would be in the general, purposely vague terms suitable for an inaugural address. They were comfortable.

"Now, gentlemen," he said, "in essence my remarks on the Hill will be a request for the Congress to approve the enlargement of the Supreme Court from nine to eleven members."

He felt a stir, and his eye went at once to Paul Anderson, who seemed to have been jarred upright in his chair by the words.

His glance moved to Sprague and found the Secretary of the Treasury's lips moving rapidly and a flush creeping into his lean cheeks. He had been right about those two.

He went on, almost hurriedly. "You all know the reasons behind my proposal. I believe it is time some action was taken to alter the Court so that it is more readily adaptable to reflecting the times in which we are living. That is, I believe the majority of the Court at this time is wrong. Wrong about its interpretation of the Constitution and wrong because it refuses to move into the new and terrible era which the Cold War has forced on us. However, there are other reasons for the request I shall make to the Congress, and the most important is that the Court as now constituted is unable to keep up with its work. It needs help—it needs more manpower, young and vigorous manpower, if it is going to do the job it must do. In the past four years it has refused an astounding number of writs of certiorari. We must have a Supreme Court physically able to review cases which in the name of simple justice deserve review by the highest court in the land."

He saw that both Anderson and Sprague were tense, waiting for Presidential permission to comment. Tom Morgan's mouth was open; the Vice-President was still trying to grasp the magnitude of the President's proposal. McAdam had the look of serenity which meant the Senate Majority Leader was mentally counting votes, wrestling with the tribal idiosyncrasies of his flock. Henry Adam Smith, who wanted nothing but to remain as Speaker of the House the rest of his life, looked angry, but John Alden Hughes knew that his anger would become determination to deliver the vote. He heard Bill Ball utter a "By God!" but it was an ejaculation of surprise, not of indignation; the Majority Leader of the House would go along with Pennsylvania's favorite son—and with Speaker Smith—when the chips were down. Aside from Treasury's Sprague, the rest of the Cabinet didn't matter because, except for Charlie Mayborn, they were not interested in becoming involved in issues outside their spheres. And Mayborn, the coauthor of the Court-packing bill, was delighted; the President could tell that by the way he was leaning back in his chair, his eyes half closed.

"That's about all, gentlemen," the President said. "As I said, the details are in my address—and there isn't much time for me to

113

discuss it any more fully." He hoped his use of the word *discuss* would be hint enough that he was not inviting comment.

But Paul Anderson did not take such hints. "Mr. President," he said in a kind of woeful cry, and as he spoke the chairman of the House Judiciary Committee was lifting his ponderous body to his feet, with one hand pushing back his shock of blond hair.

"Yes, Paul," the President said, in a tone he hoped was even.

"Mr. President, this is quite a surprise to us all, I'm sure. It is not quite the way we've grown used to having things done." Anderson's voice was more than petulant; it had taken on a chiding note.

"I'm sorry, Paul. It's something I believe in quite strongly, and I wanted to give it the impact of making it the theme of my inaugural address. I didn't want any anticlimaxes. That's why I haven't talked to anybody until now." What he meant was that he didn't want any leaks from big-mouthed members of Congress. Anderson understood that.

"Yes, sir. But some of us may not immediately feel strongly enough without further consultation with you, Mr. President. Your proposal is a sensational one, if I may say so, sir. Speaking entirely for myself, sir, I will have to meditate on it. Yes, sir, I will have to meditate on it."

"I'm sure you will, Paul." The President was speaking lightly now. "I want you to. I'm confident everyone in this room will give it considerable thought. And naturally, Paul, I shall want to discuss it with all of you as things progress."

Paul Anderson looked at the President with his heavy-lidded blue eyes; his heavy breathing was like the wheeze of a bellows in the quiet dining room. Paul Anderson looked at the President for a long moment, and then he sat down.

"Mr. President?" It was Secretary of the Treasury Sprague's turn. After Sprague, the President decided, he would have to shut them off.

"Yes, Larry?" In the lift of the Presidential eyebrow and the small note of impatience in his tone, Sprague was warned to be brief.

"Just one thing, Mr. President." Sprague's voice was the voice of an accountant reading down a column of figures. "I know how you feel about this, Mr. President. But in the near future, sometime soon, would it not be advisable to consider alternatives—the matter of a compromise if compromise becomes necessary?"

"Certainly, Larry. I certainly hope that we will go into all aspects of the matter as time goes on. But, of course, you must know that the question of alternatives has been gone into quite thoroughly. Charlie Mayborn and I have made a most exhaustive survey of the situation. Certainly there will be discussions—about tactics. When you have all been filled in on the details, I'm sure there will be no question of alternatives."

"Yes. I see." But Sprague didn't see, not yet and perhaps never. "But, Mr. President . . ."

"Larry, I'm sorry." The President made his voice as apologetic as his impatience permitted. "I've just got to cut it off now. I've got too many other things to do." He looked around the table, with its faces now turned blank and noncommittal. "Gentlemen, thank you for coming. I'll see you all up on the Hill, I hope."

He walked out with them into the lobby and out onto the North Portico, shaking hands, acknowledging proffers of good luck in his inaugural address, the hearty host bidding his privileged guests adieu for the moment. Outside, the air was freezingly crisp in the wan January sunlight, and the snow seemed as high as a man on the White House lawn and across the bare asphalt of Pennsylvania Avenue in Lafayette Park.

"Two feet of snow, John," said Vice-President Tom Morgan, who had given young John Alden Hughes his first subcommittee chairmanship in the Senate, and who could not be expected always to address him as Mr. President. "Two feet," Morgan repeated. "In Montana it would be a flurry, but in this goddamned town you'd think they'd dropped the hydrogen bomb."

"Are things pretty bad around town?" the President asked.

"The *Post* says three thousand cars stranded on the streets," Morgan said. "Maybe you should declare Washington a disaster area." He buttoned his overcoat about his tall, spare frame. "I'm just going to duck across to the Hay Adams to dress for the big event. I'll see you soon, John."

The President stood there for a few minutes in the biting cold that felt so good after the heavy heat of the dining room and watched his guests getting into their cars as one by one they rolled up to the portico. Paul Anderson was saying something to

Senator Pilney, and his words were caught up by the brisk wind and carried to the President at the top of the steps.

Anderson's voice was a growl and only partly distinct at the distance: ". . . tell you this, Fred," he was saying, and then, after a muffled few words, "about time to get off the bandwagon."

The President smiled as he turned and went back into the White House. So far the morning had gone predictably.

Wilfred Grier, an electrician with the Washington contracting firm of Berzelius and Company, suffered severe burns on the right hand while testing the electrical heating apparatus installed at the base of the inauguration platform on the east steps of the Capitol. Another electrician took over and discovered a short circuit, which was repaired in a few minutes. In his office in the House Wing, Speaker Henry Adam Smith drank a straight shot of Jack Daniels Black Label bourbon and then put the bottle in one of the pockets of his overcoat. Senate Majority Leader Chester W. McAdam studied with horrible fascination a thermometer outside his office window, which informed him the temperature had fallen in the last hour from twenty-one degrees above zero to fourteen degrees above zero. Alpheus P. Ward, chairman of the Senate Judiciary Committee, told his secretary wearily, "Yes, I'll take it," and picked up a phone and said, "Hello, Pete" to Peter J. Underwood, a political columnist whose prose more or less adorned six hundred newspapers. No, the Senator told Pete, there had been nothing special at the breakfast with the President; he supposed the two Judiciary chairmen had been there because they had been around the Hill so long. Yes, there had been some discussion of the President's inaugural address, but, of course, he never revealed what went on at a White House meeting. (Except, of course, if it could do Alpheus P. Ward some good.) House Majority Leader William C. Ball picked up his phone with resigned reluctance and then spent the next ten minutes listening to the bellowed grievances of the president of Philadelphia's biggest bank, who had received only seventeen tickets to the inauguration.

In the office of White House Press Secretary Mike Blair, thirty-seven correspondents regularly assigned to the President of the United States were telling Mike Blair in voices of strident anger that he couldn't do this to them.

"I can't help it, gentlemen. That's the way it is," Mike Blair said into the onrushing tide of words. "You won't get the speech until the President starts delivering it. Now, what do you suggest I do about it?"

"Goddammit, tell him we've got to have it!" shouted Danny Congdon of the *Star*. "I never heard of such a silly goddamned thing. We could have that thing in type right now."

"Hasn't the President's momma finished reading it yet?" asked Jack Sparks of the New York *Daily News*.

"Okay," Mike Blair said amiably. "Let's cut that crap—right now."

"But why, Mike? Why?" pleaded Don Schwed of *The New York Times*. "The speech must be ready by now. I understand your girls have been working on it in the Fish Room since six o'clock this morning."

"I'm sorry, Don," Mike Blair said. "I can't help what you understand. The speech will be handed out to everybody the moment the President starts making it."

"What's he going to say?" asked the new man from the Des Moines *Register and Tribune*. "Is he going to declare war on Mexico?"

"Should I call my wife and tell her to get the kids into the bomb shelter?" asked Ralph Udall of the Philadelphia *Bulletin*.

"Ah, shove it," said Tom Beasley of the *Chicago Tribune*.

"Whatever you say, Tom," Mike Blair said. "But now we've all got to go—that is, if you people are coming up with us."

Thirty-four of the White House correspondents were standing outside the North Portico a few minutes later; a man from each of the wire services and a woman from the *Post* had remained behind to do features on an empty White House. The reporters clustered around the White House policemen in their heavy blue uniform overcoats and the casual-looking Secret Service agents in well-cut mufti. Inaugural Chairman Dennis J. Flaherty, in top hat and black chesterfield, was talking to Secretary of State Douglas C. Wilson, who had arrived a few minutes before.

"The Boss figured it would be more convenient for the boys on the Hill to just be there when he arrived instead of riding up to the Hill with him," Flaherty was saying. "They'll ride back with us all, of course, for the grand parade. It's a grand day after all, isn't it, Mr. Secretary?"

"It is, Dennis, a real good one." The Secretary of State turned aside to spit out his chew of tobacco. He had learned to chew at Yale when he was on the baseball team, and he did not find the habit incongruous in a man who was an expert on abstract art, spoke seven languages, wrote pretty fair blank verse and bore a name that had been in the *Social Register* for a century. Wilson turned back to Flaherty, who managed to keep the awe out of his round face. "It's damned cold, though. I hope it won't discourage too many people. It's always fine to have a good crowd watching the parade."

"They're there," Flaherty said. "I made what you might call a survey, Mr. Secretary. They're fifteen deep on the Avenue and the bleachers are almost full. And it's going to be colder than the Kennedy inaugural, so just think of that."

By the time the President appeared on the portico in high silk hat and black topcoat over his cutaway, all the Cabinet members were back in their limousines and a woman reporter from the *New York Herald Tribune* had a nosebleed, which was receiving the undivided attention of eleven male journalists. On the President's arm was Mary Elizabeth Hughes, hatless and with a light-brown mink coat over a navy-blue dress. Behind them were Vice-President Tom Morgan and Mrs. Morgan, the latter in a leopardskin coat that bulged with her plump body. Then came John Alden Hughes I and the President's mother, both tall and straight, both silver-haired. The President's father held the hand of Martha Hughes, seven, and the President's mother was leaning on the arm of Barbara Hughes, eleven. Behind this quartet was Jimmy Hughes, stooping to hear a question from Bounce Hughes, four, and bringing up the rear were Dr. Geoffrey Parker Osborne and his wife, the President's sister Pauline, with their two children, Geoffrey, seven, and Julia, six.

"All set for the tribal rites," the *Times* man said to no one in particular.

On the ride up Pennsylvania Avenue to the Capitol, Bounce Hughes, riding in the second limousine with his grandparents, unaccountably wet his pants and collapsed into tears. But he recovered shortly when his grandmother produced a change of underpants and trousers from the glove compartment and swiftly restored the boy to the proper aridity. "Julia, my dear, you think of everything," John Alden Hughes I said absent-mindedly.

Most of the crowd in the bleachers along the parade route was standing, but not necessarily in tribute to the President. The bleacher seats were covered with several inches of snow. As the parade climbed the hill to the Capitol, those in the procession could look down the side streets where the snow was unplowed and where stalled cars blocked all passage. Just as the parade turned into the Capitol grounds, Postmaster General Tom Dugan reached under a blanket on the floor of his limousine for a miniature bottle of Scotch and, holding his head below window level, drained the bottle.

Chief Justice Robert McNair Bacon was among the dignitaries who greeted the Presidential party when they were escorted into a large room in the Capitol rotunda. Mr. Justice Frank Mitchell, standing in the informal receiving line next to Mr. Justice David Benjamin Feldman, remarked that "All else having failed, Hughes is now determined to give old Bacon pneumonia." Justice Feldman did not smile. Mr. Justice Francis Copley Dalton, standing on the other side of Justice Feldman, did not hear the remark but he dutifully returned Justice Mitchell's wink. Francis was hoping that Beatrice was not too cold, standing in a corner of the inaugural stand. She had insisted on coming—"After all, Francis dear, actresses are interested in all kinds of performances, and your Mr. Hughes always puts on a good one."

The President left his topcoat and hat in an anteroom before he stepped out onto the inaugural stand with the First Lady. The roar from the crowd was most satisfactory; the East Plaza of the Capitol was packed with humanity, and despite the cold, most of the people had been there for two hours. The President stood there, his youthful face alight, while motherly females in the crowd feared he was catching his death of cold, and assorted newspaper, radio and TV reporters cursed an adoring populace that could prolong the most cruelly uncomfortable journalistic assignment of the year.

It was noted as significant by the analysts in the press section that when Chief Justice Bacon administered the oath, President Hughes's gaze was directed not at the adoring throng, but directly, aggressively, at the Chief Justice. The President's voice rose almost to a shout as he pronounced the words "and will, to the best of my ability, *preserve, protect* and *defend* the Constitution of the United States." A few minutes later, the President began his inaugural address, and from nowhere appeared a regiment of messengers handing out mimeographed copies of the speech. In the clutching, bumping, cursing melee that followed, three Western Union boys fainted, Assistant Press Secretary John Ames suffered abrasions about the face, and a TV technician fell from the hood of a jeep, spraining his left ankle.

In the press section, only editors and columnists with deadlines eight hours away listened to the words of the President as he announced his attack on the Supreme Court of the United States: "These vital statutes have been outlawed, but the problems remain with us. . . . It is not a question, my fellow countrymen, of altering the basic law of the land but of taking action that will ensure among all branches of the government a more enlightened, a more modern viewpoint. . . . I offer you with all earnestness the means to adapt our legal forms and the interpretation of those forms by the judiciary to the vital needs of the nation in these times of national peril. . . . A free government must have the power to govern, without illogical and blind obstruction from any branch of that government."

In the House majority cloakroom, where he had been listening to the President's address on the radio, Representative Henry Frederick Watson of Missouri got up slowly from his chair and walked out of the room. He sauntered up and down the corridor for a few minutes, then re-entered the cloakroom and walked through it and through the door onto the House floor. Two clerks were riffling through a tall pile of documents at a desk below the Speaker's rostrum. Watson walked up to them.

"You got the bill that goes with the President's speech?" he said.

"Yes, sir, Congressman," one of the clerks said. "We've got a whole flock of copies right here. We're just going to distribute them to the desks."

"Gimme one," Watson said.

The clerk handed him two copies. Watson took them to the nearest desk, stuck one copy in his pocket, then took out his pen and scribbled his name on the other. He picked up the endorsed copy, walked over to the bill hopper and dropped it in. If all went well, the President's plan to pack the Supreme Court would become known as the Watson Bill.

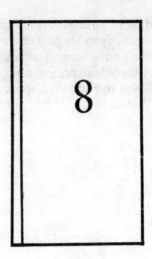

8

A DMITTEDLY, THE EDITORIAL in the liberal *Post* was bitterly to
the point regarding Congress's record of slavish obedience
to directives from the White House. "Congress?" asked the *Post*.
"Congress would strip to the skin and leap en masse into the
Potomac if the President so suggested!"

Francis Dalton put aside the newspaper on the seat and settled
down in the cab with a sigh. On this fateful morning after, the
reaction to the President's Court-packing plan was as startled
and as strident as John Alden Hughes had gleefully anticipated.
Francis had read as many comments as he could digest this morning; he would save the rest for tonight, when new ones would be
emblazoned on newsprint and come crackling over the airwaves
on radio and TV.

Francis wished he could be convinced that the President's plan
was the *right* one for what needed to be done. But he had not been
able to put down the vague doubts that had crept unwelcome into
his thoughts when John Hughes outlined it to him. There was
considerable logic in it, the kind of logic Francis Dalton had always tried to apply to his appraisals of the law and to the almost
constant need for improving, for modernizing, the law. It was the

kind of logic that had steered him in his opinions on the Court, the kind of logic he believed he could see in the amendments and changes to the law enacted by men of their particular times to suit those particular times. Jefferson *could* have thought of something like the Hughes plan under these same circumstances. In any case, Jefferson's mind would have been open about it. Not only in the present time, but in the future, the enlargement of the Court by two members would give its judgments the elasticity required by a nation always on the move. With two more places on the bench falling vacant regularly through death and retirement, the Presidents of the future would have more elbowroom in keeping the Court fresh and vital and more responsive to new ideas. The President's plan was practical, *modern.* Yet he was stirred by disquiet. The plan had a look of tampering with something basic. At the same time he told himself it was needed, Francis was gnawed by a nagging little fear that it was expedient, that it created a dangerous precedent, that it implied the right of a President—a man—to dictate the interpretation of the laws. There were other things, too. Was Hughes in danger of embracing too fervently the wrong strategy in seeking to drive his plan through Congress? Francis distrusted the President's affection for the word "efficiency," despite Hughes's casual reference to it as a kind of gimmick. There were too many holes waiting to be shot in the argument that adding two justices to the bench would enable the Court to speed up its labors, to hear more cases. This Bacon Court worked hard; Francis had discovered that early.

Beatrice had once jokingly chided Francis about the soft life the justices led. "Why, you only work four hours a day," she said. "Two weeks out of four you don't show up in the courtroom at all to hear cases. You take a month off in winter and three months off in the summer. Darling, it's the nicest-possible way I can think of to earn thirty-five thousand a year—and five hundred more if you're the Chief Justice, although the Lord knows why *he* should get more than my Francis." That, of course, was all Beatrice and the public saw on the surface—although Beatrice knew better when she was not in a teasing mood. What the public didn't know—and what Hughes seemed determined to ignore as he mapped his strategy—was that the nine justices of the Supreme Court, with a couple of exceptions, quite possibly were the hardest-working government employees in Washington. Francis Dalton had found that out to his surprise, although law school and law practice had given him a better view of the Court's activities outside the public eye. In his two years on the bench, Francis had gradually grown accustomed to working at least sixty hours a week; he did not begrudge this toil; it was the very breath of his existence. But if the President became too careless with his use of that word "efficiency," there would be proper repercussions.

It always impressed Francis, when he was reminded by circumstances, that every one of the nine justices in fact participated in every stage of the consideration of a case. Each member of the Court considered every application for review, and there were nearly fifty of these petitions crossing his desk every week from October to June. To be sure, each had his law clerk prepare a memorandum on the issue; but this was of the utmost necessity because of the numerous petitions which were obviously of faint merit. And the final decision on whether to review or not to review was the justice's. Then there was the interminable reading of briefs from both sides and the hundreds of pages of transcript of the lower court's proceedings. Then the listening to oral arguments, four days a week, four hours a day, for two weeks out of every four. Then the long discussions, at Friday conference, of the cases heard that week, the voting, and finally the writing of opinions which should take no more than three weeks but which sometimes took as long as six months. And each justice was writing an average of twenty-five opinions a term.

Francis' mind dwelt with momentary irritation upon Baker and Gillette, whose procrastinations in writing opinions were by now a Court legend. But, he reminded himself, it had always been thus. He recalled now a story the then Secretary of State Dean Acheson had told at Holy Cross about the days when he clerked for the immortal Brandeis. Acheson had been dispatched to the study of Justice Van Devanter with a message, and when he reached that chamber he found it filled with little piles of books. "All over the floor," Acheson related, "there were these little piles—two books, three books, six books, eight books, all over the floor, each pile with a piece of paper with something written on top of it.

"Van Devanter said, 'Be careful. That is my opinion. Be careful.'

"So I carefully threaded my way around these books and finally sat down beside him. He said, 'Do you see that pile over there with three or four little piles around it?' I said yes. He said, 'If you had upset that, it would take me a month to get it together again.' And this was the way the justice was constructing his opinion."

But then, of course, there was Brandeis himself, who did a day's work before breakfast, and whose clerks stayed up most of the night to prepare papers so that they could slip them under the great jurist's door before going to bed.

Francis' smile was wry as he pondered his own labors, and those of the painstaking Bacon and even of the voluble Baker. The Court perhaps could qualify as a whipping boy for a number of reasons, but there were too many people in Washington aware of its brain-numbing toil for any claim of sluggishness to prevail. And from a purely personal viewpoint, it was bad enough that this should be Friday—conference day—but he had spent half an hour vainly trying to dislodge the Corvette from the snowbank which was his N Street driveway. He would do what he could for the President's plan, but at the moment he just wanted to get through the day.

Besides, it looked as if it was going to be a long, hard pull. Francis had no doubt that Hughes would be able to bull and cajole his Court-packing plan through his captive Congress, but there would be no victory by default. The picture—on the front page of the *Post*—of the venerable Senator Frank Hoar of Ohio epitomized the contemptuous opposition of the tiny group of diehards from the other side of the aisle. Hoar had made no statement to the press, except that he wanted to read the President's message again, but an alert photographer had caught his encounter with a little knot of Congressmen in the Capitol rotunda right after the inauguration. The resulting photograph showed the usually dignified Hoar holding his bobbed nose with one hand while giving the ancient thumbs-down gesture with the other. Senator Dan Lewis of Oregon had found *his* voice, however. "Of course I shall oppose it," he had thundered at the gathered reporters. "I'll oppose it to my dying breath, just as I would oppose the insane proposals of any other dictator."

On the President's side, the reaction was predictable, practically automatic. Senate Majority Leader McAdam, crisp as always, said merely that he approved the bill and was sure it would pass. House Speaker Smith described the bill as "the long-awaited answer to judicial obstructionism," and added, "My boys are anxious to vote on it." All the other party stalwarts followed the leaders in varying degrees of enthusiasm. But—was there a straw in the wind in the reaction of Representative Richard Lane of Oklahoma, who had been the President's favorite golfing partner for more than ten years? Lane's comment made Francis uneasy; he told the press that the President's proposal required "considerable study," and added that "at the moment I must confess to some misgivings." Chairman Anderson of House Judiciary sounded unhappy, too. "We'll just have to give it a hard look," he said. "After all, there is the responsibility of protecting the judiciary." Anderson was not as pompous as he sounded in cold type.

But—to work, Francis reminded himself, as the cab turned into First Street past the magnificently ugly Library of Congress with its erminelike mantle of snow. He was glad he and Beatrice had escaped after less than an hour at only one of the four inaugural balls. ("Who's the only guy in Washington with six balls?" was this year's replay of the old gag.) He wanted to go, because he honestly wanted to help honor a man who had been his friend long before moving into the White House. But it was a pleasurable relief to flee to N Street with Beatrice and Grady and Helen Bishop for the chicken sandwiches and champagne Mrs. Robinson had laid out on the buffet before going home. His friends' and the public's reaction to his relationship with Bea was just as they both wanted it to be; that is, it was understood that they saw each other "occasionally," just as Francis occasionally had been seen at other concerts and dinners with other unattached females. "For once I'd like not to be an *item* in somebody's column," Beatrice had said. "I want to keep us to ourselves, Francis."

It was a relief, on Fridays, not to have to go to the robing room first. Besides, it was so late that Francis merely stepped into his office long enough to drop his hat and coat and to leave Jake Moriarty to his chores with only a hasty "Good morning, Jake,

126

see you later." Despite his general listlessness, Francis felt the old excitement bequeathed by political campaigns as he strode down the corridor to the conference room. Today, the Court should be buzzing.

He found, however, that his anticipation was to be prolonged. For the first time in his memory, he was the first justice in the room; glancing at his watch, he was surprised to see that he was five minutes early. It didn't matter; he was glad of a chance to relax, to be alone, to push important matters out of his mind for a few precious minutes. Francis always felt comfortable, cozily so, in the big oak-paneled room with its floor-to-ceiling bookcases stacked with the bound volumes of all past cases heard by the Supreme Court, its fireplace glowing at one end, its black baize-covered table and nine black leather swivel chairs, and the great Chief Justice John Marshall looking down from his framed portrait on the wall. There were times when the present Court could have used the relaxing influence of John Marshall, whose happy custom was to start each conference with a tot of rum if it was raining anywhere in the United States. "It is *always* raining somewhere in this great country of ours," Marshall had reminded his associates. Now, of course, strict abstention reigned in the room and even smoking was banned, largely at the insistence of the cranky little Henry Clay Robson.

Francis was not sure it was wise for the justices to lock themselves in this room in such terrible isolation. It might be safer to have a couple of clerks lurking about just to prevent mayhem. But the rule was: no stenographers, no clerks, no pages; it had been imposed in 1910 when the practice had been to have two pages on hand as messenger boys and an attendant at a table in one corner to serve coffee and other drinks. In that year, the Court had been outraged when a lawyer had sold at a profit a block of stock in a company involved in litigation on the morning the decision was announced. His broker compounded the sin by reporting the lawyer's action to a few choice clients, and there had been a run on the stock. Since the justices were not inclined to blame one another for the leak, they decided one of the pages was the culprit, and they ruled that thenceforth pages were to be banned from the conference room. Poor little page, Francis reflected; he was the innocent victim of the circumstance that even

Supreme Court justices are capable of the uninformed, snap decision. For subsequently the lawyer had assured the Court there had been no leak. His trained ear had merely furnished his trained brain with the gist of the decision after hearing only the first paragraph, and he had departed the courtroom forthwith to telephone his broker. However, the Court had not seen fit to review its decision banishing outsiders, and now when a message was sent or received the junior justice—meaning Francis—acted as doorkeeper. Francis relished the job as a welcome excuse to stretch his legs, and he was sure the others envied him; Hume was always harking back to "the good old days when I could unstick my bottom from that chair."

When the door opened, it was Bacon, and he did not walk into the room—he marched in. His eyes were bluer than ever, but their customary chill was replaced by a flash of fire, and his pince-nez seemed to be trembling on the bridge of his Roman nose. Chief Justice Robert McNair Bacon was in a fury.

"Good morning, Chief," Francis said.

Bacon seemed to be looking at him as though seeing him for the first time, but his manners were adequate to any occasion. "Morning, Mr. Justice," he said shortly, and his hand was out for Francis to shake. "Well, Mr. Justice, I presume you are fully aware of the latest dictatorial vagary of your friend Mr. Hughes."

Francis had a wild impulse to grin, but he repulsed it. "Yes, I suppose I am, sir, if you mean the President's plan to enlarge the Court."

"*Enlarge* the Court?" Bacon's glare was such as to almost cause his eyes to pop out of their sockets. "You *are* generous, Mr. Justice. *Pack* the Court is what I mean, and pack the Court is what that man intends to do—if he is so permitted. Mr. Justice, is it possible that you are sincerely innocent of that man's Machiavellian mentality?"

Francis dared a smile now. "Machiavellian? I'm afraid I never thought of the President in quite that way, Chief. But he does seem determined to give us a little help."

"Help! That man give us *help?* My dear Mr. Justice, if you have troubled to read the text of Hughes's message and of the tawdry little bill he has thrown to his servile Congress, you must have perceived that he is determined to wreck the Court—to make of it an obedient adjunct of the executive department. God save the Court from such help!"

"I don't think he quite expressed it that way, Chief." It was a senseless argument, but Francis had heard a surprising number of senseless arguments in this room, and his respect for Bacon had never been confused with awe. "As I understood it, the President hopes to improve the Court's—ah—capacity"—*not* efficiency, Francis insisted to himself—"by giving it new freshness and vigor."

Bacon started to reply, but paused as the door opened and Baker came in, followed by Hume and Robson. The door closed, but opened almost immediately to admit Feldman, ear held close to Gillette's lips, and then Whitfield and Mitchell. Francis saw that Bacon was struggling to hold himself in as the justices performed the traditional hand-shaking rite, each with the others.

But Mitchell's hearty Nevada voice was booming out before Bacon had a chance to go on. "How do you like that Johnny Hughes," boomed Mitchell, "trying to get some fresh thinkers on this little ol' Court! Damned if ol' Johnny doesn't keep things moving all the time."

Bacon's lips were pressed hard together; even at such a time the Chief Justice could not deign to acknowledge Frank Mitchell. But David Benjamin Feldman was not so snobbish.

"I judge you regard the President's proposal as something rather humorous," Feldman said, his grudging banker's look turned bleakly on Mitchell. "I would have another word for it—tragic."

"Yes, you would," Mitchell said. "You would, Benny." Above all else, Mr. Justice Feldman detested being called Benny. Mitchell was still wearing his broad cowboy grin. "It's humorous, yes, because it scares the pants off people who would be struck dead by a new idea. But it's a serious and straightforward proposal, with a great deal of horse-sense merit, to people who believe you have to do something once in awhile to preserve what we've got."

"Tragic?" Henry Clay Robson's girllike twang was cutting. "Really, David, aren't you being rather dramatic, emotional? I don't quite accept the theory that the Supreme Court of the United States exists through some kind of divine right."

Bacon had to get into it. "I suppose there are those who have scant respect for democratic institutions except in so far as they may be used to further one's own ends," he broke in. Now his voice had regained its usual icy contempt. "But I hope I shall always be in the forefront of those who would defend this Court against debasement by the politicians."

"I should hope you would, Robert," Robson said, his voice drily mild. "But I'm afraid I don't agree that anyone has suggested debasing this Court. I don't pretend to have formed a final opinion, but there are times, I confess, when I think it might be a good idea to give a certain amount of study to the reorganization of the Court."

"You believe that adding two new justices to the membership would be a form of reorganization?" Bacon asked, icily sarcastic.

"I don't know that I do, Robert—but obviously you do."

The shot set Bacon's pince-nez to trembling anew. "Sir, I reserve the right to put my own words in my own mouth. I call it packing, sir!"

"All right, it's packing," Mitchell said. "And after listening to some of you this morning, I say I'm all for it."

Bacon turned to Hume, who had eased himself quietly into his chair and was staring out the window. The Chief Justice's manner was most respectful; Francis reflected that if there was anyone on the Court capable of frightening Bacon, that man was the mild, scholarly, strong-minded William Allen Hume.

"Allen, you've given it some thought, surely," Bacon said.

Hume looked up at the Chief Justice's towering figure with its wavy white hair and its fullback shoulders. "Yes, I have, Robert. Certainly." He smiled. "My ivory tower has excellent communications. But I don't believe I have anything to add to the discussion at the present. Besides, the decision is the prerogative of the Congress, isn't it?"

One strikeout for Bacon, Francis thought. Hume was not a brawler.

Bacon retreated slowly. "Yes, of course, Allen. But I hope we can be excused a certain personal interest, a certain personal loyalty to this Court."

"Yes, Robert," Hume said. "Of course. And we are all loyal to the Court, of course." Even Robson and Mitchell, he seemed to be reminding Bacon.

Gillette was trying to clear his throat, but the sound came out as a wheeze from deep in his round body. "I suggest, gentlemen, that we are wasting polite words on this—project," he said, the words seeming to require extraordinary effort. (Glutton! Francis told himself.) "John Hughes is simply and cold-bloodedly determined to set himself up as a dictator of the Court's opinions. He seeks to create a Court that will give slavish approval to every unconstitutional measure he persuades Congress to inflict on the country."

Mitchell's voice was gravelly, and contemptuous. "Speech! Speech! Gillette, you sound as if you're running for dogcatcher in some neon-lit suburb of Los Angeles. Hasn't it ever occurred to you that in these times you're in danger of losing something a little more important than the right to eat five big meals a day? You liberals and your talk of freedoms—it's never occurred to you that the Constitution was written by men who recognized the need for sacrifice and discipline and strong action in order to preserve the most important freedom of all, the freedom to exist!"

"And so we should permit a dictatorial President to tamper with the judicial process!" Gillette shot back. "And so we should place our freedoms, our inalienable rights, in the doubtful custody of John Alden Hughes!"

Francis looked hard at Gillette. Such talk should have sounded silly coming from the portly Californian, and yet it didn't. Francis detested Gillette and Gillette's pat philosophy which determinedly overlooked license, and yet Gillette's words made him uncomfortable this morning. He wished he had more time to think, away from all this talk, but Baker's nasal tones broke in on his consciousness.

"It's despicable, that's what it is," Baker said, his face one large flushed pout. "That man is seeking personal and political vengeance on those members of the Court who have dared to challenge his thirst for personal power. We refuse to do his unconstitutional bidding, and so he will send among us intruders who will."

Mitchell was standing there, legs wide apart, a grin on his face. "Joe, maybe you should have a bodyguard to protect you against this tyrant. I've got a couple of no-good ranch hands I can detach for the assignment."

Robson spoke up with prim sharpness. "Really, all this twaddle is becoming most—disgusting. The President has sent up a piece of legislative matter which he deems advisable and needful, and we stand about screeching our opinions like children in a schoolyard. If we cannot discuss the matter with at least the intelligence of stockbrokers or insurance salesmen, I would suggest we terminate this collective harangue."

Francis glanced at Hume and found the Hoosier's lips parted in his gentle smile. Hume turned to Chief Justice Bacon. "Robert, I don't associate myself with all of Mr. Justice Robson's remarks, but I think you may agree that we are making very little progress in settling the issue. Perhaps we can employ ourselves more usefully."

"Yes, of course," Bacon said. He seemed uncertain of where to go next.

It was Angus Whitfield who showed him the way. Silent up to now, the old Minnesotan's deep bass flared with impatience. "We've got a lot of work to do today. For God's sake, let's get started."

The conference got things done, but it was not a happy conference. Bacon could not be polite to either Robson or Mitchell, and Feldman sulked in his seat. Whitfield, impatient and determinedly businesslike, kept things moving. There were, first, sixty-eight entries on the assignment sheet listing the cases the Court was being asked to review: a few cases in the Court's original jurisdiction—those affecting states or foreign representatives—and the rest appellate cases from lower courts which raised some Federal question. All the justices had presumably studied the petitions on the sheet, and their opinions on whether or not to review should have been clear-cut. But as usual, the Ohio Rotarian, Joseph T. Baker, and the indolent Californian, George W. Gillette, wasted valuable time with their vague, circuitous statements. Robson, neat and orderly, his mind fine-honed by a solitary, well-read childhood and a decade among the pedagogues of the closed-shop Ivy League, tried not to show his impatience with these two judicial dolts, but it was too much for his impatient IQ.

"Mr. Justice Baker, I do not see why we should linger over a defendant whose guilt was betrayed by his own counsel," Robson suggested at one point. And at another, "My dear Mr. Justice Gillette, I should like to propose that we are not examining the qualifications of a potential candidate for the city council of Laguna Beach." Bacon, as annoyed as Robson at the feckless delaying tactics of the pair, could only grunt uncomfortably and offer the recommendation that "we cease these interruptions and get on with the business before the Court."

Despite his weariness, Francis found fascination again in the petitions for review from paupers in the country's various prisons. There were eight of these today, two of them scribbled almost illegibly on postcards, one painstakingly transcribed on a typewriter with the letter "r" missing—it was carefully written in in red ink—and the others following the proper form but obviously with little care for legalisms. When he first joined the Court, Francis had been warmed by the discovery that the Court processed nearly a thousand of these informal pleas a year; the printing of briefs and records of these cases was financed with a part of the $25 fee paid by lawyers when they were admitted to practice before the Court. Most of the applications were without substance, but Francis took pride in the fact there was not a single member of the Court who did not spare time and attention for these pleas. None of the applications was approved today, although Francis was surprised to note that Baker, with his country-club mentality, was somehow still capable of joining Whitfield and Hume in pressing for acceptance of one of the postcard pleas.

"The record clearly shows that this man knows what he is talking about, even if he doesn't know how to express himself," Baker argued. "His guilt may well be plain, but I suggest there are enough signs of legal uncertainty in the judge's charge to the jury to indicate that the man's trial fell considerably short of fairness."

Hume's argument was dry and brief. "I can only repeat what Mr. Justice Baker has said," Hume said. "The issue here, if you will, is whether a defendant whose guilt is obvious deserves a fair trial. He does."

It was a good thing, Francis was thinking, that only four affirmative votes were necessary to accept the review of a case. Otherwise, the Court might spend its entire time twiddling its thumbs in an empty courtroom. It was curious that the Court could make up its mind on a decision in a case it was reviewing, but seemed to hate the thought of deciding to take a case. Anyway, by the time the justices had finished their voting on the petitions of certiorari, it was time for lunch; the Court had voted to review exactly seven cases.

As he walked into the justices' private dining room, Francis noted that Robson was not among the community eaters. The little man from Florida apparently was lunching in his office again. Everybody else was on hand, however, as though the Court was drawing together in this hour of attack from the executive department. Francis had ordered a small steak from the conference room, and he was glad to find that Mitchell, sitting next to him, seemed preoccupied with his lamb chops. Bacon, too, was silent, and Hume was digesting a copy of *The Yale Law Journal* along with his cottage cheese and fruit. No one seemed to want to resume the acrimonious debate that had opened the weekly conference. Good, Francis thought; he felt that if he were to proselytize successfully, it would have to be in private, and these hot-headed scenes were no help. Besides, it was too early to get to work on anything as complicated as the President's proposal.

Francis found himself alongside Hume as the Court returned to the conference room for its discussion and vote on the cases heard that week, and he was surprised at the Hoosier's amiable garrulity.

"It was an excellent speech, didn't you think so, Mr. Justice?" Hume asked.

Francis looked at Hume. "Why—yes, I thought so. I think it was typical—and quite logical."

"Yes, it was," Hume said. "President Hughes is not an idiot, despite the wishful thinking of some people we both know. He is an activist who knows that the time to act is when you are strongest."

"He's strong enough," Francis said. "November showed that. The people seem to approve what he's doing."

"They do. They do. They've made that plain. And Mr. Hughes is confident enough that he can dare to be—direct." A small smile played over Hume's face. "After all, Mr. Justice, it's the votes that count, isn't it—in the country and on the Supreme Court?"

They were back in the conference room then, and Francis was spared a reply to a question that defied an answer. He was still pondering it when the Chief Justice irritably called the conference to order and the Court started its usual disagreeable discussion of the cases on which it intended to vote.

The meeting followed its usual pattern. As the junior justice, Francis ended each discussion with an exposition of his views; for the most part it was routine stuff, since few of the cases being considered were of major importance. Francis did persist in a faint hope that the Court might be more lenient in the case of the Baptist college in Biloxi which had been granted four million dollars for a dormitory for its physics students on the grounds that anything connected with the production of scientists was in the national interest. "And besides," Francis pointed out, "the dormitory is just for sleeping." But it was evident—in the crackling commentary of Bacon, Feldman and Baker and the quiet agreement from Hume—that once more the administration was to be foiled in its efforts to give financial assistance to private schools.

"I suggest that it is useless to waste our time in argument," Bacon said in his snappish way. "After all, this is the same Court that in the Jamieson case ruled that the expenditure of public monies for the benefit of private schools is a clear violation of the constitutional admonition calling for the separation of church and state."

Bacon's comments were hardly necessary. The vote was the usual five-to-four against the administration, a decision softened only slightly by Hume's tolerant admission that "The need is there; unfortunately it cannot be filled in the manner the government has chosen in this case."

As usual, Francis and Hume locked horns about individual rights; they did so at almost every Friday conference. This time the case involved one Slade, a lawyer, who had refused to answer a Congressional committee's question about evidence that he had once joined the Communist party. Slade had been disbarred and the issue revolved around the state's power to disbar a lawyer on those grounds.

Hume's tone was low, as always, in launching his attack on what he called "another violation" of the First Amendment. "I would still dare to hope," he said, "that this Court can find it possible to abandon its policy of going into a balancing act when confronted by cases such as this. I must insist, as I have insisted before, that nowhere in the Constitution is the Supreme Court of the United States given the power to decide whether individual liberties may be abridged merely because they conflict with the interest of the state."

Francis was cool and confident in his rebuttal. "It is a matter of logic," he said. "There is just no other way to approach such a case when the state's power conflicts with an individual right. When the Court faces a claim of a violation of free speech, it must weigh the claim against the effect that claim—if supported—will have on the state interest."

The vote was five-to-four in upholding the disbarment. Hume was smiling gently as he had his last say, but his words were sharp. "Here is another decision which takes its place with those too many others whose effect is the violation of the Bill of Rights," he said. "It is a flagrant violation, committed in a manner precisely contrary to the explicit commands of the First Amendment."

But it was Hume who furnished the only humorous relief there was in that long, stiff session that continued for nearly eight hours. Holding for the majority that the simultaneous transportation of two women across a state line for purposes of prostitution should be punished by only one sentence instead of two, Justice Feldman insisted there was only one offense involved.

"The state line was crossed only once," Feldman pointed out.

"Ah, yes," Hume put in merrily, "but should we make it easier to transport them by the dozen?"

Mr. Justice Francis Copley Dalton, packing his briefcase for a weary return to Georgetown and a martini with Beatrice, found himself suddenly grateful that so far John Alden Hughes had not stretched his trade-restraining hand in the direction of the nation's lively ladies. So far, that is, Francis reminded himself.

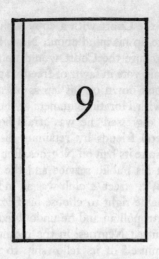

9

GEORGE HAD RECOMMENDED THE MAN, in professional jargon, as one of the country's few "really significant" writers. Mr. Justice William Allen Hume, at ease in the living room of his Chevy Chase home, was not quite sure these days what "significant" meant to his son, but there was no doubt that in *The Undecided* Felix McCovey revealed himself as a sharp-eyed observer who knew how to record his observations with considerable pungency. It was no use being offended because an author sprinkled his prose with words like "fuck"; many people used these words, including a late member of the Supreme Court of the United States whose passions otherwise had run to Greek poetry and Aztec ruins. In a novel about the Chicago slums, an author undoubtedly would find it difficult to remain faithful to his characters without acknowledging the obscenity that sprinkled their patois. At any rate, it was a rather good novel; McCovey had created some magnificent characters. Hume reflected he probably would not have read the book had he not been a Supreme Court justice. It had, in effect, been forced on him by counsel for the state of New York, who had forgone an oral argument concerning the state's ban on the book in favor of presenting each member of the Court with a copy which he could read for himself and make up his mind about. Now, halfway through the book, Hume was sure the Court would uphold the ban, despite his virtually certain vote in favor of freedom of expression.

He put the book down on his lap as his mind returned to his lunch that day with Horatio Summers at the Metropolitan Club. Again, his mind digressed; he was afraid he had offended some of his more liberal friends by retaining his membership in the Metropolitan despite its ban on Negroes. But he could see no connection between his public service and the membership policies of a private club; in effect, a club was an individual, with the individual's inalienable right to choose his friends and companions. He liked the Metropolitan and he undoubtedly would like it just as well if it admitted Negroes; in the meantime he was not going to deprive himself of its fellowship to support a viewpoint which abridged one of the rights of man for which he fought daily.

Horatio, bless him, had tried to restrain himself, but he had been too full of his viewpoint; besides, Horatio was so sincerely an old and trusted friend that he could not be self-conscious about the fact that he was talking to a Supreme Court justice at the same time he was protesting to a friend. Summers had been full, mostly, of the President's Court plan; it was just what was needed, and if the Court itself was offended by it, the justices had only themselves to blame. The President had tried to "play ball" with them and they had rebuffed him, and now he was going to get what he wanted despite their "stuffed-shirt" obstructionism.

"Stuffed-shirt?" Hume's broad sense of humor had been nudged, despite Horatio's seriousness. "But Horatio, you've always complained that I'm too liberal, too far to the left."

Horatio had not been embarrassed. "Yes, stuffed-shirt. You know damn well you and I never agreed on the definition of liberal, Allen. They call me a conservative, but as far as I'm concerned I'm more of a liberal than most of your bleeding-heart pals. To me, a liberal is a man who wants to get things done in these times and is not always splitting hairs about how to do 'em. You know how I feel about you, Allen, but to my mind people like you and old Bacon and old Scrooge Feldman are standing in the path of progress."

"Yes, I see what you mean, Horatio," Hume had replied. "I suppose the Constitution is pretty old-fashioned these days, going back as it does to 1789." His smile was sincere; he *was* enjoying himself.

"Now, you know damned well that isn't what I mean, Allen," Horatio had stormed. "That's the difference between you and me —to me the Constitution means what *it* says, whereas the Supreme Court claims it means what the Court says."

That was the heart of the controversy raging in the country, Hume reflected. It was a battle which seemed to him senseless. Throughout the Bill of Rights, its authors had used plain language, easily understood: "Congress shall make no law . . . abridging the freedom of speech," for example. "No law" meant no law, regardless of the circumstances or the momentary needs of the state. To Hume, there could not be the shadow of a doubt that the fathers of the Constitution—men who knew what words meant and used them purposely—intended their interdictions to be absolute. It was not a question of whether you were liberal or conservative—whatever *those* labels meant—there was no legal way in which to circumvent the meaning of those words. Those five-to-four decisions were not an attempt by the Court to foist its own laws on the country but merely a formal reminder that the Constitution was explicit in certain of its prohibitions. And it was entirely beside the point that William Allen Hume should find personal satisfaction in those prohibitions.

He could understand Horatio's attitude. In the first place, Horatio had an orderly mind, and a rather good one beneath his old-shoe manner and speech; during four years as Governor of Indiana, Horatio had gained a reputation as a man who got things done. He was not only a practical politician, but a practical businessman as well; to Horatio it was a waste of time to split legal hairs, as he put it. And in these uncertain times, Horatio had even less patience with hair splitting; Hume could understand Horatio's deep, almost frantic concern for the country, even if he could not accept Horatio's and John Alden Hughes's insistence that it was a period of clear and present danger and thus a time for extraordinary measures aimed at protecting the state by any means. Horatio was fond of repeating that the Walsh Act had worked, as though that excused its flagrant disregard for individual rights. "The people wanted it—they showed that in November," Horatio had thundered at lunch, and it had been impossible to persuade him that even if the electorate temporarily favored an unconstitutional law, that approval did not give the law validity.

"The people were in favor of the Alien and Sedition Act," Hume had reminded Horatio. "Did that make it right?"

"Certainly not," Horatio had replied comfortably. "That was a bad law. The Walsh Act was a good law, aimed at protecting the nation's welfare." It was odd to hear such a straightforward man mouthing such sophistry.

Of course the people had wanted the Walsh Act, and of course it had worked during its year of operation. Big labor had become so big that its leaders no longer wanted the orderly conduct of its business disrupted by strikes, and of course management was delighted to enter into a cartel with big labor to protect its own interests. The idea of a government board to impose compulsory arbitration and with authority to levy heavy penalties for refusal to abide by its decisions gave both big labor and big business the escape hatch they wanted. And there had been no strikes and very little unrest. But the Court had no choice but to invalidate the Walsh Act, again on the ground of the abridging of individual rights. The government could not interfere either with the individual's right to run his own business or with the workers' right to bargain collectively. Hughes had all but admitted that, and then had gone on to insist that the times had outmoded those rights in some respects. Hume had a healthy respect, even admiration, for Hughes; he was saddened by the knowledge that such a man, sincerely devoted to the betterment of the underprivileged and with so much of the common touch in his makeup, could employ the same methods authoritarians had always sought to use to get things done.

Hughes often puzzled Hume, especially in their social encounters. He smiled now, recalling their conversation at the White House dinner for the judiciary which followed closely the Court's decision throwing out the Walsh Act. "I'm surprised at you, Mr.

Justice," Hughes had remarked with that meaningful jocularity that was one of his political arts. "A good conservative like you deserting the cause." Hughes's remark amazed him, not because of its casual impropriety, but because it reflected a general, and quite erroneous, viewpoint. It always baffled Hume that people should consider him a conservative.

He wished he did not have to consider himself tagged with any label, but he supposed he would qualify, by his own definition, as a liberal. That is, he believed a liberal was any person who opposed arbitrary and extralegal power assumed by either a "liberal" or a "conservative" executive. He had always preferred to think of himself as a Jeffersonian Constitutionalist, but since both sides insisted that Jefferson was the first authentic liberal on the American scene, he supposed he would have to accept the label. The difference, he supposed, was that he was a Jeffersonian without any reservations, without the convenient habit of rationalizing any deviations from the philosophy when those deviations served a special interest.

Despite this unswerving devotion to the specific, the absolute, in the Constitution, however, his appointment to the Court had been both hailed and decried because of his supposed conservatism. On one side, he was seen as the justice who would lead the Court away from its wild and woolly leftism; on the other, his vote was seen as another in the campaign to maintain the status quo. His father, leaning against the counter of the little Indiana hardware store, would have been amused. He had instilled in his son the doctrine of the protection of the citizen by the constant invoking of the Bill of Rights, and that was the doctrine William Allen Hume had followed through his career as Governor and, later, as Senator from Indiana. Nowadays, Hume wondered if his political attitudes had not been fostered by the fact that his family's poverty had required him to work at a variety of odd jobs in order to get through the university and law school. He certainly had always been a firm believer in free enterprise, in a minimum of government, in the free exercise of the citizen's energy and initiative. He had always opposed government interference in those affairs he believed were the sole domain of the individual, whether he was a steelworker or a coupon clipper.

He reached up and turned off the lamp over his shoulder; he had lost interest in the prose of Felix McCovey. His opponents had even called him a reactionary; he smiled now at the thought. To be sure, he had fought the "liberals" both in Indiana and in Washington when they sought to invade the citizen's private domain, and yet his social welfare legislation and his dealings with labor had been of considerable concern to many of the conservatives whose interests he presumably was serving. It was the times, he reflected. There had been no normality since World War II, and in the middle of national abnormality it had been difficult for people to think clearly. His conservatism had always been of the type that threw up the Bill of Rights as a barricade against governmental infringements, and yet he had gained a reputation as an old fossil standing in the path of the progress decreed for the nation by a philosophy of benevolent Big Brotherism. And now he was being denounced as a turncoat politician —by the President as a "liberal" and by the electorate, which wanted ultimate security, as a pinko. It was the old story of whose ox was gored, he supposed. Tactics such as the President's arrests of those Sons of Slaves agitators in the South might be deplored when occurring in the Soviet Union, but here at home they were necessary to preserve the public order. It was one of a piece with the fierce determination of the official liberal to impose rightist governments abroad—as a protection against Communist infiltration—and his anguished cries against any encroachment on pure democracy in the United States.

Well, he was glad he was privileged to sit in on it, even from the lofty isolation of the Supreme Court bench. Things could not always be the way one wanted them, and it was Hume's opinion that that probably was a good thing. The citizenry might be in a state of constant disagreement, and voices might sometimes grow too strident for national dignity, but in its own way the noise was an assurance that the country was still vital, still bursting with energy. Ideas were popping up all over the land, and it didn't matter that so many of them were unintelligent or bad; what mattered was that the country was still producing them.

He confessed unashamedly, too, that he loved Washington. It had become his city during his fifteen years on the bench. "It's full of phonies," Eric was fond of reminding him, and his clear-minded son, with the impatience of his crisp Manhattan law practice, was right. But it was also full of hard-working, dedicated public servants, who risked fortune and health because each one of them had an idea to contribute to the amiable chaos that was the Federal government. Hume could understand why elected and appointive officials hated to leave Washington when they lost their jobs, and scurried about seeking desks in public relations and consultants' offices; things happened in this strange city whose atmosphere and attitude were more Indianapolis and Richmond than London or Paris but which yet remained the capital of the world. Foreign diplomats came, contemptuous or pleading, but grudgingly accepting the city's importance to them, and no state governor dared ignore it lest he suddenly find his state without Federal funds for a new bridge. Twice now, Hume had walked the six-mile length of Rock Creek Park and he honestly believed this unspoiled refuge of the oak tree, winding through the center of the yammering city, was the finest in the world. Eric was always demanding that the city do away with its many traffic circles which so enraged motorists, but Hume was prepared to block such progress to preserve his right to look at them on a spring morning. There were too many statues for some people, but not for Hume; he liked even the more hideous chunks of marble and bronze because they were things that at one time Washington wanted in its midst and therefore were a part of history. He even didn't mind the gymnasium in the Supreme Court with its steam cabinet, rowing machine and exercise bicycle—after all, he had only been in it once.

The phone rang in his library and he could hear Dorothy's footsteps as she hurried down the carpeted hall to answer it, and he hoped it wouldn't be for him, but it was.

"William?" Dorothy was standing in the doorway, unwilling as always to break in on his thoughts. His wife was the only one who called him William, and Hume was always pleased by the thought. He had been Allen to his hometown friends because his father was William, and the name had gone with him through college and into politics. Dorothy had made her decision the first time he had had a date with her, during his senior year at Indiana University. "I think you're old enough now to be called by your first name, William," she said.

He turned now and smiled at his wife through the semigloom. "Yes, dear, I'm just sitting here wasting my time. Is it White with a problem?" That was unfair; his law clerk seldom had a problem he couldn't tackle alone.

Dorothy was grinning as she came into the room, her slender figure gliding across the floor. "I'm afraid it's much worse than that, William. It's Senator Hoar."

"Hoar?" Hume was surprised. He knew Frank Hoar, of course, and liked him for his single-minded devotion to economy and efficiency in government, but they were not particularly close friends. He got up from his chair, stretching his long legs. "Wonder what he wants," he said partly to himself.

Dorothy laughed. "I suppose one of his spies caught you wasting paper."

"Saucy girl," Hume said and kissed her cheek as he went by. "Don't be irreverent."

He walked into the library and picked up the phone. "Hello, Frank," he said. "It's nice to hear from you."

Hoar's voice, hoarse and faintly irritable, crackled on the wire. "Allen, sorry to bother you." He would be, too, Hume thought. "I just wanted to sound you out, Allen," Hoar said.

"Why . . . certainly, Frank." Hume was honestly puzzled. "It's no bother. But, about what?"

Hoar sounded a little uncertain now. "Well, Allen, you know how some of us are feeling . . . we'd sort of like to see how you feel. About that Court bill of the President's."

"Oh." For the moment Hume could think of nothing else to say.

"Now, Allen, I know you hate to get mixed up in anything outside the Court. You know I wouldn't want to drag you into anything. But some of us think it's a damned bad bill and we'd like to get your opinion."

"Oh, I see, Frank." Well, well, Hume thought. "Frank, I don't really—I'm afraid you caught me by surprise."

"Yes. Yes, I suppose so. But I'm not pressuring you, Allen. That is"—hurriedly, because it obviously had occurred to him that Supreme Court justices could not be pressured—"that is, this is just a private chat. Off the record, as it were, Allen. Just a friendly talk between friends."

"Of course." Hume could not let Hoar remain ill at ease. "I understand, Frank. But I don't quite know what to say."

"Sure, I get you. But, Allen, I wonder if you'd be good enough to tell me what your first reaction is. Do you think it's a good bill?"

Be careful, Hume told himself. Don't get involved here. This is a matter for the Congress. It is none of your business. And then he couldn't help it. "Frank, I don't like to comment on such things. You can understand that. But no, I don't think it is a good bill." Why did he say that, when he had warned himself?

"Good, Allen." Hoar's scratchy tone expressed approving delight. "I was sure you'd say that, Allen. Know what kind of a man you are. Never had any doubts when you were in the Senate."

Hume smiled. Good, honest, straightforward Frank Hoar. No matter what he said, he could never be accused of being patronizing, but merely of enjoying a man who agreed with him.

"Thank you, Frank," Hume said. "I don't quite see what practical comfort it will give you, though."

"Oh, it does—it will. Tell me, Allen, on what grounds do you call it a bad bill?"

"Why, I think it's quite simple." Certainly there was no harm in explaining his viewpoint. "The President has advanced this bill as a measure to improve the efficiency of the Court. His argument has no validity. There is no reason to believe the addition of two more justices will make the Court more efficient; it may even contribute to inefficiency."

"Right. Thought so. The damned shyster." Hoar coughed apologetically. "Excuse me. Didn't mean that. Thinking out loud. But I'm glad to hear a man who knows something about it put it just like that."

"Yes." Now Hume felt uncertain. "But, of course, it's none of my affair. Officially, that is. I'm afraid it's your problem, Frank, the problem of the Congress."

"Yes, yes, it is. It's our problem, all right. But, Allen, wouldn't you say it was the problem of the people, too, all the people?"

"Why, I suppose so. Certainly I hope the people will be interested and will express themselves. But the Congress represents the people."

"Yes. Sometimes I wonder. I hope I don't represent some of those idiots in my state. But, Allen, you're one of the people and, what's more, you're an expert on the subject. Don't you think you should be represented?"

"Why . . . certainly, I am interested. Naturally."

"All right. Now, Allen, I'm not going to annoy you with a lot of speechmaking or arguments. But we need help, Allen. Hughes has got the Hill in his pocket, you know that. Some of those characters dassn't take a pee without asking Big Brother. We need help to try to pound some sense into their concrete skulls."

Hume tried his best to sound jovial. "Frank, I can't start hanging around the cloakrooms telling your people how to vote." He shuddered at the thought.

"Now, Allen, you know I wouldn't suggest anything of the kind." Not much, Hume thought. "What I was going to suggest was that you might like to express an opinion—as a private citizen."

"Oh, and what would that opinion be?"

"That it is a bad bill, that's all."

"Oh, and as a private citizen? You don't think it would occur to anyone that I was also a justice of the Supreme Court?"

Hoar laughed. It was not a comfortable laugh. "Now, Allen, you know what I mean. Of course you're a member of the Court. But you're also a private citizen. Both as a member of the Court and as a private citizen, you have the right to say so if you think something is bad."

"Frank, I understand. But I don't see how I can do any such thing. It may be perfectly proper, but I just don't like the idea. I never liked the idea of Supreme Court justices expressing ex officio opinions. We're supposed to attend to our knitting."

"I know that, Allen. I know that. We wouldn't want you to go out and take the stump and start making a lot of damnfool speeches like Robson and that young Dalton. You know that. Allen, here's what I want to suggest, and I don't want an answer now. Take your time, sleep on it—we've got weeks to fight this out. All I'd like is for you to issue a statement, sometime, saying I asked your opinion on the bill and you were giving it."

"Frank, I don't see how . . ."

"Now, Allen, just don't answer me now. Just don't say anything at all except that you'll think about it, that you'll consider it."

Hume sighed. "All right, Frank. I'll think about it. Naturally, I'll think about it, after your call. But I can't promise a thing, Frank. I just don't like the idea."

"All right, all right. That's all I ask—that you think about it. Don't say anything more, Allen." Hoar took a long moment to clear his gravelly throat. "I'll say goodbye now, Allen, because I don't want to bother you. You know you can get in touch with me any time. And, Allen, thank you. Thanks very much." Hoar couldn't wait to get away.

Hume hung up and remained sitting at his desk, a hand to his high forehead, his mouth pursed. Curiously, he thought first of Dorothy. She wouldn't ask him about the call, but it was unusual for her husband to get telephone calls from senators, especially Frank Hoar, and Dorothy was an intelligent woman. She had been a politician's wife for a long time, and she had never been slow at reaching conclusions. She couldn't ask, though. And because of that, he would tell her what Frank wanted. She would not offer an opinion unless asked, and he would not ask her—not yet. It was something he had to think about, alone, for a while. Perhaps for a long while.

It had seemed that he had not wanted to think about the President's Court plan before Hoar called. Hoar's call had reminded him that he had to think about it. He knew now he was opposed to it. It was a bad bill and a willful bill. It was not needed, at least for the reason Hughes had advanced. It implied that the executive could work his will not only on the legislative but on the judicial. It as much as said that when the Supreme Court did not function to suit the executive, the executive could, in effect, march up Pennsylvania Avenue and take charge. Even if it were needed, even if the times indeed were as perilous as Hughes insisted, the bill was still an evil precedent. If Hughes were a saint, this tampering with the Court might be justified, but what would happen if an authentic man on horseback invaded the White House?

But should he—did he have a right to—get involved in the fight that was brewing? Could a member of the Supreme Court maintain his awful and necessary isolation from the public churnings of government if he took a public stand on an issue not

147

before the Court? Hume had always disapproved of the peripatetic Robson and his speeches in far-flung hamlets on the international situation, and he had been disappointed in Francis Dalton's emphasis on the need for what he called "national discipline" in his speeches to bar associations. To Hume it had always seemed that the only opinions a Supreme Court justice should express were those that came from the bench.

Yet, as Hoar had shrewdly pointed out, he was a citizen—and an expert on the Supreme Court. The implication, of course, was that a proper duty lay there, waiting to be done. If he had reason to believe that the bill was a bad one and that it would not fill the advertised need, was it not his duty to say so publicly so that the people could be informed? The wry thought occurred that many of his opinions from the bench had been filled with phrases demanding that no one should interfere with the public's right to be informed. Did he have the right to interfere with his own right to inform the public? He wondered why Hoar had not called the Chief Justice, and he immediately knew the answer. First, nobody would have to call Bacon; he would express himself trenchantly when the time came—which was when Bacon got around to it. Second, Hoar knew that in the public's view Bacon was a cranky old man whose opinions were likely to be prejudiced by his oft-expressed dislike for John Alden Hughes.

Yes, he opposed the bill, despite the wistfulness the thought of fresh new—and young—justices induced in him. He had always taken delight in the open-mindedness of the new justices as they arrived on the Court; Dalton was a special favorite with him because of his fresh, unhackneyed approach to the point at issue. Usually he and Dalton were on opposite sides because of Dalton's insistence on looking first to the needs of the state, but Hume admired Dalton's keen mind and his genuine feeling for the ordinary man. On such a court as this, it was important to have one or two, or more, freshman justices with fresh viewpoints; otherwise there was the danger that the arguments within the Court would become mere trite premises memorized through constant use. Hume was quite aware that with justices like Bacon and Feldman, in particular, the tendency was to overlook the nice specifics of a difficult case in their determination to be guided only by their timeworn principles. He did not agree with Francis Dalton that the Supreme Court should be careful not to interfere with the legislative in its responsibility for governing. "I merely ask that the Court indulge in a certain amount of self-restraint," Dalton was fond of saying. "We should not say to Congress, you cannot do this, until we have looked into the reasons why it sought to do it." Hume could only reply that the Constitution did not entrust power either to Congress or to the Supreme Court to weigh all the considerations and then decide what the law should be. To Hume, the law was the law, and the Constitution was the Constitution, regardless of how adversely its application might affect the state. But he had hope for the young Irishman from Massachusetts. More, he had faith in him. Hume had seen justices mature and become intimate with the Constitution on the bench, and because it took a really good mind to so mature, he was sure Dalton would come to a new understanding of the basics in the nation's laws pertaining to human liberties. He hoped it was not merely because he was so warmly fond of Dalton that he felt this way. Anyway, for a moment he could expect once again to line up against Dalton; there was little doubt this vital Irishman would do what he could to help his friend the President. Hume stopped himself in the middle of a disapproving thought. He could not decry Dalton's lobbying for the bill if he himself decided to help fight it. He got up and walked out of the library and across the hall to the living room because he wanted to be with Dorothy.

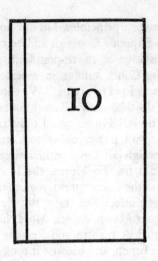

10

FOR ALL HIS ARISTOCRATIC LINEAMENTS, President Hughes as always was managing to look and sound old-shoe on the television screens. The press conference was his first since he unveiled the Court plan, and he had come to the cameras after a postinauguration week during which a storm of protest over the plan had dominated the newspapers and caused the radio and TV commentators to raise their voices a strident note higher. All over the country, Francis reflected, obsolete politicians had crawled out of the woodwork to pronounce the nation's doom if Congress knuckled under to John Alden Hughes. Protest meetings were springing up across the land, and cries of dictatorship rang out in grange halls and in the opposition cloakrooms of the state legislatures. Yet, sitting in his Georgetown living room with Beatrice and Jimmy Hughes, Francis was impressed with the President's bland self-assurance.

It was evident from the very outset, when the first question of the conference—put with considerable politeness by Jack Smalley of UPI—inquired whether the President was not concerned with the hostile reaction to his Court plan.

Hughes donned the smile that had been charming reporters in both the Senate and the White House for more than ten years.

"Concerned?" he asked. "Why, I hadn't given it much thought. I suppose you mean that bleating the newspapers are making so much of. I'm sorry, Jack"—ah, Francis reflected, the importance of that first-name familiarity—"I don't really have time to notice it. They're the same voices I heard during both of my campaigns for the Presidency."

"You *can* tell the players without a program," Jimmy Hughes put in. "Even with your eyes closed."

"Yes, sir," Smalley said, still trying, "but the volume seems to be a lot louder, sir."

Again Hughes laughed, his strong white teeth gleaming in the television lights (and, thought Francis, causing orgasms all over the country). "Oh, perhaps they are louder, but that was to be expected," the President said. "It's a last gathering of the do-nothings. Why, gentlemen, your own newspapers show that by the prominence they give to every stray obscure member of my own party who suggests he may have misgivings."

Nor did Hughes seem troubled when it was pointed out to him by the man from the *Times* that several bar associations had condemned the bill and that an occasional bishop of the Roman Catholic Church had come out against it.

"I never worry about the bar associations, having once belonged to one," Hughes remarked lightly, and the tastelessly barren walls of the State Department auditorium rang with the anticipated laughter. Then, more solemnly, "As for my good friends in the Catholic Church, I think we understand each other. They know that the White House during the past four years has fought a good fight to end discrimination in the allotment of aid to education."

"And watch out," said Francis, "lest the White House take that carrot away."

When it was over, and they had adjourned to the dining room for Beatrice's ragout, Beatrice's voice was high with wonderment. "Is he really unconcerned about all those attacks in the newspapers?" she said. "I should think it would be as bad for his Court plan as a lot of bad reviews would be for a play."

"Those editorials can't scare Brother John," Jimmy Hughes

said. "You know how he is—he's licked the press in two elections now, and he's convinced newspapers don't have any influence any more. He says he knew the press would be against him—that he'd have been uneasy if it wasn't."

"Or, as he so often puts it," Francis said, " 'who was the last editorial writer elected President?' "

"Well, it would frighten me," Beatrice said. "My life has been dominated by critics."

"I confess I'm a little concerned," Francis said. "It seems to me this is a little different. Always before, the President's opponents have been on the defensive; now they're taking the offensive. They're no longer trying to explain that they aren't, either, do-nothings; they're going after the President for something he's done and putting him in the position of having to justify it."

"I put that to Charlie Mayborn during one of my infrequent audiences with that glorified pavement-pounder, and he dismissed it," Jimmy said. "He looked at me with a kindly avuncular eye and said shortly, 'Not much different about it, Jimmy. They're squealing just like they always squeal when the Boss wants to do something.' Life is not complicated for the Attorney General; he just wants what Brother John wants."

Jimmy looked at his watch. "I do have to eat and run, you nice people." He stood up. "Bea, that was an enormously good stew; I feel almost too full to cope with Mr. Ian Kerr's grandiose ideas for spending my money on his Village theater. He awaits me now at the Statler with a flock of sharp-eyed Manhattan lawyers. Shall I see you later, at the Pratts'—both of you?"

"Sorry you have to hurry, Jimmy," Francis said. "You'll see Bea, at least; I've got to go over to the White House for a meeting, but I hope to make it later. Much later, I'm afraid."

"Of course—the board of strategy is meeting," Jimmy said. They were walking with him to the door now. "Reports from the tribal chieftains. Francis, you're damned nice to help John on this; I hope it's something you feel it's all right for you to do. John thinks a lot of your advice, but sometimes I wonder if he always considers the proprieties."

Francis smiled. "Oh, he's considerate. It's only natural of him to ask an old friend to sit in on these things. And, of course, it's up to me to worry about the proprieties." Why did that last sound a little sharp, a little defensive?

Jimmy looked at Francis. "Sure, old boy. But you are good to help, and you're my friend, too." He turned to Bea. "You've fed me well, Bea. I'll buy you a steak at Duke Zeibert's any time you say."

When the door had closed, Francis and Beatrice walked back and sat on the sofa in the living room for their coffee, and as Beatrice was pouring from the big silver urn, Francis kissed her cheek.

"Yum-yum," he said. "You smell good, Miss Krasnov. Isn't this comfortable? I feel like an old married man."

"Thank you, darling. That's the way I intend to fix it so that you'll feel—forever." She handed him his cup. "Francis." Her look was full of a kind of earnest, concerned affection. "Oh— I don't really know how to put this—but, are you all right, dear? About this Court plan, and helping the President, I mean."

"Bea, dear." Francis' laugh was merry with surprise. "All right? I'm not quite sure what you mean."

"Oh, Francis, perhaps I don't know what I mean, either. But it's such a momentous thing and I know how you feel—all that really wonderful rectitude of yours, darling—and I just wonder if you're a little worried about things. And"—quickly—"if I could help."

Francis put down his cup. His voice was low. "Yes, Bea, I guess I know what you mean. And the answer is no, I'm not worried—not particularly. I think about it a great deal and there are some questions that perhaps have not been completely resolved in my mind. But basically, I'm all right—as you put it." He smiled. "But I do want you to help, anyway—any time."

"My lion." Beatrice seemed flustered. "You are so sweet to *say* you know what I mean when I sound so silly. But, Francis, I want to be sure you are doing what you want to do and that you're sure it's what you want to do. You're so loyal, darling, and I know the President wants your help—that's a tribute, isn't it? But—I just want you to be completely happy about it."

Sipping his coffee again, Francis thought: When is anybody completely happy about doing anything? And he was confounded by the swift answer: When you are a Supreme Court justice. Period. And not mucking about in politics on the side.

"Bea, there are always problems concerned with anything one does," he said. "I have to solve those problems. As always, they're concerned with legal philosophies, and how I feel about the role of a judicial officer. That's about it, really. But I'll try not to be undignified. And, of course, I do owe the President a great deal."

"My lion, I have no doubts about you. I thought your statement supporting the plan was excellent. So succinct. And you did it just right, of course, having Jake Moriarty merely hand it to the press instead of getting up in front of a lot of television cameras."

"It was hard, for an old political ham like me. As a matter of fact, Bea, this may shape up as quite a hard fight. I've talked with a lot of people during the past several days, and I don't think it will be as easy as John Hughes expects. He's not getting every vote he counted on, not yet."

"It must be fun, in a way, getting back to old, familiar ground and counting political noses, Francis."

Counting political noses; well, he had been doing that, to some extent. But not with his robes on. Francis' voice was casual, now. "Oh, of course, I've only been working on the fringes, Bea. I contact only those people on the Hill I know well. People, for instance, like Bailey of Massachusetts and Sanders of New Hampshire. And then, of course, there are certain friends of mine in industry and in the professions who are interested in politics."

"Yes, like Tom Nelson, I suppose," Beatrice said. "He fascinates me. He's a genuine member of the Establishment, isn't he?"

"The Establishment?" Francis laughed. "Dick Rovere really started something way back there, didn't he? Well, I suppose there is an Establishment of a sort. There always has been, for that matter. It's a rather picturesque name for the group that has always existed—people with money, people with power and influence who are not politicians but who, shall we say, take an interest in where certain politicians are going."

Beatrice laughed a trilling little laugh. "Francis, you are so proper. You mean people who put up the money and get together and decide who's going to run for what. Like your Tom Nelson."

Francis laughed back. "*Touché*, Bea. You punctured my stuffed shirt. Yes, of course, they're the money men of national politics. Politicians couldn't afford to be politicians without them, and the money men know it, and so the money men have a great deal to do not only with who's going to run for what but with how the country is going to be run after the election. Tom Nelson probably is the most influential of the lot, and I happened to meet him while I was still in college, lucky thing for me." He took a sip of his coffee, as his thoughts went back to those early years. "You know, it's a curious thing. I worked in Tom Nelson's law office after I got out of Harvard Law, and I had the impression that he was not exactly interested in my getting into politics. But I later realized, years later, that actually his supposedly hands-off attitude had influenced me to become a politician. It's flattering, in a way; for forty years Tom Nelson has been choosing candidates in just this way, all over the country. He sits in his office in Boston, and very few people in the country have ever heard of him, but the politicians know him and respect him and, of course, are careful not to cross him. I suppose, in a sense, he made me; it doesn't bother me particularly. Tom Nelson may have more integrity than any man I ever knew. Since somebody has to be the money man, I'm glad he stepped forward."

Beatrice said, "He does sound—fascinating. But just a little sinister, darling? I mean, this kind of secret power-behind-the-throne kind of thing."

Francis laughed. "Bea, my sweet, dear thing, you're mistaking real life with a play script. Men like Tom Nelson are facts of political life. Sure, some of them have political axes to grind—most of them do, actually. Some of them, perhaps, are sinister characters. But they have a stake in the country, too, and they have a right to be interested in where the country is going. I don't think it's always wise to have one little group dominating the financial affairs of a political party, because that leads to corruption on the legislative level, but the fact is that these days it's almost impossible for anyone, for any group, to get away with anything significantly evil. There are too many newspapers, too many magazines, too many radio and TV stations and—probably most important of all—too many Congressional investigating committees and inquisitive members of Congress. Politicians do their little favors for the Tom Nelsons of the country, and, probably, their votes are based to a large extent on the economic philosophies of the Tom Nelsons, but they won't go for anything raw. They won't, first, because most politicians—at least, in the Congress—are not made that way, but also because they know the American people won't let them get away with it."

"Yes, that's good. It's nice to have you put it that way, Francis. It's nice that we can have a certain—oh, trust—in the people we elect. I'm so silly, really. Sometimes I think I'm an awful prude, politically."

"But not with me, I hope, my sweet. Will you love me when I'm a crusty *old* Supreme Court justice?"

"More, darling. I'll even polish your silver-headed canes—after we make love. Francis, how is it, working on the Court plan?"

"Oh, not too bad, Bea. As a Supreme Court justice, of course, I can't go lurking about the Capitol cloakrooms, and that's a relief. I have the utmost respect for the legislative process, but I've never really enjoyed being involved in it. At its best, legislating is an untidy business, full of idiotic postures, and I've always felt it was something that should be gotten over with as soon as possible. I suppose I got very little enjoyment out of my tenure in the Massachusetts General Court—how's that for an ill-fitting name for a legislature?—and as Governor I suppose my major satisfaction in dealing with the General Court came only when I counted the votes and found I had enough for something I wanted."

"Francis, I'm glad you're not so damned—neat—with me."

"Dirty girl," Francis said. They both moved toward each other at the same time and their kiss was long.

They were all there when Francis was ushered into the President's second-floor oval study by the handsome blond Secret Service agent whom he knew only as Pete, but who came from East Boston and whose smile seemed perpetual. Chet McAdam and Speaker Henry Smith were seated on the sofa facing the President's big desk, with a coffee table between them and the desk; Harry Weiss and Charlie Mayborn, as usual, were seated in cane-bottomed chairs at either side of the desk, flanking the President in his big high-backed swivel chair.

"Come in, come in, Francis," the President's voice boomed. "Nobody's said anything important yet." Hughes looked vital and important as always, his voice filled with a serene self-confidence. He was wearing an old black turtleneck sweater that usually was his uniform on deep-sea fishing trips, and his black hair was mussed, as usual.

"Mr. Justice, it's good to see you." Chet McAdam was on his feet, tall, thick and heavy of body, with a heavy face that seemed to be dragged down by its own weight.

"Good evening, Chet." Francis was always pleased that the Senate Majority Leader should seem as glad to see him as he was to see McAdam. Their friendship was not a long one, dating back only to Hughes's first Presidential campaign, but it had developed into a warm and easy intimacy through the happy discovery that they worked together well. And it was Chet McAdam who had strongly backed Francis for the chore at The Hague of wringing its United Nations dues out of the Soviet Union. When the crackpot Senator Davis had opposed Francis' nomination for the Court, McAdam had remarked caustically, "Old men who are not too smart always envy young men who are. Attorney General Dalton's nomination will be approved unanimously by the Judiciary Committee." It was, of course.

And here was Henry Adam Smith, the tiny, small-bored Kentuckian with the black horn-rimmed glasses and the deceptively absent-minded stare. "Evenin', Mr. Justice," the Speaker said, his voice casual and neighborly cordial. "Hello, Francis," Harry Weiss said, and "Welcome to the club meeting," said Charlie Mayborn, who always thought in terms of small, exclusive political clubs.

Francis gave his overcoat and hat to the footman who appeared from nowhere, and sat down in a wing chair next to Mayborn. He liked this room, with its disorder of ships' models, family portraits, scimitars from Oriental potentates and golf bags heaped against the walls. Interior decorators held their pretty heads over it, but it was an easygoing room.

"You seemed quite comfortable at your news conference, Mr. President," Francis said. Sometimes he addressed Hughes as

"John" in private, but even then he reserved the familiarity for familiar occasions; he disliked to impose his friendship on the *office* of the President.

Hughes smiled. "I guess I managed not to fall on my face. The boys are never very hard on me, of course."

"They're hard enough," Mayborn said in his grunt. "You fielded that Catholic Church thing fine."

Chet McAdam looked uncomfortable. "Yes, sir, you did," he said. "But I don't like everybody getting into the act."

Hughes's smile was wider. "I know, Chet. You like things tidy—because you're the man who has to deliver. But people like to sound off, you know. And the newspapers encourage them."

"The hell with the newspapers," Speaker Smith said in his curiously bass voice. "Any time they endorse a project, it's the kiss of death."

"Speaking of projects—although not necessarily the kiss of death—what about it, Henry?" The President gestured toward Smith with his hand, as though introducing a lecturer.

Smith was ready, as always, with his facts. "Well, first, the major problem," he said. "As we might have expected, that's Paul Anderson. It doesn't look so good in the House with Anderson stubborning up. Anderson's come up with a majority of three against the bill in Judiciary. That's pretty upsetting when you realize how we've always been able to get what we wanted there. We can influence the committee hearings on the bill, of course, but we can't control them. Anderson is in complete charge."

"It's a little better," the President said. "You were afraid the majority might be five. But that's damned little comfort. Well, perhaps we'll have to strong-arm the House. I don't think we'd have any trouble rounding up the necessary votes on a petition to discharge the committee. I even think we could get the two-thirds vote to suspend the rules."

"Yes, sir, we could," Smith said. "We've got those kind of votes. But I'm against it, and so is Bill Ball." (The easygoing House Majority Leader *would* be against it, Francis reflected. Too much work and too many harsh voices.) Smith said, "We could steamroller the bill through the House all right, but it would make a lot of people sore and we'd probably have trouble when the bill came back from the Senate."

"Charlie?" The President looked over at Mayborn.

"I don't know," Mayborn said. "I'm tempted to go along and try to push the bill through the House first. The House is always easier to handle than the Senate, because the boys have to run for re-election every two years and they want the people to recognize them as being on your side. Besides, if we make the House deliver, it'll be a good psychological twist of the arm to the Senate."

McAdam stirred on the sofa and the President said, "All right, Chet."

"I'm probably looking for trouble early, Mr. President," McAdam said, his voice sawing away. "But I have to string along with Henry. I say let the Senate take up the bill first, although God knows I could use Charlie's psychological advantage of having the House put it over. But overall we can't borrow more trouble than we've already got. Henry here and Bill Ball are against any dragooning operation, and they know what they're talking about. They live with those boys in the House twenty-four hours a day."

"We sure do," Smith put in. "After twelve years as Speaker, I know a little something about the moods of the House, and right now I don't like it. Besides, except in dire emergency I try to lead rather than drive my boys. I don't think it is a dire emergency, and when we have the choice between the hard way and the easy way, I think we ought to take the easy way."

The President put a hand up to brush a lock of hair back from his forehead. "Damn!" he said. "Anderson worked fast. I suppose I could see it coming at that breakfast. Chet, you can manage it, I suppose."

McAdam's shrug was that of the politician who was resigned to the facts. "If that's the way we have to do, that's the way it'll have to be done."

"All right." The President clapped his hands together softly. "Then the Senate will take up the bill first. We tried to manage it otherwise"—he nodded at Speaker Smith—"and you did an all-out job, Henry, but I guess we just couldn't manage it. We can't waste any more time. Chet, how does it look in the Senate?"

"Not as comfortable as I'd hoped it would look." McAdam cleared his throat. "We're having some trouble with the liberals in the party and even with some of the moderates we've always counted on in the past." He turned to Francis. "It was damned hard, losing regulars like Bailey and Sanders," then, quickly, "No fault of yours, of course—from what you said, they were lost from the start."

"Yes, confound it," the President said.

Francis said, "I'll admit they surprised me. But there wasn't much I could do." Now there was a bad taste in his mouth as he recalled the genteel pressure he had tried to apply to the two recalcitrant New Englanders, who were presumed to belong to the Hughes-Dalton team. It had seemed that Senator Ralph Bailey of Massachusetts would be a sure vote for the Court plan. He was a genuine and energetic conservative, who had been swept into office in the conservative tide created by John Alden Hughes. Hughes had done much for the state's textile industry, and Bailey would need more help in the future. Francis had gone to him in quiet confidence; he and Bailey were good friends, and over the years they had exchanged important favors. But Bailey had been an unhappy surprise.

Francis said, "Bailey told me, 'Now, Francis, I know you're here because Hughes has some question about how I stand on the Court bill. Well, I'll clear that up right now. I consider the bill obnoxious and dictatorial and an outrageous insult to the Supreme Court.' I talked to him for more than an hour, but I couldn't budge him. Of course, Massachusetts is turning liberal again."

"Yes," the President said. "They need you up there to maintain discipline, Francis. And then there's Sanders, of course; it's hard to depend on those professional hayseeds."

"Unfortunately, they don't consider themselves hayseeds, but rugged individualists," Francis said. "It's a posture that seems to work well in New Hampshire, perhaps because the state clings to its artificial agricultural personality. And, of course, Sanders has a lot of power, thanks more to seniority than to intelligence." Yet, Francis thought, even Sanders should have had the intelligence to consider the importance of John Alden Hughes's influence. Hughes had seen to it that he got help from the Congressional Campaign Committee when he was in trouble the year before, for instance. Yet when Francis went to him, he had been met by sly platitudes.

"It took some time to pin Sanders down," Francis said. "But I finally forced him to—confirm my fears. 'I just don't reckon I can vote for that there bill,' he told me, 'I just don't reckon I can, Frank.'" Among other things, Francis did not like to be called Frank.

"Well, perhaps we can do some arm twisting, although I doubt it," the President said. "Bailey at least has a brain, but he's terribly stubborn when he thinks one of his principles is in danger of being trampled." Hughes seemed momentarily wistful. "I can't blame the man for that." Then, "But Sanders is a damned fool as well as an ingrate. We'll have to deal with them." He turned to Harry Weiss and lifted an eyebrow, and Harry Weiss nodded. Weiss was in charge of patronage.

Once again, Francis felt that little prickle of irritation, mixed with embarrassment. Bailey *was* a man of principle, though he might be in error on this issue. Was any issue so important that a man should be punished for standing by principle? In power politics, the answer was yes—you had to *get things done.*

"I do respect Bailey," Francis said. "He's an honest man. I hate to think of him—being 'dealt with.'"

The President's look was hard. "So do I, Francis," he said briefly. Then his voice matched his look. "But it has to be done."

"I suppose so," Francis said. Damn the art of the possible! he was thinking.

"Yes—and, Francis, I wonder if you'd have a little chat with Bailey and talk around what happens to sheep that stray." The President's voice was casual now, and the smile was back.

Francis smiled back. That was the best way to handle it. "Well, Mr. President, I'd rather not. I say that quite respectfully. I'll be glad to talk to Bailey and try to swing him around to your viewpoint"—why not *our* viewpoint? he wondered in swift passing—"but I don't think I want to threaten him, however gently."

"No?" The President was still smiling, but the monosyllable was curt. "Why not, Francis?"

Francis could feel McAdam's friendly gaze on him, and the impatient stares of Mayborn and Weiss. Smith, he knew, would be looking at the floor, as he always did when an incident was of no concern to him.

Francis would keep on his smile. "Mr. President, I can't say that I don't approve of those methods. I know they're used because they have to be used in practical politics. But I have tried to steer clear of that kind of politics since I went to the bench. I have to put it this way: that while the methods may be all right, they are not suitable—ah—weapons for a member of the Supreme Court."

"Yes, I see." The President looked over at Speaker Smith. His movement was not even one of impatience, yet Francis could see and feel his careful, almost snublike, disapproval. Yet Hughes must recognize his, Francis', position.

"Henry, exactly what is the situation in the House as far as roll-call votes go?" The President suddenly was unperturbed, determinedly so.

"It's good—once we get past that Judiciary Committee," Smith said comfortably. "Bill Ball and I have a poll, and it comes out a majority of a hundred and nine for the bill. We could improve on that with a little more pressure if we had to; I think we could manage two-thirds of the membership if it came to a really tough showdown."

"Good." Hughes suddenly seemed to remember something. "Chet, dammit, you were giving us your countdown in the Senate when we took a detour to discuss Bailey and Sanders. I think I know what it is, but how about it?"

As McAdam started to speak, the President looked at Francis and smiled. Francis smiled back. That was the way things went in this business, Francis reflected; bitterness over differences of opinion was always brief unless the issue was a vital one.

"As I said, my figures aren't as comforting as Henry's," McAdam said. (Besides, McAdam is more cautious, Francis told himself.) "We're going to have to work on the liberals and moderates pretty vigorously. Still, we've got the leadership and we've got the hard core, and unless Tom Morgan and I have lost our grip, we should be able to talk a lot of the doubtful ones into camp. Tom is soft-soaping his way through the list and doing a good job; I don't suppose we've ever had a Vice-President who worked as hard as Tom."

"Yes, bless him," the President said. "He's not here tonight, as you know, because he's out soft-soaping a powwow of some labor types. How many have we got solid in the Senate, Chet?"

"I'd say forty-three. Thirty are more or less solidly against it. That means the balance of power will be wielded by the people in the center. Most of them belong to the right party, of course, and we should be able to do business with some of them on the basis of party loyalty, party regularity."

Mayborn broke in. "I should hope so, after what the President did for them last November."

McAdam smiled. "We'll remind 'em, Charlie. Don't worry."

It was as if all the rest were waiting for the President to draw Francis back into the conference, and, casually, the President did so. Casually, but with the special manner Francis had come to recognize as special—a softening of his speech into a kind of easy respect which Francis knew Hughes felt and knew Hughes wanted to show for a justice of the Supreme Court. After the incident over the case of Bailey and Sanders, the decently deferential tone was back in Hughes's voice as he turned to Francis.

"Francis, have you had a chance to talk to Tom Nelson?"

Francis warmed to the manner of the asking; John Alden Hughes knew that Francis would have made it a point to talk to Tom Nelson as soon as possible on the matters the President had mentioned; it was typically decent of him to assume the role of a man who had asked a favor of, if not his peer, at least of a dignitary whose favors were not lightly asked.

"Yes, I have," Francis said. Now he felt comfortable again; now he could talk the business these men were talking without feeling ill at ease. "Nelson saw to it that Hays got some financial help in that Connecticut primary fight. Nelson says he'll have a good chat with Hays. As you know, Nelson has known Hays for a long time, long before Hays went to the Senate, and they've always been—friendly. I got the impression Nelson felt Hays was uneasy, but thought he would go along."

"Good. How about that broker friend of yours in Chicago —Estabrook, is it?" Again the President's tone was deferential. Among other things, Francis reflected, he was putting Charlie Mayborn and Harry Weiss in their places.

"Yes, Bob Estabrook. Well, again it's a case of the side the man's bread is buttered on. Estabrook is new, but he pretty well runs the finances of the machine, and he's already mentioned the Court plan, in passing, to Senator Childs. He says it's instinctive for Childs to be opposed to the bill, but he doesn't expect any trouble; Estabrook had a mutual friend suggest to Childs that he couldn't expect to be renominated if he voted against the bill."

Hughes's smile was warm. "I've got to know that Estabrook, Francis. I'd like to know him as you do, of course—as a man slightly above the battle—but he sounds as if he's got the makings of a real politician. All right, what else, gentlemen?"

"Well, I think you've taken care of Paul Smart with that flood control project for West Virginia," Chet McAdam said. "That should give us a solid majority in the Senate Judiciary."

Hughes grinned. "Yes, I used a little polite strong-arming there —if Mr. Justice Dalton will excuse the phrase." His tone again was amiably deferential. "I had a little talk with Governor Nash. The Governor said he was delighted with the flood control money—and that he would see to it that Smart would be equally delighted."

"I should think so." Mayborn's voice had the dry quality of the professional. "Smart hates Nash's guts, but he can't afford to have Nash hogging the credit for that flood money. It's patronage that makes the strange bedfellows."

"Yes, you can't practice the art of the possible without it," the President said. "Now we have got to practice that art on some of the out-and-out liberals and the independents. We may be able to count on the independents, anyway, but it is maddening the way they make such a production of thinking things over. I'd like them in our camp immediately, for psychological purposes."

"Mr. President." Francis was surprised to hear himself cut in so sharply.

"Francis?" Hughes seemed merely interested.

"Mr. President, it does seem to me we've got to do more than wait and hope for the independents to throw in with your plan." Francis had been thinking this over for several days now, and he wanted to get it out, put it before these professionals. "Of course I know you mean to have their votes. It's important. But the only one with national influence—and influence within the Senate —is Claude Wilkins. I think you've got to have him because I think he can bring in the others, plus some moderates and liberals to boot."

"He's already come out against it, of course," Harry Weiss said blandly.

"Yes, he has," Francis said. His mind saw again the news photo of the great thinker—"America's Honest Man," they called him—standing on the Capitol steps and telling the reporters that he saw "basic dangers" in the President's plan. "That is, he's indicated he'll be against it. But he hasn't denounced it out of hand."

Hughes put a cigarette in his mouth and then took it out and examined it. "That's true. He reserved the final word, as usual. But I'm not sure I share your hopes, Francis."

"Well, I think it's worth looking into," Francis said. Claude Wilkins was worth any effort, he was thinking. "I don't know why, but I believe that if he were approached properly he wouldn't oppose the bill. It would be difficult, of course, because Claude is such an individualist and so burning in his zeal that he hates to work with others. But I believe that if you, Mr. President, went over the arguments in favor of the bill, especially the fact that you believe no other approach would work—if you did that, I think Claude might at least think it over. Claude wants a Court bill as much as you do, Mr. President; it's quite possible he'll take your bill rather than nothing—if he's approached correctly."

Mayborn broke in. "I'm hanged if I see why we need Wilkins so badly; he's an awful pain in the neck to work with."

"Well, we do need him—I agree with Francis," the President said. "I hope I'd have thought of it myself eventually. The situation is a ticklish one for the opposition. We want Wilkins so they can't have him. The liberals have put up a united front against the bill, and they've picked up some defectors from our side. But there you are—it's strictly a liberal front, a partisan front, and the liberals were thoroughly discredited in November. A party that has just taken a walloping at the polls cannot carry on an effective fight, not only because its forces are so slender but also because their voices are the same voices the voters have habitually ignored. They can't even put up a respectable fight, let alone squeeze out a majority, unless they get some considerable help from the conservatives and the moderates. They can't win if theirs is merely a liberal cause; they've got to give it political catholicism. Francis has put his finger on it; that's why we need Wilkins."

"I don't like it," Mayborn said. "It doesn't sound like Wilkins—I can't see him going along with anybody, especially when he's already expressed doubts on the bill. Wilkins has never operated that way; he's a lone wolf. He makes up his mind and that's it. I don't see him being persuaded."

"I know what you mean," the President said. (Let Hughes take it from here, Francis was thinking.) "Claude is a man who follows a political platform—that is, his own political pattern. But I think it might be worth while to have a pretty frank talk with him. I think I may be able to persuade him that the bill deserves a little more thought before he starts flailing away at it. It seems to me I can put it to him that way. You know how Wilkins is; he's jealous of his reputation as a thinker. It's a piece of ham that's pardonable in a man like that." He turned to Francis. "Mr. Justice, sir, I commend your perspicacity. I was wondering what to do about Wilkins. Now I may be able to think of something. I just may."

I may be able to think of something. Suddenly the old unease intruded on Francis. Think of what? "Of course, he's got his own bill," Francis said.

"Sure." Hughes smiled. "But perhaps there are things he can do in good conscience. I should think he could continue to demand that some legislation be passed to make the Court more responsive to public needs. Even if he continues to push his own bill—that impossible amendment requiring a seven-to-two vote of the Court to invalidate an act of Congress—it won't do us as much harm as if he joined forces with the liberals. After all, it doesn't matter much what Wilkins does so long as he doesn't join the opposition and give it respectability."

Harry Weiss said, "We might be able to swing it. Wilkins sure as hell would hate to do those liberals any favors. That's on our side." Harry Weiss saw no point in any vigorous argument among the board of strategists; they had too many other problems on their hands. Besides, the President was the boss. Harry Weiss always kept that in mind.

"We'll swing it if we can," the President said. "Now, Charlie, tell me—are you worried about the bill?"

Mayborn's jaw shot out. "Certainly not, Mr. President. We're going to have to work at it, but I'm sure we can do it. I'm not worried at all. Some things bother me sometimes, and I say so. But I'm not worried—overall. After all the yacking is done with, I think we'll have the votes."

"Fine. Splendid." For a moment Hughes reminded Francis of his baseball coach at Holy Cross, who had been full of florid phrases like "old school fight" and "splendid." In locker room sessions like this, a President had to be something of a baseball coach.

"Just one more thing, Mr. President." Mayborn's tone had a faintly desperate air, the air of a man determined to broach a sensitive subject again despite the danger. "You know how I feel about going out and mounting the attack. I still feel you should go on television again as soon as possible and keep going on television and keep the issue in front of the country."

Mayborn's desperation was natural, Francis thought, as he watched Hughes's face change again into an impersonal grimness. The President had been sold on the idea of keeping silent, after his inauguration speech, by his mother. It was the premise of Julia Hughes that the opposition would talk itself out and that when this had happened the President could step in, at the deliciously psychological moment, and put his enemies to rout with a couple of stirring speeches designed to clear up the confusion left by the opposition's oratory. The President felt as strongly about this as if it had been his own plan, and he had rebuffed both Mayborn and Weiss when they had attempted to get him to change his mind. Moreover, the President was aware of the feeling among some in his administration that his mother exerted too much influence on him.

The President's voice was low when he answered Mayborn. "Charlie, we've gone all over that before and you know how I feel about it. Quite aside from the fact that I feel it wouldn't be suitable—from the viewpoint of the dignity of my office—I don't think this is the time for television speeches. I have offered my bill and I have offered sound arguments for its passage. I'll continue to discuss it at press conferences. But it is a matter for the Congress, at least in these early stages. I don't plan to speak in behalf of the bill in the near future."

Mayborn started to speak, obviously to acquiesce, but stopped as Hughes's face broke into a wide grin. "Oh hell, Charlie, let's not fight about it," the President said. "I know how you feel, and I respect you for it. You know I want you to speak out for what you believe should be done. But we're going to have these little problems, and we'll have to argue them out, and then I'll have to make the decisions. But I don't think they're important enough to lose sleep over. By God, gentlemen, the fight has just started. The Court problem is there and the country wants it solved. The party is riding the greatest crest of popularity in its history. We've got practically everything on our side."

He paused and turned his back on his guests and walked over to the window behind his desk and looked out on the floodlit Washington Monument, a shaft glaring in its whiteness even against the snow-covered ground. His back was still to his guests when he spoke.

"But the party doesn't really matter, gentlemen. The important thing is that I have the people on my side."

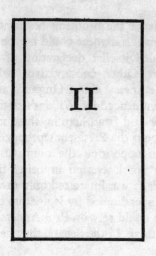

II

SENATOR FRANK HOAR OF OHIO knew of the doubts that gnawed on that great independent and thinker, Claude Wilkins—and he knew also that there might be something he could do about exploiting them. Hoar believed he could negotiate with Wilkins—not in the sense of making a deal, because Wilkins did not deal—but on the basis of an association of right-minded legislators interested in the country's welfare—and other things. He knew that the President had temporarily muzzled Wilkins, and he did not hold it against the Senator from Utah. In Wilkins's case, Hoar knew, it was not a question of being expedient—as it seemed—but of a second, honest thought which persuaded him to give the Court plan the benefit of a further, more judicious appraisal. Hoar respected Wilkins's desire to alter the function of the Court legislation, even though Hoar did not agree with any such proposal, and he knew that Wilkins could not cast away the chance of winning the President over to his particular amendment. Yet, Wilkins could be had; meanwhile, there were other fish to be caught if the angling was done right.

As Hoar sprawled at his ease on the black leather sofa of Suite 423 of the New Senate Office Building, he contemplated with considerable confidence the problems besetting his loyal opposition. Wilkins's original statement could not be recalled, although Wilkins had amended its flat declaration of opposition to the Court-packing plan. Other conservatives, who Hoar believed were inclined to be uneasy about Hughes's autocratic methods, had been strongly influenced by Wilkins's restive posture. Whatever Wilkins did or said from here in, these men were going to remain ill at ease about the President's proposal. These men were needed to give the opposition the nonpartisan flavor vital to success. Hoar was not interested in being the public hero in this particular fight; he was interested only in winning it, and the winning had to be spearheaded by legislators of another political stripe. He knew he could rely on Paul Anderson in the House—if the bill ever got there. In the Senate, they had to have Wilkins, eventually if not now.

And so, when Senator Frank Hoar greeted his guests as they came shambling into his private office, he had honed down his plan to an edge of pragmatic, political fineness. He could depend on them all, he was thinking, as he greeted them by name—young Martin of Oklahoma, who hated Hughes almost as fiercely as Hoar did; Dan Lewis of Oregon, angular and irascible, another good hater; and Minority Leader Cliff Sampson of Nebraska, able and coldly efficient despite his moody bouts with the bottle. They got down to the business immediately; each of them was burning with his own particular brand of impatience.

"Gentlemen, I suggested this meeting because I believe the time has come to organize our strategy and to expand our organization," Hoar said. "I thank you, Cliff, for coming over here and sparing my arthritis." Sampson nodded absent-mindedly; Cliff was content to run the machinery of the opposition and let Hoar do the heavy thinking. "Gentlemen, you know the odds we are faced with. We have not only the conservatives to battle, although God knows with their tremendous majority they would be tough enough alone. We've also got to argue with and try to convince the moderates to throw in with us. You know the situation as well as I do. This is a time of deep crises, both at home and abroad. People are worried as hell. And in such times the moderates who usually stay away from the extremists tend to become more willing to go along with them, especially the extremists of the right. I would point out, in passing, that John Alden Hughes once was regarded as a moderate."

Bill Martin's handsome young face registered no emotion, but the sound from his throat was a growl, "Yes, until he acquired a little power."

"To be sure." Hoar wanted to get on with it. "Anyway, you find nowadays that the membership and officers of the right-wing groups include a hell of a lot of respectable community leaders who in the past have always been moderates. They feel that the basic doctrines of the extreme right coincide with theirs, even though they still have reservations about the fringe issues. They throw in with the extreme right because it gives them a feeling of security. Those are the people, here in the Congress, that we've got to reach to help us in our fight."

Dan Lewis stirred in his chair. "I hate to do business with some of those sons of bitches," he said. "They've given us a hard time."

Hoar gave Lewis a sympathetic look. "Sure they have, Dan. Nobody knows it better than I. But we can do business with them, and we've got to do business with them if we're going to lick Hughes. Now, we've talked this over some before, and I think you'll agree with a plan I've evolved. We've got to be sensible enough to let the boys in the other party do the front-line fighting in this thing. If we lie low and keep our mouths shut for a while, while encouraging the defectors on the other side to take up the cudgels for us, we're going to see some savage internecine fighting among our opposition. They'll be clawing at each other like a bunch of wild animals."

"Who've we got that we can be sure of, Frank?" Cliff Sampson asked.

"We've got enough for a start. Anderson, for instance, can handle the House if it comes to that, but we don't have to be concerned about the House yet. Here in the Senate we can count on a good half-dozen, either defectors from Hughes's camp or independents. There's Pugh of Maine and Giles of Florida and Harvey of Missouri and Prescott of New York; and among the independents we can figure on Rockwell of Montana and George of South Dakota. They've all shown they're ready and willing to raise a little hell. Our job is to stand aside for the present and let 'em holler."

"There's not a leader in the bunch, though, Frank," young Martin said. "They'll fight well enough, but they need direction."

"We'll give 'em a leader," Hoar said, his voice a grim snap. "We'll give 'em a leader pretty soon. We'll give 'em Claude Wilkins."

"Wilkins?" Cliff Sampson looked up from studying his pot belly. "I thought you knew Hughes got to him."

Hoar's grin was a savage one. "I know, all right, Cliff. But getting to Wilkins and holding onto him are two different things. Just take my word for it, gentlemen, Wilkins will be out there leading the parade."

The three men looked at him, and Hoar could see in their faces what they were thinking. They were thinking that Frank Hoar had a scheme, that he was plotting something. Well, maybe. But mostly, he just knew Claude Wilkins and he knew what Wilkins would do.

"I hope you're right, Frank," Dan Lewis said. "I'll go along."

"Count me in, Frank," Sampson said.

"Good enough for me," Martin said.

"All right, gentlemen, then let's map a little strategy," Hoar said. "We've got a few little problems with some of our people outside the Congress. We're going to have to do some telephoning."

"Yes, Finlay," Cliff Sampson said, and it was Finlay they tackled first. Hughes had barely announced his Court plan to the nation when former President Herbert Finlay was holding a press conference in his Los Angeles hotel suite and telling reporters in his deep, booming tones that Hughes was trying to wreck the country. He had let it be known also that he was planning a series of radio and television speeches to further denounce Hughes's bill.

"I know one thing," Cliff Sampson said. "Neither you nor I can approach the old cuss, Frank. He hates our guts. And vice versa, I may add."

"Right, we'll have to stay out of it as much as possible, Cliff,"

Hoar said. He looked at Lewis. "I think that leaves it up to you, Dan. The Old Man has nothing against Martin, but you've known him for a long time, Dan, and he's always thought a lot of you."

"I suppose so," Lewis said gloomily. "Damn. I hate to tackle the old grizzly, though. He's been mean as hell ever since Hughes clobbered him four years ago."

"There's the telephone, Dan," Hoar said. "You're the sacrificial lamb."

Lewis lifted his wrestlerlike body out of his armchair and walked over to the desk as Hoar stood up to make room for him. Hoar picked up the phone and told his secretary, "Get me Finlay in Los Angeles." He winked at Lewis as he handed the man from Oregon the phone. "Gently, gently," Hoar whispered in his fellow plotter's voice.

There was silence in the room, then, as Lewis held the phone with the helpless look on his face that comes to most men waiting to complete a transcontinental telephone connection. Then, "Yes, yes—this is Senator Lewis on the line. Yes, ma'am, *I am on the line.*"

His audience heard the click-clicking as the call was transferred, and there was no difficulty in catching Herbert Finlay's voice as he came on the wire, "Lewis—Dan, are you there?" impatiently, irascibly.

"Hello, Mr. President," Lewis said, his voice an unguent. "I'm right here."

Like talking to a goddamn kid, young Bill Martin was thinking.

There was a sequence of growls on the other end of the line. "Yes, we're working on that now, Mr. President," Lewis said. "It's beginning to look a lot better." Lewis paused as Finlay interrupted with another booming remark. "Sure, we know how evil the bill is. We're putting a lot of work in on it."

Another pause for Finlay's comment. Then, "Well, Mr. President, that's what I called you about. We've got a little plan that we think is going to spread confusion in their ranks. We hope we can get your support on it."

"What's the plan?" asked Finlay with a snap. Lewis held the phone a little away from his ear. In measured tones, speaking slowly and precisely, he told the former President what had been decided at the strategy meeting. "It's kind of a conspiracy of silence," Lewis said. "We think it will confound Hughes."

"Who's there with you?" the voice barked. "Who decided on this plan? I don't like people trying to shut me up."

Nervousness sabotaged Lewis's syntax. "Well, there's me." He paused, then hurriedly, "There's Frank Hoar and Cliff Sampson and Bill Martin."

Finlay's reaction had the sound of an explosion. "Hoar and Sampson! By God, I might have known it. They're still trying to shunt me into the background. They've been undercutting me ever since I was President. Well, I won't have it, I tell you. By God, I won't have it. There are still a few people in this country who listen to me, and I'm going to fight that Court-packing plan tooth and nail."

Lewis's voice was soothing, but firm. "Now, Mr. President, I just have to talk turkey to you. Nobody's trying to undercut you. I explained the situation. We've got those defectors and we've got some other conservatives. You must agree that protests from Hughes's own political wing will have far more effect, for the present, than anything we can say or do. You're a practical man, and I know you don't want personal feelings to stand in the way of defeating this Court plan. You never let them influence you when you were in the White House. It's our only chance right now, Mr. President. It's a wonderful idea. We're unanimous about it. It'll drive Hughes crazy."

"Herbert Finlay, old fool," Cliff Sampson said to himself.

For a full minute there was silence on the other end of the wire. Lewis was afraid Finlay had dropped the phone on his desk and walked away from the conversation. He looked over at Hoar and raised an eyebrow. Hoar raised an eyebrow back at him.

"All right." The exploding phrase startled Dan Lewis. "All right, Dan, I'll go along. I want more than anything else in this life of mine to defeat that evil bill, and I suppose your plan has considerable merit—*if* those conservatives catch fire. I'll give it a chance. I've got a radio speech next week, but I'll just mention the Court bill in passing. But I won't wait forever, Dan. By God,

I'm not going to sit back and twiddle my thumbs if your plan doesn't work."

"Fine, Mr. President," Lewis said. "We knew the party could depend on you. It always has."

"Yes, I wish I could depend on the party."

Lewis hurried on, warned by the bitterness in Finlay's tone. "We're going to put this show on the road, Mr. President—but with a cast from the other side of the street. We'll keep you in touch. We'll call you every day or so to fill you in."

"*You* call me, Dan. Not Hoar or Sampson." Finlay hung up.

Lewis cradled the phone and his sigh was a shudder. "Damn. That was a tough one. But he's convinced. We don't have to worry about him—not for a while, anyway."

"The old gamecock," Frank Hoar said. "There's life in the little joker yet. Why the hell would the people desert a fighter like that?"

Bill Martin said, "He was old hat. Hughes made conservatism respectable."

Hoar said, "Yes. I suppose Hughes could have made marijuana smoking respectable with that goddamned grin and that handsome family."

They had two more telephone calls to make, and they had no trouble with either Jim Clayton or the National Chairman, John Ellsworth. Clayton had not fully recovered from his defeat by Hughes in November, and his reaction was that of a numbed patient, unable to argue with the doctor. He'd keep his silence. Ellsworth was a little more balky, but Hoar, who did the talking to him, knew the national chairman was merely making it plain that he would go along only as a favor to the strategists and not because he had been ordered to. It was an order, all right, but Hoar didn't mind letting Ellsworth save face. Ellsworth was a good organizer and a good money-raiser. Let him have his little vanities. And Clayton should have been grateful they had even consulted him.

When the meeting broke up, Cliff Sampson lingered behind. "I hope you're right about Claude Wilkins," he said. "Our plan is O.K. only if those defectors and those independents get a leader."

"They'll get one," Hoar said. "Just trust me, Cliff."

175

． ． ．

They had lunch in the dining room of the Carroll Arms Hotel, and Frank Hoar broke it to Claude Wilkins with the pumpkin pie and coffee.

"Claude, I won't horse around," Hoar said. "You think you're going to nominate those two new justices of the Supreme Court, but you're not."

Wilkins was as startled as Hoar had hoped. His short slight body actually jumped in the chair, and as his hand jammed the coffee cup down onto the saucer, a little geyser shot up from the cup onto his blue polka-dot bow tie. Irrelevantly, Hoar's swift thought was that the impeccable Claude Wilkins with his white crew-cut hair would not be so impeccable this afternoon.

For a moment, Wilkins merely stared across the table at Hoar. When he spoke, his voice was low, but Hoar could feel the tenseness of it.

"Just what are you talking about, Frank?" Wilkins asked.

"You know what I'm talking about, Claude," Hoar said. "You think you're getting those two judges in return for keeping quiet about the Court bill. And I'm telling you that you've been had."

Wilkins's smile was gray, but it was a smile. Good man, thought Hoar. "All right, Frank, tell me your fairy story. I think we can both agree your motives are ulterior."

"Sure, Claude. You know me. I wish to hell Hughes was planning to keep his promise, because if the bill passes, I know your judges would be all right. But he's going to welsh on you, Claude. You can depend on my word, and you can check it with the White House, naturally. The judges will be nominated by Chet McAdam, after screening by Harry Weiss."

"I'm not saying I know what you're talking about, Frank. You know I don't make deals. But where did you get this— fable?"

"From the horse's mouth, Claude, or rather from the mouth of somebody who knows what the horse is doing. I can't tell you who the person is, Claude. You know that. But I'm not a liar. You know that, too." One of the most important things in politics, Frank Hoar was thinking, was to have a Congressman in the opposition party who owed you a favor. And who, in this case, was privately opposed to the President's Court-packing plan.

Wilkins was getting over his shock, but he was thinking hard before speaking. Hoar felt genuine sympathy for this neat man with the face of golden tan and the completely decent instincts. Wilkins was right. He did not make deals. This business of nominating judges, Hoar knew, was Wilkins's insurance that if he stood aside for Hughes's Court-packing, he would still have the right to say what kind of judges the President would appoint. In politics, when a man of principle was faced with the danger of seeing that principle violated, he had to lay plans to obtain the best half-a-loaf in the house.

"All right, Frank." Wilkins's tone was even and low-pitched. "I suppose I should thank you for your interest, even if I don't admit you know what you're talking about. I don't, of course, discuss any conversation I have with the President. I never have."

"Of course, Claude. I pick up these bits of information, and if they can help a friend I pass them on. Anyway, I suppose it's academic. It looks as if Hughes has the votes in his pocket."

"Yes, Yes, Hughes has the votes, all right. He has them now. But I don't know, Frank. They still have to run around the track. And now I guess I'd better be getting back to work."

Claude Wilkins could not think about it until he got back to his office and closed the door against intrusion. It was incredible. No, it was not incredible. It was quite believable. It was the kind of thing that happened. It happened to you rather often when you represented a maverick political party that never was represented in the White House. Even now, despite his anger, he could not hold it against John Alden Hughes. Nobody knew what it was like to be President except the man in the office. He, Claude Wilkins, would not judge a man, would not judge a man's actions or his deceit, when he did not know all the facts of life about that awesome office. A President could not always be rigidly principled; he understood that much. A President had too many politicians to please, to keep in line, to cosset with his patronage. He had to make the political deals that were possible in order to achieve the possible. In the long run, too, Chester W. McAdam of New York was more important to the things Hughes wanted to get done than was Claude Wilkins of Utah. Wilkins felt no bitterness about that. It was a fact of life.

He walked over and stood looking out the window and across the street to the Taft bell tower in the broad sloping park. Just like the man, he thought—monolithic, solid. What had happened to Robert A. Taft's breed of conservatives? He could feel no great rage over the double-cross—but was it a double-cross? Hughes had not made the offer unequivocally. He had said merely that he thought "it could be arranged" for Wilkins to "have something to say" about the new judges. It was the way a President had to put things, and it was considered strong enough. And yet, if necessary, the President could report sadly that it couldn't be arranged after all. He had accepted the offer because he had felt there was no other choice by which he could work his way with the President's bill. If he had refused it, he would have dealt himself and his way of thinking out of the game. He believed Hughes was a man of morality and principle, but he did not trust the kind of judge Hughes would appoint to the bench. They would not be bad judges, because Hughes was not an evil man, but they would be Hughes's judges who would vote Hughes's way, not because Hughes was standing over them, not because they were beholden to Hughes, but because that would be the way they thought. He, Claude Wilkins, had to grasp at this straw, at this chance to keep his hand in if the bill passed.

He picked up the telephone on the desk. "Miss Mahoney, please get me Mr. Weiss at the White House."

Weiss's voice was on the line almost immediately. "Hello, Senator, it's nice to have you call," Weiss said.

"Thank you, Harry. Harry, I want to know something. Has the President arranged to have Senator McAdam do the nominating of the two new judges—if the bill passes?"

There was a long moment of silence on the other end of the line. There seemed to be a quaver in Weiss's voice when he spoke. "Senator—you've got me cold. I don't know what you're talking about."

"All right, Harry. Please find out for me, and please call me back."

Weiss started to say something, but Wilkins cut him off, gently. "That's all, Harry. Please find out for me. Goodbye, sir."

It could not have been more than three minutes before the

telephone buzzed and Wilkins picked it up to hear Miss Mahoney say, "It's the President, sir," and then John Alden Hughes's hearty, virile voice barged in on the line.

"Claude, I want you to do something for me. Will you come and have dinner at the White House tonight?"

Wilkins's smile was a genuine one. Hughes's charm was unmistakable. "Mr. President, thank you, but I think we can do business on the telephone. I just want to know one thing. Who is going to nominate those two judges?"

There was nothing subdued about Hughes's tone. "That's what I want to talk to you about, Claude. I want to talk about it at dinner."

"No, Mr. President. I don't want to seem rude or disrespectful to your office—or to you. I just want an answer to my question."

Now there was a pause, but it was a short one. A President could not be embarrassed easily. "Very well, Claude. I can understand how you feel. I think I told you I had reason to believe we could give you the privilege of nominating the new justices. I was wrong, Claude. I was wrong. It couldn't be managed. Claude, you know how those things are. In this office, a man can't always do what he wants to do—what he thinks is best."

"Yes, I understand, Mr. President. Thank you for telling me. I can only presume you would have told me without my calling—before it was too late."

"I suppose I would have, Claude. I would have tried to tell you. But it would have been hard, Claude. I need you very badly."

"Thank you, sir. I'm sorry I can't oblige. I have always tried to oblige, but this time I cannot."

"You're cashing in your chips, then?" The President's voice sounded wistful now, almost boyish.

"Yes, I'm cashing in my chips."

"I'm sorry, Claude. The bill is going to pass, you know. We'd like you on the winning side."

"It is not going to pass, Mr. President. I shall fight it until I am exhausted."

"I'm sorry again, Claude. Please call me any time. Goodbye."

"Goodbye, Mr. President."

Claude Wilkins hung up the phone, and when Miss Mahoney buzzed he told her he did not want to be disturbed for a while. He had tried and he had failed. He had feared the President's bill and he had taken out the insurance so that he could act if the bill passed and salvage some good out of it. It was not a cheap compromise he had agreed to, but one which might have preserved the Court's integrity. But it didn't work out because when you played power politics, as the President was doing, your favors had to be reserved for the men with the most power. After all these years, Wilkins felt rather a fool not to have recognized that in the beginning. Hughes's charm, he supposed.

He was as much at fault as the President, he admitted. He had *wanted* to make those nominations. It had pleased his ego. He felt he was the best man to do so, and he had been pleased, and warmed, when the President seemed to recognize his superior judgment. No man is safe from his own vanity, he reflected.

Yet though he felt slight anger at the President, his feelings were hurt. He had fought long and valiantly on the side of the conservatives in the massive effort to pull the country out of the morass of misguided liberalism—the exaggerated policies which had followed the New Deal, the Fair Deal and the New Frontier and which had stunned even the staunchest advocates of those earlier programs. As a young lawyer in Salt Lake City, he had been a liberal with a careful eye on the national pocketbook. But his liberalism had been diluted by his disillusionment with men like Herbert Finlay. Their spending had been wild and senseless, and they had constantly sought accommodations abroad which weakened the nation, which left it no place to gather up its forces and make a stand. He had fought for John Alden Hughes's election because Hughes, in effect, had told the enemy abroad and the disruptive influences at home: this far and no farther. Hughes had promised, in effect, reaction—a return to certain basic principles of government—and he had delivered. Wilkins had been with him every step of the way until the last two years, when Hughes's attempts to foist violations of the Constitution on the Supreme Court and the country had brought a prickling, sweating kind of fear. He had not expected gratitude from Hughes, and so he was not hurt when he got none, but he had expected constitutional discretion. He recognized the need for solving the problem of the Court's intransigence on some issues, but he had become suspicious of the President's motives. You did not arrive at good government by taking the path down which John Alden Hughes was striding. Hughes had made of the Presidency too much of a personal thing; he was forever grasping for new powers, new domination over the legislative and judicial branches. Wilkins had refused to be silent while Hughes tried to upset the precarious balance of power.

He picked up the phone and dialed for an outside line, and in a few seconds he heard Frank Hoar's scratchy voice on the wire.

"Senator, I want to thank you for your information," Wilkins said. "It proved out."

Hoar's voice sounded embarrassed. "Oh—well—sure, Claude. Hell, you're welcome."

"I've decided to throw in with you gentlemen," Wilkins said. "I think we have all got to work together."

"Wonderful, Claude. By damn, wonderful. I knew you'd be with us. I knew you wouldn't take that raw stuff."

"Yes, well, I seemed to have been willing to take it, at first. But, Frank, the answer is yes. I'll join up."

"Good, the floor is all yours, Claude."

"That's what I want to make sure of," Wilkins said. "When I think of you and your associates, I see only men with whom I've disagreed on practically everything but the day of the week. I find myself in strange company. I must warn you that I am joining up to lead, Frank. I can only see disaster ahead if you try to spearhead this opposition yourself—yourself or anyone in your party. I repeat, Frank—I am joining up to lead this fight."

The voice of Senator Frank Hoar came over the line like a purr. "Lead on, Claude, lead on."

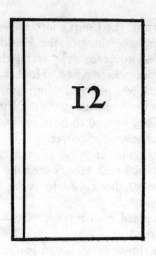

12

USUALLY, FRANCIS WAS GRATEFUL for the tradition that kept Supreme Court justices out of the limelight and rigidly decreed their isolation from the public workings of government. But he had been fretfully impatient with the necessity of having to watch the opening of the Senate Judiciary Committee's hearings on television. He wanted to be in that spacious chamber with its marble pillars so he could observe the reactions of the committee members and sense the atmosphere of the spectators. He had dispatched Jake Moriarty to watch things for him, but it was not quite the same as being there himself. Jake was a good man, but he had never had to worry about such things—things that were vital in the life and death of a politician. And especially a Massachusetts politician. As legislator and as Governor, Francis had used television to the utmost, but he had always insisted on a large number of personal appearances at rallies and clambakes so that he could appraise the voters' varying moods. The television screen lacked the personality to make him feel he was a participant in the important infighting.

Actually, things were going well, as he had had every reason to expect they would. Despite the hullabaloo in the press and from pulpit and black-tie dinner, John Alden Hughes was still in command of the situation. Losing Claude Wilkins was bad, but it didn't have to be fatal if the administration moved forward with the attack. Congress was still scared to death of the President's popularity; after all, November was still recent enough to be a potent reminder of the dangers of opposing the people's nearly unanimous choice. As of now, Hughes had the votes he needed—by a relatively comfortable margin. But his army could not loll in the trenches; it must go over the top.

Mayborn was a vigorous first witness for the administration. He was a politician and he was talking to politicians, a chore the Attorney General always performed with comfortable efficiency. It didn't cow Mayborn that among the faces ranged along the committee dais were those of the Court plan's bitterest enemies —Frank Hoar, Dan Lewis, Bill Martin and now, Claude Wilkins. Mayborn could never be at his best unless he was dealing with the best the opposition could offer. He made his point succinctly —that the situation within the Supreme Court was such that immediate remedial action was necessary. His airy presumption was that everybody demanded a solution to the problem, which was nearly correct. He offered the President's plan to appoint two new justices as one which provided the speediest solution to the problem and yet would not alter the traditional, constitutional, posture of the court.

"We do not suggest—as some others have suggested—that there be any tampering with the majority rule on the Court," he said. "We do not suggest tampering with the Constitution by bulling through an amendment to a document that has stood the test of time. We merely ask that the Congress take the necessary action to bring a new efficiency to the Court, to bring it up to date, to make it more nearly representative of the dynamic aspirations—yes, and fears—of the people."

And he stood his ground well during the questioning, savage beneath the veneer of senatorial courtesy. The senators were well prepared for Mayborn and for the other witnesses who followed him. The American Bar Association had offered its help to Frank Hoar, and Hoar had established a research staff of bright young men from the association's membership. Predictably, these researchers had come up with a filing case full of inconsistencies and contradictions in the political and legal pasts of the administration's witnesses, and Hoar, Lewis and Bill Martin took turns throwing them up to the Presidential troops.

Wilkins's role was clear from the start. He was always the first inquisitor on the opposing side, a privilege bestowed by Hoar and Company which brought a glare of baffled irritability to the face of the committee chairman, the heavy-handed but dependable Alpheus P. Ward. Ward, a graduate of the same rough-and-tumble Illinois political school as Mayborn, properly suspected every maneuver, or seeming maneuver, on the opposing side. His short, thick-bodied frame stirred restlessly every time Wilkins asked a question in his precise, demanding tone, and he was quick to question the relevancy of the remarks Wilkins uttered in an offhand manner after he had finished with the witness. "Let's save our speeches for the Senate floor," Ward growled. Wilkins politely ignored this dictum, and he was ready with a kind of summation of all the evils of the bill each time one of his colleagues wound up his own questioning of the witness. Wilkins made it difficult for Ward to contain his brutal temper and his penchant for the coarse remark, but he had been warned by both the President and Majority Leader McAdam under no circumstances to seem to be belaboring the beloved Wilkins.

Francis' statement in support of the President's plan was read by Mayborn at the outset. For that chore, Mayborn adopted a more sonorous tone than he usually employed, and Francis thought the result was to make the statement seem stuffier than a justice's dignity required. When Mayborn finished, Alpheus Ward cleared his throat self-consciously and said, "Ah, yes, quite impressive. I'm sure we are all pleased to have Mr. Justice Dalton's statement. It is always important to have the opinion of an expert. Ah, are there any questions, gentlemen?" As expected, there had been none; it was obvious the opposition was not going to risk harassing a Supreme Court justice, even *in absentia*.

For the public, the opening of the hearings was a climactic moment in the struggle, but Francis knew they were important for each side only as a forum for argument. The issue would not be decided in the Senate Caucus Room but in Congressional cloakrooms, hotel suites and restaurants. By now, both sides had set up elaborate yet simply operating organizations, and it was within these organizations, with their military-like chains of command, that the important moves, the tactics of the whispered word and the midnight drink, were mapped. To the Presidential chiefs of staff had been added Majority Leader McAdam and, almost absent-mindedly, Vice-President Morgan. Speaker of the House Smith and House Majority Leader Ball were keeping quiet watch on the House, attending the strategy meetings but not fully participating until the time should come when their own cohorts would get their marching orders. Paul Anderson's successful roundup of a majority of anti votes in his House Judiciary Committee was still to be reckoned with, but in the House at large the President had the votes. Once the Senate had been conquered, no one doubted that the more docile House would take whatever action was necessary to blast the bill out of Anderson's committee. Across no-man's-land, Claude Wilkins ostensibly had no formal link with the liberal opposition, but he directed its operations with a firm hand through liaison with his friend Frank Hoar; it was a powerful liaison between the only two men with enough power and prestige to keep the unruly anti-Hughes forces in line. A steering committee had been hammered together and young Martin had been named whip. The state of a senator's thinking at any given moment was passed on to Martin, and he drafted daily reports showing the score and pinpointing areas where the opposition was either gaining or losing ground. And each day the opposition senators went out to consolidate those areas or to try to bully or cajole stubborn would-be recruits into line.

In all this quiet, closed-door bustle, President John Alden Hughes again proved himself the master tactician in what Francis admitted was a rather sordid little department of political infighting. While his commanders went their way, wheeling and dealing, the President sat in the White House and invoked his prerogative of doling out reward and punishment to the Congressional ranks.

Francis had not been on hand at the White House when the showdown came with Chet McAdam over the projected two new justices; he was glad he had escaped that. But McAdam had telephoned Francis after the meeting and then had hustled over to the Court to fill him in.

"Hoar did a beautiful job," McAdam told Francis. "He saw that I was informed that he knew about the President's offer to Wilkins—to let Wilkins name the new justices *if it could be arranged*. Dammit, I don't know where Frank Hoar gets his information." McAdam grinned. "Same places I get mine, I suppose. Anyway, I went down to the White House and put it to the President bluntly. I told him what I'd heard and how about it."

McAdam leaned forward in his chair. "Perhaps you don't know it, Francis, but last year the President promised me the next vacancy on the Court."

Francis hadn't known it; now he was both delighted and concerned to hear it. "Chet, I didn't know it—but I'm glad to hear it. The Court would be a better one with you on the bench."

"Thank you, Francis." McAdam's manner was dry. "I don't know whether that opinion is general. Anyway, I got the pledge because of the job I did in forcing through all those goddamned White House bills last year. Eleven musts, all together. Well, I put it to Hughes, and I must say he was decent about it. He said he was about to call me and discuss it with me—ask me whether some accommodation, as he called it, could be arranged with Wilkins to get him on our side."

McAdam took out his handkerchief and blew his nose hard. "Goddammit, Francis, I came close to blowing up. I reminded him of his promise to me and said I couldn't help feeling betrayed. That's the word I used, Francis—betrayed."

"Chet," Francis said. "My God, I don't know what to say. It sounds pretty awful."

"Yes—that is, it did, Francis. But, by God, Hughes was all right. He said right away he would not renege unless I gave him permission to do so—that he'd made that plain to Wilkins. I don't know whether he did or not. You know how the President talks sometimes."

Yes, Francis thought, I do know how he talks sometimes. I was afraid that night about how he might talk, to Wilkins. Then he caught himself: But I've talked that way myself, when I was a politician. He was silent.

"Anyway, I put it to him straight," McAdam said. "I said

there wasn't the chance of a snowball in hell of any retirements from the Court in the near future and, by God, I was damned sure that Wilkins wouldn't ever put me on the Court once the bill passed. The guy hates my guts; I suppose he's got a right to. I've had to be pretty brutal down there on the Senate floor getting things done for John Alden Hughes, and Wilkins wouldn't give me the time of day. I told the President, 'I did all this for you; it seems to me I've got a right to hold you to your promise.'"

McAdam took out his handkerchief again and wiped his brow. "It turned out all right, Francis. It turned out better than I had hoped, actually. Hughes said, 'All right, Chet, I thought I could work this out, but obviously I can't. You'll get your place on the bench, Chet—one of the new justiceships.' I said fine, but I don't want Wilkins messing in it, and he said very well, I could put in a nomination for the second Court post and my nomination would be put up at the top of the list."

Francis looked at Chet McAdam, and for the first time he felt sorry for him, even as he shared his friend's satisfaction. McAdam had worked for the President, had done his bidding, and he had almost become a victim of the political philosophy upon which he himself had operated so often: do what is necessary to get things done. Francis understood what the President had tried to do—win a new and powerful supporter for his cause, a supporter of unquestioned integrity and judgment, and then try to sell the deal to his creditor, McAdam. It was not unreasonable for Hughes to suppose he could persuade McAdam to go along; in the White House, where you had to get things done somehow, a President might expect a commander in the field to understand. The trouble, Francis reflected, was that when you were President you never had to wait in line for another job, as the Chet McAdams must. The Chet McAdams could not understand because they weren't President. And so the President had had to make another big decision; hurtful though it was, he could afford to lose Wilkins—he could not afford to lose a leader in the Senate who had proved his rugged competence.

"Fine, Chet," Francis said. "I'm glad it turned out all right." But, he thought, it is too bad to lose Claude Wilkins.

McAdam seemed to be reading Francis' mind. "Yes," he said.

"Thank you, Francis. It's too bad, though. We could have used Wilkins, of course. I don't suppose Hughes is going to do him any favors now."

Reluctantly, but with the icy realism of politics, Hughes indeed proceeded to deal with Claude Wilkins. The time had come for final administration approval of the Indian Head Dam project in Utah, a Federal gift to the state for which Wilkins had worked mightily and which some of his more ebullient constituents had suggested be renamed after its senatorial sponsor. The day after his telephone conversation with Wilkins, however, Hughes put through another phone call—this time to Utah's junior senator, the amiably ineffectual Cameron McLachlen. That afternoon, McLachlen had a half-hour chat with the President at the White House, and then Hughes stood with McLachlen on the steps of the West Wing while the junior senator announced that the Indian Head Dam would become a reality. A few days later, President Hughes dropped in at a luncheon meeting of the American Public Power Association to pay tribute to Cameron McLachlen for his unceasing efforts to bring power projects to his state.

A Minnesota banker, financial angel of a political foe of Paul Anderson's, was nominated as Ambassador to Norway. Harry Weiss was forced to inform a New Jersey liberal that the Pentagon was taking another hard look at a military contract before awarding it to a Newark company. Senators were deluged with mail from governors, mayors and county officials in their home states asking for their help "at the White House" in obtaining approval of projects described as vitally needed but which in most cases the senators had never heard of. It was made clear to the party organizations in those states whose senators were opposed to the Court bill that there would be a major shuffling of the patronage setup if they were unable to talk their senators into line.

Senator Frank Hoar was seriously concerned by the effectiveness this jungle warfare was having on his recruiting campaign. Senators who had seemed amiably reasonable a week ago suddenly turned coy or even irritable when approached by Hoar's missionaries. There was no doubt that Hughes had spread considerable terror among them, and Hoar accepted their fright as a reasonable reaction to the threats imperiling their political careers. He had always been blessed with the luck of a considerable backing from both labor and business, and he had not had to cut as many corners as most of his colleagues. But he understood their problems and he recognized his responsibility to help them resist. Hoar had snared Wilkins, but he was, after all, a politician; what was needed now was a figure who could more or less compare with the stature of the President of the United States. There was only one place to go; to answer the pressure on them, the besieged senators had to be able to turn to the Supreme Court for backing.

It took some time to lay their plans and to prepare their arguments. It was not, therefore, until the evening of the third day of the hearings that Frank Hoar, Claude Wilkins and Dan Lewis appeared by gracious invitation at the squarish, ivy-covered brick house in Chevy Chase which was the retreat of Mr. Justice William Allen Hume. The answer had been a cordial "Of course, Frank," when Hoar had called to ask permission for his committee to wait upon the justice; now Hume was courtly and smiling as he ushered them into his library with its huge mahogany rolltop desk and polished Victorian furniture.

"I suppose we'd better get right down to business, Allen," Hoar said with nervous gruffness.

"Of course. Please do. But I hope you'll let me give you some coffee and brandy later." Hume's manner *seemed* promising.

Hoar said, "Well, we talked this over, a little, once before. I think you know, generally, what we have in mind." He paused, but Hume didn't speak. "Now, Allen, we've had to come to you for help. We didn't want to press you, but we have to."

Hume smiled. "Yes, I know how you dislike to press people, Frank."

"Hm, well, yes." Hoar was well aware he had no reputation for gentleness. "But the fact is, as I said, we have to—uh—intrude. We don't want to, but we have to. Allen, we believe we can lick this Court bill. We think if we can get the country so it understands the bill for what it is—a coldly calculated attempt to dominate the Supreme Court—we think if the people get to understand that, they will encourage their representatives in Congress to oppose it. But we can't do it alone. We took a shellacking last November, and because of that we haven't got the votes in the other party that we ordinarily could expect to get on an issue of this kind. The boys are scared to death of Hughes. They're afraid to buck his popularity."

"Yes, of course," Hume said. "Even Roosevelt never had the hold Mr. Hughes has on the people."

"Right. And of course, the White House is always a potent force when it gets behind any piece of legislation. The President wants it—when the people hear that, they think it must be all right. What we need is somebody on the same level as the Presidency, somebody the people respect in much the same way, to come out and tell them not to swallow this bill."

"I suppose I have to ask you who that somebody is—just for the record." Hume was quite serious.

"Yes, sir, Allen, it's you. We want to ask you, with all possible respect and deference, to testify against the bill before the Judiciary Committee of the Senate."

Hume looked at Hoar, as though asking him to understand. "My answer has to be no, regretfully. I'm sorry, because I'd like to help. But I could not approve of any member of the Court's testifying before a Congressional committee either for or against a piece of legislation."

Hoar was forming his lips to reply, but Wilkins's voice broke in, clear and precise, yet gently soothing.

"Yes. We understand, of course, Mr. Justice. We ask you to appear, and yet in a sense we are not so much making that request as we are asking you for your counsel in this matter."

Hume looked over at Wilkins and smiled his gentle smile. "Sir, you are . . . graceful. And I am complimented. I was complimented in the Senate whenever another senator saw fit to ask my advice. I have told Senator Hoar that I am opposed to the bill. It could work much mischief, in years to come if not now. I want to help. But there you are, a Supreme Court justice is under sentence of isolation, and rightfully so."

Wilkins was taking over, with Hoar's relieved consent. Dan Lewis merely sat there, coldly attentive. "As I said, Mr. Justice," Wilkins said, "we understand your position. But this is a serious time. What the President seeks to do is a serious thing, so serious that at one time I had hoped to gain admission to his camp in order to salvage what good was possible from a bill that seemed certain to pass. I was prepared to be a hostage, for a ransom." His short laugh was dry. "It didn't work, for which I blame only my own vanity. But, Mr. Justice, we must try to find something that will work. Naturally, we turn to you—to the enormous prestige and dignity and influence of the Supreme Court as well as to your own high standing with the people. I ask you, sir, if you will not testify—and I accept your refusal—will you not sit with us and try to suggest an alternative which would permit the country to become aware of your opposition?"

He can't help talking like that, Frank Hoar thought, that's the way Wilkins thinks—cautiously and with respect for the issues, and for others. Wilkins was a man whose thoughts were polite.

"I understand, Senator Wilkins," Hume said. "But I can't help wondering why you haven't discussed the matter with the Chief Justice. Surely, he would be the man to be approached first."

Wilkins smiled carefully. "Frankly, sir, we feel that you are much easier to talk to. Chief Justice Bacon is inclined to be a trifle Jovian when conversing with mere senators. At the same time, Mr. Justice, if you will permit my saying so, there is a considerable segment of opinion which holds that your influence across the land is as great if not greater than that of the Chief Justice. When the editorialists call you 'the great dissenter,' I believe the emphasis is on the word great. It is you, sir, more than the Chief Justice who has become known as the defender of the Constitution."

Hume's smile was a little wider now; he knew Wilkins was aware that he suspected the flattery. "Well, I must thank you again, sir," Hume said, his tone even. "The praise is undeserved, but I accept it in the spirit in which it is offered—by America's Honest Man."

Wilkins bowed. "An unfortunate appellation. I do not agree that honesty is so rare that its possession should distinguish a man."

"I hope not, Senator. Nevertheless, the name fits you. But to return to your problem, although I cannot conceive of involving myself in a legislative process, there may be an alternative. It is most apparent to me that the President's grounds for seeking passage of his Court plan are false. His talk about the refusals of writs of certiorari is nonsense, and his complaints about the alleged infirmity of some of the justices are gratuitously insulting."

Hoar jumped in. "Will you say that? Will you say that in a public statement?"

Hume's glance at Hoar was almost casual. "I don't think so, Frank. I think such a statement would be the prerogative of the Chief Justice."

"Well, how about Justice Dalton?" Hoar was in pursuit now. "By God, he's come out for the Court plan. He didn't worry about Bacon's prerogatives."

"Frank, I won't discuss what any other justice has done or may do," Hume said. "I will not criticize Justice Dalton; every honest man has good reasons for what he does, and I have absolutely no doubts about Justice Dalton's honesty or integrity."

"To be sure," Wilkins said, taking over again. "My own respect for that young man is considerable. But, Mr. Justice, if you won't make a public statement, will you help us in another way? Will you ask the Chief Justice to do so?"

Hume sighed. "I'm afraid the answer to that has to be no, also. But just a moment, gentlemen. I will go this far. If you wish, you may telephone the Chief Justice, tell him you're calling from my home and say that although I am opposed to the bill, I have declined to say so publicly because I believe that is a matter for the consideration of the Chief Justice."

Hoar was on his feet. "O.K. Fine. I'll call him right now." He looked over at Wilkins and Lewis, and both nodded.

Hoar did his job well, Hume noted. He repeated Hume's message almost word for word, before reverting to pure Frank Hoar and admonishing Robert McNair Bacon with the crackling tagline, "You can't let them ruin your Court!" Bacon's replies were terse almost to the point of irritation, but it was clear to Hoar that the Chief Justice welcomed Hume's counsel and his deference. Bacon wanted to do something to make his weight felt in the Court fight and he was ready to go along. But there was one condition.

Hoar put down the phone and, holding his hand over the mouthpiece, said to Hume, "He says he'll write the letter if you'll sign it with him."

Hume slowly looked over at his other guests, at Dan Lewis with the half-scowl on his face, at the expressionless Claude Wilkins fingering his bow tie. "Very well," he said to Hoar. "Tell him I'll sign. But say that I suggested he also try to get signatures from the other like-minded justices—Feldman, Gillette and Baker."

Hoar spoke into the telephone again. "Justice Hume says all right, he'll sign," he said. "And he says how about getting Feldman and Gillette and Baker to sign, too." The Senator from Ohio was the old familiar cloakroom operator again. He listened for a moment and then, "No, sir, not to me. I think you'd better address the letter to Senator Wilkins." Another pause. And then, "Yes, sir, we all think it would be better that way."

Frank Hoar hung up the phone and took out his handkerchief and wiped his brow. "Allen, did you say something about brandy —or maybe a little bourbon and branch water?"

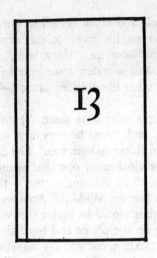

13

I DON'T KNOW HOW YOU MANAGE, with your red hair and your Gaelic countenance, to look and sound like Frank Roosevelt, but it's all there." As usual, Claude Wilkins's tone was neat and precise, but Francis Dalton unwillingly conceded that there was honest respect, even admiration, in the man's earnest phrases. This man sitting across the luncheon table from him in Paul Young's carefully elegant restaurant was incapable of an insincere statement. How, Francis wondered, did the man manage to keep getting re-elected?

He smiled across the table at the Senator from Utah; almost, he felt like bowing. "I'm not sure I want your compliment to include an identity of philosophies," Francis said, "but I can't help but be honestly flattered, Senator."

Claude Wilkins smiled back. "You should be, Mr. Justice. Frank Roosevelt had no equal in the art of—communicating, as they say nowadays. If there had been television networks in his day, I'm afraid we'd have elected him king. In a way, it's a frightening medium when employed politically."

"I'm afraid it frightened me a little last night," Francis said. "Those college students were sharp as well as articulate."

"Now, sir, I can't believe you were frightened. If so, you managed to conceal it artfully." Wilkins stared for a moment at the roll in his hand. "It's a catchy title for a panel program—*Campus Conversation*. It manages to imply that the subjects discussed are those the students are talking about. That interests the parents with boys and girls in college. I suppose they are as worried as they were in my college days that their children are flirting with dangerous philosophies."

"The kids didn't sound very dangerous to me," Francis said. "I'm afraid I wasn't that sensible when I was that age."

"Sensible? Oh, yes. Of course, they were generally in agreement with your views, Mr. Justice. I would say there wasn't a dangerous liberal in the lot. That helped, I should think."

"Oh, come now, Senator. They were in favor, as I am, of enlarging the Court. Yet I've heard from your side that the President's proposal is dangerous radicalism."

"Quite right, Mr. Justice. It is. But I hope I don't have to remind you that radicalism is not exclusively associated with what is loosely known as the liberal approach. The boys on the panel with you were all conservatives; and, like you, they espoused a radically conservative philosophy."

Francis smiled. "I suppose they said the same thing about most college students in the New Deal years."

This time Claude Wilkins's earnestness was too strong to permit an answering smile. "They did, and to a large extent they were right, sir. I willingly wear the mantle of the liberal independent, but in my humble opinion only about one-half of Frank Roosevelt's programs and policies were correct. The rest were dangerous. Dangerous to our system of government, which relies so heavily on checks and balances."

Francis said, "We agree on that point, sir—if not for the same reasons. But today—speaking of the philosophy of the student of today—his attitude seems to reflect that of the nation at large."

"Yes—and I must add, unfortunately. But you're right, Mr. Justice. I suppose more than anything else it was the students of a few years back, come to voting age, who swept President Hughes and his running mates into office. It took time; I believe our contemporary historians agree the conservative trend on the campus was first perceivable around 1960. But eventually the trend became a national attitude. I suppose it will take just as long for the pendulum to swing back."

"If it does swing back." Francis kept on his smile.

"Oh, it will." Wilkins's smile had returned. "It always does. We live in that hope, sir."

"Yet, we all must deal with today's attitudes, Senator, and those attitudes indicate that you are on the losing side in the Court controversy."

"Yes, I suppose I am. So far the President seems to have the troops, so to speak." Wilkins cut a piece of lamb chop, and seemed intent on spearing it with his fork. "Yes, you seem to have the votes—and yet it is too early for our side to despair. In any case, I don't believe in abandoning a fight, even though it be doomed to failure, if I believe in what I am fighting for." He popped the piece of lamb chop into his mouth.

Francis leaned back in his chair. "Well, I suppose all I can do is sigh heavily and mourn the loss of a powerful ally. If that bourbon old-fashioned didn't persuade you to my arguments, I'm sure a lamb chop won't. Besides, Senator, I'm about talked out after that preluncheon oration I directed at you."

"The lamb chop is every bit as good as the bourbon, Mr. Justice. But—we disagree, don't we? Amiably, I hope."

"Amiably of course, Senator. Even if I had the presumption, I couldn't be angry with such a distinguished opponent. I just hoped to persuade you to the right side. You've been on it so often."

"Thank you, Mr. Justice. You remain charmingly Rooseveltian to the end. But I am forced to abandon humility and say that I dare hope I am on the right side this time, also. I shall do my best."

I shall do my best, Francis was thinking as he walked down Connecticut Avenue toward the White House. And, by God, he will, too. The delightful, courtly old warrior. He'll do his best to lick this Court plan because he couldn't do any less. We've lost a good man. We've lost class and political grace in an age when those qualities have become scarce. Well, I did *my* best. I did my *honest* best. I didn't try any tricks on him. I just told him what I thought and why I thought it. We've lost his vote, and his voice, and his prestige, but we've gained back a little of his respect.

He wanted to feel *better* about things—about his personal role in the controversy—and it had helped, a little, to talk with Wilkins. Wilkins had been not only amiable, but most respectful. Francis' train of thought stopped suddenly, jarringly. My God, have I been poking about to find someone who would treat me with respect? Am I that concerned about what I am doing? He discovered he had stopped short at Connecticut and I Streets, and he was relieved to find that a red light gave him the ostensible reason for it. No, he needn't feel displeased with himself; he was doing nothing he should be ashamed of. He was helping where he could, and quietly; he had so far preserved his dignity, the dignity of the Court. Francis smiled at the wry thought, the determined effort to convince himself of his purity. Would all this soul-searching be necessary if he were sure, if he had no doubts? My God, he thought, I *am* becoming a quibbler with myself, a hairsplitter. Instead of all this self-interrogation, let's put it this way: I am in favor of the President's Court plan, with certain reservations concerning my own participation in the campaign to put it over. The Court needs freshening; it is too much preoccupied with consideration of the so-called absolutes in the Constitution, which are at best only implied. It worries me that a President should be forced to *tamper* with the judiciary, but the dangers inherent in the tampering are not as serious as the orators claim. Men named to the Supreme Court are, after all, not small men, men of small character and will; no matter how many justices may be added to the Court, each justice will be free, as usual, to reach his own independent conclusion on each issue; a President may name a politically amiable man to the Supreme Court bench, but once that man sits down on that bench, there is nothing any President, including John Alden Hughes, can do to make that man decide one way or another.

He did feel better. He must keep the logic of that argument in mind and not permit himself to become confused—and embarrassed?—by irrelevancies. It was the way he had put it to Beatrice last night, and she had accepted its clarity of thought as well as its practical, politically sophisticated logic.

"You know, Francis, you are still pretty much of a politician," Beatrice said. "And I'm glad of that. I don't think any branch of the government can operate successfully in this rather hectic society of ours without adding a pinch of politics to its recipes. It's just that, in the past few weeks, I've worried about your seeming to be too active in the President's behalf; I know it doesn't affect your dignity or the dignity of the Court, but that's because I know you so well. I'm afraid of what the public will think."

"Well, of course, I have to risk that, Bea," Francis had told her. "I have to be loyal to what I believe in."

Beatrice had looked at him, as she often did when she was trying to get inside him, behind his words. "Darling, I know that," she said. She smiled, but her face remained earnest. "You are so loyal, Francis. I just want to reassure myself that you *are* being loyal to what *you* believe in, and not merely to the President."

Francis had laughed, and told her not to worry. He *was* loyal to Hughes, but he believed he was in a position where he could be independent of that loyalty. And, of course, Bea had her real doubts about the merit of the Court plan. "It disturbs me, Francis, because I know you are so much for it," she said. "But—oh, I suppose I'm being the individualistic actress about it. I don't quite like the implication that a President is imposing his will on anybody."

There was the rub, Francis thought. It was difficult to explain —sometimes even to himself—that this was not the case of a man willfully attempting to have his way with the Court, but of a man taking modern action in a modern day to deal with modern problems. He sighed. It was damned difficult, sometimes.

As usual these days, Francis walked down Seventeenth Street, past the Old State Department Building, and detoured around to the southwest gate of the White House. He had suggested that there was no point in advertising his frequent visits to the White House, despite his all-out speechmaking for the Court plan. The President had agreed that it would be too conspicuous for him to enter through the West Wing lobby, always jammed with reporters—"although I don't think we're kidding anybody, Francis." Possibly not, Francis had replied, but it would emphasize his participation in the Court campaign if he had to run that journalistic gauntlet every few days. And the *News* had already suggested editorially that there was something sinister about "secret meetings" in the President's office.

Francis was five minutes early for the meeting when he stepped through the ground-floor door under the South Portico, but the Secret Service agent who opened the door for him told him he was to go right over to the President's West Wing office. "Are the others there already?" Francis asked, and in typical Secret Service fashion the agent replied that he didn't know, Mr. Justice, but his orders were to ask Mr. Justice Dalton to go right in. So Francis strolled past Doc Allen's office and out onto the colonnade running along the swimming pool, and when he got to the French door which gave the President his view of the Rose Garden, the door was opened for him by Vice-President Morgan.

The President was seated at his big mahogany desk, feet resting on his wastebasket, with Majority Leader Chet McAdam, Speaker Henry Adam Smith and House Majority Leader Bill Ball, and, of course, Charlie Mayborn and Harry Weiss.

John Alden Hughes waved a vigorous hand at Francis. "Make yourself comfortable, Francis. I shooed the Iranian Ambassador out early before he could ask for more money." Tom Morgan, the born host, took Francis' hat and coat; the guests at Morgan's Montana ranch, Francis was thinking, must be the most waited on in the country.

"Chet?" Hughes was looking over at McAdam. "Could we interrupt a few minutes to hear Francis' report on his chat with Claude Wilkins?"

"It won't take long," Francis said. "The answer is a polite, well-dressed no. Wilkins will not reconsider. He is unutterably opposed to the Court plan. He will fight it, to quote, with all his strength."

"Yes." The President looked over at Chet McAdam, sitting in a straight chair with its back propped against the green wall. "I don't suppose any of us expected anything different."

Francis looked over at McAdam, too, at a face empty of emotion. McAdam would not stir. Wilkins was important, but McAdam would not budge from the patronage he considered his just due. More, the President had made it quite plain on that day less than a year ago that McAdam would receive his reward. The story was well known by now to the inner circle—how

199

Ed O'Hara, the National Chairman, had gone to McAdam with the President's thanks for getting the White House program passed almost unscathed by opposition sniping. Whether prompted or not by the White House, O'Hara had exercised the prerogative of the National Chairman to inform McAdam that he could ask for any reward within reason. And McAdam had promptly demanded a seat on the Supreme Court bench, a post which he said would be the climax of his lifelong ambition. O'Hara had heartily encouraged McAdam in his request, and a few days later had phoned him with the word that Hughes had promised him the first vacancy on the Court. So overjoyed was McAdam that he had spread the good news among his intimates on the Hill, and by now the promise had become such public property that there would be trouble in Congress if the President reneged on it. Not that Hughes wanted to renege; he had shown that in his prompt reassurance to McAdam even when he knew it probably would cost him Wilkins's support. No, only McAdam could open the escape hatch and he would not.

"I knew you couldn't sway him," McAdam said, his voice toneless. "Wilkins won't play unless he can call the tune. He wants to name those two judges."

The President's voice was quiet, and almost as toneless. "Well, he can't. I thought it could be arranged, Chet. I honestly believed I could talk to you and you'd be willing to take something else. But I realize I had no right to think that. You had a perfect right to hold me to my promise. I don't regret trying. I had to try. But it didn't work and that's that."

Francis said, "It probably doesn't matter. I gather that even if he got the right to make the nominations, Wilkins wouldn't go along now. I brought the matter up—not offering him anything, but expressing regret it had turned out the way it had—and he said it was unimportant now. He said his suggestion had been one born of desperation and he said, rather quietly, 'I'm not desperate now.' "

"All right." The President's voice was crisp now. "I don't know what he's basing his new-found hope on, but it doesn't matter. Chet, what about our tame union leader?"

McAdam let his chair down gently. "He'll go along—naturally. He says he'll arrange to organize the citizens' group and make sure he gets named chairman. He's making a batch of phone calls today. I think we can leave it up to him. Whatever else you may say about Joe Harris, he pays his debts."

"He called me this morning," Harry Weiss put in hurriedly. "He said he was glad to do what he could and asked me to give his best wishes to 'my friend, the President.' "

"Fine," the President said. "Thanks, Harry. Remind me to drop him a note when he gets the citizens' group off the ground." His tone and manner were dry.

McAdam moved to get the meeting back on the subject of legislative progress; after thirty years in Congress it was McAdam's determined and calculated opinion that efforts spent elsewhere but on Capitol Hill were merely window dressing. To McAdam, the only important thing was keeping the faithful in line.

"If you don't mind, Mr. President, I'd like to report on our latest poll," McAdam said. Hughes nodded. "We're holding our own," McAdam said. "And that's what I don't like."

"You don't like it?" A Presidential eyebrow was lifted.

"No, sir, not with an issue like this. The way it looks, if it came to a vote now, we'd have a comfortable margin—maybe as many as twenty-five votes. But it's not coming to a vote now, and in the meantime we're not stepping ahead. The margin on our side is exactly what it was three days ago, and three days before that. It's too damned static to suit me."

"But the margin is still on our side," Francis noted.

"Yes, and I repeat, that's what I don't like," McAdam said. "We ought to be gaining votes—we've *got* to pick up some more votes to make up for the votes that'll become more and more doubtful as time goes on. I don't know when the hell we'll force this thing to a vote; the way those hearings are going, the bill may be in committee for another month. Meanwhile, we should be building up a cushion. Well, we're not only not doing that, but the drive seems to be stalled. We put on that first push and we built up our margin, and now we seem to be standing still. I don't like that to happen this early in the game."

"Is it that important, Chet?" asked the President. "After all, we've got to allow time for oratory."

"Yes, we have. And if it were almost any other issue, I wouldn't be worried. Hell, the kind of oratory you hear on the Senate floor is enough to make Bill Borah quiver in his grave. It's the usual stuff, the usual appeals to prejudice and self-interest, quotations from the Bible, cries of alarm. I don't think it'll have any direct effect at all. It's the indirect effect I'm worried about. What that oratory is doing is giving the people time to think over this issue. I don't like that. I happen to believe in this plan, but I can understand the fears of those who don't like it. You let the people start thinking about things and pretty soon they'll be writing letters to their Congressmen and sending telegrams, and the gentlemen on the Hill will look at the pile of protest mail on their desks and they'll get scared and wonder whether they dare to vote for the bill. That's all right. That's the democratic way of doing things, slowly and surely, with everybody getting a chance to have his say. But with our margin static, it sure as hell is not going to do us any good. It's got to hurt us. It always hurts the side that's ahead. It happens in every election. For thirty years now, I've made sure that my opponent takes that early lead."

"Well, Chet, what do we do?" The President was still crisp, anxious to push ahead.

"Well, sir, we've just got to fight a little harder." McAdam looked hard at the President, half lying now in his big swivel chair, his long legs stretched out to his foot perch on the waste-basket. "If you don't mind my saying so, Mr. President, *you've* got to fight a little harder."

The President looked back at McAdam, his mouth a little straighter. Francis knew what McAdam was up to, and this was the time for it, because the President's mother, after winning her point on no Presidential speeches for the present, had flown off to Palm Springs and was not around to protect her victory.

"Go on, Chet," the President said. "I may as well hear you out."

"Well, sir, you're our best bet." McAdam's tone was a little harder, but he seemed to be searching for the kindliest-possible words. "Our best argument for the Court bill is that you want it, that it's something you believe is best for the country. We can orate all we want to up on the Hill, but none of us is you, none of us is the President who was just re-elected by the greatest landslide in history. The Court bill is not Chet McAdam or Henry Adam Smith, Mr. President, it's John Alden Hughes. You've told the country you want it, and you're the most popular President in history. But, sir, I don't think you can merely tell the people you want it—once. You have to keep reminding them. You have to keep reminding them that it's *your* bill, that it's something John Alden Hughes wants, and wants very badly. I think the people will give it to you, but with the opposition that's developed I think you have got to let them know how important it is to you."

"I asked for it," the President said. His voice was tinged with impatience. "I will not get out and brawl with some of those nuts who are inveighing against it."

"Yes, sir, you asked for it. As I said—you asked for it once. And you don't have to do any brawling, Mr. President. We've got a victory dinner for the party coming up. You're due to make a speech at that dinner. Any time you wish, you can speak to the nation by television from the dignified atmosphere of the White House. Mr. President, I repeat: we're not using our best weapon in this fight. We aren't facing the facts, which is that the elections last November were a personal triumph for you, not for the party. Hell, we all got in because we had you on the ticket. It's as simple as that. One major thing we've got to do is build up more resentment against the Supreme Court for blocking your program. And only you can do that, Mr. President. None of the rest of us has enough prestige to go around getting really tough with the Court."

"Chet, I do not like the idea of dissipating the prestige of the Presidency." The President's voice was quiet but it had a ring. "I believe strongly that that prestige should be nurtured and saved for important moments, important occasions. I'm going to have to spend some of that prestige, as you well know, on the German question. It is going to be a difficult piece of work to make clear to the people the danger of Germany's flirting with the Soviet Union. That kind of *rapprochement* brought on World War II, and we've got to be on guard against it. And yet, we have to be careful, because a whole generation has been brought up to regard Germany as a kind of sentinel against Communism. We may have to give them nuclear arms."

Hughes lowered his feet from the wastebasket and leaned forward on the desk. "Gentlemen, it is all these problems that have made the Court bill a must—one of the actions necessary to permit us to go ahead and at the same time strengthen the national security. We have got to do something soon to achieve general automation in industry, or the Soviet Union is going to leave us behind in the production of those materials that go into building up national security. The Sons of Slaves are raising hell all over the country, raising tempers, too. I appreciate their problems, but we cannot have a situation where riots organized almost as armed insurrections spring up all over the land. The case of the Soviet spy, Gleason, is being hawked by the Kremlin all over the world as a propaganda weapon; it never seems to occur to our friends in London and New Delhi that not only was the man convicted by due process, but he also picked up, by the guile of his legal advisors, some rather extralegal rights usually denied the man who steals a pound of hamburger. We are being assailed by our friends in the name of civil rights—but how far should civil rights go?"

The President paused and leaned back again in his chair. Francis was annoyed that his thoughts should dwell briefly on Beatrice's remark concerning the Gleason case: "But aren't we secure enough to *make sure* he's had every safeguard?" The man had had every safeguard; you did not vulgarly parade a lot of artificial gestures of legal coddling to please the Communist hireling in Caracas who had just thrown a rock through the window of the American Embassy.

Hughes's low voice broke the silence. "These are monumental problems, gentlemen. They are my responsibility to handle. But I'll need help in that handling from the people. I am going to have to go to them and ask their help. In the meantime, I can't dissipate whatever influence I may have with them, whatever credit I have."

But Chet McAdam was not giving up. "Yes, sir, I know. It's going to be touch and go. I'm as worried about it as you are, and I wish I could help you with it. But I still do think, Mr. President—and I say this with all respect—that we need you, now, in this Court fight. Congress is still scared of you at this point. The boys' memories are still fresh—they haven't forgotten what happened in November. The one thing they fear is that you'll get out and put the enormous prestige of the Presidency on the line for this Court plan—and keep up the pressure constantly."

Unaccountably, it seemed, the President turned toward Francis. But it gave Francis a start. The President couldn't possibly know of the long dinner session Francis had had with McAdam at which Francis pushed the idea of the President's more vigorous participation in the campaign for the Court plan. It was not that Francis cared whether the President knew how he felt; he had made that pretty clear in the past few weeks. Hughes knew Francis wanted him to take the stump. But Francis didn't want the President to feel, unreasonably, that his favorite Supreme Court justice had been conspiring against him behind his back.

"Francis, I suppose you feel pretty much the same," the President said. "That is, you haven't changed your mind, have you?"

"No, sir." Let's all get in on this, with all our strength, Francis thought. "I've wanted you to speak out from the start. I think Chet has made some telling points." Especially the one I gave him about building up resentment against the Court, he was thinking.

"Yes, well, we'll go back to it later," Hughes said. He started to speak, then paused as the door from the hall opened. It was Mike Blair, and the Press Secretary had a yellow sheet of news wire in his hand.

"I'm sorry to interrupt, sir," Mike Blair said. He walked toward the President's desk. "But this just came in over both UPI and AP. I was pretty sure you'd want to see it." He handed the piece of paper to the President.

Hughes glanced at it, then adjusted his glasses and brought his feet down off the wastebasket. As he read, two new lines appeared in his soaring brow. He stopped reading and looked out over his glasses at the men in the room.

"Here, Mike," he said. "Read it to them."

Mike Blair stood by the desk and read it:

CHIEF JUSTICE ROBERT MCNAIR BACON AND FOUR OTHER MEMBERS OF THE SUPREME COURT TODAY ISSUED A STATEMENT STRONGLY DENOUNCING THE PRESIDENT'S PROPOSAL TO ENLARGE THE COURT, AND

CHARGING THAT "THIS PLAN TO PACK THE SUPREME COURT IS A DICTA-TORIAL ACT ON THE PART OF THE EXECUTIVE BRANCH OF THE GOVERN-MENT."

BESIDES THE CHIEF JUSTICE, THE STATEMENT WAS SIGNED BY ASSO-CIATE JUSTICES WILLIAM ALLEN HUME, JOSEPH T. BAKER, GEORGE W. GILLETTE AND DAVID BENJAMIN FELDMAN. TOGETHER THEY COM-POSE THE MAJORITY WHICH HAS RULED UNCONSTITUTIONAL SEVERAL OF THE PRESIDENT'S CONTROVERSIAL PIECES OF LEGISLATION BY A 5 TO 4 MARGIN.

THE STATEMENT, HANDED TO REPORTERS IN THE SUPREME COURT PRESSROOM BY ALBERT W. WEEKS, SECRETARY TO JUSTICE BACON, RE-PLIED IN DETAIL TO EACH OF THE SEVEN POINTS ADVANCED BY PRESI-DENT HUGHES AS ARGUMENTS FOR HIS PLAN. FOR INSTANCE, THE JUSTICES DENIED THAT THE COURT HAD BEEN FORCED TO REFUSE PETI-TIONS OF CERTIORARI BECAUSE THE COURT WAS OVERWORKED AND SUBMITTED A LENGTHY EXPLANATION OF HOW THE PETITIONS WERE HANDLED.

SIMILARLY, THE STATEMENT TOOK ISSUE WITH THE PRESIDENT'S CONTENTION THAT ADDING TWO NEW JUSTICES TO THE COURT WOULD INCREASE ITS EFFICIENCY. ON THE CONTRARY, THE JUSTICES SAID, EN-LARGING THE COURT WOULD DECREASE THE COURT'S EFFICIENCY, AND THEY QUOTED THE LATE CHIEF JUSTICE CHARLES EVANS HUGHES TO STRENGTHEN THEIR POINT.

"All right, Mike, that's enough," the President cut in. "We can read the rest in the *Star*. Thank you for bringing it in to us."

When Mike Blair had left, closing the door softly behind him, Vice-President Morgan said, "My God!" Chet McAdam looked up at the ceiling, while next to him Speaker Smith pursed his lips in a soundless whistle.

The President stood up and ran a hand through his black hair. The lines had left his forehead, but his mouth was still a straight line. "Well, gentlemen, that would seem to be that," he said. "I think perhaps we can now talk about what should go into those speeches I'm going to make—very soon."

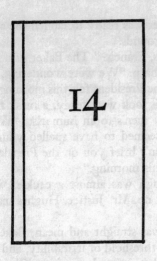

14

As Francis might have expected, Baker—the eternal Rotarian—was in his glory. Francis had sauntered almost absentmindedly into the robing room, his head filled with exultant thoughts of the trenchant phrases soon to burst upon the opposition from the awesome dignity of the White House. With his mind thus occupied, he should have been prepared for Baker, but he wasn't. In the midst of his own thoughts, he had pushed aside all mental reference to what *The New York Times* was already calling "The Statement of the Five."

When Francis entered the room, the sound of the murmuring that greeted him was of the volume and tone of uneasily controlled argument. Momentarily, Francis was surprised; he felt his brows lift quizzically as he automatically started his handshaking round. There was a pause in the muted hubbub of conversation, but he felt the effort that went into it and the tension behind the sudden grace of mien and manner—except for Hume, of course; his courtly bow and firm handshake were as always pleasant and easily cordial.

Baker grinned hugely as he shook Francis' hand, and there was a coarse amiability in the tone of his "Good morning, Francis, old boy." But Baker was ready to launch the attack once Francis had completed his rounds.

"Read the papers, Francis?" The Baker grin was still there, but now his look was sharp. "We were wondering, some of us, if you could tell us how the President felt this morning."

Francis hoped his look was steady, a mask for the loathing he felt for this hearty men's-room humorist. "Why, yes, I've read the papers—they seemed to have spelled your name right, Joe. But I'm afraid I can't brief you on the President's mood, since I haven't seen him this morning."

Baker's short laugh was almost a cackle. "Ha! Well, maybe you'd better check up, Mr. Justice. Hughes may need somebody to hold his hand."

Bacon's mouth was straight and mean; Baker had pricked the Chief Justice's low threshold of irritability, and there was a harshness in the voice that came down from Olympus. "Mr. Justice Baker, let us not be vulgar. I suggest that vulgarity be best left to the politicians."

"To be sure." Little Henry Clay Robson's voice was matter-of-fact. "Politicians like Senators Hoar and Martin, perhaps?" His look in return for Bacon's glare was innocent. "Francis, you can't be surprised that we've been discussing the forthright public statement of some of our colleagues."

"Oh, of course." Francis' smile was easy. "I've read it, of course. It seemed to me to be a good one, for those who think that way."

Now it was Feldman's turn, but his interposition was dry. "We thought perhaps we should make our sentiments known—ah, as it were, to counteract your vigorous activities, Francis."

Francis looked over at Hume's gently neutral face, then turned to Feldman's bankerish scowl. Why is so much respect accorded bankers, he wondered—people who deal only with money all their lives? "Why, I think that's natural. I should think we all have enough character to be willing to express an opinion. As I said, I think it was a fine statement. It contained, I think, a little of all of you who signed it."

Frank Mitchell's laugh was an ugly explosion. "*Touché*, Francis. I'll bet old Joe Baker thought of that business about the dictator—and Gillette about how hard we all work." He turned to

Gillette and seemed to be appraising the Californian's rotund trunk. "Are you tired, George?"

Gillette's face reddened and his reply came in a kind of strangled wheeze. "Always the comedian, aren't you, Frank? Well, if I'm tired, it's not from a hangover."

Mitchell was maddeningly equable. "Sure enough, you're right. But you ought to try a little bourbon and branch water, George. It'd help your disposition. You stuff yourself on too many desserts."

"Gentlemen!" The Chief Justice's voice was a whip. "Let's stop this childish bickering." He turned to Francis; he seemed to be peering down from a great height.

"I hope you know, Mr. Justice, that the step we have taken would not have been necessary had not the President already—ah—recruited a most active advocate from this Court."

The tough, nasty old devil, Francis was thinking. But his toughness was something to admire. "I suppose I know what you mean, Chief," he said. "If you mean that I have spoken out, as an interested citizen, then I must point out that that is my right. I'm not going to apologize because you have implied that somehow I have violated the dignity of this Court. I should think your statement was necessary because that is how you five justices felt about the issue, not because I had spoken out."

"Then your thinking is in error." Bacon's retort was swift. "I have never believed in a member of the Supreme Court getting involved in politics. But after considerable wrestling with my conscience I decided that I could not permit the people of this country erroneously to conclude that one member spoke for the entire Court."

"That's reasonable," Francis said. "But I happen to think you are wrong about getting involved, as you put it, in politics. Politics in this country is the art of government. The Supreme Court is a part of our government, and when any legislation is proposed that affects this Court, I believe it is the duty of a member of the Court, as well as his inalienable privilege, to express an opinion publicly."

Bacon's smile was mean. "Yes, of course. Your career has been —ah—political. I suppose in a sense you are still more politician than jurist, *Mr. Justice*."

Francis was contemptuously confident that Bacon could not stir him to anger. "I should think not, Chief, even though you choose to italicize, as it were, my present title. In any event, that can be left to history. But I should hope that I have enough of the politician in me—an honorable calling, by the way, which seeks always to understand people—to leaven my purely legal approach to my present chores."

He was being a bit of a ham, but Francis couldn't resist a quick glance at Robson and Mitchell, and he was warmed by Robson's barely perceptible nod and Mitchell's swift grin. But it was old Angus Whitfield who stepped in, as his impatience so often caused him to do.

"Goddammit to hell's fire Maria!" Whitfield's voice was a roar that came from deep in his barrel chest and seemed to make the few white hairs on his gleaming skull tremble. "Goddammit, Bacon, what's all this rot about politicians? By God, I was a politician and a goddamned good one, and I'll not claw at my topknot to any snotty lawyer who's never been human enough even to go fishing."

"Wowee!" It was Mitchell with his hoarse Nevada shriek. "Give 'em hell, Angus. Grab him by the horns."

Bacon turned to Whitfield, his face gray, his blue eyes icy and unblinking. "Mr. Justice Whitfield, I find it difficult to excuse your language. This is not a low saloon, but the robing room of the Supreme Court of the United States."

"Is that so?" Whitfield's jaw was out. "Well, by God, I'll thank you not to pass judgment on my language, Mr. Justice Bacon. I'll talk the way I goddamn please, wherever I am, and especially when you start your goddamned frozen-faced nit picking."

"Indeed?" Bacon seemed now to be slightly patronizing. "And I suppose you support the arguments of Mr. Justice Dalton?"

Whitfield grunted an old man's coarse laugh. "Don't worry about me, Bacon; when I arrive at an opinion, I'll let everyone know in language that even a stuffed shirt like you can understand."

"By God!" Mitchell's delighted voice boomed about in the chamber, and suddenly there was a cracking thud as his big hand came down like a pile driver on Baker's back. Baker's mouth flew open and crimson dyed his face as he turned, choking, to the Nevadan.

"You goddamn son of a bitch!" Baker's right arm went back and when he swung, there was a fist at the end of it that grazed Mitchell's ear. As Mitchell's big hands flew up swiftly, Baker aimed a second roundhouse with his left. "You bastard!" he shrieked. "Keep your goddamn hands off me."

Mitchell had both arms around Baker by the time Hume was trying to step between them on one side and Francis was tugging at both of them on the other.

"Gentlemen, please!" Hume said.

"All right—Frank, Joe," Francis said.

"Stop it! Stop that at once!" Bacon roared.

And little Henry Clay Robson, surprisingly trying to force his tiny body into the melee, murmured, "What would people think?"

What, indeed, would people think, Francis reflected from his place on the bench as he looked down on some of those people filling every one of the one hundred and eighty-eight seats reserved with cautiously judicial niggardliness for the public. It would, he thought, make a hell of a headline in the *Post*, and with his politician's bent for filling others' shoes, he found himself writing the headline: JUSTICE SLUGGED IN SUPREME COURT BRAWL. It was not quite a brawl, of course, because it had subsided as suddenly as it had erupted, with Mitchell predictably offering swift apology to Baker, and Baker just as predictably accepting the apology with the short and ungracious "Very well, sir." Bacon, of course, had been in a fury, but after his first outcry there hadn't been much he could do except relieve himself of muffled growls, because Hume had been there, taking charge in a voice soothing yet firm. "This sort of thing is inexcusable, gentlemen," Hume had told the two red-faced justices, and Mitchell had had the look of a law-breaking schoolboy, while Baker, although sulky and wheezing, had kept his eyes to the floor until Mitchell apologized. The matter then had been taken completely out of Bacon's hands by Angus Whitfield's irascible growl demanding, "Let's get on with it, gentlemen. We can't hang about here all day." Then, as the justices donned or adjusted their robes, Francis had managed a brief interlude with the matter-of-fact Hume, who had refused to hold Francis responsible for the fray.

"Thank you," Francis said, "but I'm afraid I goaded Bacon into speaking more vigorously than he might have."

"No, it's the sort of thing that could have happened anyway," Hume said mildly. "After all, we've had four years of controversy on this Court. Five-to-four decisions are not conducive to the general serenity. There has been frustration on one side and, I'm afraid, a certain arrogance on the other. There is plenty of blame to go around."

"I could have been more conciliatory, or at least kept my mouth shut," Francis said.

"No, no—you couldn't have. The Supreme Court is not that kind of organism. It is, after all, a collection of rugged individualists, all with their own staunch beliefs. In times of tension like these, I always think of what the late Justice Jackson said—that the Court functions less as one deliberative body than as nine, with each justice working largely in isolation. Emerging from this isolation into the robing room or the conference room, we are apt to be appalled by what we often regard as the malicious inability of our colleagues to see our point of view."

"True enough." Francis smiled at some thoughts he had entertained during several of the more acrimonious conferences. "Some of us tend to believe that our colleagues disagree with us out of pure cantankerousness. But Baker—I should have been more careful not to let him get so involved."

"There was nothing you could do, Mr. Justice. Unfortunately, Baker has his troubles—outside."

The prim Hume, of course, avoided discussion of Baker's "troubles," and yet all the justices were aware of them because of Baker's occasional compulsion to discuss them. Although it seemed incredible to Francis, the hearty, painfully jovial Baker had a young wife who flitted relentlessly from one love affair to another. Between late nights in the arms of her latest insurance salesman, she nagged Baker about his age and the probability of his death in the near future. Appallingly, her concern seemed to be not with the fact that poor Baker was to be plucked from this vale of tears but that by so surrendering to untimely death he would leave her unprotected. "She's always asking me what she's going to do when I'm dead," Baker had once confided to Francis in one of those swift appeals for sympathy so uncharacteristic of the country-club-locker-room manner he usually wore.

"Well, Mr. Justice, it's good to have your support—or at least, your tolerance—on one issue," Francis said. He was aware that no one seemed in a hurry to leave the privacy of the robing room.

Hume's face was solemn, but friendly. "I'm sorry we can't agree more, Francis. I admire your arguments too much to hold you lightly, and it would be an achievement if I could recruit you as a convert to the way of thinking whose majority on this Court is so pathetically slender."

"Why, thank you, Allen." Francis felt a suffusion of warmth throughout his body. He had been aware of a mutual respect between them, but to have Hume use the word *admire* was a tribute. He said, "I suppose the best way I can put it is to say that I never enjoy disagreeing with one of your opinions. I wish we could be on the same side."

Hume smiled. "I think we *are* on the same side, Francis. The differing opinions we offer—they're merely exercises in hair-splitting. But I know that what you believe you believe earnestly and sincerely, and what you do you do because you believe it is the right thing to do. I may call you wrong, but I could never call you expedient. Since I flatter myself that I try to believe and act in the same fashion, I believe that puts us on the same side."

"Thank you again," Francis said. "I'm glad you see it that way. Yet, we don't agree, do we?"

"Oh—I wonder if it should be put that way." Hume was thoughtful. "We disagree on certain questions before the Court; I don't think we disagree on such things as honesty and integrity in our separate, peculiar interpretations of the law. I like to think, Francis, that we are—all of us on this Court—our own creatures, creatures of our own thinking, that we arrive at our conclusions honestly, independently, because of what each of us believes. That is the important thing."

Creatures of our own thinking, Francis repeated to himself. Yes, that was the important thing—that we *arrive at our conclu-*

sions honestly, independently. He felt a warm pride at Hume's words, yet at that moment, unwelcome, there passed through his mind the image of John Alden Hughes, and a vague discomfort jabbed at his consciousness. He wanted to brush it aside, so as to enjoy this moment, but it stayed with him.

"I think that's true," Francis said. "We may differ, but I agree that our differences are honest. I believe there can be mutual respect on this Court." Respect for poor Baker, yes, and for Gillette and for Feldman—for all of them; yes, Francis could feel that. For better or for worse, they *were* their own creatures. Wrong at times, perhaps, but wrong with integrity. Suddenly, his mind created a picture of those meetings at the White House and he thought: Can they—do they—feel this for me? They should; they most certainly should—but do they?

Hume was still smiling. "There is, I am sure, mutual respect within the Court," he said. His words had a comforting tone. Is he trying to comfort me? Francis asked himself. Hume went on, unhurriedly. "We all believe in the basic freedoms; I believe that is true, though we may interpret them, define them, differently. Of that I'm sure."

Francis managed to smile back. "But, there are of course times when you may feel some of us are bent on infringing those freedoms. There are times when you seem to feel some of us are too —practical—in defining those freedoms."

"Practical?" Hume raised an eyebrow. "I hope I'm a practical man, too. No, I should not make practicality an accusation. I admire your practicality. I merely hope that, someday, you will slow down to my pace. There can be no hurry, really, where man's rights are concerned, because those rights are too delicate to be subjected to haste. That is all I suggest."

Bacon was clearing his throat impatiently, then, and as the Court began its slow march to the courtroom, it was as though Hume's words kept repeating themselves in Francis' ears. Did packing the Supreme Court *to keep it abreast of the times* subject man's delicate rights to the harsh dictation of haste? Was there such a thing, *practically*, as hurrying when man's rights were at stake? Was there such a thing as infringing a man's rights *a little?* Bosh! Francis reflected. Hume was talking his lofty philosophy again. He was not talking law. He, Francis, had no intention, by anything he did, by any opinion he handed down, of bruising man's delicate rights, or of infringing them even a little, but of protecting the national interest, of putting the community above the wants of the selfish individual. As he took his seat on the bench, Francis rebuked himself for again permitting Hume's arguments to unsettle him. The reasonable man, he told himself, should guard always against attempts to influence him against his own honest thinking. Irritably, he reflected that such vigilance would not be necessary if the Court were not a pack of garrulous old maids. He was surprised, and ashamed, now, to find he was angry at Hume without being able to explain why.

Yet, with all his unease over Hume's arguments, Francis felt again the pleasant tingle at being a part of all this. It was his life; he couldn't tolerate any other. The citizenry sometimes seemed one big national debating society, and his concern was deep for what it might do to the country, but it was vivid and vital and hard-working. And as a Supreme Court justice, he was taking a part in trying to wrest reason from the confusion of these conflicting ideas. He listened to the lawyer pleading below him with half his mind while he thought of how much he loved this Court, with its neoclassic architectural pretensions somehow given a kind of human grace by the motto over the façade: EQUAL JUSTICE UNDER LAW. He loved its fusty traditions—the page boys in their blue knickerbockers who were hired when they were five feet one inch tall and fired when they grew taller than five feet six inches, lest they tower over the shortest justice. He had affection for every one of the special police detail of fifty-four red-faced individuals, and for the men in the Court's own printshop in the basement—for the smell in the printshop. And he was warmed by the comforting knowledge that no leak had ever come from that highly restricted area despite the fact that its employees were privy to every opinion printed there. For the first time in a life well sprinkled with political honors, Francis felt that he had at last found something that meant everything to him. The Court was everything to him, everything he had ever wanted or would ever want. He found himself smiling at the thought of Beatrice. Did the Court mean more to him than Beatrice? No, of course not. That is, there was no conflict. The

Court was everything to him in one way; Beatrice was everything to him in another. He told himself again there was no conflict, as though reassuring himself, because another thought had intruded and he did not like thinking about Freddie Adams. He did not like thinking about Beatrice's second husband, because Freddie was an ugly threat to Beatrice. To Beatrice—and to him? He didn't have to answer that now. And he would see Beatrice tonight. She was coming back from New York tonight. That was enough to think about now.

Jimmy Hughes was drunk. To Francis Dalton, who had known the President's brother in campaign planes and on the platforms of dusty convention halls and in early-morning sessions in Georgetown drawing rooms, the signs were obvious. Jimmy Hughes had reached the point where he was making a determined effort not to appear drunk. He was choosing his words carefully and moving prudently and working hard at the job of checking the sarcastic smile that was the hallmark of Jimmy Hughes in his cups. But the inevitable had arrived in the exquisite elegance of the French Embassy, in this atmosphere of exquisite monotony. Jimmy was still drinking martinis, although he had had five at dinner at Duke Zeibert's and at least one each time he fled to Bassin's between the acts of *Hey There!* at the National. Now a lock of the black hair streaked with gray was beginning to slip down onto Jimmy's handsome brow, and his eyes had the familiar glistening look. Jimmy had not wanted to go on to this reception to which the theater party had been charmingly summoned by Mme. Paquette; he had pleaded with Francis and Beatrice to make a detour with him to observe the belly dancers at the Casino Royal. "I'd love to," Beatrice told Jimmy, "but let's just make an appearance. To show off our good manners." And so Jimmy had come along with them and had barely taken the time to shake the hands of his host and hostess before making for the bar.

Now, after two quick ones at the bar, Jimmy was moving about the big room with its crystal chandeliers and its profusion of Louis Seize, making that big effort not to relax too far.

"He seems all right," Beatrice said. "Or—does he?"

"I don't know," Francis said. "He's being careful. That could be bad."

"Let's hope." Beatrice touched Francis' arm lightly. "You know, darling, we haven't had much time with each other since the airport—dashing right off to the theater and now here. I've wanted to tell you that I love you."

Francis gazed at her, thinking, What a superbly sweet woman. "About time, too. I told you as we were coming in."

"You know I couldn't say anything then. Your Charlie Mayborn was right on top of us."

"Chicken," Francis said. "Anyway, I accept your tardy proffer of affection."

"Francis, you're full of beans tonight. Is the Court plan going well? I mean, even after that big statement from Bacon and Hume and the rest?"

"I think so. The statement was no help, of course, but I think it was inevitable—or something like it was. After all, Congress was well aware of how those justices felt about it. The statement probably will have some effect on public opinion, but I'm not sure it will be translated into votes on the Hill. The President has an effect on public opinion, too, and our friends on the Hill only have to think back to November for a reminder."

"Darling—tell me if I'm prying; you know I try not to—but how are things, well, *in* the Court?"

Francis grinned down at her. "Beatrice, you're a real gossip. You'd love me to tell you we have fistfights every day in the robing room, wouldn't you?"

"Yup. And I love you for not telling me."

"Good, because I wouldn't, of course. But if it will give you any satisfaction, I'll leak the intelligence that we are not one big happy family. Or, I might put it this way: The Court plan does not go unmentioned in our scholarly discussions."

"Mr. Justice, stop huddling with that beautiful woman!" It was Molly Evans, one hand grasping Jimmy Hughes's wrist. "I insist you spread yourself around."

"Hello, Molly," Beatrice said. "I've got him pinned down."

"Molly, you look wonderful," Francis said. She did, too; she looked so much at home in this elegance with her tall, slender figure in its straight and simple dress. Molly was a pusher with credentials.

"Every time I make for the bar, this woman intercepts me," Jimmy Hughes said. His smile as he looked at Molly was a fond one, and he gestured with his empty martini glass. "First it was Mother and now it's my big brother—with an assist from Molly. I'm terrified at the thought that they all may make something of me yet."

"I hope not," Beatrice said. She put a hand on his arm. "I like you this way. Don't you dare stop being fun."

Francis looked at Jimmy and for a moment was startled by the look of fright on his face. He looks harassed, hemmed-in, Francis thought. He wants to go somewhere but he doesn't know quite where. "Molly's motives are more simple, Jimmy," Francis said. "She's just a girl-type girl who likes men."

"Mm." Molly cuddled against Jimmy Hughes's arm. "I love men. I think it's unfair of Jimmy to try to get away from me."

"Whoops!" Jimmy Hughes said. "I was going to get another drink, but there's old gumshoe Harry Weiss. Do you suppose he'll tell my brother on me?"

Francis looked over to where Weiss was standing with Charlie Mayborn. He smiled at Jimmy. "Don't be hard on poor Harry. Besides, he's giving his full attention to the Attorney General."

"What's he drinking—yogurt?" Jimmy said. "And isn't he out rather late?"

"Jimmy, be sweet," Beatrice said. "Be your gaily handsome self."

Jimmy turned to Francis. "Francis, you're one of my oldest friends. Do you think I'm a bad advertisement for my brother—for the President of the United States?"

It was such a sudden switch that Francis could almost feel the silence. "Jimmy, don't start pulling my leg at this late date," he said. He was embarrassed, yet he felt a new sympathy and affection for Jimmy. It must be a difficult role, being brother to the President.

"Oh, I know." Jimmy seemed to be trying to brush it off, and yet his face was serious. "That was a pretty silly thing to ask." The old familiar grin came then. "It's just that I wish I could get rid of this feeling that he is so godawful right all the time—about me."

"Jimmy, you are being silly," Molly Evans said. "You know the President is fond of you."

"Yes, of course." Jimmy was still grinning. "I do know that. John has always been fine. But perhaps he'd be fonder of me if I were in Samoa."

"There's that Mr. Hoff over there," Beatrice said. "Isn't he the new lawyer for that Russian spy, Gleason?"

Francis looked over and found the short, fat Hoff talking to the Indian Ambassador. "Yes, that's the one," he said. "The newspapers quote him as saying he's gathering new evidence."

"He'll have to hurry," Jimmy Hughes said. "The new date has been set for the execution." He turned to Francis. "And you boys on the Supreme Court have already turned down the appeal. What would it take to have you consider it again, Francis?" Jimmy smiled. "If that's a proper question."

"Oh, it's proper enough," Francis said, returning the smile. "I honestly don't know, Jimmy. It would take something pretty important."

Molly Evans was not going to be left out of the conversation. "All I read about nowadays are Communists," she said. "The other day it was that awful man, Atkinson."

"Darling, Atkinson isn't a Communist," Jimmy Hughes said. "He's a Nazi."

"Oh—never mind," Molly Evans said. "It's the same thing, really. I'm so glad the District commissioners wouldn't let him speak in East Potomac Park. Really, he is such a monster."

Beatrice's brow had a worried line in it. "Yes, of course, he is a dreadful man," she said. "But—can they, should they, prevent him from making a speech?"

"Better ask Francis," Jimmy Hughes said. "Atkinson says he's going to take it to the Supreme Court."

Francis' voice was hurried. "Not now, please. Really, children, if you don't behave I'll have you all arrested for contempt of court."

Beatrice touched his arm. "Yes, sir, Mr. Justice. I'll behave. Just count me as one of the confused multitude—it seems to me that these days both the left and the right want to do over my country tomorrow. I wish they'd let me think it over first. Don't you, Jimmy?"

Jimmy bowed carefully. "Bea, I love you, but I'm going to flee."

Francis got two Scotches-on-the-rocks and handed one to Beatrice.

"Miss Krasnov, let's gulp this one and go home," he said.

"Yes yes yes, my pet. Let's hurry."

But there, suddenly, was Ian Kerr barring their way. He was in his kilts and he was waving a newspaper.

"Beatrice, my love," Ian said, and leaned forward to kiss Beatrice's cheek. "Hello, Mr. Justice. Beatrice, you've been keeping things from your friends." He clutched the newspaper to his chest. "It's right here, Beatrice. You've gone and let the papers find out before you told your friends."

"Ian, you delicious oaf, what are you talking about?" Beatrice said.

"Sweetie, don't be coy. It's right here, in Dolly Drake's column. Freddie is going to write his memoirs. His life and loves. Isn't it crazy? He's going to call it *Me and My Actresses*."

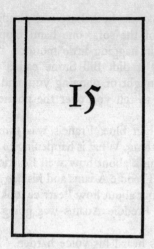

15

"BUT, BEA—MY GOD! How did this gruesome thing ever happen? How did it get out? Why on earth didn't you tell me —before that kilted little ghoul came charging up?"

"Darling, I wanted to. Please, darling. I wanted to tell you at once—as soon as I saw you. But Jimmy Hughes was in the car with us all the way from the airport, and there wasn't a single moment all evening when we were really alone."

Francis found himself examining the mantel of his fireplace as though he had never seen it before—and, incongruously, reminding himself that his father had shipped it down to Georgetown after salvaging it from the wreckage of the Hollis house on Main Street. He couldn't think coherently; his thoughts would not come in any reasonable continuity. On the way home, he had tried to absorb Beatrice's first, tentative efforts to discuss Dolly Drake's item about Freddie, and he had been unable to do so. And, more impatient with himself than with Beatrice, he had told her, "Wait. Please wait, Bea. Wait until we get home." The rest of the way home there had been only a hurtful silence.

"Bea, I'm trying so hard to think. It was such a shock."

"I know, darling. I wouldn't have wanted you to find out that way." Beatrice's look was both hurt and pleading as she sat upright on the edge of the sofa, one hand tapping her cigarette against the ashtray in nagging little motions. "I never imagined it would happen as it did. Bill Stone called me before I left New York and I thought of phoning you, and then I didn't because I didn't want to tell you over the phone, and I'd be here tonight."

She looks so well in blue, Francis was thinking. She always looks so well, in anything. What is happening to us?

But he couldn't think about how well Beatrice looked. He had to keep his mind on Freddie Adams and his *Me and My Actresses*. It did no good to think about how Beatrice looked and how much he loved her when Freddie Adams was going to write a nasty little book about her.

He felt as well as heard his voice harden. "I'd better hear all about it, Bea. You'd better tell me the whole story."

She looked up at him, the hurt look in her face now tinged with surprise. "Yes, of course, Francis. I'll tell you everything I know. It's what I've been wanting to do all day." Her voice was low, but it had a quality that told of her effort to make it so.

He looked away from her, purposefully, and he tried to keep the chill out of his voice, but it was there. "Yes. Bill Stone called you . . ."

Now Beatrice's voice had a careful recitative quality. "Yes, he called me at ten o'clock this morning. He had just talked to Freddie's lawyer. Freddie's agent had been negotiating with a publisher, and the publisher had agreed to pay Freddie an advance of fifteen thousand dollars for his—memoirs. Freddie's lawyer pointed out that Freddie had a reputation as a—a kind of ladies' man. He said the agent had assured the publisher that Freddie would be rather frank—that the book would, in his, Freddie's lawyer's words, tell all."

"God! Good God!" Francis was staring again at the mantel, and his words were ugly expletives that tasted bad in his mouth.

"Francis, please." Beatrice's voice was small, and when he turned to her Francis had to force himself not to break down and take her in his arms. He looked at her, not knowing what was in his face, but trying to keep the ugliness he felt out of it.

"Francis, you must let me tell you. I've got to, so you'll know, so no one else can surprise you." He loathed himself for his coldness toward her distress, but forced himself to keep his distance.

"Yes, of course," he said. "I've got to hear it all. Go on."

Beatrice looked at him; it was almost a stare, almost defiant. She rubbed out her cigarette carefully in the ashtray. "Freddie's lawyer said they had been patient with me but it was obvious that I was going to be hard-boiled—his term, again—about increasing the alimony. Bill said he took an injured tone—as though we had deceived him."

She lit another cigarette with a quick motion of the table lighter. Francis wondered if that was the first time he had failed to light her cigarette for her. She went on, in that toneless, grade-school-assembly-hall voice. "Freddie's lawyer said that they had had some preliminary discussions with the publisher about the book before they contacted me about increasing the alimony. He said after they talked to Bill they thought we would be—reasonable—and so they broke off the negotiations with the publisher. But then he said we had shown bad faith by quibbling about—about Freddie's financial needs."

Francis kept looking at her. He couldn't take his eyes off her, and yet he wouldn't let himself feel anything. It was not the time for feeling anything. How could he feel anything when he was thinking about the robing room and the pages who were fired when they grew too tall and the careful dignity of that courtroom—when his mind was so filled with everything that meant everything, and which he could lose, which he might have to sacrifice, if there was a Beatrice Hart in his life. When it had been up to him alone, he had always qualified for the honorable status the voters had given him, the voters and then the President of the United States. He had kept himself clean, and it had been easy, because that was the way he wanted to be, the only way he could be once he took the path to public service. And now there was someone else in his life, and if she remained in his life he no longer would have the sole prerogative of keeping the slate unblemished. Beatrice's life had to be reckoned with—her life with people like Freddie Adams. Her life would become a part of his life, a part of his record.

"It was quite horrible." Francis was aware now that there had been a pause in Beatrice's recitation, as her voice broke into his thoughts. "Bill said he tried to keep calm and he told Freddie's lawyer that they weren't being practical, that they had no assurance that the book would be as successful as they hoped, that it wouldn't bring as much money as—as Freddie could get from me."

Poor Bill Stone, Francis was thinking. Dealing with people like that, and being forced to use Beatrice's money as a lever. He would *not* think of Beatrice, now. He couldn't think of her, he couldn't pity her, until he knew everything. He had to hear it all, so he would know the complete ugliness of it.

"Bill said Freddie's lawyer laughed at him," Beatrice said, just the edge of anger in her tone. "He told Bill the publisher had assured them the book would be a best seller. He said it was the kind of juicy stuff people love to read about. He said there would be a first printing of fifty thousand and they would hire a high-pressure press agent to sell the book. Also, it seems there are two movie companies interested in it—*The Freddie Adams Story.* After all, he told Bill, they even did George Raft."

Francis broke in, although he knew the answer to the question he was posing. "You know, of course, that if the book is libelous, you'd have legal redress. You could sue Freddie for his last penny."

"Yes. And besides—it's an invasion of privacy, isn't it? But Bill said you'd understand about that. We could sue, but by that time it would be all over the papers, and the book would be out. And even if we took action before publication, the publicity would be just as bad as the book would be. The publicity's started already, as you learned from Ian Kerr."

"Yes, yes. Of course. I understand that. I suppose it's obvious that Freddie is doing all this just to hold a sword over your head so you'll come up with the money he wants."

Beatrice sounded hesitant. "Yes, Bill thinks so. But he's worried. He's afraid that if the publisher and the movies make it sound attractive enough, Freddie will go through with it. Bill says Freddie can hire some lawyers to go over the manuscript and make sure, or reasonably sure, that he is protected."

"God, I suppose so." Francis could see how it could be done.

It was all very well for Freddie's lawyer to talk about juicy stuff, but Freddie could be very careful and make certain not to overstep the bounds, and still the book would be a sensation. You could say some things, by implication, anyway, and get away with it. You could get around it. The strong point on Freddie's side was that Beatrice didn't want *any* kind of scandal, *any* kind of publicity, and neither did the Supreme Court justice who was in love with her. Whatever happened, Freddie couldn't lose. And even if Beatrice settled with him, the filthy gossip would continue, in bars and restaurants and in Georgetown drawing rooms. And Francis would be aware of it, by a look and a sudden silence when he walked in the door, even in the robing room of the Supreme Court of the United States.

He looked at Beatrice, but not into her eyes; the way her eyes looked tonight made him want to cry. "It's not very good, Bea. It looks as if we can't win—it looks as if Freddie has already won." He tried, but he couldn't stop the huge sigh from escaping.

"Oh, Francis. My poor, dear Francis. That was what I was afraid of. All the way on the plane, I was afraid we couldn't win. I didn't want to believe it. But now you've said it; now I have to believe it."

"Bea, my very dear." He wanted to take her into his arms, but he couldn't. He didn't dare to touch her, because this was a time for cold, clear thinking, and he would not be able to think if he touched her. It stirred his anger, and now his laugh was a short, impatient burst of sound. "Goddamn him. Goddamn Freddie. He holds all the cards. We have to believe in his strength this time. He knows, now, that he can wreck us if he chooses."

"Francis." Beatrice's voice was calm, but the quality of it told of its artificiality, the effort that created it. "That is what I have been thinking—all day, all evening. That Freddie can wreck us. *Us.* What we want to be to each other."

Her voice frightened him. "Bea, what do you mean? I said—wreck us. I didn't mean it—that way. How can he wreck us?" *How can he wreck us?* he asked, knowing the answer, but ragingly refusing to face it.

"Francis—he can. We have to face it. We have to look at that side of it—it's the only side, really. It's the only important

225

thing, because nothing else matters to me but you—you and your life, what you are. I cannot let you be hurt."

"Bea." He found both arms going out to her, in a gesture of supplication, as though he wanted help, wanted her to deny what she had just said, what was terribly implied by her words. "You are overwrought. He cannot wreck *us.*" *Yes he can, goddammit. Goddamn him.*

She was still sitting up straight, her body determined to be strong. "Please, Francis, you—you aren't being realistic. Freddie, in one way or another, obviously intends to smear my name all over the gossip columns and probably across the front pages. He's already started. We've got to do something before he smears you, you and your career."

He walked to the sofa and sat down and took her hand, and she let him take it. That was all. She just let him take it; she did not give it to him. Her hand was cold and she did not look at him but stared ahead at the mantel. "Bea, I don't understand. I will not understand what you are saying, what you are trying to do." But he did understand and he would understand, because even though it angered him, he was interested in the simplicity of her solution; it would solve everything—from the selfish viewpoint of Mr. Justice Dalton.

"Darling, I wish you had not taken my hand. I wish you had not sat down here with me. You're making it hard for me to say what I think should be done. But I am going to say it. I must say it, because you know what has to be done, too. You know, even if you won't admit you know."

He put a hand to her chin and turned her face to him. Her eyes were bright and moist but they were—businesslike. "Yes, Bea, I know what you're suggesting. But I won't let you put it into so many words. Of course it would be a solution. There is always that kind of solution. But I will not let you make it our solution." Why didn't he take her into his arms? Was it because he wanted to hear more? Was it because those thoughts kept jabbing at him, those thoughts about the robing room and an obligation to your government and how there were things that disqualified a public servant from serving that government?

She took her hand gently out of his and stood up and walked over to the mantel and leaned against it—for support? "Francis, please—you must be realistic. You can't let this hurt you. I won't let you. I won't let you offer yourself up as a—sacrifice."

He looked at her hard. "And I won't let you suggest what you want to suggest, Bea. I love you. I won't say that is all that matters. Other things matter, too—but they are outside of us, outside of what we are to each other. They're my problems, not yours, not ours."

"No, darling, they're our problem—mine, too. Francis, I have to say this to you, even though it tears me apart. I can't let you have a love that destroys you, because you're more than just Francis Dalton, whom I love. You know that; you've spoken to me so many times of how you feel about people in government service. And I've always understood and respected you, admired you, for it. You can't change how you think. You can't change the man that is you. You can't alter your moral stand on what is right and what is wrong for a man in government."

Francis cut in, his voice harsh with self-impatience, self-irritation. "Bea, I can't let you struggle so with yourself as well as with me. I'm confused and disturbed, but I can't let you struggle. We mustn't think this way." He started to get up, but Beatrice said, "Please, Francis, don't get up. Just sit there so we can talk. We've got to talk this way, with a part of the room between us."

"All right." He managed a little smile. "I'll sit here." Did he actually *want* to hear more?

She wouldn't look at him. "I have to finish, Francis. I have to tell you that I love you. There's never been anyone else, ever. And I know you love me. I couldn't be coy about that, because I can be sure—you've made me sure. But, Francis, there's another part of you that can't be denied. You can't deny it. If you did, you'd be untrue to everything you've ever stood for. You're a member of the Supreme Court and you're proud of it. You have a terrible responsibility to that Court. You have to deserve to be on that bench. You have to satisfy yourself completely that you deserve it."

She stopped and lit another cigarette. "Francis, what I have to say is that this thing with Freddie has changed things. I have to put it bluntly or I won't be able to say it at all. If he goes through with this smear campaign, we'll have to postpone all our plans."

His voice was steady, carefully so. His rage at what had happened was cold now, now that she had said the words he feared so much. "Bea, you mean we won't be able to get married?"

She cut in as he started to say something more. "Please, Francis, hear me out. I love you, but that is what I do mean. Oh, Francis, Francis—don't you see? You don't belong only to me. You also belong to the state. The state, the people—however you want to call the organism that employs you—they've entrusted you with a position of responsibility and honor. Honor, Francis. You have to be faithful to that trust. You can't let scandal touch you—not because you're Francis Dalton, but because you are Mr. Justice Dalton, a servant of the state. You've sworn to protect your government not only from its enemies at home and abroad but also from yourself—from anything about you, anything that might attach itself to you, that would detract from the reputation of the state."

He got up and stood in front of the sofa, looking at her. Poor darling, he was thinking. Poor honest, decent Beatrice Hart. And she has to talk that way because that is the way she was born. That is the kind of woman she is. But I have had a hand in it, too, with all my puritanical talk about my honored position and my grave responsibilities and my petty criticism of public officials who stooped to being human and kissed the wrong girl. Now, again, he could hear Alice O'Sullivan over the lunch table: *You not only licked the Yankees, but you appropriated their stiff-necked righteousness. . . . I hope you won't let all this Puritanism stand in your way when you meet the authentic, bottled-in-bond Somebody. Don't be stuffy . . . you'll screw it all up.*

He said, "Bea, I have to stop you now. You can't talk any more of this—rubbish." He went to her, in long strides, and she seemed to be retreating from him without moving, but he took her in his arms. For a moment, she was just there—not coming into his arms, but merely being in them. But then she came to him and he held her as close as he could, the two of them just standing there silent—and together.

After a long time, she stirred and his arms loosened about her and she looked up at him and now there was a brimming in her eyes. "My dearest dear," he said, and he kissed her with hurting gentleness.

"Francis, please," she said.

"No, Bea. No, my darling," he said. "I can't let you talk any more. I don't want to hear that kind of talk. We'll talk about what *we* will do about it—what we will do together, you and I."

"Oh, darling, thank you." She pressed her face hard to his shoulder. "I have to thank you—just for wanting me. For still wanting me, as I still want you. But we do have to talk, darling. I can't let you—win, completely, for your sake—for both our sakes, really, darling."

"Then let's sit down." He took her hand and led her to the sofa, and plucked a cigarette from the box and lit it for her and put it to her lips. I am still frightened, he thought, but now it's an honest fear, a man's fear. It won't hurt me the way that other fear was hurting me. I'm no longer afraid for myself, but for us.

"Francis, you know—we can't just ignore this in the hope it will go away. It won't go away, darling. Freddie's vicious, because he's never quite grown up."

"No, I know it won't go away. I don't fool myself. But I want us to face it together, somehow."

"Francis, are you sure?" She looked at him gravely, searchingly.

He thought: Am I sure? And felt happy relief when the answer came so swiftly. "Yes, I am. That is, I'm sure I want us, whatever happens. I'm not sure of how the situation should be—handled. I don't want a scandal, Bea. I'd be lying if I said it didn't matter, and you'd know it. I want somehow to avoid a scandal, but I don't know how to do it."

"You mustn't have a scandal. That's the whole point. It's even more complicated, more perilous now—now with you involved in the President's campaign for his Court plan. They'll be ready to jump on you. You know that. They couldn't wait to use your —involvement with me—to hurt you and the President."

"I know that, Bea. It frightens me." He smiled as he heard her little gasp. "It frightens me, Bea—but what I feel is not panic. I have to be concerned about my position, because it affects a man I respect and admire who is in the White House and who doesn't deserve to be hurt by criticism I may have earned. I want to save John Hughes from that. But I want to do it without sacrificing us. I will not sacrifice us, no matter what."

"But, Francis, if they crowd you . . ."

"If they crowd me, we'll see. I hope the situation won't arise. But if they do crowd me, I'll do whatever has to be done."

"Francis! You will not—you cannot—sacrifice yourself, your position." Her voice was high with sudden fear.

"Bea, you mustn't be panicky, either." He took both her hands in his. "I haven't said what I'll do, if *anything* becomes necessary. I'm going to see to it that it doesn't come to that. Somehow, I'm going to see to it. But there is to be no more talk about sacrificing us. I won't hear of it, I won't listen to it." He started to think: *But if only this hadn't happened* . . . But he put the thought away contemptuously, glad to put it away.

"Darling, you mustn't do this all alone. I won't let you. I've got to help."

He looked at her. "You'll help, Bea. You are helping. By being with me. At my side."

"No, no, Francis. That's just it." Her eyes were wide with concern. "That's something I have to do for you—*not* to be at your side. For a while."

"Not be at my side? Bea, we've discussed all that, and dismissed it. I love you. I want you with me."

"And I love you and I want to be with you. But I can't be with you, darling, not now. Not for a while. I mustn't dare to—for your sake, for *our* sake. No, let me finish, darling. Don't you see? For a while we've got to stop seeing each other—until, somehow, we resolve this—this sordid little problem. I've got to go back to New York and stay there and help Bill Stone fight my battle with Freddie. Not because he needs me particularly, but because we can't be in the same town, darling. We can't give Freddie and his pet columnists any grounds—any more grounds —for their ugly little gossip."

"But, Bea, I don't want you to leave." No, he didn't want her to leave. But she was right. She should go back to New York, to her Gramercy Park apartment, and wait. And he should wait here, alone. She was right. And—goddamn his selfishness—he was relieved.

"Oh, darling, I don't want to leave, either. You know that. But I must. It's logical, it's reasonable, and you are a reasonable man."

Yes, he was a reasonable man. He had always been a reasonable man. And Bea was talking reason. She was right. Bless her, God bless her, she was so right and so wonderfully *good*. And he was *relieved*.

"All right. All right, Bea. You're right. It will, I suppose—help—if we aren't seeing each other. It can be our first counter-blow against that goddamned Freddie. Goddamn him again for forcing us to be apart."

"Yes, darling, goddamn him. But we do have to be sensible, and it won't be forever—we'll be doing it so that we can be together forever. You've got to let me do what I can, however pitifully small it is."

"Small." Francis felt hoarse with a mixture of anger and frustration and, suddenly, a new surge of love for her. "It isn't small. It's you taking the blame for what's happened. It's you implying that somehow you could hurt me by being with me, by being seen with me."

"No, Francis, it's just me facing facts. And I'm honest enough to realize that it could hurt you, in some people's dirty minds, if we were seen together. Francis, I do feel pretty pure, really, but I do face facts. I have been foolish enough to acquire a past. That was my fault, darling, even though you are too wonderful to admit it. And now I have a chance to make up for it, a little—to become, oh, Caesar's wife and all that. I owe that to you. I'm proud of the way you feel, and I want to help you to continue to feel that way."

"My dearest," Francis said. "You are—pretty wonderful. I hope I deserve you."

Beatrice grinned. "So do I, darling. But you won't if you keep on insisting on compromising me. Darling, I feel so silly for having practically wept all over your nice dinner jacket. I've got to start acting more adult. And the first step is to go home; it's already three o'clock."

"Go home! Bea . . ." Francis looked startled.

"Yes, darling, go home to the Carlton. We've got to start somewhere, and you've got to help me by getting my coat and calling me a cab."

"Calling you a cab? Bea." He started to say that it took hours to get a cab in Georgetown at three o'clock in the morning, and was outraged at the colossal irrelevancy of the thought.

"Darling Francis, my lion." Bea grinned up at him. "Please don't be difficult. We do have to *start*. Let me, darling. Help me."

Beatrice Hart, Francis was thinking, I have to deserve you someday.

"All right." He smiled back at her. "All right, I'll let you go. But before I get your coat and call your cab, promise me something."

"Of course, darling. What is it?"

"That I can kiss you—chastely—good night." Francis grinned.

Beatrice grinned. "Chastely, hell! Now go get my coat, Mr. Justice Dalton, so we can get the performance started."

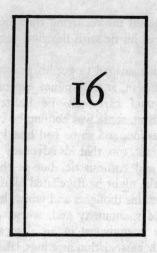

16

EVENTS WERE PILING ON TOP OF EACH OTHER too fast; frantically, Francis wanted to stand up and cry "Stop!" so there
would be the time and the serenity of atmosphere to think of Beatrice. Washington, in the midst of the battle over the President's
Court-packing plan, was like the swift assembly line of a monstrous Chaplin-style factory, turning out events and crises hourly,
and ever quickening the pace to meet the demands of the politicians' speedup. Beatrice was back in her apartment in New York,
and he tried to picture her in the cloistered confines of Gramercy
Park, seeking to see her in the pursuit of everyday minutiae so
that he could regain something of his old familiarity with her. But
instead his mind was too filled with reports from Bill Stone that
Freddie was going ahead with the book while continuing negotiations for the alimony increase; this was Freddie, adept at the
show business tactic of cat-and-mouse. Francis cringed for Beatrice at the little paragraphs in the gossip columns about Freddie's
book; his own name had not been mentioned yet, but he scarcely
noticed the omission. When and if his name came into the gossip,
he felt now it would have little effect on him. It no longer seemed

important, and he hated the recurring thought that he could be safe, if he had severed his tie with Beatrice; yet the thought continued to recur.

Somehow, Francis managed to get his pressing chores done in behalf of the Court plan, at only minor expense to his work on the bench. He *would* carry on, he insistently repeated to himself. At the moment, there was nothing he could do about the Freddie Adams situation, and so he had best keep busy at other things. He told himself, too, that his advocacy of the Court plan was still vigorous and enthusiastic, but in the honesty of the gloomy middle of the night he flagellated himself for the doubts he permitted to assail his thoughts and which he knew were robbing his speeches of spontaneity and, worse, of the ability—or willingness?—to be unequivocal in his advocacy. He made his rounds dutifully to bar association meetings, labor conventions and chambers of commerce, where he greeted and was greeted by old friends ready to yield to genteel pressure—and somehow his proselytizing fell flat. He seemed to keep hearing Hume's words, bland in tone but vital in their meaning: *creatures of our own thinking,* conclusions arrived at *honestly and independently,* the *delicate* rights of man. But Hume was wrong; in his insistence on his pet absolutes, the Hoosier would permit if not condone the kind of license—or at least the kind of extravagant exercise of those rights —that was perilous to a country beset on all sides by a worldwide nationalism menacingly sleek with nuclear stockpiles. How could the country be held together, in the face of the discipline of the Communist imperialists and the new regimented forces of the nationalistic neutrals, so-called, unless the country submitted to its own brand of discipline? To Francis, the attractive liberals were merely that; the charm of their free-wheeling, free-thinking philosophies and measures for the public welfare made no provision for the national belt-tightening required by the times. He hammered away at this thesis wherever he spoke—and yet somehow always fell short of spelling out his absolute support for the President's Court plan. Sometimes he told himself that it would not be fitting for a Supreme Court justice to so spell out his advocacy, but he knew he was merely trying to rationalize a mind experimenting with doubts. The country was prosperous, but it was fearful and nervous about the threats from abroad and, because of the violence of such agitators as the Sons of Slaves and the supporters of the spy Gleason and the Nazi Atkinson, about the creeping danger of anarchy at home. Francis could tell himself that something had to be done to give the President a freer hand in gaining the legislation needed to cope with these threats. He was convinced the Court had become obstructionist. He believed that somehow something had to be done so that the executive and the judicial branches could find an accommodation. It had to be the President's plan, he told himself. And yet . . .

Yet, the administration was maintaining its lead, and Francis felt he could take some of the credit. McAdam wasn't satisfied, of course; the Senate Majority Leader still harped on the static situation, and besides, in many years on Capitol Hill, McAdam had learned never to be satisfied where politicians were concerned. It worried McAdam, too, that Claude Wilkins had emerged so spectacularly as the leader of the opposition; the administration could match Wilkins's efforts with its own, but the independent had too much prestige for the administration to risk any blows below his belt or even to quarrel too acrimoniously with his stand. It no longer baffled McAdam that the liberals should be so quiescent; he now recognized the strategy which called for them to work behind the scenes while using Wilkins's oratory as a front for their opposition. It was the liberals the President had trounced in November, not the independents, and although Wilkins's was only one of three or four independent voices being heard, his credit with both moderates and conservatives was such that he was being listened to far beyond his party's strength at the polls.

On both sides, the crises erupted, big and small—and often amusing. The liberals' strategy of lying low in public was threatened for a hectic several hours by the angry stubbornness of Jim Clayton, still smarting over his humiliating defeat by John Alden Hughes. The liberals' Presidential ex-candidate was scheduled as the main speaker at the annual dinner of the party's national committee at the Sheraton-Park Hotel, and to Senator Frank Hoar came the sudden and startling intelligence that Clayton had drafted a fiery denunciation of the Court plan, with chiding asides to the electorate that it was getting only what it deserved for deserting the liberal cause. The news came late; Clayton was arriving in Washington that afternoon for his speech, and a phone call to his home in Des Moines brought word he had left sooner than expected.

"The son of a bitch," Cliff Sampson said. "That bastard wants to screw us up."

Hoar was inclined to agree with the Minority Leader; Clayton had a persecution complex—and no wonder. But they had to get to him.

Hoar looked at Sampson and dismissed him as the answer. Sampson would take a couple of drinks and then, probably, punch Clayton on the nose.

"I'll see him," Hoar said.

He met Clayton at the airport and Clayton was immediately suspicious.

"What the hell are you meeting me for?" he asked irritably. "You never do anything, Frank Hoar, unless you want to interfere with somebody."

"Jim, goddammit, come and get in my car," Hoar said. Clayton tired a man out. "I just want to talk to you for the good of the party."

It took two hours of talk in Clayton's suite in the Mayflower and Hoar had to send out for reinforcements: young Bill Martin, who lent the influence of an authentic fire-eater, and Dan Lewis, who had always had a soothing effect on Clayton. The three Senators, happily parading their man-to-man, Western ties as representatives of Ohio, Oklahoma and Oregon, thus had a head start in their argument with the Iowan, and at the outset there was considerable talk of an anti-Wall Street nature. Clayton sometimes suspected Hoar's Western credentials as a delegate from Ohio, but Hoar as usual leaned heavily on his Nebraskan birth. Clayton's bad temper was soothed as the first order of business, and then Senator Martin led the attack with an appeal to party loyalty based on the party's burning hatred for John Alden Hughes. As rewritten by Hoar and Lewis, the speech delivered by Jim Clayton was a wondrous collection of generalities which only mildly suggested that the Court-packing plan was sinful.

Francis did not have the same luck with Lawrence Sprague. The Secretary of the Treasury, in his chilly way, had been leery of the Court-packing plan from the beginning, but Hughes insisted on trying to bring Sprague into the campaign. Francis dutifully informed the President that Sprague was showing reluctance, but Hughes was blithely unconcerned. "I won't put it on the basis of the President directing him to help out," Hughes told Francis. "I'm damned if I feel I have to do that. Sprague is a good man, but he is my appointee, after all, and I think he should cooperate. Please handle him, Francis."

Francis winced. He felt he could have handled Sprague if he had been permitted to pass on the speech the President wanted Sprague to deliver to the American Bankers' Association. The speech had been written by Ed O'Hara, but for some reason the usually trenchant National Chairman had drafted an implausible and specious appeal which Francis knew would outrage Sprague's frosty nature.

Sprague read the speech carefully, his pointed nose quivering, then tossed it aside.

"I won't make a speech like that," Sprague said. "I wouldn't make a speech like that to a crowd of settlement-house workers."

And Francis was unable to sway him, despite the President's reluctant acquiescence to the suggestion that the speech was a White House request.

"I won't do it," Sprague said. "I'll have it out with the President." He grinned. "Why don't you give it to our Secretary of State, the lugubrious Douglas Colfax Wilson? If you can get the son of a bitch out of church, that is."

Francis was in the President's study the night Claude Wilkins addressed the AFL-CIO convention in Miami. There were only four of them in the room—the President, Francis, Charlie Mayborn and Harry Weiss. It was a confident little gathering. Mayborn, more the politician now and less the Attorney General, was full of hearty gloating over Hughes's decision to take the stump, and Weiss seemed encouraged by the day's reports from the Hill, which told of Chet McAdam's latest successes in pressuring senators on the patronage front. The President was relaxed, pleased now that he was about to go charging into battle.

"I'm not admitting I wasn't right in the first place, Charlie," Hughes said. "I'm not going to let you burst with smugness. But I must confess I relish a little action."

"It's what we need," Mayborn said, every syllable a comfortable one. "No use wasting time with our second team."

The President grinned. "All right, Charlie. I'm properly soothed. You'll have to have it out with Mother when she gets back, though."

"Yes." Mayborn's happy thoughts seemed to come to a pause. "I suppose she's kind of—disappointed."

"Disappointed! She's sore," the President said. "But you know, she has great restraint. She's quite a guy."

"A lady," Mayborn said. "There aren't many left." Mayborn meant it.

Wilkins was everything the opposition had promised—an old-fashioned spellbinder who yet was completely at home before a television camera. His phrases were florid, but they were delivered in such a clean-cut style that they did not seem outdated. There was a kind of genius in Wilkins's ability to indulge in such bathos as the sorrowful "I am speaking tonight from the depths of a soul filled with bitterness." And there was a force curiously not out of keeping with the ultramodern medium when he spoke of the attempt to "foist judicial sycophants upon the nation" and bitterly charged the President with "an attempt to rape the Supreme Court."

When it was over, Hughes's sigh could be heard all over the room.

"I don't know how that man does it, but he's brought William Jennings Bryan back into style," the President said.

"He's good," Mayborn said—and then, his valuable, politically one-track mind working, "I wish we had him. He gets to the folks."

"An honorable foe," Hughes said. "I'd like him on our side merely because of what he is. It's curious, that bow tie wouldn't do a thing for most people, but it seems to add to the man's integrity. I remember, it was the same way with Elmer Davis."

"Well, we did our best," Francis said. "I don't think he'd have ever come along. The Court plan isn't his cup of tea."

"I wonder." Hughes's nervous hand clawed at his unruly black hair. "I wonder if I did my best. You did what you could, as well as it could be done, Francis, but I'm afraid I was rather clumsy."

Francis started to speak, but the reassuring words wouldn't come. The President's approach to Wilkins *had* been clumsy, considering Wilkins's character. Even if Wilkins had gone along, he'd have insisted on directing the show, and it was more likely he'd have dropped out. Wilkins didn't trust the Court plan.

Mayborn was the practical politician. "We made the pitch. It's the kind of thing you try to do. That's the way things are done. It didn't work because Chet McAdam wouldn't get out of the way. No sense in your feeling guilty, Mr. President."

"Oh, I don't—really." Hughes was cheerful. "But I see now that it was a blunder. I knew McAdam better than that and yet I tried to fool myself. I'd just feel better if I'd put it to Wilkins as the respectable piece of political logic I believe it is."

"He'd have turned you down cold, sir," Harry Weiss put in. "Even Claude Wilkins doesn't do anything for nothing."

"I wonder," Hughes said. "Even now I wouldn't mind having Wilkins's advice on those two new judges—if we get them. I don't like to talk this way, because it sounds disloyal to McAdam, but there you are. Chet could be a problem."

Mayborn's throat-clearing was a massive business. "I've been worried about that, too. It's not a question of suspecting Chet's loyalty or integrity. It's just—well, chemistry."

Right, Francis was thinking. Or, how safe is a reformed liberal?

"It's something I have to face, and yet I can't think what can be done about it," the President said. "McAdam was first elected to the House as a liberal and he was an authentic one, a real fighter. He came around to our conservative side when the tide was turning, but when it was still risky to talk that way in New York State. That recommends him. And yet—early environment and indoctrination can be a lasting thing, even when a man makes an about-face. And he's still a typical New York politician. It would not be incredible if he reverted."

"It sure wouldn't," Mayborn said. "Especially if he made the Court. The Supreme Court is about the safest place in the world to revert to political type. Too late to do anything about it if he does. And then he'd probably be dragging another like-minded judge onto the bench with him. It's a problem."

"Well, it's a problem I can't do much about, if anything," Hughes said. "McAdam has been promised the job, and he's been promised he'll be the chief consultant on the other appointment. That's that."

"Yes, that's that." Mayborn seemed thoughtful. "Unless, of course, something happens to cancel out the promise."

"Yes?" Hughes's left eyebrow was up.

"Like McAdam suddenly getting scared of the voters and reverting while he's still in the Senate." Mayborn's voice was matter-of-fact. "Seems to me that would relieve you of the responsibility of making good on the promise."

Hughes looked hard at Mayborn. "All right, Charlie, this is ugly talk and I don't like it, but I suppose we have to talk it and hear it sometimes. At any rate, I have to tolerate it because there is no point in my Court plan if I don't get the kind of justices I want. Yes, I think that's a responsibility I can expect Chet McAdam to share. You're good for me, Charlie. You make me think the unpleasant thoughts that are necessary in politics. We'll have to see. I think Chet will turn out all right. He's been very good under those pressures from New York."

"Yes, sir—so far." Mayborn's face was naked of expression. "I guess we have every reason to depend on him."

"And after all, we can't have Claude Wilkins now," the President said.

Hughes got up to signify that the meeting was over, but said, "Francis, could you stay for a few minutes?"

Francis said, "Of course, sir," and Mayborn and Weiss, filing out, looked determinedly unconcerned.

"Francis, let's have a drop of brandy," the President said. He dug into a drawer of his desk and came out with a bottle, then got up and took a couple of brandy snifters out of the glass-doored cabinet he used to store his guns. "Sit down here, Francis," he said, gesturing at the chair alongside his desk on his right.

"Cheers!" Francis said, and they both took a sip of their brandy.

Hughes sighed, leaning back in his chair. "Man, I am tired, but I'm beginning to get my second wind. I suppose it's because I'm about to take a stronger role in this dogfight."

"You've always been happier up front where the noses are being bloodied," Francis said. "Sometimes I think you enjoy campaigning more than you do counting the votes on Election Day."

Hughes laughed. "I enjoy campaigning, all right, but perhaps not that much. Those twenty-two-hour days in the Midwest tire me even in recollection. I have a couple of things on my mind. First, I'm a little worried about you."

"Worried about me?" Francis' surprise was sincere. "I don't understand. Why, sir?"

"Hell, Francis, you're one of the few men I know who could address me as John, and I wouldn't be upset about the office losing dignity. Those were pretty good days—the John-and-Francis days."

Francis said, "Well, things have changed—you are the President now."

Hughes smiled. "I understand, Francis. You're a man with your own set of rules, too. But, Francis, you do seem a little tired lately, a little sluggish."

Francis smiled. "I suppose I hadn't been aware of it. I'm sure I feel all right."

"No, you're honest, Francis, and I'm afraid you don't feel too all right—about everything. You're doing a good job for me, on the Court plan. It's taking up a lot of your time, and I shouldn't complain. But I have to notice and I have to tell you I've noticed that your work doesn't seem to have the old zip these days. Is something worrying you—about the plan, about our tactics?"

"No." It wasn't a complete lie, because Francis could not have put his finger on what was bothering him, and so there was no use in even implying that he was bothered. "Nothing bothers me —specifically."

"Specifically? Then, perhaps, something is troubling you generally?"

"Mr. President . . ." Francis felt the urgency in his tone. "I can't even say that. I suppose the only thing I can say is that perhaps I feel differently about what my role should be, how I should operate, than you do. I try to do my work for the Court plan with a consciousness of the position I hold."

"Oh." It was a flat monosyllable. "And that means—" Hughes's face was a little more set.

"I don't suppose it means anything significantly different from the way you see it, Mr. President. As I see it, I have to be more discreet in how I operate—and more discreet in how I phrase my public utterances. It's just that."

"I see." Hughes leaned forward. "And I suppose that's why I've noticed, in your speeches, a kind of—tentativeness. A disposition to rely more on lofty phrases, moralistic generalities. You don't feel you should demand, in so many words, that my Court plan be passed."

This is getting sticky, Francis thought, but if that is the way it has to be, all right.

"I don't suppose I've thought of it in that way," Francis said. "But yes, I expect that is it. What I mean is, I don't believe I can operate as, say, Chet McAdam operates, or Charlie Mayborn, or Harry Weiss."

"I see, Francis. I thought I saw before, but now I do see. You are conscious of your robes, is that it?"

"I suppose that's one way to put it. I'm conscious of my office, not of who I am as a person." Little prickling sensations of irritation traveled up the back of Francis' neck.

"Yes." The Washington monosyllable of polite impatience, Francis reflected. Hughes leaned back in his chair and sighed. "All right. I have to say that I had expected a little more of you. A more enthusiastic advocacy, perhaps. A taking off of the gloves and slugging away. You were always good at it, you know." He held up a hand. "Well, all right. Let it stand, for now; there's no use arguing about it. Except." He paused and reached for a cigarette and held it between thumb and forefinger to examine it. "Except I do have to remind you of something. When a President needs help, he feels an urgency about it. He wants that help, and he is determined to get it. He feels it is fitting to ask—and get— that help from his friends. From people he has helped." Again, as Francis started to speak, he held up his hand. "No, let me finish, please. And so what I have to say, Francis, is that if I decide I need even more help from you, I shall have to ask you to make the effort."

The hot prickling irritation gave way to something icy. "Yes, sir, I understand," Francis said. "And I shall have to decide whether it is right and proper for me to give it to you."

Hughes looked at him for a long moment, then took the lighter from the desk and lit his cigarette. "Yes," he said, his words coming through the little cloud of smoke. "Yes, you will. You will have to tell me how you feel."

Francis said nothing. He could not have said anything—not anything with grace in it. And yet the hot irritation and the something icy had been replaced by a sadness. John Hughes was his old friend. He did not want to hurt his friend. He did not want anything to happen to their friendship. Not because John Hughes was President, but because he was John Hughes.

Suddenly, then—as had happened so often—John Hughes smiled. "It's all right, Francis. I do respect you. You know that. And—we are friends, of course. That doesn't change." He leaned forward again on the desk, his hands clasped before him. "But I'm the President, and a President has to be tough—with everybody—when he wants to get something done. That always comes first."

"Yes," Francis said. "I understand." He had been close enough to John Hughes, in the White House, to know it was true.

Hughes stood up. "Francis, I'm falling asleep. I've got to get to bed." He walked over in front of the desk and as Francis stood up, he gave Francis his hand. "Thank you for staying. I suppose I do—lean on you, quite a bit. A habit you get into with old campaign friends."

"Thank you, Mr. President," Francis said. "We all do our best."

"Yes," Hughes said. They stood there looking at each other for a moment, and Hughes smiled and Francis smiled, and as Francis started to walk toward the door, Hughes stopped him.

"Francis, somebody showed me a little clipping about Beatrice's husband—Freddie Adams—today. That's a hell of a thing. I'm damned sorry for Beatrice's sake—and for yours. Somebody should kick that bastard in the ass."

Francis stopped and turned. Hughes's face was solemn, but friendly. "Yes," Francis said, "it's not very pretty. He's a vicious man."

"Yes, vicious for pay. I am damned sorry to hear about it. You know how fond I am of Beatrice."

"Thank you, Mr. President. It's nice to hear you say that."

"I say it because I mean it. Beatrice is a great lady. I hope it won't hurt her too much, but I'm afraid it won't do her any good."

"We're doing what we can—Bill Stone and I," Francis said. "We may be able to handle him."

"Good. I hope so. She doesn't deserve to be hurt."

"No, she doesn't." As he said it, Francis was aware of the deep look the President was giving him. There was a moment's silence and then the President coughed a dry cough.

"No, Francis—and neither do you deserve to be hurt," Hughes said. "I don't want you to be hurt. You're not only a Supreme Court justice, you're my friend. Watch out you don't get hurt."

Francis looked at the President. He knew what John Hughes meant, as President of the United States. What Hughes meant was *You had better not get hurt, Francis, or else.*

"Thank you." Francis' words were short. "I'll watch out— Mr. President. Good night." He walked to the door and opened it and went out.

Charlie Mayborn hated to fly, and he would still hate to fly after Jerry Bates had finished reassuring him, and Francis was amused as always by the sales job the President's personal pilot was doing on the Attorney General.

"I tell you, I feel a lot safer in this little ol' *Bounce* than I do driving my car," Colonel Bates was saying. "I don't take half as good care of my car as we do this little ol' plane. And boy, those other drivers!"

"Yes." Mayborn wanted specifics. "I've read about all the safety precautions—but what exactly do you fellows do, Colonel?"

"Well, sir, take last week. We flew the *Bounce* up to Friendship Airport in Baltimore to practice emergency landings. First we made an instrument landing, the kind we'd have to make if we couldn't see where we were going. Then we made a practice bad approach, as if the field was closed in. We made believe an engine was on fire and we went through all the emergency procedures to put it out. We landed with one engine dead and then another one limping. Hell, Mr. Attorney General, it was like eatin' ice cream and cake. We practice every chance we get, just to make sure."

"I shouldn't think you men would need any more practice," Francis said, leading Bates on for Mayborn's sake. "Didn't you and your copilot both fly the Hump during the war?"

Bates grinned easily. "Yes, sir, we sure did. Six thousand hours of it, over the toughest Himalayan terrain you can find. We learned how to fly, all right. But the pilot who gets cocky is the pilot who should quit flying. Ernie and I, we like to make sure. Hell, Mr. Justice, we got eighty-six men in our maintenance crew. Commercial airlines change their jet engines every twelve hundred to two thousand hours; we change ours every eight hundred. Nothing can happen to this little ol' plane—and we keep making sure it can't." He turned to Mayborn. "You're safer in this plane, Mr. Attorney General, than you would be crossing Fourteenth at F Street."

"What's on the luncheon menu?" Francis asked.

"Steak for you gentlemen," Bates said. "But, let's see—just going to Chicago. I don't suppose the Boss will want anything but his regular little ol' bowl of chili. Man, he *likes* that chili. He should of been a Texan. Chili—we always have about a dozen cans of chili in the galley, and some beer, and always plenty of vanilla ice cream. That's what the Boss likes. I guess, being rich and all, he got enough steaks when he was a kid."

Bates turned and pointed to the fuel truck moving away from the plane. "Look at that truck, Mr. Attorney General. The fuel in that truck was sealed twenty-four hours ago, for security. Before we fueled up, we drained off about a gallon of the stuff and analyzed it to make sure it was just right—not too much of any one component. The fuel truck is always under guard, just like the *Bounce*." He interrupted himself. "There's the President's car now. Gotta go, gentlemen."

Inside the *Bounce*, Francis looked about him as he fastened the safety belt attached to the roomy beige armchair. A few steps behind them, John Alden Hughes was settling himself into his upholstered high-backed chair before the mahogany desk with its radiotelephone, typewriter, dictating machine and the silver carafe which Francis knew contained a mixture of orange and lemon juice.

The President looked over at Francis and Mayborn, sitting side by side. "Everything all right, Charlie?"

Mayborn managed a smile. "Yes, sir, I guess so. It's a nice day, anyway."

"Jerry Bates has just been giving him aid and comfort," Francis said. "I think he may have sold Charlie on flying."

"Pay attention to Jerry," the President said. "He's the cream of the Air Force, Charlie."

"Yes, sir," Mayborn said. He grinned. "I just wish those Wright brothers had gone into politics, instead."

"Oh, well, some Russian would have invented it if they hadn't," the President said. "Charlie, after we get up I want to go over this speech of mine once more." His voice was comforting. "I'll come over and sit down with you. I want to get a little more of the ring of victory in it; after all, this is a victory dinner."

"Yes, sir," Mayborn said. "Just so long as we don't tone down the stuff about the Court plan." He looked around him, like a wise old owl, seemingly interested only in the wallpaper covering the sides of the cabin with its pictures of the Capitol, Big Ben, the Eiffel Tower and an assortment of Kremlin domes. Mayborn liked to talk about victory as much as the next politician, but for the present, and for the near future, the only thing that was important to the Attorney General was the Court plan.

"I promise to be good," the President said. "We won't alter the approach, Charlie, but I do want to pass out a few bouquets to the boys who worked so hard."

But throughout most of the flight, the President was busy with the radiotelephone. Francis assumed he was talking to the Joint War Room in Washington about the incidents along the Yugoslav-Hungarian border. They appeared to be the usual thing—a few rifle shots and menacing postures—but the situation was so fluid in Eastern Europe that they could have important significance. The Yugoslavs were worried about those German talks with the Soviets, too, and there was a trigger-happy excitement in the atmosphere. The Yugoslavs—and the Czechs and the Poles and the Romanians—were sensitive about the possible danger to their frontiers of any German-Soviet decision to do business with each other.

Francis peered far forward and repressed a shudder at the sight of the solemn Army warrant officer, sitting upright in his seat, looking straight ahead. He was, Francis knew, one of the five warrant officers who guarded night and day the slim black case that contained the complicated codes by which the President of the United States could send American missiles with nuclear warheads hissing to any part of the world. The black case was at the President's hand wherever he traveled, and although its presence gave Francis reassurance, it also lent a frightful quality to the flights of his imagination. It was at least sobering to know that even when the President slept in the White House, one of the five warrant officers was outside in the great hall, the case in his hand, and when he sailed on his yacht there was a warrant officer in sailor's garb aboard. With the warning time for a nuclear assault reduced to fifteen minutes, that was the way it had to be, for the President alone was authorized to touch off the nation's atomic warheads.

Francis had been present for one scare, at the annual diplomatic reception at the White House. Soviet planes had buzzed an American civilian transport over captive Bulgaria, and the word was brought to John Alden Hughes as he and Liz stood in the East Room greeting their beribboned guests. The President had excused himself while he turned to his military aide for a few words, and as the aide wheeled to leave the room, Francis had caught Hughes glancing over at the warrant officer, in dress blues, standing against one wall of the brilliant room.

The Yugoslav-Hungarian scare must have been on Francis' mind all day, because when he walked into the ballroom of the Conrad Hilton Hotel with the Presidential party, he found himself looking for the bearer of the codes. He saw him almost at once, standing against the curtain behind and a little to the right of the chair where the President would be sitting. Now this youth —no, it was a different one than the one on the plane because the shift had changed—was wearing black tie and dinner jacket, as unostentatious as the well-groomed Secret Service agents hovering nearby. As he looked around the hall, Francis couldn't help thinking that this young Army guard was the most important man in the room, next to the President, and probably considerably more wholesome than his fellow guests.

Everybody was there, at a hundred dollars a plate. Certainly, the big jobholders were on hand, from the Cabinet members on down—even Treasury's tight-fisted and impatient Sprague didn't miss affairs such as this. They all had the fat-cat look, Francis was thinking, until he interrupted his thought to remind himself that there was nothing lean about his own success. And, of course, they were the human grist for the political mill, without whom no victory dinner would have been possible: state and county chairmen, the big-city bosses like Detroit's Sam Silverman and Kansas City's Esau Henry—Silverman was throwing a huge hamlike hand in greeting to Francis—Congressmen, a large assortment of agency heads like John C. Roberts of the SEC and Torbert Hayes of the FCC. No force had been required to bring men like this to the dinner; they were well aware of the fact that without the party they would be friendless. Nevertheless, force had been applied; the word had been passed that the purchase of dinner tickets was a party duty for every jobholder earning ten thousand dollars a year or more, and though there had been scattered grumbling, the faithful had toed the line for the dinner here in Chicago and for the more than one thousand other victory dinners across the bountiful, and frightened, land. There were the farm leaders and the labor leaders and the education leaders, and scores of other lobbyists from industry and management, the NAACP, airplane makers, steel tycoons, junk dealers, uniform makers.

"Lucky guys." Making his slow way to his table, Francis turned to find Jack Smalley of UPI at his elbow. "How do you like that, Mr. Justice?" Smalley said. "In the old days only a Vanderbilt or an Astor dared to spend a hundred bucks on a small steak."

Francis winked at the journalist. "Come now, Jack, this is a privilege."

"Yeah, Mr. Justice—and besides, it's good job insurance." Smalley winked back. "Except for Supreme Court justices, of course."

"Thanks, Jack. I was hoping you'd recognize my party loyalty."

Smalley was more intent now. "Sure I do, Mr. Justice. You may be the only one in the hall who doesn't have to be here. By God, even old Archibald Welles is here. Now, don't tell me our aristocratic CIA boss is looking for spies."

Francis followed Smalley's pointing finger and picked out the Central Intelligence director seated at a table with the Secretary of State and some younger men who looked fresh out of Princeton. Welles, his pince-nez glinting, seemed uncomfortable in his surroundings despite the Ivy League look of his tablemates. He looked like a professor emeritus of English Lit who had lost his way.

"My, I hope he doesn't hear any naughty words," Francis said. "Jack, did you hear about the CIA agent who was assigned to Moscow? He'd only been there a couple of weeks when he attended a big dinner at the Kremlin—the Hall of St. George. He was seated between two women, one the stout and well-scrubbed wife of a minor Soviet official, and the other the most beautiful girl our hero had ever seen. Well, the agent dutifully conversed with the Soviet official's wife for a while, but then the vodka began to have its way with him and he went at the chore of charming the beauty on his left. She seemed most approachable, and the agent was so carried away with her charms that he laid a tentative hand on her knee. When she didn't protest, he began to move his hand up her thigh. At about the halfway point, the girl suddenly reached into her handbag, took out a pencil and a little memo pad and scribbled something on it. She handed the paper to the CIA man, who put on his glasses to read what he thought would be a sweet assignment of a trysting place later in the evening. But the note read: *Please don't change expression when you reach my balls—I'm Carruthers of CIA.* Be good, Jack, I've got to go."

The President was magnificent. Even allowing for his prejudice, Francis was impressed with John Alden Hughes's expert handling of his own personality and of his canny points of emphasis as he pursued his argument for the Court plan. There could be no denying the youth of the man on the platform, and Hughes, casually elegant in black tie and with that lock of black hair continually to be brushed back from his brow, did not attempt to deny it. Rather, his boyish smile and his swift, graceful movements emphasized both the attractiveness and the energy of that youth. But as he interspersed his remarks with references to the victory of November, it was clear that here was no untried young man pushing wild, socialistic ideas that would lead the nation to bankruptcy. Here, instead, was a young man who had interpreted the yearnings of the nation's youth, its demand for sobriety in government and caution in spending, its demand for a return to basic principles and morality in international dealing. Here was the man who had refused an invitation to visit the

Soviet Union, and who had ignored the Russians' feelers for a summit conference. Here was the man who had acted swiftly in Albania, who had had the courage and moral fiber to rap the Russians' knuckles and to speak frankly to a burgeoning, muscular Germany when its nationalism endangered the Western alliance. Here was the man who had stopped the strikes until the Supreme Court interfered, who had quelled the race riots in the South, and who had balanced the budget. And here, finally, was a winner for the party—the man who had led the party to the greatest triumph in the history of American politics. Could anyone ask for more?

But Hughes asked more from those who listened to him. His speech was a rallying call to all those groups who had supported the party, and who had benefited hugely from that support. He spoke frankly to these groups. The officeholders were told they were where they were because of the program led by John Alden Hughes. The farmers, the labor leaders, the NAACP— the tribal chieftains who had gone along with Hughes because there was no other path to follow—all these were told again the facts of political life. They were told that it would be futile for them to harbor their little resentments, because only through the party and through John Alden Hughes could they continue to exist as effective forces in the nation's political life.

"We won in November," he told them all. "The opposition has been routed. Can anyone listening to me have any doubts that we will win now? We are the majority party today because we gave the nation what it wanted, what it has been crying for over the long years of spend-and-tax and of seeking accommodations with the tyrants of Communist imperialism. Do we now permit a little band of stubborn men in the ivory tower of the Supreme Court to stand in our way—in the way of a great nation as it marches to its destiny?"

"No! No!" they shouted, believing in him, anxious to trumpet their loyalty. And John Alden Hughes went on: "I say to you that nothing can beat us, no one can stand up to us, if you follow me on this plan to streamline the Supreme Court. No one can beat us if we stand together, if you give me your support. And if you do not, if we do not stand together, then I warn you solemnly that the people will find other instruments to achieve their ends, other and bolder men to lead them."

He leaned forward on the lectern, his face earnest and yet with a faint smile on his lips. "A columnist the other day called me a willful man, drunk with the power of veto," he recalled. "I know that you who are listening to me do not have to be told who has assumed the power to veto. I know I do not have to tell this nation what branch of its government has stood between the people and their ambitions, their yearnings, and struck down those programs which would have realized those ambitions for them."

He reminded the farmers of what they wanted, the labor leaders of what they wanted, the housing leaders of what they wanted, and told them bluntly that "You'll never get it until we modernize the Supreme Court. Don't tell *me* what you want," he told them. "I know what you want. Tell the Supreme Court, through your Congress. See to it that your elected representatives *represent* you."

Hughes was confident of victory in the Court fight, and he said so; his bronzed, smiling face and his easy manner exuded that confidence. "But my confidence is based on what all of you will do for yourselves in this battle," he told them. "I am confident you will do your job, as you have done it in the past. I remind you only that that job must be done—and now."

As for the cries of dictatorship that issued weakly from the opposition, John Alden Hughes had a scornful smile for "those two-bit peddlers of fear, those timid souls who want only to stand still, who are afraid of marching ahead with this great country of ours." His voice softened, and grew low. "I would dare to believe that the people trusted me last November. I would dare to hope that they trust me now."

And the shout rose again: "Yes! Yes!"—the cry of people who wanted to trust someone, of people, in this hall, at least, who needed to trust someone for their own sakes.

"You all know me," the President said quietly. "You have known me now for a great many years. We have been good neighbors to one another. We have gone together, arm in arm, doing the things that needed to be done, putting out the fires together, rebuilding from the economic ruins together. I cannot believe that you can fear me. I cannot believe that with the Free World in peril, anyone can fear that the President of the United States would seek to undermine the pillars of democracy. No, the nation knows and the world knows that you and I, together, seek only to make this land of ours stronger, to make the republic more workable than ever before, to save our children from the future planned for them by our enemies."

At O'Hare Field the next morning, waiting for the President to arrive for the flight back to Washington, Francis struck up a conversation with the man next to him at the lunch counter, where he was having a third cup of coffee. The man wore a brown leather jacket and his flannel shirt was open at the neck; Francis guessed that he was in his early thirties.

"Did you hear the President's speech last night?" Francis asked him.

The man looked at him and there was a sudden fire in his eyes.

"You're damned right I did, Mac," he said. "I heard every word of it. They oughta take those Supreme Court justices out and shoot 'em!"

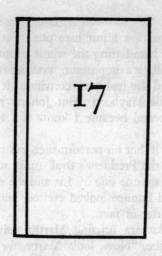

17

B Y URGENT REQUEST OF CHARLIE MAYBORN, the President's second speech was pure corn—the phrase was the President's, used over and over again during the brief interludes he snatched to go over the speech with Mayborn, Francis and Harry Weiss. "I'm a little disappointed in you, Charlie—or, perhaps, in me," John Alden Hughes said. "I didn't think I was the type." Mayborn merely rolled his eyes and muttered something about "getting to the folks." Anyway, Francis decided, Hughes *was* the type—or could be at the turn of a switch—whether he wanted to be or not. Having served his time in what Beatrice called the cornfields, Francis now found a personal relief in being able silently to disapprove of such tactics on principle, but the practical politician stirring within him knew there was a time and a place for corn, providing the performer was up to it. Indisputably, John Alden Hughes filled the bill.

The setting was the fireside, but Franklin Delano Roosevelt had never dared what John Alden Hughes managed so well, so sincerely. Liz Hughes, her patrician features showing the lines of outrage, had inveighed against it in private conversation with Francis. "Oh, Francis, we've always managed not to do this sort of thing," she said. "It's so—vulgar. Dragging the children in is the worst, of course, but I just hate posing as the little wife. I love Johnny, but I hate letting the whole country play voyeur." Francis said, "Well, it's important, you know," and Liz had sighed and admitted she had been convinced it was by both her husband and Charlie Mayborn. "But Johnny hates it, too," she said. "I know that and because I know it I feel a little better about it."

Hughes did hate it, but his performance was perfect. The "fireside" actually was the President's oval study, with Hughes in an easy chair, flanked on one side by Liz and the children on a long sofa. Four-year-old Bounce looked excited, but Martha and Barbara were quite matter-of-fact.

Francis heard Barbara briefing Martha privately before the television appearance. "Now, look, Marty, we can't look silly," Barbara told her. "I'm eleven and you're going on eight and we've got to be dignified. If we aren't, Bounce will raise Cain." Martha was haughtily cooperative. "Just worry about yourself," she told Barbara. "And if Bounce misbehaves, I'll pinch his bottom good."

But, thanks to Liz Hughes, there was no crisis. Mayborn had wanted the children to sit through the entire telecast, but Liz put her foot down. "Absolutely not," she told the red-faced Attorney General. "They'd be at each other's throats, and I'm sure Bounce would get excited and wet his pants. Off they go to bed after the introduction."

"All right," Mayborn said, then brightened. "Say, that's a good idea. You taking them off to bed, like it's supposed to be."

Liz gave him a hard eye, but said nothing.

But that was the way it developed. The President, looking boyishly mussed and yet with a hint of a father's harassed mien, introduced his family, and had barely finished when Liz spoke up. "And now these children are going off to bed," she told the viewers, managing a beatific smile. "They've stayed up much too late already."

Mayborn, tense on a straight-backed chair, nudged Francis. "A great girl," he muttered in his politician's stage whisper. "A smart girl."

Mayborn also obviously heartily approved of the President's

speech. It was a folksy, man-to-man approach with simple language and just the right touch of neighborliness. Hughes explained what the Supreme Court was and how it should operate. It should not make laws, he explained carefully, but merely interpret them; it had no right to strike down laws because of personal prejudice. It had no right to interfere with the common welfare or the common security. "We've got to stop this trend," he said. "You and I—all of us—we've got to let the Court know that this is a government of the people and by the people."

Thus it went for most of the half hour, and at the end Hughes essayed a facetious reply to some of his detractors. "Now, some of my enemies have been attacking me because they say I'm a rich man," he said. "Well, I can't deny that I have had certain advantages. I wouldn't think of denying it; after all, this administration is dedicated to the goal that all Americans should acquire more of the nation's wealth. I hope no one will turn on you—my fellow Americans—when you get rich."

He laughed, the hearty, confident, happy laugh of the Hughes family. "Anyway, they've got it all wrong. I'm really just a barefoot boy, who was born in a log cabin, and there have been only minor improvements made—air conditioning, a swimming pool, a bowling alley and a small golf course."

Small's was out with a survey three days later, reporting that the viewers loved the log cabin bit, and presenting a picture of a populace grinning its joy over having a man in the White House with a sense of humor. And the rating was the highest ever achieved for a Presidential speech. Both Harry Weiss and Chet McAdam were inclined to be fretful over the slow response over the land, however. There was no immediate avalanche of mail, and only a trickle of telegrams. Both the President and Mayborn were unconcerned; they pointed out that despite the President's careful enunciation of the issue, it remained a confusing one and the voters had to take time to frame their opinions. Francis agreed with Mayborn that these days people took longer to react; but he remained a trifle uneasy. In the past, Hughes's television appearances had always evoked an immediate and spontaneous response.

There was plenty of activity, but progress on the Court plan remained slow. The Judiciary Committee hearings in the Senate were proceeding, in Mayborn's words, "as though those jokers have all summer." In the chairman's seat, Alpheus Ward did his best to whip his colleagues along, but he was helpless in the face of the opposition's superb organization, which had collected a flood of witnesses and which insisted on interrogating them at maddening length. The bright young men from the American Bar Association who had been loaned to the opposition worked day and night at their research and thus armed the antis on the committee with scores of questions whose answers were as time-consuming as complicated interrogation could make them.

Desperate, Mayborn and Weiss went to Ward and pleaded with him to maneuver the committee into limiting the hearings by resolution. But the Senator from Illinois, always irascible and often pugnacious, met their plea with a most uncharacteristic bleat of helplessness.

"Now, gentlemen, you know I can't do anything of the kind," he told them. "I don't have to tell you how difficult it is to get a group of senators to go along on anything. These men, gentle-men, are members of the world's most exclusive club. They have rights and prerogatives, and they have minds of their own. They like to have plenty of time to express their opinions. I can't help you, gentlemen. I'm sorry, but I can't. Haste makes waste, gentlemen, and this committee will not waste its opportunity to go into this matter carefully, and at length."

Mayborn was furious. "The sanctimonious old son of a bitch," he told Francis. "He hates the guts of almost everybody on that committee, but now suddenly he's found his dignity. He's just scared, is all. The son of a bitch has a majority on that commit-tee, but he's scared to test it. That guy is so goddamn mean he won't even help his friends."

Francis tried his luck with Ward, but Ward was adamant, and irritable. "Now, Mr. Justice, I like you and I respect you," he said. "But neither Charlie Mayborn nor that smart little Jew boy, Weiss, is going to tell me how to run my committee. I'm be-hind the President, and I'm doing the best I can, but, by God, I'm going to do it the right way. This is the United States Senate, not some goddamned smoke-filled room at the White House."

What happened in the Senate dining room a few days later, then, was surprising. Or perhaps it wasn't, Francis concluded;

perhaps Alpheus Ward had been wilting under the pressure. At any rate, the explosion that was always so close to the surface in the judiciary chairman finally occurred.

Ward was lunching at the same table with Frank Hoar, and as the men settled down to their lamb chops, there was the usual switch from pleasantries to the Court plan. Hoar, a burr under Ward's saddle on the committee, observed pleasantly that "We seem to be making progress, Alph."

Ward grunted, but said nothing.

"Don't you agree, Alph?" Hoar asked, pressing his colleague.

Ward looked across the table at Hoar. "You know damn well I don't agree, Frank. You goddamn liberals are making a farce of the hearings."

"We're inquiring into the matter," Hoar said, his voice comfortable. "This is important Senate business, Alph."

Ward's voice was a snort. "Sure, sure it is. Important Senate business. Where the hell were you pinkos on that Highland Communist case?"

Hoar's face struggled to produce a strained smile. "Alph, I hope you're not calling me a pinko." Then his judicial calm deserted him, and his voice became a snarl. "At least I'm not a goddamned errand boy for a pretty-boy dictator."

"You son of a bitch!" Ward was up on his feet, his face red and mottled with little bumps. He reached over a long arm and, with a swipe like that of a clumsy bear, slapped at the side of Hoar's head.

Hoar turned to avoid the blow, and it was this maneuver that caused him to slip off his chair onto the floor. In the confusion of bodies that followed, Hoar was lifted to his feet by a corps of Senatorial colleagues, while three others clutched at the steaming Ward. It took long minutes of careful argument, while a cordon of senators screened the participants with their hulks, before apologies were torn from both men and a reluctant handshake was accomplished. But both men had enough enemies that the *Star* could put together a Page One story hawked by the startling headline: SENATORIAL FISTS FLY; WARD SLUGS HOAR.

Chet McAdam phoned the President to tell him about it. Hughes was disturbed; he knew both Hoar and Ward would be ashamed of themselves after a night's sleep, and because he had known both well in the peculiar intimacy of the Senate, he could understand how bitterly they would berate themselves in private.

"The boys are getting rough," he said.

"Yes, and I don't like it." McAdam's voice held a sincere grief. "I know the issue is a bitter one, but I don't like senators slugging each other. It's a sign I hate to see—a sign that this thing is really dividing people. I hope we can heal the wounds after this is all over."

"Yes." The President was silent for a moment. It would not help him, or the country, if the Hill should deteriorate into a snarling, brawling dog pit. More practically, this kind of thing was bad for the Court bill; it took people's minds off the main issue. It started people—people in Congress—thinking that the important business was to make peace, rather than to pursue the objective.

"Have you talked to them, Chet?" the President asked.

"I talked to Hoar. Ward's gone home and he's not answering the phone. I'll see him tomorrow. Hoar is annoyed at himself as much as at Ward. It's too damned bad."

"I know—they're both good men, Chet."

"Damned good, Mr. President. Frank Hoar—well, he's on the other side of the fence, but he's a decent gentleman. I respect him."

"Yes, so do I." And I'd like him on our side, for once, the President was thinking. "Work on them, Chet."

"I will, Mr. President. By God, I'm beginning to wish this was all over."

The President hung up. He was more concerned, now. He didn't like McAdam wishing it was all over. There was too much to be done. He sat for a while, thinking: I hope Chet McAdam is tough enough.

Everybody, of course, was being as tough as he could in this fight, but sometimes the President wondered whether they were all as tough as they had to be—as tough as he was.

August Brandt was tough, but was his toughness enough to cope both with the farmers' eternal recalcitrance and with his own Iowa-bred suspicion of the necessary machinations of politics? The Secretary of Agriculture was working hard; Hughes knew that. Brandt had gone at the farm leaders in his bull-like way, his power augmented by his superbly knowing grasp of farm problems. He had put it bluntly to Richards of the Farm Bureau, the hulking, slow-moving Billy Joe Lucas of the Grange and the radical-thinking Jake Ewart of the Farmers' Union. He had reminded them with pitiless logic that the farmers were richer now than they had ever been, thanks to the weeding out of the inefficient, the incompetents, and that they were no longer hog-tied by harassing government controls. What they were they owed to John Alden Hughes, Brandt told them. Without Hughes, they would still be stumbling about in the morass of government regulations. They owed it to Hughes to support the Court bill.

But the reaction had been lukewarm, at best. All three farm-group leaders had made speeches for the Court plan, but the speeches had been too careful. They sounded like men hedging their bets, cautious lest they stir up the suspicions of their wary constituents. Richards had spent a long hour with the President, pledging him complete support, but between the lines he had not been able to resist voicing a warning about "trouble with some of those guys." His public words were strong, but they lacked the ring of words a man has put his heart into. Billy Joe Lucas had been too considerate of his members; he had spent too much time urging them to study the matter and too little telling them that he expected them to arrive at the inevitable decision. Ewart clearly was afraid of his membership; he made his dutiful speeches and issued his dutiful statements, but he was continually tracking down Brandt to tell him of another batch of telegrams from farmers opposing the plan.

What troubled Hughes most was Brandt's confidence. It was difficult, wrenching, to doubt the man's sincerity, and yet the signs were so ominous that Hughes wondered why a shrewd operator like Brandt saw so little significance in them.

"Now, Mr. President, what you call unrest among the farmers —I don't see it, I honestly don't," Brandt told him. "All I know —and that's plenty—is that Richards and Lucas and Ewart say the farmers will go along. Sure, they admit some rumbles here and there, but that's only natural. Sure, there's an argument going on. But don't forget that Richards and Lucas and Ewart have been around for a long time. You have to be shrewd, you have to know your business, to survive that long in a cutthroat business like running a farm pressure group. Of course, I've looked around myself, and I've heard some grumbling. But the organizations seems to me to be safe enough. We've just got to depend on the leaders—depend on their knowing their business."

"Yes, August, I guess we have. I hope to God they're right, though." They'd better be, the President thought. "But, August, keep after it."

The situation with labor was just as worrisome, and might prove more so. Joe Harris was being most cooperative, even subservient, but the fact was the President did not trust the president of the AFL-CIO. He had not trusted Joe Harris since that day five years ago in a St. Louis hotel room when he treated Harris to the same candor that had won him support for his candidacy from a majority of those forces which made up the nation's spectrum of pressure groups. Smiling and with complete sincerity, Hughes had suggested that the AFL-CIO throw in with him as a full partner, trusting him to do what was right for labor in return for its plighting of troth.

"Like hell." Harris had mouthed the words matter-of-factly. "I don't do that again, Senator. I've been screwed by too many goddamn politicians in the past."

Hughes had stared for a moment, unbelieving, at Joe Harris's tall, spare figure, at the brown doe's eyes blinking behind the horn-rimmed glasses, at this man who had argued and cajoled and slugged and clawed his way up from the lower East Side. There had been a long silence, while in the background Hughes could hear Francis Dalton clearing his throat, and then everybody had pitched in with placating phrases. A compromise had been reached, but Harris had served notice that he and his organization would retain their independence and reserve the right to upset the apple cart when labor's whim suggested it. To be sure, the AFL-CIO had gone along then and since, but the President had never deceived himself about its motives. Power lay with the winner, and since the winner obviously would be John Alden Hughes, labor had to pose for its picture with him to get its share of that power. By now, Joe Harris had forced himself to be pleasant, if not ingratiating, with the President— always careful to do the little chores required while smilingly sending along his regards. He seemed to be working vigorously at the head of the citizens' group for the Court plan. But the results so far had been sparse; was it because Joe Harris had finally decided the opportune time had come to drag his feet?

With the honesty he always brought to his thoughts, Hughes realized he had never liked Harris for another reason—Harris was too powerful, and it was not convenient having a man that powerful so close to the White House. It could interfere. He was sure, too, that Harris had never liked him. After the years spent in that garment loft, Joe Harris was suspicious of charm, and Hughes knew Harris had never really felt comfortable in the White House when in the presence of that charm. Harry Weiss had once reported, in those early years, that Joe Harris had spoken bitterly of "that guy's Ivy League horseshit talk." Moreover, the President had become aware in the last year or two that Harris had detected the signs of the President's uneasiness over the labor leader's increasing force of impact on the national community, and in little ways Harris had sought to build up this uneasiness—by following an act of acquiescence with a little word or a legislative thrust intended to make it clear to the President that Joe Harris still could be troublesome.

Harry Weiss had wanted the President to let Harris in on the Court plan before making it public, and Hughes had declined to do so on the basis that if he did it for one he'd have to do it for all. And Harris's reaction had been predictable. Undoubtedly, he had heard rumors of the plan before Inauguration Day, for during a call at the White House shortly after the New Year, Joe had suggested as much. The President had grinned and managed to intimate without leaking an important word of his plan that something was afoot, adding, "I think I can deal with the Court, Joe." Harris, of course, had pressed him, but Hughes had kept on his smile and gone on to reassure Joe that he could safely leave the great issue to the strategists in the White House. Harris had not exploded when the Court plan was unveiled; after all, he favored a constitutional amendment to do much the same thing, and Harris was careful as well as tough. But he passed the word through Harry Weiss that, although he would do everything he could to help, he was saddened by the President's lack of confidence in his discretion. Then Joe had turned cheerfully—almost too cheerfully—to organizing the citizens' group behind the plan.

The President could find no fault in Harris's statement endorsing the Court plan; it could only be described as ringing, in the best tradition of the Harris prose, which is to say it had about it the authentic hoarse-throated aggressiveness. And in a later public statement, Harris had urged all like-minded pressure groups to go along. Yet Hughes was baffled; there was no sign, anywhere along the line, that Harris was putting on the heat. No bleats were heard about AFL-CIO pressures on the Hill, where such pressures would do the most good. Weiss had suggested the comforting thought that Harris had learned a certain subtlety in applying those pressures and thus Congress was not as aware of them as it had been in the past, but Hughes dismissed this premise. If Joe Harris were doing his job, it would have to be done with a meat-ax, with threats and warnings, and the sound of his blows would be heard all over Washington.

"No," the President told Weiss, "I'm afraid Harris and his boys are sitting on their larded hams, smoking their expensive cigars. I suppose I'll have to have it out with Joe shortly."

"I'd like to wait a little while, Mr. President." Harry Weiss was brutal when brutality was necessary, but he liked to give the administration's allies as much time as could be managed to fall into line; he had a fetish about saving face. "I'll drop some hints around and see what comes of it."

"All right, Harry," the President said. "But I'm more than a little concerned. The silence is deafening." He could not trust Joe Harris; his old animosity toward the labor leader was bolstered by a feeling coming from deep down in his instinct that Harris had never been pleased by the almost absolute power enjoyed by his candidate in the White House. Harris, he knew, was too shrewd to come out into the open with even a hint of his misgivings, but, given a chance, Joe would delight in helping to whittle away the influence and prestige of the man he had helped elect. Hughes knew his history well enough to realize that while labor might do very well under a strong President with whom it cooperated, its leaders were always suspicious that the Presidential power might be turned against them. Harris had gone along enthusiastically with the no-strike legislation, but only because labor got its price in advance—higher wages on an annual increase basis, and a shorter work week. But labor could not but be restive under a law that made the President supreme over its ambitions. Harris had not been quite disappointed enough when the Supreme Court invalidated the Walsh Act.

As for the South, Hughes hoped things were not turning out as his mother had warned him, but the curiously ambiguous attitudes of some of Dixie's legislators, entrenched behind the seniority system, seemed ominously significant. He had won the South by protecting the South, by posting the Go Slow sign along the road to integration. But he was beginning to wonder how long the South's gratitude could resist the Southern legislators' natural tendency to seek selfish autonomy in the halls of Congress. The South had not been too happy about either his farm program or his recent efforts to placate the electorate in the big Northern cities with housing and urban reform measures. Discoursing from his position of prestige as a Kentuckian, Speaker Smith had argued as patiently as possible with his Southern cousins the necessity for winning votes in the North to pass measures on the Hill that would benefit the South, and the South had gone along —but grudgingly. The President realized, too, that the South mistrusted him on the fundamental ground that he was not one with Dixie, that not only was he an Ivy Leaguer from the North but his past was one in which he had clashed repeatedly with the traditional arguments of the party which for so long had owned the South, by dint of both tradition and like-minded opinions. Burke of Alabama had pointed up another of the glandular causes of the South's uneasiness—that since Hughes was in his second term and could not run for re-election, he no longer needed the South and would cast Dixie aside when it became expedient to do so. Chet McAdam, Speaker Smith and all the rest of his hierarchy of leaders had answered this argument well with the counter argument that everybody in Congress, including the Southerners, had to take cognizance of Hughes's victory in November. With the Congressional elections coming up in less than two years, they argued, it behooved all the faithful to clutch tight the coattails of their victorious President lest they be rejected by the voters for infidelity to the cause. Still, the South remained restive; noted for their florid oratory and their fiery response when the battle was joined, Southerners on both sides of the Hill had been niggardly in their support in those cliché-filled debates at which they could have shown their loyalty. Perhaps oratory was not that important; but for John Alden Hughes there was something oddly uncharacteristic in the South's matter-of-fact attitude toward the Court bill.

"You can't trust the South," his mother told him. "Those Southern gentlemen will always worry about themselves first." The President had nodded absent-mindedly, mentally exulting over his electoral vote in Dixie, and thanking heaven and a rousing campaign for it. Now he was not so sure he could depend on the Hill's Southern delegation, even as the South's overwhelming choice for President.

A buzzer on his desk sounded, and the President spoke into the box.

Sarah James's voice on the other end said, "Mr. Weiss would like to see you, Mr. President."

"Mr. Weiss—oh, sure, tell him to come in."

Weiss must have been just outside the door in the appointment secretary's office, because the door was opened almost the moment the President finished issuing the invitation.

Weiss's face was flushed, and his hands seemed to be shaking, as he walked toward the desk, arms held out.

"Mr. President—excuse me, but this is the damnedest thing."

"Harry—what's up? You seem all wrought up."

"Mr. President, Ed Hawley over at AP just called. He says the Supreme Court has just upheld you on that Sons of Slaves case in Chicago."

Self-preservation, Chet McAdam was thinking as he walked swiftly down the corridor to his office in the Old Senate Office Building—everybody had it, even the Supreme Court. The good old instinct of self-preservation. His bafflement had receded now with his discovery of the cause of this spectacular about-face, but he found his relief tinged with annoyance. This would complicate matters.

Henry Smith and Bill Ball were waiting for him in the office, and they were silent as McAdam slammed the door shut and walked over and threw himself into an easy chair.

"Well, gentlemen?" McAdam looked at them crossly. "Cat got your tongues?"

Ball laughed. The House Majority Leader almost always showed agitation in that fashion. "How about you, Chet? Guess you're as surprised as we are."

"What do you think, Chet?" Speaker Smith said.

"Hell, I don't know." McAdam threw one leg over the arm of the chair. "The perverse bastards."

"I guess that sums it up," Smith said. "I'd have bet a thousand dollars the Court would overthrow those convictions—and give Hughes another chance to nail down its coffin. Now what? Here's the Supreme Court, all of a sudden, going along with the President. Here he is, clouting them on the head every hour on the hour, and suddenly they're on his side."

"It was Bacon—you know that, of course."

The other two men nodded. "Bacon delivered the opinion, too," Ball said. "Sam Jenkins of Justice was there, and he called me up as soon as he could get to a phone. He said it was the damnedest thing—he couldn't believe his ears. He said he didn't know which he felt more, horror or astonishment. He said he couldn't believe that out of the blue the Court was abandoning its stand, discarding all its stiff little doctrines, to climb into bed with John Alden Hughes."

"That's one we didn't figure on," Smith said. "And we should have—remember, Chet, when you said a few weeks ago it was a wonder the Court didn't give Hughes what he wanted, just to ease the pressure?"

"Yup. It was just an idle thought, though," McAdam said. "I'd like to take credit for prescience, but it never occurred to me again. Until today."

"Goddamned cute." Smith's voice was irritable. "Hughes wants to change the Court, so the Court—to save itself from destruction, or self-destruction—merely reverses itself. Sure it was only five-to-four, but there you are. The Supreme Court finally has started thinking like John Alden Hughes. That's what people will be saying."

"Yes." McAdam wished he had more time to think. "You think that's what people will be saying, Henry?"

"Of course that's what they'll think." Smith seemed impatient.

"I ran into more than a dozen representatives on the way here, and every one of them said the same thing! 'That takes some of the pressure off us, doesn't it?' That's what they said. They acted as if the party was over, as if nothing more had to be done."

"Yes, I'm not surprised," McAdam said. It was coming to him, but hard. "It's just a step from talk like that to talk about compromising. A constitutional amendment, maybe mandatory retirement for a justice at, say, seventy-five. To a lot of people, I suppose that'll mean we're off the hook."

"Well, why not?" Bill Ball spoke up sharply. "Why the hell not? It looks to me as if Hughes had gotten what he wants without changing the Court, without adding those new extra members. Why the hell keep running when you've reached your destination?"

Both other men looked at Ball, saying nothing. McAdam cleared his throat. "Well, there's something to what you say, I suppose. And if other people are thinking that way, we'll have to, too, if we're going to be able to answer them—or do business with them." He laughed. "Dammit to hell, this is almost funny. Here we'd all been counting on liberal opinions from the Court to give us more ammunition for our campaign, and the sons of bitches have double-crossed us. I've got to call the President pretty soon, I don't know whether I'm going to enjoy that."

"Hell, he ought to be happy," Ball said. "He's won a great victory after all these years. He should feel pretty good."

McAdam looked at Ball. "Bill, you don't know John Alden Hughes like I do. I think I'll get in touch with Harry Weiss first—see how things are developing."

But Harry Weiss was not immediately available when McAdam called a little later. Weiss was in the President's office with the President and Charlie Mayborn. The President had set out to get a conservative Supreme Court; now he apparently had one. But no one in the office was pleased.

The President's feelings surged within him—astonishment and anger. He had been confident that the Court would continue to thwart him, and now, when the Court had betrayed that confidence, he was outraged. John Alden Hughes was not one who lightly ascribed cupidity to others, even to other politicians, but he had gone to the wars often enough to acquire an unerring eye for what he considered duplicity. This sudden reversal on the part of the Court could not be merely that; it had to be a political trick. If it had been Hume who had reversed his vote, the President might have been able to accept it, but he expected nothing of the sort from Bacon, and the fact that it was Bacon who had changed sides warmed the political suspicion that was in him.

"There is nothing sincere about this," he said, to no one in particular. "This is Bacon, trying to beat my bill. It's a clever political trick."

"It's clever, all right," Mayborn said. Mayborn was subdued.

"And it's a trick, Charlie. I know Bacon. He's a dangerous man. I don't trust him. I could never trust him."

Weiss stirred in his chair. In his pragmatic way, Harry Weiss was always able to come around to seeing the necessity for changing directions if circumstances prescribed it. His mind was not only a brilliant one; it was well larded with common sense. Weiss respected people, and he was careful in his dealings with them even when he had to be brutal. He put himself in their shoes, and tried to think as they were thinking. Harry Weiss was a humanist without quite knowing it.

"But what about it?" Harry Weiss asked. "Suppose it is a trick. Suppose it is a matter of the Court's buying the status quo. Even if that is so, can't we—negotiate a little? Can't we do business with the Court? I'm for our Court plan, without change. But if we can achieve the same result without it, by merely accepting a change, however motivated, in the Court's complexion—if we can get the job done that way, why not do it?"

"No, Harry." The President's hand came down flat on his desk. "I won't take that. That is not the kind of Court I want. That is not the kind of Court I set out to get. Aside from everything else, a five-to-four majority is not enough. It's got to be better than that; our plan is the only way."

"Yes, sir, but if this sabotages our plan? We've got to be ready with something else." Harry Weiss's value was that he was always ready with something else.

"No—I'm not interested in something else, Harry. I want a Court that will cooperate with me. I want a friendly and sympathetic Court, a Court with which I see eye to eye on the great matters of our time. A Court like the one Governor Adams had in Pennsylvania. Adams was very much like several members of the Court of Appeals, and they saw things as he did. Adams got things done."

The buzzer sounded, and the President spoke into the box. "If that's Mr. Justice Dalton, ask him to come in."

Francis walked in with what he thought was a brisk stride, but he was tired. It had been a long and hard day, the climax of those longer days of keeping faith with the rule of the Supreme Court that there be no leaks of its decisions to anyone. No leaks to *anyone*—not even the President of the United States—is the way Francis had interpreted the rule, because he knew that was how it was meant to be.

"Hello, Francis." The President stood up and grasped his hand. "I'm always glad to meet a man of integrity. I know you're not worried, Francis, but I'll tell you this: I'm not the kind of President who expects anyone to break a confidence in my favor, and I have a special respect for the oath of a Supreme Court justice."

Hughes was smiling, and Francis smiled back. "Thanks, Mr. President," he said. He was too tired to say more, although he had come to the White House prepared to fight for the inviolability of that oath.

"Francis, I've read as much of the opinion as I have to for a moment, but I suppose it's all right to ask you for an expert briefing."

"Well, the case was simple, as you know," Francis said. "The big issue, in view of this new Federal statute dealing with incitement to riot, revolved around the fact that the state didn't request Federal assistance. In a nutshell, all sixteen convictions were upheld because the majority felt that the statute was valid and that, at least in this instance, the government was correct in its conclusion that the state could not preserve order."

"Could have, perhaps," Mayborn put in. "But those timid Chicago liberals were not about to make the Negro voters mad."

"Francis, you say *apparently* convinced," the President said. "Are you referring to Bacon?"

"Well, sir, I don't know. I'm just being properly cautious, I

268

suppose. After all, I hesitate to impugn anyone's motives. Besides, there has been something about Bacon lately . . . "

"What, Francis?" The President's voice was sharp now.

"I don't really know, to be truthful. But more and more he has become the Chief Justice in fact as well as in title. He's taken hold more. He's stepped up and dominated the Court. Before— oh, until a few weeks ago—he deferred to Allen Hume. I think he respects Hume greatly, and he has realized that his own gruff manner is not as suited to preserving harmony on the Court as is Hume's great gentleness. But lately, without showing any diminution of respect for Hume, Bacon has been more—well, more the boss. His manner has been more relaxed, too, but he has kept things moving by adding that little pinch of graciousness to his characteristic firmness. He seems, all at once, to be newly aware of his responsibility. You know, he loves that Court, Mr. President."

"Yes. Yes, I suppose he does. He *is* capable of that." The President was talking as if to himself.

"Well, that's about it. Bacon, I think, is a real liberal, but he also has become conscious of what he feels is unrest in the country, an unrest that is a clear and present danger. I think that awakening, plus his determination to save the Court in its present form, probably combined to cause him to vote as he did."

"Yes. Well, I won't say to you what I said to the others, Francis." The President smiled. "But I'm afraid I'm not quite as trustful as you are."

The phone rang and the President said, "Yes, put him on," and then, "Hello, Chet, what's *your* bad news?" The conversation lasted for four or five minutes, with the President interrupting McAdam's presentation only for an occasional "Yes" or a "Go ahead, Chet, I'm listening."

The President hung up and looked at the three men sitting in front of his desk. "McAdam has heard from the troops—and some of them are in favor of a retreat. Chet is willing to carry on—but he does have an idea for a compromise."

"Already," Mayborn said, in a murmur. "Damn."

The President continued, seeming not to have heard Mayborn. "In effect, what Chet said was that it might be a good idea to settle this thing right now. Those are his exact words, by the way. Settle this thing right now." Francis sensed the anger rising in the President's tone. "He said it looked as if it might get worse than ever, but that if I gave him the go-ahead, he could get me a compromise. What he suggests is that constitutional amendment making retirement from the bench mandatory at seventy-five."

"That would take care of Bacon and Feldman," Harry Weiss said. It was Weiss's business to know the ages of people.

"To be sure." The President's voice was a snap. "And it would take care of Whitfield and Robson, too—two justices who have been voting with us ever since I moved into the White House."

Francis put in, "Yes, but of course you'd appoint their successors."

The President smiled. "Half a loaf. Better than none, I suppose, is what I should say. No, gentlemen, I'm not saying that. Do you realize how long it would take the states to ratify a constitutional amendment? By that time—if it passed—it would be too late. Gentlemen, I am not about to compromise—not at this point, and not at any point until I have run my race."

"Old Chet has had a scare," Mayborn said. "You know Chet—he's apt to be a defeatist, trying to run that bunch up on the Hill. He'll come out of it. We don't have any proof yet that this reversal is going to change any votes."

"I think that's a fair statement," Francis said. "At least we should wait a while and see what develops. The people on our side are not going to switch to the other side overnight. Senators don't do things that way."

"There is also another point, quite important to me," the President said. "This administration is going to have to take the responsibility for whatever Court bill is passed. If that is so, then I want that bill to be my kind of bill. Some men are too old for the Court at sixty. Some, like Whitfield and Robson, are an asset to the Court even though they are well beyond the age prescribed for retirement by this constitutional amendment. I don't want to be responsible, some year in the future, for banishing a good man—perhaps a great justice—from the bench merely because he's reached the age of seventy-five."

"We've got to wait," Francis said. "We can't afford to run

scared yet. I don't really know what that Sons of Slaves decision means. Perhaps it means that the Court will gradually become more conservative. Perhaps Bacon's vote on this case will lead others to vote in a like manner on other cases. Perhaps Bacon has honestly had a change of heart, and of mind. I have to believe he has. But we don't know yet. We can't know yet. And frankly, it's hard for me to believe that the Court is ready to do a complete about-face. It is not that kind of Court. No Supreme Court has been that kind of court."

"We won't retreat one step," the President said. "My instinct tells me not to trust this reversal, not to trust Robert McNair Bacon." He turned to Francis. "With all respect to your recent observation of him, Francis."

"Good," Mayborn said. "I'll talk to McAdam. The poor guy must be tired, anyway. I don't really think he's going to drag his feet now."

"I hope not," the President said.

"Besides, there's too much in it for him," Mayborn said, merely making a statement.

"Yes, there is," the President said. "I hope Chet realizes that."

"I think he does," Mayborn said. "We're all in this together, and if we all do our part we'll pull this one." He turned to Francis. "Naturally, you knew about this Bacon switch pretty well in advance, didn't you, Francis?"

"Of course." Francis was thinking about Beatrice. "As usual, we all saw each other's printed opinions a few days before they were handed down. You know that, Charlie."

"Yep, I do." Mayborn sighed, and, as if talking to himself, "Another five-to-four decision. Too bad you didn't vote against the convictions, Francis. That would have given us what we wanted."

Francis looked at Mayborn, trying not to understand what the Attorney General meant, but understanding too well. Suddenly he felt nauseated; a bad taste seeped up into his mouth.

"Charlie . . ." he said, and his voice was icy, but another voice cut in.

"All right," the voice said, and Francis was surprised to hear the President speaking in such a low voice. "All right, Charlie, that was in extremely bad taste. You must know that. I appreciate your viewpoint, but none of us—including you, I am sure—can condone any mention of the means you have suggested. I must ask you to apologize, Charlie."

Mayborn looked at the President, a swift, seeing-all look.

"Yes, sir," he said. "I overstepped. It just came out. You think these things, in an idle kind of way, and if you're not careful they come out." His look switched to Francis. "Francis, I apologize. *I* know I didn't mean it, and I hope you do."

Francis looked down at the floor. He still felt sick, but somehow he must say something and get out of that office.

He looked up at Mayborn after what seemed an eternity. "All right, Charlie," he said. "I understand. And thank you."

"Good." The President stood up and walked around his desk and stood half leaning on it. "We all have to be careful. We have to be careful to remember who we are—and what we are."

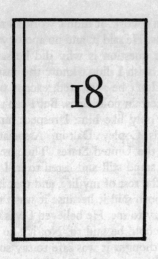

18

WHY MUST BEA'S LINE BE BUSY! Francis took an angry sip of his Scotch, and its harsh taste stirred his instinct. Three drinks at that horrible party for Chet McAdam at the Mayflower and now this was his second since coming home. Well, he was not going to try to drink himself out of anything. He put the old-fashioned glass down on the coffee table and got up and walked into the kitchen and poured himself a glass of milk and drank it swiftly. He grinned despite himself; he was being pretty dramatic about a couple of extra drinks of Scotch. What was so tragically wrong about drinking alone on a night like this?

I don't really know whether I want to be left alone, Francis was thinking. Tonight it would be much better to talk to somebody, even that pretty blonde at the party, whom I bored. Perhaps I should go out on the town so that I won't have to be alone with myself, thinking about Charlie Mayborn. I wish I could be merely indignant with Mayborn and let it go at that. It would be so much easier. So much easier to berate him as a hack politician with no ethics. So much better to let my dignity remain outraged and to peer down at the Charlie Mayborns of the world from Olympian heights. That gives me comfort, just to think

273

about it. But it won't work. It didn't work all the way home and it's not working now. He said it, and no apology can wipe it away. He said it, and the question is why did he say it? How could he dare to say it? I wish I didn't know the answer. I wish it was a question that couldn't be answered, except with a reply about the boorishness of certain politicians. But I can't call Charlie Mayborn a boor. I not only like him; I respect him. No, that is not the answer, Francis Copley Dalton, Associate Justice of the Supreme Court of the United States. The answer is uglier than that, and I have to stand still and listen to it. I have to stand still and listen to it for the rest of my life, and that is going to be very hard. Charlie Mayborn said it because it was the sort of thing he believed he could say to me. He believed I was the kind of justice that kind of thing could be said to. No, it's no use getting angry again. If Mayborn thought it was safe to say something like that, I must have given him grounds. Charlie is a smart politician. He knows people. He knows the people to whom it is safe to say this and that. I have got to think about that—sometime later—and decide if I am really that bad, if I am really that kind of man. Later, I have got to argue that one out. Right now I want to talk to Bea.

He walked back into the little living room and sat down again on the sofa, his feet up on the coffee table. Why didn't that damned operator call? He'd wait a few minutes and then put in the call again. He mustn't take a chance on Bea's going out before he talked to her. Distractedly, his thoughts wandered to Chet McAdam. Chet had always been cautious, but he had seemed particularly concerned about the Court bill during their hastily-snatched conversation at the Mayflower. Chet thought they could still do it, but he hadn't seemed happy about it. Perhaps it was because he was tired; Chet had looked tired, and Francis told him so.

"I am tired," McAdam said. "This has been a tough day, Francis. Trying to keep the troops in line after that Sons of Slaves decision." He took a long drink from the glass in his hand.

"How does it look, Chet?"

"Well, it's hard to say right now. Those who never had much stomach for the Court bill want out, of course. They figure the

Court decision gives them an excuse. But the others are pretty firm. Waiting, of course, to see what develops."

"Can we still make it, Chet?"

McAdam sighed; it was a sigh that was almost strenuous, as though it had positive energy behind it. "I won't say your guess is as good as mine, Francis. I'm up close to it, and I'm supposed to know. Yes, I suppose so. I guess we can. But it means a lot more work, and now we can't afford any more setbacks. We've used them all up—like time-outs in a football game. From now on it's going to be tight."

"What about the Judiciary Committee? Will they vote it out?"

"As of now? Yes, as of now I think they would. Those hearings are nothing but a lot of goddamned chaos, a kind of shouting delaying action, but I think we've got the votes. As of now. We just can't slip up anywhere, that's all."

"The President seems to feel the country is still on his side."

McAdam looked at Francis, eyebrows lowered over his puffy eyelids. "Yes, I know he does. I wish I had his confidence." He sighed again. "Oh hell, I guess we've still got the people. The big noise is being made by the lobbyists, outfits like ADA and so forth. But I don't like the mail being slow. The President has received a lot of letters in favor of the plan, sure—but not enough. Not enough, Francis. It's nowhere near the way it used to be. Hell, he used to say he wanted something and they had to ship the overflow mail to the National Guard Armory."

"But people don't write as much these days, Chet. All the polls say that."

"And the polls are right. But not in the case of John Alden Hughes, Francis. The people don't write to anybody else, but they write to the President. That's what I keep reminding myself of—and it doesn't make me happy." McAdam looked over Francis' shoulder, in the time-honored Washington fashion of the politician keeping track of who is around that he should talk to. "Hell, Francis, there's Charlie Mayborn. I've got to see him. See you later."

No you won't, Francis said to himself. He had slipped through the crowd to the bar and ordered a Scotch on the rocks and drunk it at one gulp. Nobody at this party was going to see him later—not with Charlie Mayborn here. He was no longer angry with Charlie Mayborn, but he was taking no chances on seeing him tonight. Mayborn reminded him of something, of what kind of man some people thought he was, and he needed time to decide if those people had a right to their appraisal of him. He took the first door he found and walked out into the corridor and headed for the cloakroom. It was time to go home.

The telephone rang its harsh, somehow frightening, ring, and Francis jumped, then grabbed the receiver. Yes, yes, this was Justice Dalton, yes, yes, yes.

"Darling!" It was Bea's voice at last, after all that parley with the operator.

"Beatrice, my dear," Francis said. Then quickly, "I damn well wanted to talk to you. I'm so glad you're home."

"Of course I'm home, darling. I'm so glad I am. Three calls in one day! My cup runneth over. Darling—you're not all right."

"Beatrice, I love you."

"And I love you, darling. But you're not—*all right*." He warmed at the concern in her low tone. He mustn't be a cry baby.

"Oh—I guess I am. Now. Now that I'm talking to you, Bea. It's just been—a damned hellish day."

Bea's voice was soothing, loving. "Of course, pet. I read about everything. It must have been hectic. Poor lamb."

Oh hell, he might as well tell her. He *wanted* to tell her. She was the only one that mattered to him, and so he should tell her.

"Bea, it was pretty rugged." He realized his voice sounded hoarse. "To put it as prettily as possible, Charlie Mayborn suggested that I might have—played along with the President."

"Played along? What did he mean?"

"Charlie implied I had been disloyal to Hughes, that I should have voted against the government so Hughes would have another defeat to use in his demand for his Court bill."

"Francis, how horrible!" There was a kind of breathless shock in Beatrice's voice. "Oh, darling, how nasty. How utterly nasty! Oh, my poor lamb. How could he?"

"Well, he could and he did." Francis tried to make his voice dry. "He could, apparently, because I seemed to him to be the kind of man he could say that kind of thing to. That's the terrible thing about it."

"Francis—why he's a monster! No wonder you've had a bad day. But don't worry about it, darling. Charlie Mayborn must have forgotten whom he was talking to—he was thinking in terms of what he would have done himself. Even Charlie Mayborn knows you're—oh, a tower of rectitude. That's how everybody knows you. You know that, even if you don't proclaim it to the world."

"Bea dear, I thought I was." That was what made him so tired. He thought he was, and Charlie Mayborn had dared to suggest he wasn't. And a man doesn't dare suggest such a thing without grounds. "I guess I didn't impress Charlie that way."

"Damn Charlie Mayborn! Damn all the Charlie Mayborns of the world. Francis, I won't let you torture yourself about this. The whole thing is so ridiculous it would be laughable if it weren't so—so utterly dreadful and in bad taste and nasty."

Dear Bea. She did believe in what he was. He believed in what he was, but she believed in him more, because she didn't know some of the things he did. But he wanted her to believe, because it would help him to believe.

"Bea, thank you," he said. "I suppose I have to say I called you because I knew you'd say what you've said. I just wanted to make sure. I want you and me to believe, anyway."

"And we do, darling. *I* do, and *you* do. But, darling, so does everybody else. You've earned that reputation, Francis. Everybody believes, even politicians like Charlie Mayborn—except that the Charlie Mayborns are always running, always trying to arrange a gimmick, no matter how tasteless they may appear, no matter how false they are to their own beliefs."

"Bea, I hope you're right. No, you've made it so that I do know you're right. I needed you to make me know that, and you've done it—you've made me believe."

"Francis, I won't have you doubting yourself. It's not like you, it's not worthy of you. You judged the Sons of Slaves case on its merits, regardless of anything else. I know it must have crossed your mind that it wouldn't help the President's case— but you went ahead and did what had to be done, because you are Francis Dalton, darling, and you do what's right to do."

"Bea—yes, I do. I always try to do what I sincerely believe is right. I can say that, now, now that I'm talking to you, knowing you won't say I'm stuffy."

"Stuffy!" Beatrice's trilling little laugh filled him with delight. "My lamb, you are terribly correct—about the law—but if you don't stop being silly, I'll write my memoirs and expose your stuffiness."

"Good. I'd like people to know I'm human. Bea, sometimes it's difficult to be human and still be a good judge."

"No, it isn't. Not for you, Francis. I know this about you—you are all human, but when it comes to the law you are all judge. Sometimes, as you know, I disagree with you—I suppose because I tend to be emotional about things. But I know, Francis, that you never mistake emotion for your understanding of the law. Even when I don't approve of what you do, I know you are doing what you believe you have to do. You'll always do the right thing, according to the way you see it. And that is why I love you—because, first of all, I respect you."

Warmth cosseted Francis; if he could just take her into his arms. "Bea, I love you," he said. There was nothing else to say. Nothing that should be said but that.

"And I love you, Francis. Because of what you are. Darling, are you all right, now?"

"Yes, I'm all right, now. Thank you, Doctor Krasnov."

Bea laughed. "And thank you, Mr. Justice." Her voice sobered. "You've just done something wonderful, darling. You've made the girl who loves you feel important."

"You are. Most important to me. You make me feel ten feet tall. I do so want to see you. How are things going?"

"Oh, Francis, I do so want to see you, too. But we can't yet, not for a while. Because things are going pretty much as before. I have just got to stay here in New York—for as long as it takes to handle Freddie."

"Of course. Freddie. He hasn't relented? He won't compromise?"

"No, but that doesn't matter now, Francis." She was so positive now. "It doesn't matter at all because I'm going to fight him. I'm not going to let him dictate to me—to us. I've decided that I'm right. That is, I knew it all along, but now I've decided to do something about it. I'm not going to let Freddie walk over me, Francis. I should have realized before I couldn't allow that."

"No—you couldn't, Bea." He had known all along she couldn't. Beatrice Hart—*his* Beatrice Hart—was not like that. But, God, the publicity—he couldn't repress a shudder. Angrily, then, he put the thought aside. The hell with the publicity. Somehow it had to be worked out. It would be worked out. He had to have Bea. He said, "You're doing the right thing, dear. You can't negotiate with somebody like Freddie."

"That's what I decided, Francis." Her voice changed and there was something tremulous in it as she went on. "Oh, it's going to be such a mess, and sometimes I feel so—sordid. But I can't let him win, Francis. He's wrong. I can't let him win when he's wrong."

No, he thought, Bea couldn't. She was the kind of woman who believed strongly in fighting for what was right.

"Bea, I knew that's what you'd do," he said. "I'm glad you're fighting him."

"Are you, Francis? Are you really? I do want to know that I'm doing what *you* think is right."

"I do think it is right. I don't think you could do anything else."

And when they had said goodbye, and he had hung up the receiver, he tried not to think about the headlines.

She mustn't be schoolgirl-idiotic about it, Beatrice thought, but she *would* be a *good* wife for a Supreme Court justice. They didn't award Ph.Ds in the theater, but if you weren't a complete yokel or sex machine you acquired poise, and after hours you spent enough time with outsiders who knew something about the world so that the native intelligence inherited from Jacob and Esther Krasnov was continually nourished by the hard-crusted bread of contemporary facts. Without making any particular point of it, except to satisfy her curiosity about what happened beyond the proscenium arch, she had moved easily—and with easy acceptance—among politicians and diplomats long before she met Francis, so that when she did meet him she was ready for him on more or less equal terms. And the proof was that they got along

279

—so beautifully, so effortlessly. She sat there and the good days and nights kept flooding her memory, filling her with joy.

She poured herself another cup of coffee and walked over to the high, floor-to-ceiling window and looked down on the gray gloom of Gramercy Park, here and there splashed with lamplit traces of green. She would not have been like Henry Clay Robson's wife, that was sure. She supposed there was such a thing as a woman's being too damned intellectual, as Franny Robson proved with such insistence. It was bad enough that she talked so much, dropping literary names all over the floor, but the woman was unsquelchable—even by the President of the United States. There had been that dinner last spring when Beatrice's own cheeks flamed for Franny Robson and yet Franny had taken the Presidential rebuke in stride, almost impassively. She had been going on and on about an obscure Uzbek author who had made been made captive by some haughty reviewer on the *Times* and was currently the rage among the *avant-avant-garde* types, and worse still, she had been pouring her lecture into the ear of the Indonesian Ambassador who was sickening enough with his verbal curtsies to the Soviet Union. Beatrice had not blamed John Alden Hughes when he broke in to protest impatiently, "Oh, for God's sake, Franny, don't you know any American writers?" So shortly Franny had shifted the conversation to television, inveighing against its vulgar corruption of the American people, and quoting *Harper's* and the *Atlantic Monthly* at length to illustrate her points. The trouble was, Beatrice reflected, that the people who watched westerns on TV did not read *Harper's* and the *Atlantic* and thus were not exposed to reform. If the country needed to be saved from TV, which Beatrice doubted, the evangelism would have to come from Dick Tracy or Little Orphan Annie. No, Li'l Abner wouldn't do; he was untrustworthy as somehow too sophisticated for his patched britches.

And what was she doing worrying about TV and finding fault with Franny Robson, when she should be trying to organize her thoughts for her session with Bill Stone? She had to pull herself together and think the practical thoughts necessary to the negotiations with Freddie. It was no good striding about the house thinking what a beast Freddie was. He *was* a beast, and that was that, but calling him names didn't accomplish anything. She wished she could just give him all the money she had and then forget it, but she knew that couldn't work. She could not let Freddie get away with it; such a surrender would be alien to everything she was. Freddie was wrong and she was right, and she could not let him win by default. The money didn't matter, at least not that much, but it did matter that Freddie was trying to take advantage of her. She had never confused generosity with foolishness, and she would not do so now. Francis would not want her to. It was curious, but he would not. He might have wanted out, for reasons she would not have agreed with but which she knew were terribly valid to him, but Francis was too incorrigibly on the side of right to condone any crawling to Freddie. And he did not want out—that was the important thing. He wanted her to fight. He even wanted to help her fight.

She welcomed the ringing phone and she picked it up eagerly, and when she heard Jimmy Hughes's voice, her greeting was almost gushing.

"I just wanted to talk to a nice girl," Jimmy said.

"Oh, Jimmy, you're an angel to call me," she said. "I want to be reminded I have such nice civilized friends."

"I'm nothing of the sort; I'm a porcine predator tracking down my prey."

"If you want to take me to dinner, the answer is yes, yes, yes."

"I do want to take you to dinner, and stop acting as if it doesn't really matter that I'm me and not Francis Dalton. I know you loyal types."

"Oh, Jimmy—don't be so nice and silly." It *was* nice to hear someone speak Francis' name. Say Francis Dalton again, she pleaded silently. "Jimmy, you know I'm always glad to see you."

"Well, fine. I don't deceive myself, you little hussy, but I'll be in New York Thursday night and I think I've got enough money to take you to Le Pavillon. I'm tired of Washington. I want to be seen with a pretty girl in an expensive saloon."

"I accept, you porcine predator, and I'm so sorry you're tired. I'll do my best to keep you awake. I've got a new soft-shoe number."

"Just a smile every fifteen minutes will do. Sweetie, how *are* you?"

"All right, Jimmy. I'm all right." She felt, suddenly, so wretched. "Oh, Jimmy, no I'm not. I feel so dreadful, and I'm so glad you called just so I could stop thinking of myself—and of fighting Freddie."

"Poor dear. Bea, you're a nice, sweet girl, and it shouldn't happen to you. I've talked to Francis; he told me about it."

"I'm glad, Jimmy. I'm glad he wanted to talk to somebody about it, too. I've got Bill Stone, and I've tried not to be too East Lynnish and he's been an angel, but I suppose I have been rather a bore. But I like knowing that Francis wants somebody to talk about it to, too; I want it to mean that much to him."

"It means very much to him. He's terribly worried about you. He's blaming himself a lot."

"Blaming himself? But how could he, Jimmy? Nothing is Francis' fault. He hasn't done anything. It's I who've been such a fool."

"Oh, you know—Francis is a bit of a bloody idiot about such things. He feels you wouldn't be concerned if he hadn't yacked on to you so much about the dignity of his position and his responsibility to the state, and all that rot."

"Oh, poor Francis." Poor, poor dear, she thought. Merely because he can't help being himself—being decent and honest, and dear. "Jimmy, you mustn't let him talk like that; it's so unfair to him."

"I suppose so, Bea; but he is—has been—rather an idiot. A nice one, but an idiot. Oh, I do understand him, Bea, perhaps because I don't have his rectitude. He's got what I suppose they used to call a code. Sounds silly, but I think with Francis that is it, honestly. Trouble is he wore it too often on his sleeve, for you to admire—and it frightened you. He didn't expect that, sweetie, and now he's chewing on himself for being so stuffy— with you. I told him he was a bloody ass for going on like that with you, but I suppose I do see his point."

"That is it, Jimmy. You've got to understand Francis. He is so—oh, respectable, in such a nice, decent, attractive way. It's not flag waving with him, Jimmy; it's just the way he was made."

"I know, sweetie. I'm not throwing him over. I've had experience with people like Francis all my life—Mother and Johnny and, in a lesser sense, Father. They all irritate the hell out of me, but I can't not like them for it. I can't not respect them. I don't want them to be like me, but I just wish they could be a little more—human."

"Francis is very human, Jimmy. I know that, and so do you. And we can't criticize him for being responsible. For years everybody has been yelling for responsibility and decency in government, and then we get someone like Francis and we don't appreciate him."

"Yes, I know. It's silly, but I understand your Francis."

"It isn't silly to Francis, Jimmy. His—rectitude is almost frightening, but it's real. It's honest. He's not striking a pose."

"Bea, you're a wonderful woman. You may be a great one. I wish you were my girl."

"Jimmy, thank you, you awful, lovely man. Let's not be this philosophical Thursday night."

"No, we won't. And Pauline is going to be in town and she'll meet us after dinner for some pub-crawling, so it'll be dreadfully respectable."

"Oh, good. Jimmy, you showed awfully good taste in picking out a sister."

"Pauline's great. She did what she wanted without causing a big row with Mother. I wish I had that faculty."

"You've got one just as good, Jimmy. You make people feel good."

"Stop it, Bea. Look, I've got to get back to work. Johnny has me toiling on that Food for the World thing. I work with a virginal schoolteacher from Racine, Wisconsin, who thinks passionate thoughts about my brother. I think I should tell Liz."

"Jimmy, everybody thinks passionate thoughts about your brother. Call me when you get in so I can powder my nose."

"Right—and, Bea"—Jimmy paused—"I can't believe Francis Dalton is going to be a damned fool permanently."

After she had hung up the telephone, she sat there with her hand to her cheek, and she realized how happy she had been talking to Jimmy. It was hard to cast Jimmy Hughes in a paternal role, but he was just what she needed, since she couldn't have Jacob Krasnov. She needed to be taken care of, to be comforted, to have somebody talk sense to her as well as give her casual affection.

She got up and got a cigarette and lit it and walked slowly around the living room, strolling really, to help her thoughts. She did need being taken care of, and Francis had always been the one she knew instinctively could do the job. Over the years she had not realized she was lonely until she met Francis and discovered how much of her life he filled and how he wrapped her in a comfortable, protective cloak of caring. She had been busy, and she had had neither the time nor the inclination to feel sorry for herself. More, she had usually been merry. She was doing what she wanted to do, and doing it well, and she liked the people she worked with. It was a tough world she lived in, often ruthless and hard, and she knew that others had valid criticisms of it, but she could judge it only in the light of how it treated her, and it had turned toward her a smiling face and, often enough for such a competitive world, a helping hand. She had never had a serious row with anyone on the stage or *of* the stage, although she had been told she couldn't work with this one or that one. Those warnings had frightened her, but she had tackled the job as she always had done in the past, with an open mind and with the determination to do her job as well as it could be done so that she would not be a burden to anyone. Roy Smithwick had been the toughest, but she had held her tongue, and by opening night he had almost completely ceased his irritable mutterings, and at the final curtain he had turned to her and said angrily, "I've had less trouble with you than any goddamned woman I ever played with." She realized later that she could not have expected a wilder compliment.

Poor Freddie. And poor Robert. It was easier to feel sorry for Freddie, bereft as he was of any decent instincts, amoral, because she now realized he had never had anything decent to lose. Freddie had not deteriorated; his was a pathetic case because of the mental quirk that prevented him from ever reaching a point where there was anything to deteriorate. And yet she could feel sorry for Robert, too, despite his coldly calculating ways, because he was so desperately anxious to get somewhere, to arrive. As her first husband, Robert had always had that chip on his shoulder so incongruous at times with his little-boy manner. She had arrived and Robert was on his way up, but still a mere reporter—as he put it, so defensively. She had thought him brilliant and witty, and she had been childishly enchanted with the idea of helping him, of inspiring him on his road to the heights. But her solicitude, her casual seeing to it that he met the right people, her honest excitement at reading everything he wrote, had seemed to irritate him. He had used her, of course, but something good deep inside him must have given him concern about this using; he had taken it out angrily on her.

"It's plain enough," Bill Stone had told her during the divorce proceedings. "The bastard feels guilty. He let you give him a boost, and now he's being eaten up with the realization that he got to be the editor of that paper at twenty-eight not because he was a genius but because you put him on display in your show window."

She had laughed at Bill, but she knew he was right. Robert had blurted it out during their last scene.

"And one more thing," he had told her. "You like to think you've been a little kingmaker, the inspiration that got me where I am today. Well, I'm sick of all that. I'm sick of your patronizing me."

At this point, she found it impossible to be hurt.

Anyway, she had not had to pay Robert any alimony, although she had made the offer.

"No, thanks," he told her. "This may come as a jolt to your ego, but I don't need you any more."

She had been so hurt, then, that she had fired back, "I think that is quite obvious, Robert," and been sorry a moment later, for she could foretell what Jacob Krasnov would tell her a few weeks later when she fled to Columbus and fell into his arms.

"*Nu*, Beatrice, that was not my daughter speaking," her father told her. "It was a fact, yes, that he no longer needed you and so he was going. But you did not say it as a fact, Beatrice. You said it to hurt him. In this world, we don't have to hurt people on purpose; the world hurts them every day, by accident."

It warmed her now, to think of her father, and the thought brought another—of Michael Dalton. There had been that same, comfortable feeling of warmth when Francis introduced her to his father in his Georgetown living room, that same feeling of being protected, but with Irish charm thrown in.

"Miss Hart, you're a whole lot prettier than the pictures,"

Michael Dalton told her, and then leaned forward and kissed her on the cheek.

"There," he said. "I haven't kissed a beautiful woman since my Bridget died."

Michael Dalton liked her; Beatrice was sure of that. It was evident in the easy grace with which he treated her. After the first few minutes she was no longer a famous actress to Michael Dalton, but more a pretty contemporary of his daughters, and before long he was complaining to her, in the same tone he used with Sheila and Kathy, about the general disrepair of Francis' house.

"A fine place for a former Governor of Massachusetts to be living in," Michael Dalton told her. "The plaster in the bathroom is a disgrace, and the toilet itself is cracked."

And it was not at all corn when Michael Dalton did the conventional thing and turned to Francis to suggest "And maybe you'd better try to get this young girl to marry you, Francis, before you get too old to give me a grandson."

In the kitchen later, where Michael Dalton was refilling his beer glass and Beatrice was replenishing the tray of what Francis' brother Mike called "horse's dovers," the Dalton patriarch had been easily confidential. "Francis, now, could never make up his mind about a girl," he said. "But he seems fond of you, Beatrice. I'd count it a favor if you didn't let him get away."

Beatrice thought about Jacob Krasnov and Michael Dalton and Jimmy Hughes for a long time, because it made her feel good to do so, and then she called Bill Stone.

"You sound wonderful, Bea," Bill Stone said. "I knew you'd bounce back."

"Not quite that, Bill," she said. "I've not quite bounced back. But I'm determined to live. And I've spent most of the evening talking to Francis and to Jimmy Hughes and thinking about the nice people I know."

She could see Bill's big hand tugging at his graying guardsman's mustache as he said, "They're none of them as nice as you are, child, but they all love you, including me."

"Thank you, Bill. I know I'm lucky—in spite of my worries. And now I want to talk about Freddie. I want to tell you what I want us to do tomorrow."

"Yes . . . I've got some papers here, Bea."

"Bill, never mind the papers for a while. I just want to tell you this: I don't care what kind of scandal Freddie kicks up. I don't care if he crucifies me. He's not going to get any more money out of me. I'm going to fight him. I'm going to fight him the way my father would have fought him, and Francis' father—and Francis."

There was a pause, and then over the line came the high-pitched awfulness of a rebel yell. "Goddamn!" Bill Stone yelled. "Now you're talking, child. Congratulations. Let us get to work —immediately."

The headline in the Washington *Star* fed Chief Justice Robert McNair Bacon's irritability, never undernourished: BACON IN ABOUT-FACE, it screamed. About-face indeed! Washington, accustomed to placing its roster of public figures in precise patterns, was the least expert of any city, in Bacon's opinion, in analyzing the actions of any public servant higher than a charwoman. About-face! Was it really Washington's opinion that a Supreme Court justice was an automaton, a machine, who reached his opinions on law merely by pushing the proper button? Bacon knew he was not particularly popular in the capital, yet he realized also that this would hardly have an effect on the kind of headlines the *Star* wrote, or the impression its story would give. In the urgent, black-and-white area of journalism, Bacon acknowledged, significance was swiftly deduced when anyone said anything or took any action in contradiction to what he had said and done consistently over a period of years. Calming down somewhat, he acknowledged further that technically his vote to uphold the Chicago convictions *had* been a switch. But there was a *reason* for the switch, just as there was a reason for every opinion he had ever handed down from the Supreme Court bench. He thought he had spelled out that reason with considerable lucidity in his opinion; it should have explained that the switch was made, not merely as a switch per se, but for the purpose of correctly interpreting a given situation.

"Robert." Margaret's voice came twangy from the doorway. She stood there, as though appraising his mood, and he looked up at her, and gave her the briefest of smiles to reassure her.

287

Dammit, he could not understand why Margaret was always worried about his moods. His mood was always all right when he was at home, locked away from the world behind the heavy oak door of their Massachusetts Avenue town house.

"Yes, Margaret," he said. "I'm really trying not to be angry at anyone."

"Oh, good. Robert." She remained in the doorway. "I've got to make some telephone calls, but you will watch *Macbeth* on TV with me later, won't you?"

"Yes, I suppose so. Why *Macbeth*, dammit? We've both seen it fifty times. Is that *avant garde* enough for you?" He was fond of Margaret, but sometimes she baffled him when she experimented with being wifely. Happily, these experiments were rare, and brief in duration; his perception had been accurate when he married this horse-faced intellectual on the grounds she would be less bothersome than the other females he knew.

"It's not just *Macbeth*, Robert. That new Greek actor, Mithridates, is in it. He's supposed to give the character a whole new dimension. It's not just Shakespeare the way he does it. Or at least, so I've read."

"Good, then. I hope it's incomprehensible enough to please you." He rustled the paper. "I'm just reading the *Star*. I'll be upstairs shortly and I'll do my best to be attentive."

"Reading about the decision?" Margaret was ready to pounce, and he didn't want to subject himself to one of her long-winded, convoluted discourses. Margaret had a good brain, but she suffered from the inbred ideas of the intellectuals she ran with.

"I suppose so," he said. His grin was a grimace. "I suppose you want to stick your nose in it—hear all the inside dope. Well, I shan't let you."

Margaret remained in the doorway. "Don't try to fluster me, Robert. I didn't say a thing. I'll wait for the *Times* in the morning."

"Sure, but you'd like to get an earful, wouldn't you?" He barked a little laugh.

"Robert, you are smug. I'm sure I can form my own opinion without listening to a lot of dreary legal phraseology." She paused. "I thought it interesting that the *Star* called your vote an about-face. Have you made your peace with John Hughes, Robert?"

"I have not." His voice was grim. "I still think John Alden Hughes is a damned scoundrel—no matter how I voted. And now, let me read, dammit."

Well, that was true, Bacon was thinking as he turned back to his newspaper. He let the paper fall to his lap. No, not quite. Hughes was not a scoundrel. He couldn't be—not and be President at the same time. The office didn't let a man be a scoundrel. But he still felt the same way about Hughes; he still thought his presence in the White House was a national disaster. He smiled at the thought of the *Star*'s conclusion that the decision would be a blow to Hughes. That was great. He was glad he had disconcerted the President. That was all to the good. He relished the thought of the President sitting in his study tonight, pondering the day's news and worrying, worrying anew about his Court plan.

"Damned dictator!" Bacon was surprised at the words tumbling out, aloud. Hughes affected him that way; he couldn't think of him without becoming angry.

Let John Alden Hughes worry. He, Robert Bacon, was worried about what was happening to the country under Hughes. What was happening to the country which had come so alive during those eager New Deal years when he first came to Washington to work for the Justice Department? He had been rich and a scholar to boot, a national celebrity in the comparatively obscure post as professor of law at Columbia University. He supposed he was one of the earliest eggheads, although in those days the conservatives were content to deride them with the simple epithet "professors." He was renowned for the skill and artistry he put into a teaching chore that for others would have been a routine task. And he knew that he had vision beyond the horizons of provincial partisanship. He had fought even with Roosevelt because of that vision, which saw things—since come to pass—that even the Hyde Park squire could not perceive. In that day, he supposed, he had been a wild man—and wildness had to be superlative to gain that distinction in that day. He was with Henry Wallace, and yet far ahead of him. They were great days and they lasted for a long time, but not long enough. They were torn off the calendar by a country too prosperous and comfortable, too jealous of its material possessions to risk the continuing struggle for the possession of liberty. He had wealth, much more than most, and it meant almost nothing to him although he lived well and graciously on it. The money merely freed him from material worries so he could worry about ideas, about the world.

He supposed, while he was about it, he might consider what had happened to him during those long years since he had first come to Washington. But the answer did not come simply, because the change in him had been outward only. There were the days when he exulted in his elevation to the Court of Appeals, for he was still relatively young, and in the distance the Supreme Court of the United States beckoned to his politically favored eminence. And the years on the Appeals Court were rich and satisfying. There was always the exaltation of finding the relevance of a given law to a given situation, as he did in the television case which to so many seemed to pose no problem under the Sherman Act. He brought to Appeals not only erudition but a sharply honed awareness of history—of where the United States had to go, lawfully, in the new world that had opened to it. Always, he insisted that the nation could not continue along its destined path unless the freedom of its citizens, the liberty of the individual, remained unscathed in the hurly-burly of the several confusing battles involving government, industry, labor and the enemy abroad. You did not compromise on the law, because the law as written already represented compromise achieved by competing interests, unless that law was in conflict with the basic law represented in the Bill of Rights. Allen Hume might insist on prying into petty details, but Robert McNair Bacon had always been satisfied to go along with the progress of liberalism so long as its general outline stayed within constitutional bounds.

Particularly, he had never insisted that judges know best. In the first place, on matters of crucial import, there was no necessity for the judge to don the cloak of omniscience; the Constitution was there, it said what had to be said about the fundamentals; it was the rule book, the only rule book. His celebrity grew with his opinions on the Court of Appeals, but there was no reason why it should have grown, or diminished. No medals should accrue to the judge who obeyed the directives of the Bill of Rights. Nor did his so-called "wildness" ever cause him to overlook the dangers inherent in abuse of the Bill of Rights. When the case of the six Communist leaders came before him on appeal, he upheld the convictions. The Communists had invited action against the nation's legal bible and thus had presented a "clear and present danger." It was as simple as that.

No, his legal approach had not changed one whit. But the bitterness in Robert McNair Bacon, the man, the hearty, witty companion, had come to him with the disappointments piled upon disappointments. He had waited sixteen years for his appointment to the Supreme Court while vacancies were filled for political or geographical reasons. He had always been content merely to be a judge, the best judge his talents would permit. He had thought that was enough. But, like Learned Hand, he had discovered it was not. And so by the time he returned to Washington to preside over the Supreme Court, he had lost most of his good will toward men. They had made him wait too long, while they played politics.

Well, now. He brought himself upright in the chair. Was he crying personal persecution? Had it been too easy for him, as it was for others, to feel sorry for himself merely because it was his own career that was involved? He considered the question coldly and decided upon acquittal. To be sure, he had his pride and it was monumental, but he had always been too impersonal a judge of everything, of everybody including himself, to let his pride intervene. No, the country had ignored a man of superb qualifications, a man perhaps with the greatest fund of qualifications that could be found. It might please his ego to put it that way, but that was unimportant. He should have been appointed long before he was, because he was the best-qualified. That was a fact, and at this late date he would not abandon his respect for facts.

About-face indeed! Was his opinion in the case of the Communists an about-face? Did no one any longer trouble to examine a man's record? Had he ever given anything but short shrift to those who violated the nation's fundamental principles, even when those principles had to be applied through coercion? There were laws on the books for which he had no particular love, but he had never sought to evade the law's mandate. He was not one of those fussy men, like David Benjamin Feldman, who continually nit-picked at a case in which a guilty man had had a fair trial. Perhaps there were minor errors in the record, but if they were *minor*, then a judge should not be too quick to discover them. He had always pounced on the brutal policeman and the purposefully careless prosecutor, and he would always seek to protect the evil dope peddler whose constitutional rights had been abused, but his reasons were based on the fundamentals. Otherwise, he did not quibble.

Once he had read the briefs on the Chicago Sons of Slaves case, he had had no doubt what his opinion would be. Those poor misguided Negroes, thrown into battle by their Communist bosses, had indeed incited to riot. The entire South Side of Chicago was threatened with what amounted to civil war. And the civil authorities, cowering under the threat, probably imaginary, of the Negro's power in the polling booth, had done nothing about it.

He had been given firsthand information about that, on the second night of the riots, at the Bar Association dinner at the Blackstone Hotel. There had been some fear that commercial planes might be prevented from landing at O'Hare Field by the marauding bands, but his flight had made it, and later, before the speaking part of the program, he had found himself chatting with Hugo Brown. It was the first time he had seen Hugo in more than fifteen years, and there were pleasant reminiscences about the old days when he and the younger Hugo had encountered each other in cases Hugo defended in the role of the nation's leading corporation lawyer. In semiretirement, Hugo had purchased power in the party in Illinois, and it was in the role of a member of the triumvirate which ruled the state that Hugo gave his views on the rebellion.

"It's damned brutal stuff," Hugo said, the big cigar waggling in his hand as usual. "All hell is breaking loose on the South Side. The police are having a rough time of it."

"It looks terrible from Washington," Bacon had told him. "Do you think your police can handle it?"

Hugo Brown had looked at him and shrugged. "I don't know. It's pretty bad."

Bacon had tried without success to keep the ice out of his tone. "And yet you won't ask for help—for troops, or United States marshals."

Hugo Brown gave him another look before replying. "Well, I guess *not*, sir. Do you think we've lost our minds? Those niggers would clobber us at the next election."

Bacon had walked away.

Now he stirred as he heard Margaret's voice from the hall. "Coming upstairs, Robert? It's almost time."

He said, "Yes, dear," and was getting up from his chair when the telephone rang at his elbow. He picked it up.

"Chief? Sorry to bother you at home." It was Frank Hoar.

"Hello, Frank," Bacon said. "It's no bother. But why . . . ?"

"Oh, I just called you to congratulate you." Hoar's voice sounded cozily conspiratorial.

"What? What do you mean by that?" Bacon could sense something unpleasant in Hoar's voice.

"You know, Chief. Today's vote on the Chicago case. Congratulations. You put in a lick for our side on that one, Chief."

Bacon sat there, almost numb. He felt he could not speak, that he would disintegrate if he did.

"Chief?" Hoar's voice grated on the line. "Are you there?"

Bacon sat upright in his chair, and his voice came from deep in his throat, growling all the way. "Yes, Frank, I'm here. And if you ever say anything like that to me again, or mention it to anybody, anywhere, I'll have you hauled in by your heels for contempt of the Supreme Court of the United States."

He hung up, and got up from the chair. He was trembling, but he walked across the room and through the door into the hall and shouted up the stairs, "I'm coming, Margaret."

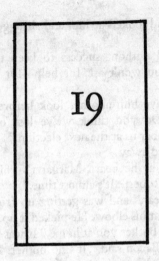

19

T HE TABLOID WASHINGTON *Daily News*, in its occasional barefoot-boy manner, summed up the President's problem editorially. "Hughes is baffled," explained an editorial writer who had made a fortune in natural gas speculation, "because for three weeks the Supreme Court has been patting him on his unwilling back." The total was impressive; in nine decisions delivered on successive opinion days the Court had upheld seven Presidential actions challenged for one reason or another by the liberal bloc. "But does the President want this kind of palship?" asked the *News*.

Hughes definitely did not; his favorite epithet for the Court was "those damned tricksters." But Francis did his best to explain. "There was never any serious division on those cases," he told the President. "They were of relatively minor importance, and you yourself, when they were challenged, said you expected no trouble from the Court on them. They're just coming at a bad time, psychologically, because they give the public the impression the Court has swung over to your viewpoint."

"Which it hasn't," Hughes said in a growl. "You're right of

294

course, Francis. Not even this Court could have ruled against me on those cases. But why did they have to come up now?"

The President might well ask this petulant question, for the Court's actions were spreading confusion in the administration ranks on the Hill. Where Chet McAdam had been confident enough to predict a margin of twenty-five or so votes for the Court bill a few weeks before, he now had to report that fifteen of those votes had become doubtful. McAdam was making his angry rounds, exhorting, pleading, threatening, but the troops were restive.

"The hell with risking my neck for that bill now," Ed Mackey of Arizona told McAdam. "I never liked it, and now we don't need it. Count me out."

Such reactions were reported daily, almost every hour on the hour, and yet the President declined to relinquish his optimism. He inveighed sarcastically against the defectors, but he insisted they could be beaten back into line. Some of his wrath he turned on Chet McAdam in curt warnings against "defeatism" in the leadership. "I expect labor to be troublesome," he said, "but it bothers me when my leadership seems so pessimistic." McAdam swallowed his anger and insisted he was merely reporting the bad news with the good.

Hughes grinned and threw an arm around McAdam's shoulders. "There isn't that much bad news, Chet. If you keep up the good fight, you'll see—those boys will be back in the fold when it's put to the test of a vote."

"I can hold my own on the Hill," McAdam said through grim lips. "But I have an awful feeling some members of the Court are meddling in this privately. Claude Wilkins has been seeing a lot of certain justices like Joe Baker and Feldman. If I knew what they were cooking up, I could do something about it, but who's going to tell me?"

"Chet, what you've got to do is protect the sure votes on your list at the same time you're working on the doubtful ones," the President said.

"My list!" McAdam's red face was doleful. "I don't have a list, as such, any more. The situation changes too often. Hell, Tom Martin has a regular IBM machine operation for the liberals; they *know* where they stand. Harry Weiss and I have to change ours every time we get a phone call. We drive a senator back into line and the next day, or that afternoon, he's wavering again. I repeat, if it could go to a vote today, we'd win it. But the Judiciary Committee is still horsing around with its hearings, and Alpheus Ward snaps at me every time I try to get him to hurry them up."

"Well, then, if we can win today we can win next week or next month," the President said. "It just needs a little effort, Chet. I know you'll put everything in it for me."

"I'm doing that, Mr. President," McAdam said, his mouth grim. "But it takes some doing. As you may have noticed when you were up on the Hill, the average senator considering a controversial bill can't think straight for that voter breathing down his neck. They're grateful to you for November, but they no sooner win one election than they have to start making plans to win the next. They're worried about all that noise being made by the opposition."

"Noise. Chet, the opposition has always made a lot of noise. And we always get the votes." The President's manner was easy.

"Yes, sir, but the boys are well aware that you can't run again—that they won't have any coattails to hang onto next time."

"Well, then, Chet, I hope you're setting them straight. I hope you're reminding them that there's an off-year election in less than two years—and that I won't go out of my way to help those who haven't helped me. I may not be able to run for a third term, but I suggest that I may be able to influence the Congressional elections while I'm still sitting in the White House."

"Mr. President, you don't have to worry about that." McAdam's face was red with agitation and fatigue. "They realize that, and I don't let them forget it."

"Good. Good, Chet. Then we don't really have to worry too much, do we?"

"Sir, we always have to worry. Nothing is sure in politics. I've got a few tame senators among the opposition—men who owe me a favor or two—and they say Hoar and Wilkins are optimistic. I don't like the opposition to be optimistic at this stage, especially when we're still supposed to have the votes."

The President smiled and followed the smile with an exaggerated wink. "And I, Chet, don't worry so long as I have you leading the troops. The people are with us, Chet, and that's important to those politicians up on the Hill. And I am not without influence when it comes to personally persuading the waverers. Meanwhile, Chet, I'm sure you can carry it off."

The trouble was, Hughes told himself, he wasn't sure of McAdam. He was almost positive that if he gave the word, Chet would hurry happily up to the Hill to arrange a compromise. He acknowledged McAdam's loyalty; what he feared was the New Yorker's ideological past. The Court plan was not the kind of bill the old, liberal McAdam would have cared for. Was he having his doubts now?

Well, he couldn't worry about McAdam all day; he still had that memo from State to read before the British Ambassador arrived. He picked up the three-page document and was halfway through the third paragraph when the door leading to the appointment secretary's office opened and Harry Weiss walked in. Hughes looked up, quelling the impatience he felt; Weiss did not interrupt except for important matters.

"Well, Harry?" The President couldn't quite manage a smile. "You look like bad news."

"I don't know, Mr. President." Weiss walked over to the desk and held out a long thin envelope. "This just came in by hand—from the Supreme Court. Feldman."

"Feldman? Another idea for reducing the national debt? Well, I'd better look at it."

The President tore off one end of the envelope and plucked out the letter, unfolding it with fingers that worked impatiently. Instinctively, he skipped the first paragraph after a glance at its conventional opening. It was all there, in the second paragraph.

"Here, read it." The President tossed the letter to Weiss, and Weiss stumbled against the desk reaching for the catch.

As Weiss read, the President leaned back in his chair and sighed.

"My God!" Weiss said.

"Yes," the President said. "He's quitting—just like that."

Weiss read aloud; his voice had the quality of a man in a trance. "Regretfully announce my intention to retire at the close of the Court's present spring term because of reasons of health."

"Reasons of health—Harry, had you heard that David Feldman was ill?"

"No, sir. Not a word. And that kind of thing is hard to keep quiet. I'm sure Francis Dalton would have told us."

"Reasons of health." The President stood up and walked over to the French door and looked out onto the Rose Garden, sere and drab in the patches where the snow had melted. "Feldman is —let's see—seventy-six. Never smoked, never drank. I played tennis with him only a couple of years ago, and he was a tiger. He still takes those walks along the canal in Georgetown, doesn't he?"

"I think so." Weiss's brow wrinkled as he attempted to sort out the odds and ends he carried in his mind for ready reference. "I think his picture was in the *Star* a couple of weeks ago, walking in the snow."

"Reasons of health." The President walked back to his desk and sat down heavily. "What do you think, Harry?"

"I wonder, sir."

"So do I. His resignation is most timely—most timely for those who are fighting the Court bill. The letter is signed by David Benjamin Feldman, but I wonder if what it says could have been dictated by Frank Hoar and Claude Wilkins."

"They're equal to it, sir. And we know Feldman is on their side."

"I wonder. Harry, I've got to read this memo and then see Sir Howard. Call Charlie Mayborn and get him over here. I want to talk to you both as soon as Sir Howard leaves."

"Chet McAdam?" Weiss lifted an eyebrow.

"No. Not Chet. Just you and Charlie. Chet is a little too involved—personally—in this one."

The President was pleased with the facility with which he had managed the past hour. Once Harry Weiss had left, he had turned off all thought of the Feldman letter, pushing that invaluable button he had used so many times during sodden, dreary campaign trips to turn his complete attention to the memo from State on the Iranian matter. Yet he felt he should take no pride in it; in this job, at this desk, you either tackled each problem in turn, with full concentration, or everything went to hell. And there had been worse times, much worse times; somehow he had managed it when word came about that lost plane over the Ukraine just before a farm speech in Des Moines. It was what they paid you for.

The memo was a good one, too; that helped. Young Boyce was always lucid and wrote swiftly to the point. And Sir Howard had always been easy to talk to; he said what he had to say without preliminaries so that there was no time for your mind to wander.

Mayborn and Weiss walked in one door even as another was closing on Sir Howard; the President waved them to chairs, leaned back in his own and said, "Well."

Mayborn's voice was hoarse. "I've just come from the Senate," he said. "Harry's secretary caught me up there. It's pretty wild on the floor."

"Yes, I suppose so," the President said. "What's going on, Charlie?"

"Well, of course, Feldman released the letter shortly after he sent it over here. It was like Christmas Day in a houseful of kids. Chet McAdam was sitting at his desk in the front row, and when the news came everybody came hustling up to congratulate him."

"On his new job—as an associate justice of the Supreme Court?"

"Yes, sir. Chet was holding court for the entire Senate, a one-man reception line. Everybody came up to shake his hand, from both parties. You should have seen Frank Hoar pounding Chet's back, and Claude Wilkins."

"A happy scene," the President said, cutting off the words shortly.

"It was kind of touching, really," Mayborn said. "There was old Chet, grinning from ear to ear and looking kind of embarrassed every time somebody addressed him as 'Mr. Justice.' Of course, everybody figures it's in the bag for Chet, now that Feldman is leaving."

"Yes—of course." The President spoke mechanically. "And I suppose they're all thinking that there's no necessity for my Court plan, now. Is that about it, Charlie?"

Mayborn looked uncomfortable, and suddenly angry. "Yes, by God, I suppose that's what those timid bastards are thinking. I didn't get a chance to talk to anybody, but I can read that Senate like a book."

"It's an easy way out for them," Harry Weiss said.

"I suppose that's the way they look at it," the President said.

"Well." Now Mayborn was embarrassed. "I suppose they'll call you on it, sir. You know, you said after the Chicago case, more or less publicly, that although the Court apparently had switched its stand you still weren't satisfied. You said a one-margin vote wasn't enough. Well, now, of course, you can get yourself another vote, by appointing a successor to Feldman. Some of those boys will figure that ought to be enough for you. They'll say all you have to do is appoint a conservative to the Court and you can forget about your bill."

"And they assume the appointment is in the bag for Chet McAdam. He would be the conservative they mean." The President sounded petulant.

"Well, yes." Mayborn coughed, hand to mouth. "Of course everybody knows Chet was promised the job, and a little bit more besides. It's no secret, Mr. President."

"No, it isn't. I realize that, Charlie. I just hate to have my hand forced, that's all." The President stood up and walked around and stood leaning against the front of his desk as he so often did when his thoughts were troubling him.

"Appoint Chet McAdam and forget about the Court bill," he said. "It all sounds so simple—and yet it isn't. It isn't at all. That way, I get no additional justices for a Court which has proved its wild liberalism and which only capriciously has given me any support. Further, the new justice succeeding to the vacancy caused by Feldman's resignation will be Chet McAdam. He's on our side now. But with his political background, how long will he stick with us?"

Mayborn and Weiss were silent.

"My way seems clear," the President said. "All I have to do is stand by my pledge and name McAdam to the Court. And then, probably, a generous Senate will offer a compromise—a constitutional amendment for a mandatory retirement age that might take years for ratification by the states. And in that meanwhile, the Supreme Court will do what it likes to my program."

Mayborn stirred in his chair, but said nothing. Weiss looked up and said, "It's tough, sir. But there it is. What else is there to do?"

"Harry, I don't know." The President walked to the French door, looked out into the Rose Garden, then turned and walked back to his desk. "I just don't like to be forced into anything. I'll pay my bills, but I don't want my creditors breathing down my neck, suggesting that payment is now in order."

One of the three telephones on the desk rang, and the President picked up the receiver. "Who? Oh." There was a pause. "All right, put him on." He turned to Mayborn and Weiss, one hand over the mouthpiece. "It's Henry Smith."

The President said, "Hello, Henry. Good of you to call," and then there was a pause. The President laughed. "I suppose this is what you'd call a delegation waiting on me by phone. All right, Henry, I'll hear your petition."

Speaker Smith was always articulate when he had something to say, and it was obvious to Mayborn and Weiss that what he was saying was important to him. The President interrupted only to say, "Yes, Henry," and once to put in, "So that's the situation, is it?" The almost completely one-way conversation lasted nearly five minutes before John Alden Hughes said quietly, "Thank you for calling, Henry. I'll be in touch with you." Then he hung up.

He turned back to Mayborn and Weiss, and now his voice had cold rage in it. "The Speaker of the House heads a little delegation which decided it was time to favor me with its views. Henry was speaking for the Vice-President and also for the Majority Leader of the House."

He was striding up and down in front of his desk now. "The delegation has explained the situation on the Hill to me. It is the consensus that Feldman's resignation has now given me all I could possibly hope for in my battle to change the complexion of the Supreme Court. It now behooves me, the delegation suggests, to appoint Chet McAdam to the Court forthwith and then to announce that I am open to compromise on the Court bill."

"Damn," Harry Weiss said, in a tone that had a strangely neutral quality. "Bill Ball. I never thought he'd join anything like that."

The President smiled. "Majority Leader William C. Ball is a politician, Harry. He recognizes an escape hatch when he sees one, even if he is beholden to me for every Pennsylvania vote he ever got."

"Everybody'll be getting into the act," Mayborn said, his voice cranky, his manner strained. "They like that easy way out."

"Who doesn't? Who doesn't?" The President's voice was low,

but the irritation in it was plain. "Especially on the Hill, they like things neat and orderly and easy. But, gentlemen, where does it leave me if I now appoint Chester McAdam to the Supreme Court? With his politics doubtful, I will still need two additional justices lest he stray from the reservation once he reaches the safety of that marble palace. I could have gambled on him with two justices to appoint. But dare I gamble on him when the Senate threatens to leave me no opportunity to balance his appointment?"

"He could turn out all right," Weiss said. "Chet has worked pretty hard for your bill, sir." Again there was the hesitancy in Weiss to be brutal until it was proved, beyond doubt, to be absolutely necessary.

"Yes, he could." The President spoke as though through a sigh. "Of course he could. I may be doing Chet an injustice. But at this desk, gentlemen, you are forced every day to do men little injustices—for the sake of what you are trying to accomplish. Every day, the President of the United States has to sit here and wonder about men, distrust them a little, set tests for them so that their steadfastness, their fidelity, can be double-checked. It is because in other jobs a man may falter a little, he may backslide a trifle, without damage to either the nation's security or its conscience. It is only the President who has to be sure, as sure as he can possibly be, when he makes a move. I respect Chet McAdam and I honor him, and I suspect him. In dire need, his presence at my side would be both a comfort and a joy. But how much does the President really know about any man? Enough, he thinks, to get the job done. Enough to trust him with his policies. And yet, never enough. Never enough, gentlemen, to set all fears aside. I know Chet McAdam, as much as it is possible to know him without being able to look into his mind and his heart. He is surely one of the statesmen of our time. And yet, gentlemen, he has glands, emotions, muscles that twitch first this way and then that way, moods, doubts, frustrations, wounds. Who can say what that complex which is man will do, always? Chet McAdam grew up on the other side; his conservatism has always been of the moderate variety. And so, though he is firmly with us today, can I be sure he will be with us tomorrow?"

The President stared at the two men, and his look offered no invitation to speak. Then his voice became more matter-of-fact. "The doubts are not mine alone, as you well know. Several of those senators who slapped Chet McAdam's back today and who can be counted on to vote for the Court bill have their doubts, too. They have expressed those doubts to me and to you, Charlie, and to you, Harry. The *Chicago Tribune* is against his appointment and so is the Los Angeles *Times*. The men who run the conservative magazines and the conservative television and radio stations are none of them more than lukewarmly in favor of the appointment. Will we continue to have their solid support if I send Chet up to the Court?"

He walked back to his chair and sat down. "I'm afraid not, gentlemen. Oh, we could weather the newspapers and the others. But we can't afford to lose a single one of those sure votes for the bill. Offend those senators and their votes are lost forever. The others on the Hill, I'm sure, can be dealt with, whatever their resentments, but those of the solid right do not merely waver—they bolt."

Mayborn's cough sounded again. "It's something we'll have to try to figure," he said. "We'll have to figure out some way of sweating it out."

"Yes, we will," the President said. "And it will take some figuring, Charlie. After all, I can't announce that I don't trust my Senate Majority Leader far enough to appoint him to the Supreme Court."

"Still, there's one thing." Weiss's smile looked like something he had stored away for use at such a moment. "Feldman's gone, or will be going. We've got rid of one of them."

The President smiled, too. "Yes, that's right. The opposition has been reduced by one. It's up to me now to capitalize on that, if I can—if I will."

"Anything we should do, now?" Mayborn asked. He was itching to be busy, to get away from the frustration of talk.

"No." The President stood up and seemed to be looking over their heads at something on the far wall of the room. "No, nothing just yet."

"Should somebody call Chet McAdam?" Weiss asked.

"No," the President said. "Not now. Not for a while. I just won't do anything for the moment."

Francis put down the phone and remained sitting upright at his desk; he was not only puzzled, but still startled, by Feldman's call. "If you are free, I should greatly appreciate it if you would come to see me." Francis could still hear the dry, slightly twangy voice of the Associate Justice from New York. The words had not been in the form of a request, but of a statement, flat and emotionless. It was strange, because Francis felt he hardly knew Feldman. It was not a question of their being on opposite sides—Feldman had usually been courteous even during the heat of debate. It was that he and Feldman didn't talk to each other; they were, in effect, strangers. Feldman had not signaled out Francis to ignore; he hardly noticed any member of the Court. Feldman lived alone, not only in his apartment at the Sheraton-Park Hotel, but within the marble walls of the Supreme Court. His liberalism was advanced in the interests of the so-called common people, but it was unlikely that David Benjamin Feldman had ever enjoyed the slightest intimacy with a common man or woman. It was not enough to explain that he had a fortune estimated in the hundreds of millions; that icy figure would have remained aloof from the world had he been a shoe salesman.

Francis got up from the chair and rang for Jake Moriarty.

"I'm going to run down the hall for a few minutes," he told Jake. Then, for the effect he knew it would have, "Feldman wants to see me."

"Feldman?" Jake Moriarty's mouth fell open as though he were a character in a comic strip.

"Yes, Feldman. I'll be right back, Jake." Francis walked out. Francis knocked on the door of Feldman's office and was surprised when it opened immediately to reveal Feldman standing there with his hand on the knob.

"Mr. Justice," Feldman said. His round face with its heavy brows looked freshly scrubbed, and that was all. "I was expecting you. It's good of you to interrupt your work for me. Please come in."

Francis walked in and Feldman gestured at a chair next to his desk, then walked slowly over to his own chair behind the desk and sat down. As always, Francis was fascinated by the tall, thin body that somehow had sprouted a round head and chubby face.

"Would you like to smoke?" Feldman pointed to a jade box of cigarettes on the desk. Francis shook his head automatically.

"I used the public entrance this morning when I came to work," Feldman said. "For the first time in years, I noticed the bronze doors. Six and a half tons apiece. We work here and we don't notice things, Mr. Justice."

"No, I'm afraid we don't." Francis paused, trying to decide what to say next. "I suppose the tourists get more out of this building than we do."

"Yes, I suppose so. Yet, some things are familiar to me. One of the panels on the door, for instance. It is my favorite—Coke barring King James I from sitting as a judge in the King's Court. It is a good reminder of the Court's independence of the executive."

"It is a good work," Francis said. Where *are* we going? he thought.

"I never cared for the oak paneling in our private offices," Feldman said, his manner that of a man finally voicing a long grievance. "I do think mahogany such as was used in the Court chamber would have been far better."

"I suppose so," Francis said. "Although again, I'm afraid I haven't noticed it particularly." My God, he thought, is he all right?

Feldman smiled, and Francis was surprised at the softness of his expression. "I suppose you notice things as you grow older, and especially when you are going to leave them," Feldman said. "I noticed things this morning. I have been here a long time, and now that I am leaving I find that I am more aware of—things."

"I was sorry to hear about your resignation," Francis said. "I think you can believe it when I say we shall all miss you."

Feldman's chubby face was solemn now. "Yes, I think I can believe that. It is a sort of family. Not always a happy one, but composed of persons of—some similarity of interests. We are all, you might say, in the same business. It is nice of you to say I shall be missed. I know I shall miss this"—he spread his hands—"and all of you." He smiled again. "The good guys and the bad guys, shall we say?"

Francis grinned. "The good guys and the bad guys—somehow we sound more human described in that fashion."

"Oh, we're all human, in our fashion—although I suppose there have been doubts about me." He held up a hand against Francis' retort. "I'm human enough, at any rate, to realize that I have not won any popularity contests within the Court, even among those who think as I do."

"It's not quite like that, Mr. Justice. There have been tense moments, but I think we all try to retain our detachment." Francis smiled again. "I know I hope my colleagues have been tolerant of me, even when it was rather difficult."

"Sometimes, sometimes, Mr. Justice. I don't think I have always been as tolerant as I should have been. But then, that is human, too." Again the smile. "Quite frankly, we have sometimes fought like cats and dogs."

"You're right, of course," Francis said. "And yet—we're still on speaking terms, aren't we? That should make us feel better about it."

"Yes, of course. I hope it does." Feldman straightened up in his chair. "Mr. Justice, I asked you to come here because I wanted to tell you something. It will come out, eventually, but I wanted to tell you now. I am dying of cancer."

Francis felt his head snap back; almost, he heard the snapping sound. He had heard it, all right, and it had startled him and shocked him, but the word had been said so matter-of-factly that he found himself considering it in the same fashion. Yet no words he thought proper seemed available to him.

"Cancer?" he said, a query in his tone. "Mr. Justice, I don't know what to say . . ."

"There's not much to say, sir, that's why. I tried not to shock you, but I suppose I did; there doesn't seem to be any polite way to put it."

"Mr. Justice, I am shocked, and most grievously moved. I really don't know what to say, how to tell you what I feel."

"No, of course you don't, Mr. Justice. I wouldn't either. What do you say when a man tells you he is dying? I not only wouldn't know what to say; I might resent the man's putting me in such a position." He put up a hand again to ward off interruption.

"But naturally you want to know, or you're wondering, why I should tell you, why I should ask you to come to me so that I could tell you I'm dying of cancer. We have not been close, sir. For that matter, I have not been close to anyone on this Court.

But, more, we have been on opposite sides. And that is why I wanted to tell you, Mr. Justice."

Francis looked at Feldman. "Yes," he said. "If I could help . . ."

"You can't, Mr. Justice. No one can. Oh, I'd tell you if you could. If anyone could help, I'd go to him, seeking help. I don't want to die." Feldman smiled his new soft smile. "Who does? We all cling to life, however poor it may be. Of course, I don't think my life is a poor one—not now. I have—actually—nothing, of course. No wife, no children, no relatives, no one to whom I have given what is necessary for friendship. Yet it is my life, and I do not consider it a poor one."

"You are not only not an evil man, you are a good man," Francis said, meaning every word. "We are all different, but goodness has nothing to do with that. Goodness is not reserved for one side or the other."

"Oh, I'm not evil." Feldman's hand flapped listlessly as though dismissing the thought as unimportant. "I don't know if that fact is worth boasting about. Whether I'm good is another matter—perhaps a matter of opinion."

"You have beliefs and principles, an honest point of view."

"Yes, I have. But again—should men be honored for things that should come naturally?" Feldman seemed bored with the discussion. "But that is neither here nor there, Mr. Justice. I asked you to come to see me, sir, because you have my respect, despite our differences, and because I have an honest respect for, shall we say, the opinions of mankind. We are opponents in the matter of the President's Court bill, and that is my concern right now. Not because we disagree; that is of no particular consequence except that it makes you the logical one for me to confide in."

"I am honored, sir," Francis said. "If I can help even in such a fashion . . ."

"You can, sir. I had a final showdown with my doctor a week ago. He insisted that I retire from the bench. He gives me a few months—possibly until summer. He wanted me to leave immediately; I said there was no point to that, but I would resign at the end of the current spring session. We left it at that—I was to tender my resignation on the last day of the term."

Feldman got up and stood in front of his chair, hands braced

307

on the desk. "I don't know how, but a man's private business becomes known in this city, sir. A few days ago I was paid a visit by Senator Hoar and Senator Wilkins. They said they had learned that I planned to retire from the bench and asked if the report was true. At first I was angered by this bald, this cruel, intrusion. But I calmed myself. They did not know the reason why I was resigning, only that I was.

"I told them yes, I was leaving the Court at the end of the session, but I had not planned to announce my retirement in advance and I would appreciate their keeping my confidence. But this was not what they wanted at all; they wanted me to announce it immediately, as part of the strategy to defeat the Court bill. They explained that if I announced now, it would further weaken the President's case and strengthen the opposition."

Feldman paused and looked at Francis hard, and then smiled again. "Sir, I am a banker, a corporation lawyer, but I am not without some of the faculties of the politician. I saw their point. They and I were opposed to the Court plan; it was our duty to do everything to defeat it." He laughed, with no mirth in the sound. "It was also a considerable pleasure, sir. I do like to win, you know. I am not quite hypocrite enough to try to deny that. But I must be fair to myself, too. I saw it as something I could do to help, something I could do—if you will—to help my country —perhaps the last thing I could do."

He sat down, suddenly, his body jarring the heavy leather-upholstered chair. "I don't like pain, sir, and it pains me sometimes to stand too long." He looked at Francis, and now there was a glint in the black eyes that had always seemed so dead. "I feel very strongly about the Court bill, sir, and about my beliefs. Some find it strange that a wealthy man such as I should be such a —flaming liberal. But I find nothing strange in it. If our system is to survive, if capitalism is to throw back the Communist enemy, the rich man has an absolute duty to employ wisely his wealth and his talents. Wealth has always been a terrible responsibility; it is more so now, now that the misuse of wealth, over the centuries, has brought us to this Armageddon with Communism. I have always had contempt for those who misused their wealth, as perhaps may have been evident in some of my opinions. But, more than that, I have always insisted that individual wealth cannot exist—does not deserve to exist—unless the underprivileged millions in the world are given their chance by, among other things, the proper use of that wealth."

Again he made the deprecatory gesture, the impatient flapping of the hand. "Enough of that. You know my views, sir. I agreed with the senators' plan to announce my retirement immediately as a means of contributing to the defeat of the Court plan. Now you know."

Francis looked at him, waiting, and when Feldman was silent he said, "But, Mr. Justice, why did you feel you had to tell me? Why me, particularly?"

Feldman leaned back in his chair, tiredly. "I wanted the President to know, but I would not tell him personally. I am telling you, Mr. Justice, so that you can tell him. The President is a politician; so, it develops, am I. We disagree, but perhaps we can do so with mutual respect. I know he suspects trickery; so would I. But I do not want his anger to become so heated that it would force him to do something for which he would later be sorry. When I die, the obituary notice will report that I died of cancer. Until then, I do not want it generally known. But the President should know, because I do not want to be responsible for placing him in a position in which, unknowingly, he might attack a man dying of cancer. It would hurt him, after my death, and it would hurt our country."

Francis looked at the man seated at the desk in front of him, and he did not see David Benjamin Feldman, Associate Justice of the Supreme Court of the United States. He saw a man he had not known before but whom, suddenly, he knew intimately. He saw a man he would never forget.

"Thank you, Mr. Justice," Francis said. "Thank you very much."

"Goodbye, sir," Feldman said.

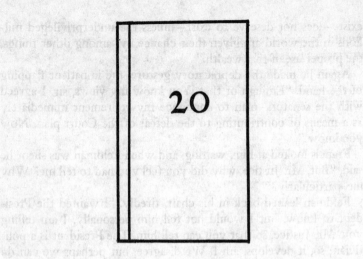

20

Francis made the appointment for Claude Wilkins; curiously, the Senator from Utah had seemed uncertain on the phone. "I've long been in the habit of just picking up the telephone and calling the President myself," he said. "But these are —difficult days, Mr. Justice." Yet when Francis had put his own call through to John Alden Hughes, the Presidential reaction had been most cordial. "Sure, tell him to come around tonight after dinner—about nine," Hughes said. "Perhaps I'd better give orders to lock up the silver, though."

The President found nothing curious in Wilkins's uncertainty. "He should feel a little uncomfortable," Hughes told Harry Weiss. "If he hadn't turned on me, we'd have had clear sailing from the very beginning." Weiss said nothing; he did not trust Claude Wilkins, as he did not trust any man in the opposition camp, but privately he acknowledged that Wilkins had had cause for his desertion of the administration. The President had not been at his best in his attempt to deal with Wilkins by offering him the voice in the Supreme Court appointments which already had been given to Chet McAdam. It was something that had probably had to be tried, on the slender chance that McAdam would cooperate by stepping aside, but it had been a dangerous attempt at finesse.

When Wilkins was ushered into the President's private study on the second floor of the White House, he found Hughes standing by the door waiting to greet him.

"Claude, it's been a long time," the President said, his hand pressing Wilkins's with just the right degree of political warmth. "I've missed our little chats."

"So have I, Mr. President," Wilkins said. "I miss the stimulation of encountering a really good mind."

"Thank you, Claude." The President grinned. "We never underrated each other, did we? Sit down—sit down, Claude."

Wilkins didn't like the idea that the two of them should be sitting side by side on the sofa; it was difficult to be convincing with a sideways look. But the President sat his guest down first, then plopped down next to him.

"I naturally assume you have a proposition, Claude." In this way, the situation *had* changed; Hughes was dispensing only a minimum of his charm in order to get down to business.

"I have, Mr. President." It *was* hard to be earnest in that side-by-side situation. "I think it is time for a—uh—proposition. There is every possibility of a stalemate, and whereas a stalemate would be a defeat for the administration and a victory of a sort for our side, I don't see that as the ideal result. The problem of the Court would remain, and, although I am chary of interfering with its functions, I admit that a less radical approach to the problem might be proper."

The President laughed his famous laugh. "Claude, you'd never know it from your speeches."

"No, I suppose not. It's a question of first things first, you know. But the situation is not pretty, Mr. President. Whichever side wins, the country is going to be seriously divided."

"I don't agree, of course, Claude. I believe the people are with me. A defeat for my Court plan, I believe, would leave the people frustrated—and, sir, determined to administer punishment at the polls to those responsible for their frustration."

"It could be, sir. It could be." Wilkins pursed his mouth and prodded at his maroon bow tie with the Y of his thumb and forefinger. "I have been—ah—fortunate in preserving some independence from the political idiosyncrasies that blow hot and cold in my constituency. But whatever happens, it will not be a happy situation."

"Well, Claude?"

"As you suggest, down to business, sir. My business is quite simple. There has been a retirement announced from the bench. The Court has shown a disposition lately to move toward the center from its liberal position. From the point of view of the administration, the situation certainly has improved. Is it not the time to accept this improvement and compromise?"

"Probably not." The President's face relaxed into a grin. "But how, Claude?"

"Sir, you want some sort of Court reform. I am not unalterably opposed to a change. I believe your purposes would be served by a proposition to which I could give my wholehearted support. I recommend a constitutional amendment which would permit Congress to override decisions of the Court affecting Congressional legislation by a two-thirds vote of both Houses after an intervening election."

Now the President's laugh was short and unpleasant. "I thought so. Claude, I believe I could have delivered your little speech verbatim, before you even entered this room."

Wilkins's neck hurt from his insistence on keeping his head turned so he could keep watch on Hughes's face. He saw now that the Presidential grin had the slight line at one corner of his mouth that made it contemptuous.

"My suggestion does not interest you, Mr. President?"

"Interest me? Oh, it interests me, Claude. It's interesting as a strategic move to get what you want—which is no change in the Court whatsoever—by appearing to give me what I want. I won't go into the matter of delay, Claude; I'll just tell you that no matter how long it took, at the end you politicians on the other side would see to it that the amendment failed of ratification. Yes, it interests me, Claude—as a piece of political strategy. But that's all. The answer, of course, is no."

The President stood up, and Wilkins realized, with a feeling of shock and embarrassment, that the interview was over.

"Claude, thank you for coming." As Wilkins stood up, the President laid a hand lightly on his arm. "We both have to keep trying, don't we? But, Claude—I have to tell you this. You deserted the ship. And I'm damned if I'm going to let you get any credit for *any* Court bill—any Court bill whatsoever. It may take a little more time to get what *I* want, Claude, but I can promise you there won't be any Wilkins Bill."

The next morning, Francis Dalton was not sure whether the President had been right, strategically, in leaking a report of his meeting with Wilkins to both *The New York Times* and the *Herald Tribune*. On the surface, it seemed a score for the President; the news stories quoting the usual "unimpeachable sources" had implied a tactical setback for the opposition in their report that Hughes had "rejected out of hand a compromise offer from a top-drawer leader of the opposition to his Court plan." It would do the opposition no good to have people reading that "Observers speculated that the offer may have indicated a weakness in the opposition." One of these observers, in fact, was quoted—anonymously, of course—as declaring that the offer was a "desperate, last-ditch move by a defeated and discredited party." Yet Francis felt an unease that the President had reached the point of no return. Now the opposition would give him no opportunity to turn back gracefully.

Jimmy Hughes was thinking much the same thing as he sat in the gallery of the Senate with Wednesday Walsh, replying to the actress's throaty comments with monosyllables. Brother Johnny had better be pretty good from here in, Jimmy Hughes reflected; he had neglected to leave the enemy an escape route. Obviously, too, the opposition was going to waste no time in mounting a new attack; Claude Wilkins himself was about to deliver himself of what his office described as an "important" speech.

Wilkins had risen to his feet with a perfunctory, almost inaudible "Mr. President," and for a long minute he leaned against his desk sweeping the Senate Chamber with a kind of negligent arrogance. About half the membership of the Senate was on hand, but as usual the Vice-President was elsewhere and young Bill Martin was presiding; Jimmy Hughes wondered if anyone had ever seriously considered invoking the Constitution's prescription that the Vice-President should preside over the Senate. It would have cramped the campaign style of such predecessors of Tom Morgan as Alben Barkley, Richard Nixon and Lyndon Johnson, for, as

Morgan put it, "You don't swing any deals sitting on that stool."

Wednesday Walsh leaned over to whisper in Jimmy Hughes's ear, "Why does he always wear a bow tie? It's so—informal."

"I know, it's not refined," Jimmy told her.

Wilkins's natty blue suit and his precise movements gave the impression of fussiness. But when he had stopped arranging the papers on his desk, his voice issued forth firm and positive.

"Mr. President, I shall not consume very much of the Senate's valuable time today," he said. "I am aware of the vital legislation which awaits our action—legislation as vital, if not more so, as that bill we are asked to believe is so necessary to preserve our way of life. I shall be brief."

Then it'll be the first time, Jimmy Hughes thought.

Wilkins surveyed the galleries, his mouth pursed, his hands resting lightly on his hips. "I stand here not so much to make a speech, in the conventional sense, as to remind the people of this great nation of ours of the grave peril which confronts them." (*Which* or *that?* Jimmy Hughes was wondering.) "It is my fear that the American people have forgotten that eternal vigilance is the price of liberty. I fear, perhaps, that it has slipped our minds in the last few years, when crises—real and manufactured —have oppressed our country. And so I believe the time has come to warn our people, again, that a dictator in all his silky power can rise in this country of ours—that a dictator can rise to all-powerful heights while our thoughts are elsewhere.

"To be sure, our thoughts are and have been on the proposal by the executive branch of this government to alter the complexion of the Supreme Court. But I greatly fear that the emphasis has been on what such a plan would do to the Court rather than what it would do *for* the President of the United States.

"Mr. President, I do not use words needlessly. I do not lightly attach a label to any man. But through my subconscious lately there has rippled a term that has kept me awake at night. The term is *man on horseback*."

Claude Wilkins paused to look up at the galleries suddenly come to life with a hundred murmurs and a scattering of handclaps. He waited while Senator Martin rapped for order, then went on: "I do not intend that my words be received as sensationalism. They are words of explanation and exposition—and warning. For I ask, Mr. President, what is a man on horseback? Do our people still know what the term means—what it means in terms of the safety of this country of ours? I do not think so, Mr. President. I think our people have forgotten that it is possible for a man on horseback to ride in the United States of America.

"I ask again: What is a *man on horseback?* And, Mr. President, I will tell you what it is. A man on horseback is a leader with dictatorial or imperialistic ambitions. According to George Stimpson's fine work, *A Book About a Thousand Things*, the term is believed to have been coined by Caleb Cushing (1800-1879), an American statesman who was Attorney General in President Franklin Pierce's Cabinet. In January, 1860, Cushing wrote a letter in which he predicted that the slavery agitation in the United States would result in a man on horseback with a drawn sword in his hand, some Atlantic Caesar, or Cromwell, or Napoleon. The term was popularized in connection with Georges Ernest Boulanger (1837-1891), a French military leader who advocated revenge on Germany. He acquired the title *man on horseback* because he habitually appeared before the public mounted on a magnificent charger. In the United States, *man on horseback* was first applied to Theodore Roosevelt in a purely political sense."

Claude Wilkins paused; he seemed suddenly occupied with a paper on his desk. Then his head shot up and his voice was a snap: "Mr. President, I could wish that our only concern today was a man on horseback of the democratic integrity of Theodore Roosevelt. I could wish that the business of the executive branch was in the hands of someone as solemnly dedicated to the preservation of our democratic way of life as Theodore Roosevelt."

The galleries' murmurs exploded into a clashing of tongues, and Senator Martin waited a long moment before gaveling for order. Claude Wilkins's eyes were closed as he leaned against his desk; he kept them closed until the galleries subsided.

Then he resumed. "But, Mr. President, unfortunately we do not have a Theodore Roosevelt in the White House. We *do* have a man on horseback. We *do* have a man who imperiously orders, 'My way or else.' We *do* have a man who tells the nation, 'Give your freedom into my hands—you are not worthy of it!'"

This time, the noise in the galleries was one deep-throated roar, and again Bill Martin, a smile on his dark, youthful face, let the galleries have their way before using his gavel. But this time Claude Wilkins's eyes were wide open as his head turned slowly to take in the galleries' reaction.

"Thank you, Mr. President," came Claude Wilkins's voice above the last scattered murmurs. "Thank you, Mr. President. That is all."

Wednesday Walsh had risen in her seat, and Jimmy Hughes touched her arm. "Better sit down, sweetie," he said.

The little actress sat down and turned to Jimmy. Her face was flushed and her mouth was working with excitement.

"But, Jimmy—he was talking about your brother. How horrible!"

"Yes," Jimmy Hughes said. "He was talking about my brother, all right." He looked at Wednesday Walsh and smiled, because the girl had to calm down. "Pretty effective," Jimmy Hughes said. But the understatement gave him no comfort. For the first time in his life, Jimmy Hughes had discovered that he could be sorry for his brother.

The New York *Post* was most acid in the almost general journalistic pursuit of John Alden Hughes. "Where does the President think he is going now?" the *Post* inquired at the end of its daily editorial on the Court plan. Francis Dalton knew where Hughes wanted to go, but the knowledge was not reassuring; it was easy enough for the President to thunder, "Drive on!" but he was providing none of the equipment necessary for the demolition of the numerous roadblocks in his path. Hughes was still confident he had the people with him, and Francis admitted this could be so. But in trying to get everything, to achieve everything he had set out to do, John Alden Hughes often seemed to be accomplishing nothing.

The most acute danger lay in the fact that in the matter of Majority Leader Chet McAdam, the President's posture was a static one. He would have to do something soon, and to Francis that could only mean calling McAdam in and handing him the Court appointment. Francis recognized there perhaps were grounds for the President to feel he should proceed with great caution; Hughes still wanted the whole loaf, and if he made his peace with

McAdam, there was the danger he might have to settle for only half, or less. At the same time that Francis was appalled at the brutality of Hughes's treatment of McAdam, he made himself see the President's position—the eternal position of the man in the White House who must use every means, exert every ounce of his power, to get what he wanted: what he believed he had to get for the good of the country. Francis felt Hughes was being most unfair to McAdam, yet he hesitated to use the word dishonorable; he realized that words like honor and dishonor took on different meanings when a man was charged with the final responsibility for the security of the country. It might be dishonorable for John Alden Hughes to discharge his honorable debt to Chet McAdam; the result could be injurious to the country. And, after all, the point could be made that a man's personal honor didn't matter when the welfare of the nation was at stake.

Yet Francis could not refrain from suggesting to the President that it was time to come to a decision on McAdam and then let McAdam in on the decision.

"It can't go on this way," Francis told Hughes. "It's hurting you, Mr. President."

Hughes was friendly but almost detached. "Do you think so, Francis? Or—and I do say this with complete good will—are you chiefly concerned about your friend McAdam?"

"I *am* concerned about my friend McAdam," Francis said. "He is an old and trusted friend, and I'd like him to be happy, if possible." He *would* not get emotional. "But I am making myself see your problem. Still, I think the status quo is dangerous."

"Yes, I think you do, Francis. I can believe that about you." For a moment there was the old sympathetic warmth in the President's tone and in his face. But the next instant he seemed intent on making light of the problem. "I don't have to do anything right now, Francis," he said, and he smiled. "You know I don't believe in letting circumstances force my hand."

"Perhaps not," Francis said. "But in this case the circumstances are of your own making, sir. Doesn't that change things a bit?"

"Perhaps, Francis. Perhaps. I don't know." Hughes lit a cigarette and took a couple of quick puffs. "I wish McAdam could be permitted to be—ah—realistic. That would solve everything. Francis, I'd thought of asking you to intercede for me with Chet."

317

"Intercede? How?" But I know what he means, Francis thought.

"Francis, I think it might be useful if you talked to McAdam and tried to talk him round to my—to our—way of thinking." Hughes was smiling again.

He had to face up to this swiftly, at once, Francis told himself. "Mr. President, I could not do that. Knowing how Chet feels, knowing his heart is set on a place on the bench, I couldn't do it." All right, that's enough, Francis warned himself. Leave it at that, and if the explosion comes, very well.

But Hughes kept on his smile. He looked at Francis and took another two quick puffs of his cigarette. "No, I don't suppose you could. I understand. But I have to say, needing help as I do, that I wish you could."

The President had dictated and dispatched his acknowledgment of Feldman's resignation. The tone of the note was warm, for Hughes had been sincerely moved by Francis' report of his conversation with Feldman. "Cancer—my God!" the President had said. He looked down at his desk, his face dark, and then looked up at Francis, pain in his eyes. "It's incredible that there should be no stronger words with which to rebuke myself than that I have been unfair to that poor man." He paused again. "This job gets no easier with the passage of time, Francis. How can a man sustain the toughness necessary to doing his job when he must constantly take time to be human?"

Mike Blair released a copy of the letter the same day it was dispatched, but the press was not satisfied.

"For Christ's sake, what about Feldman's successor?" John Sparks of the New York *Daily News* asked. "Everybody's saying it's in the bag for Chet McAdam."

"That's all we have now, Jack," Mike Blair said.

"You mean you're holding up McAdam's appointment to get space some other day?" Sparks inquired.

"Or *is* it in the bag for McAdam?" asked Ralph Udall of the Philadelphia *Bulletin*. "I smell fish."

"Go ahead and sniff, Ralph," Blair said. "That's all for today." Mike Blair wanted to know what was up; he felt it was a prerogative of the White House Press Secretary. But he was as baffled as his journalistic adversaries.

Harry Weiss and Charlie Mayborn closeted themselves with two White House aides assigned to minor matters of Congressional liaison, and the same day the aides spread a whispered rumor on the Hill that McAdam would not be appointed to the Court. House Speaker Smith called Weiss that afternoon. His voice was fierce with anger.

"Listen, Harry, what the hell is this garbage your boys are spreading that Chet won't get that Court job?"

"Garbage? What are you talking about, Henry?" Weiss's voice was calm.

"You know damn well what I'm talking about. Robinson and Tichnor are practically circularizing the Congress with the story."

"Henry, you've got me. It's news to me." Harry Weiss cringed inside at the lie. "My understanding is that Chet is the boy."

"All right, Harry. I suppose this was one of your trial balloons —you and Charlie Mayborn. If it was, you'd better tell the President it didn't work. My boys won't go for it—and neither will I."

Mayborn and Weiss thought it unnecessary to trouble the President with the reaction. Instead, the next day the word on the Hill was that Robinson and Tichnor had relayed pure gossip and that Chet McAdam positively would be the next appointee to the Supreme Court.

Smith told himself he should be mollified; after all, that's how things were done in Washington. But he called McAdam and put the question to him bluntly: Had the President told him the job was safe for him?

"Nope." McAdam was crisp. "I haven't had the slightest sign, Henry. I haven't even heard from the President for the last four days."

"Jesus Christ!" Smith said. "What the hell's going on?"

"I don't know, Henry, but that's the way it is. Goddammit, I've done that guy's work for more than four years, and now he's ignoring me."

"Did you call him, for God's sake?"

"No, I didn't. I don't think it's my place, Henry. If he wants to talk to me, he'll have to call me."

Smith was baffled by McAdam's seeming mildness; it was what happened to a man when a lifetime ambition was within his grasp and he was fearful of upsetting the applecart. But Smith told himself that he could do something, and he set about doing it with a call to Alpheus Ward.

"I can guarantee Kentucky coming out for McAdam," he told Ward. "Can you get us Illinois?"

"Of course I can," Ward said. "But do you think Chet will want us to get into this?"

"I don't know," Smith said. "But we're getting in, Alph. Get to work, boy."

It took two days of threats and cajoling, but both the Kentucky and Illinois Congressional delegations unanimously endorsed McAdam's candidacy for the Supreme Court, and Henry Smith regarded the eight-column streamer in the *Post* with angry satisfaction. McAdam was on the line shortly, and Smith was moved by his gratitude.

"I tell you, Henry, this means a hell of a lot to me," McAdam said. "I don't know how to explain it to you—in a spot like this, a man gets terribly lonely."

"Forget it, Chet," Smith said. "We're all for you—and, by God, we'll see to it that that young fellow in the White House gets the message."

"I get their message," John Alden Hughes told Weiss and Mayborn later in the day. "The pressure is on, gentlemen."

"They're pretty sore, sir," Harry Weiss said. "I tried to call Smith today and he wouldn't take the call."

"They're all that way," Mayborn said. "They've got their backs up. Hell, they wouldn't give a damn if it wasn't one of their own, but they stick together for somebody that's in the club. Besides, they don't mind embarrassing the White House a little after having to take orders for four years."

"Yes, I realize those gentlemen are not completely pure at heart," the President said. "Well, we can't give them exactly what they want. We just can't. We've got to have a couple of extra places on the Court to balance Chet's appointment, in case Chet reverts. The whole thing is no use, unless we get them. What with the Court seeming to switch, I'm afraid our supporters on the Hill would evaporate if Chet were to be safely established on the Court. They wouldn't have anything to fight for then, or at least that's the way they'd look at it."

Mayborn blew his nose loudly; he was nervous, but it was plain he felt it was time to suggest the perilous.

"I suppose we've just got to tell Chet the facts of life," he said. The President smiled. "We? You mean me, Charlie. But—you're right. I've got to have it out with Chet. After all, he's my Majority Leader in the Senate; I can't do without him indefinitely. Somehow I've got to hold onto him, and get it done my way besides."

"That's going to be tough." Mayborn had never looked so unhappy.

"Yes, it is," the President said. "It will be very tough. But I'll have to talk to Chet. I'll figure out something."

"You planning to call him up?" Mayborn asked.

"No. No, I don't think I will." Hughes paused to light a cigarette. "The ground will have to be prepared. I think I'll see what Ed O'Hara can do along those lines."

"Ed O'Hara?" Harry Weiss had small admiration for the National Chairman. "Ed's about as subtle as a meat-ax."

"True, Harry." The President grinned. "But Chet McAdam doesn't want subtlety. He wants rough-and-ready reassurance. Ed O'Hara will make Chet feel good without committing himself to anything more radical than the time of day."

It worked out pretty much as John Alden Hughes had planned. The bluff O'Hara had credit with McAdam as the man who had first suggested he might dream of a Supreme Court appointment; now he found a warm welcome in McAdam's office. "Don't worry, Chet," O'Hara had told the New Yorker, "everything will come out all right." McAdam was soothed, but he still wanted to hear from the President personally. That would come, too, John Alden Hughes reflected, as soon as I'm sure of what I want to say. It was Jimmy Hughes's turn next.

McAdam was a little less cordial with Jimmy Hughes, but Jimmy curiously was at home with politicians; as Jimmy himself put it, "They don't think I'm important enough to be dangerous." Jimmy had a purpose for his errand; he talked to McAdam for some time about getting some Federal help for an experimental theater Ian Kerr wanted to establish in Greenwich Village.

"Hell, Jimmy, your brother could do that for you," McAdam said.

"Well, perhaps," Jimmy said. "But it's not always easy to ask favors of your brother. And, after all, you're Ian's senator; you ought to get credit for it."

McAdam laughed. "Jimmy, you'd make a fine politician. Credit, hell! Whenever I get involved with the Village, I usually get nothing but blame. But sure, I'll do what I can."

That was it, then, and Jimmy could do his brother's errand. It was an errand he found distasteful, but he was glad to do it nevertheless. Since Wilkins's speech, he had thought of John Alden Hughes more as his brother and less as President of the United States, and his concern had brought them closer together—at least on Jimmy's part. Jimmy wanted to help his brother if he could.

"Chet, I know how you feel, but I thought you might like to know that my brother has been wondering why he hasn't heard from you," Jimmy said.

McAdam seemed embarrassed. "Hell, Jimmy, I'm in a tough spot. Ever since Feldman quit I've been expecting to hear from your brother. I don't want to seem to be hanging around looking for the job."

"I know, Chet. I think I understand more than you think. But —it's funny. I think my brother feels a little sensitive, too."

"Well—maybe he does." McAdam seemed surprised. "I don't know that I've thought of it that way. All I know is that when he didn't call me I got pretty sore. My feelings are hurt—I suppose that's the only way to put it."

"I don't blame you, Chet. But I think you two ought to get together. It's obvious you both want to, but neither of you wants to make the first move. Look, Chet, after all, my brother is President. Suppose I call him from here and you talk to him. Then it would be as if the call came from you, but you'd know that the President was suggesting it, as it were, through his brother."

McAdam rubbed the side of his face with his big palm. "Hell," he said. He looked hard at Jimmy Hughes, and his cough was a nervous one. "All right. Call him up, Jimmy. We'll see."

Since the President was waiting for the call, there was no delay in reaching him. When Chet took the telephone from Jimmy's hand, he found himself again warmed by the Presidential tones, even while suspicion continued to gnaw at him. He had never been sure he liked John Alden Hughes, but he never failed to be refreshed by the Hughes charm.

"Chet, will you come over and see me—right now?" The President's voice was deep with earnestness. "It's been too damn long."

"Yes, Mr. President, it's been too damn long," McAdam said.

"Then you will come over?"

"Yes, sir. I'll be over. I don't know why, but I'll be over."

And, Chester W. McAdam told himself, he *did not know* why he was going to the White House. As he sat upright on the back seat of his Cadillac limousine, and peered out at the Taft memorial bell tower, subconsciously approving the sun brightening the shaft, he tried to summon up a reason why he was doing what he was doing and why, over the years, he had done what he had done. He was sixty-two years old, and for at least forty-two of those years he had known where he was going and why he was going and why he was doing the things he did, and now the knowledge that he was uncertain brought him a pain that was part anger and part desperation. For the first time in sixty-two years, he was afraid—afraid that he was not being his own man, afraid that he was about to abandon the battle to belong to himself, to remain true to Chester W. McAdam.

Oh, he had made the little compromises, the courtly bows in the direction of expediency, but he had changed nothing in the basic framework of his beliefs. He had lost battles because of his resolute standards, because he would not compromise beyond a certain point, but he had been willing to lose them rather than pay the price for victory. And even when he had turned from the path of liberalism to the conservative road that was necessary to preserve the gains of liberalism, he had been open and above board about it. He had publicly announced his conversion, explained the reasons for it in detail, vigorously urged his constituents to follow him, and dared the opposition to make political capital of it. They had called him turncoat and traitor, and he had sloughed off the epithets. It was enough that he himself knew the epithets were false, and there was the record to show that he had not sneaked off in the night but had proclaimed in public the altered course he intended to take.

Curiously, even in this depressed mood, he could not feel that his life had been burdened with hardship. He had worked hard, of course; but hard work was his meat and drink, his hobby as well as a means of livelihood. He enjoyed a day in the field with a good gun and a good dog, and a trout stream surging against his legs, but he was always impatient to get back to work once the holiday was over. He had always had both the energy and the will to work hard, which was fortunate for a boy from Tarrytown who was neither fish nor fowl to the stiffly suspicious upstate New Yorkers and the noisy, quarrelsome hordes of Manhattan. He recalled now the question posed by his opponent in that long-ago race for the State Senate—"Who is this clerk from Tarrytown?" —and his swift answer from his seat on the platform: "He's the guy who's going to kick you out of your job, Jack Stewart!" It was this kind of thing that had worked both upstate and south of the Harlem River. He had learned his political tricks and gimmicks as he rose through the State Senate to the governorship and then to the United States Senate, but he had not had to learn to be himself—and that is what had brought him close to the voters. He had the quiet air that was necessary upstate because he was intelligent and well-mannered and had studied both books and that whole vast neighborhood while achieving honors at Syracuse. And in the garment district that made Manhattan's midtown a jungle of perilous gulches for the upstater, he had built a rapport with the surging ingredients of that melting pot by his authoritative references to his bone-numbing labors in a Binghamton mill and by the fight for urban redevelopment he had never abandoned. He had been able almost always to tell the truth, and when he had fudged a little it had been on minor matters; because he had earned a reputation for telling the truth, the people had trusted him. There was no difference between the upstater and the Manhattanite, really, he reflected; all either one wanted from his politicians was a fair shake, and he had given them one. He had been honest with them. He had not shrunk from telling them the hard facts. It warmed him now to know that his success had been a tribute not so much to his talents as to the acumen and loyalty of his constituents.

He realized that while he was well above average in intelligence, he was not and had never been an intellectual or a brilliant theoretician. He was too fascinated with politics, too convinced of the necessity for the practical approach, too aware that only the possible could be achieved when men gathered to legislate. He admitted he enjoyed engineering the deals without which the possible became the impossible. He enjoyed striking out at the opposition, embarrassing his foes, moving about carefully, behind doors, to set the stage for the political coup. He was proud of being a member of the Senate and proud that his party had selected him as its leader in the Senate. He knew he was adept at both cajoling and threatening, and at knowing when to use one weapon and when to use the other, and he knew other politicians admired him for this competence. He felt that both his native intelligence and the learning he had acquired from his stern application to scholarship at college were well above the average in the Senate, but he was satisfied that he had never risked revealing his superiority to his colleagues. He was not "one of the boys," as Tom Morgan was fond of saying, but he was glad the boys thought he was. It had hurt sometimes, but he had kept his word and he had followed his party's line. That was demanded of the man who would get things done; he had always demanded it of himself.

Idly, Chet McAdam noticed a torn flag atop the Justice Department building as his limousine moved along Pennsylvania Avenue; he'd have his secretary call somebody about it. Yes, he had always been a good party man, and that included going along with the more radical changes of John Alden Hughes. It disturbed him to reflect that he had never been sure of his liking for Hughes; it smacked of disloyalty. Yet there it was: he had never been able to quell a little feeling deep within him that Hughes was not his kind of party man. He didn't know the reason for this suspicion; perhaps it was unfairly due to the President's unconventional methods. Yet, there were other things. He had never cared for the little coterie around the President, men with Phi Beta Kappa keys and tongues like scalpels, men who seemed contemptuous of politicians, who gave the impression the Congress was a necessary evil composed of unattractive ward heelers concerned with the ordinary. But it didn't matter. He was a good party man, and the President was the head of the party. It didn't matter that his affection for the President was suspect, because it was the party that mattered, and the President had not only revived the party but given it the greatest power in its history. He was glad to serve the President for this reason; as a good party man, he owed the President his obedience, and he would do his best to see that the men he led continued to offer their support.

Now he was going to call on the President, and for the first time in his many meetings with John Alden Hughes, Chet McAdam did not know what the President had in mind. Specifically, because it had to be about the Court bill, he did not know what the President had in mind for him, Chet McAdam. He hoped the President had summoned him to tell him he would get the Court appointment, but the hope seemed timid and weak. He wanted to believe it, but he couldn't.

His limousine skirted the South Lawn of the White House and moved through the gate into the alleylike passage between the White House and the Old State Department Building that someone had grandiosely named West Executive Avenue. McAdam was glad there were no reporters at the side entrance to the West Wing offices, and he was pleased to see that Harry Weiss was waiting at the door for him. Weiss was no friend of his, but he would offer protection from any journalists prowling the corridors en route to the President's office. Reporters embarrassed Chet McAdam these days.

The President was at the door of his office, too, as he and Harry Weiss reached the end of the long hallway, and Hughes's hand was out and his manner cordial.

"Come in, come in, Chet," the President said. "I've been waiting for you."

"Good afternoon, Mr. President," McAdam said. "You see I still know my way."

Hughes grinned. "All right, Chet. It *has* been a long time, you're right." He turned to Harry Weiss as McAdam started into the office. "Harry, I'll see you later."

Good, Chet McAdam thought. Just the two of us. We'll settle this thing today.

The President caught up with McAdam and laid a hand gently on his arm to point him toward the big red leather chair on the right of the desk. "I'll take your coat and hat, Chet," he said. "You sit down." And as McAdam sat down, the President laid his guest's hat and coat on the big sofa and then walked around the desk and sat down in his big high-backed swivel chair.

"Chet, this is better—much better," the President said, smiling. "We've both been too sensitive. Here I was thinking you were sulking, and you were thinking I was avoiding you. You'd think we were a couple of old ladies."

McAdam swung one leg over the other. "It's time we got together, Mr. President. There's still work to be done, you know."

"Yes, I know. Lots of work. Chet, how is it going?"

"Not too well, but not too badly either, Mr. President." McAdam shifted in his seat. "But if you don't mind, Mr. President, we do have other things to talk about, don't we?"

"Yes, Chet, we have. And we're going to talk about them right now. I planned to talk about—that other thing, first." The President got a cigarette from the box on the desk and lighted it. "We've got to talk about you and the Supreme Court, Chet." He looked at McAdam, and paused.

"Yes, sir, I think so too, Mr. President."

"Chet, you want very much to be appointed to the Supreme Court, don't you?"

McAdam felt an eyebrow go up in surprise. "Why, yes, of course. I thought you knew that. It's a lifelong ambition."

"Yes, I knew it, Chet. Just checking, I guess." The President took a puff of his cigarette, inhaling it deeply. "Chet, you still feel the same way I do about the Court, don't you? About altering its complexion—making it more conservative?"

"Yes, sir, of course I do. It's what we've been fighting for."

"Good. Then you know that my Court plan is a must. I must have that Court plan, Chet."

"Well, sir, sure it's a must, but you've done pretty well so far even if you don't get it. The Court seems a lot more agreeable about your legislation lately, and, of course, Feldman's resignation leaves a vacancy for a conservative."

"Yes, that's true, Chet." The President's voice was almost absent-minded. "We have made—progress. But it's not enough, Chet. And it has been quite by accident. At least, the Feldman retirement was an accident. As you know, I don't trust the Court's supposed shift."

"No, I know you want the Court plan, Mr. President. I'm doing my best to get it for you. But you've already got your chance to make the Court more conservative—probably predominantly conservative—through Feldman's retirement. That's all I'm saying."

"And that's true, Chet. But the Court will not be safe until I get those two new justices—in addition to filling the vacancy caused by Feldman's retirement. I want to emphasize that. Only with my Court plan can we be sure of the kind of victory we want."

He is not going to appoint me, McAdam was thinking. I am sure of that now.

"Well, sir, I have to ask this," McAdam said. "How does that affect me—that is, my appointment to the Court?"

The President got up and took his wonted walk around the desk and then leaned against it as he talked.

"It affects you this way, Chet, and I know you'll understand. You've got to understand. If I appoint you to that vacancy, Chet, the fight for the Court plan will collapse. You won't desert me, Chet, but your troops will. No matter what you do, they'll quit. They'll argue that I've got a five-to-four margin on the Court and I should be satisfied. They will, won't they, Chet?"

"I don't know, sir." All McAdam could think about was that he was not going to get the appointment, he was not going to get the sure appointment. And he had to have it.

"Yes, you do, Chet." The President was giving McAdam plenty of time to think. "You know they'll quit."

McAdam felt desperate. "Yes, yes, I suppose they might. They might. But I'd do my best to hold them together. You know that, Mr. President."

"I know you would, Chet. But it wouldn't be enough. I've got to have better than five-to-four on that Court. My whole program depends on it."

Suddenly, McAdam felt tired. He wanted to hear the rest and get out of that office. He wanted to get it over with. It was too much of an effort to talk, against certain defeat.

"Mr. President, what do you want me to do?" McAdam's voice was limp; he felt as though he didn't care any more. He would do whatever the President wanted him to do. But now he wanted to go home.

"Chet, this is what I want to suggest. I'm obligated to you. I know that. But I still need your help. I can't do it without your help. I'm forced to appeal to you to postpone asking for payment on my note. What I propose, Chet, is that I fill the Feldman vacancy with—another conservative, like you. Then when the Court plan is passed, you'll get one of the new posts and you and I between us will decide who gets the other one. That's what I have to ask you, Chet."

"All right." He's clever, McAdam thought. This is the smart way to do it. He could not blame the President; it was a good way out of the mess. It kept the Court bill breathing. This way the President could kill two birds with one stone; he could get his Court bill and, eventually, pay his debt. Perhaps. He could, that is, if the Court bill passed. If it didn't, it was tough luck for Chet McAdam. But it was the only way. He wanted to be on the Supreme Court; all right, he would have to fight for it, just as he had always had to fight for everything.

McAdam stood up. "If that's the way you want it, Mr. President, all right. I'll go along."

"Chet, you understand, don't you?" The President was looking at him closely.

"Yes, sir, I understand."

"It will mean a fight, Chet."

"Yes, sir." Something flared briefly in McAdam's insides. "By God, I never ran away from a fight."

"Good, Chet. Fine. And thank you. I asked you for help, and you've given it to me. I won't forget that, Chet." The President stepped forward and put his hand on McAdam's arm.

"Yes, sir. I'll help. I always did and I always will. And now, Mr. President—I wonder if I could go?"

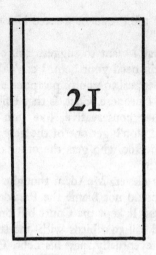

21

C HET McADAM HAD SURPRISED FRANCIS; he had seemed hardly
angry at all. When the Majority Leader's limousine pulled
up at the curb on Pennsylvania Avenue, his greeting was cheery,
hearty. "Get in, Mr. Justice," McAdam had bellowed from the
open window. "You've had enough exercise for the morning."

Leaning back on the soft gray upholstery of the Cadillac, Francis had tried not to look at McAdam too hard as he said, "You
seem particularly chipper today, Chet."

"Considering everything, huh?" McAdam's big lined face
broke into a grin. "Considering I didn't get Feldman's job, huh?
Well, Francis, it hurt like hell, but I didn't get it, and that's that.
I gave it some thought—some pretty angry thought, to be truthful—but there you are. It all boiled down to the fact that I've still
got to stick in there fighting."

"Chet, I don't quite know what to say—except that you're a,
well, a good soldier. By God, a very good soldier."

"That's the way it is—the way it has to be." McAdam puffed
twice on his big cigar. "A man can't lie down and die, can he?
Hell, I think I should have got the job; I've earned it and it was

promised to me—or at least an appointment was promised to me. From the President's point of view, I think I'd have filled the bill. But he figured otherwise. Francis, I don't go much for criticizing the President. I suppose that was the way he had to figure it. It's his program and a President has to do everything to get his program through. After all, he takes full responsibility for it, so he has to do things his way."

"I understand, Chet. But I'd understand if you were furious, too."

"Oh, I'm sore as hell, Francis. I'm human. But you can't let a thing like that get you down—or interfere with your job. I'm sore, but I realize I don't have any alternative. Either I fight for what I want—by fighting for what the President wants—or I have to cash in my chips. It's that simple."

"Is it coming any better, Chet? The Court plan, I mean?"

"Tough. It looks tough, Francis. But not that tough. Not so tough that we can't pull it off. John Alden Hughes has still got some influence on the Hill, and I'm hoping that when the time comes, that influence will tell. We've lost some votes, but I'm putting the pressure on the rest of them, and right now I think I've got the waverers a little scared. It'll take some hard work, but I'm not giving up."

"Well, you've got the Gallup Poll on your side, Chet."

"Yup—that may help, Francis. Seventy-six per cent in favor of the Court plan. It helps the morale a little, although, by God, I've seen more polls fall flat on their faces than I care to remember. To me the significant thing is that those people are not voting for the Court plan so much as they're voting for Hughes again. I'll see to it that the thought occurs to the troops on the Hill, too."

"Yes, most of them will need him in the Congressional elections next year, won't they?"

"Yessir, they will. The trouble is, Francis, some of them are thinking they may be able to sell the idea that with Feldman quitting, the President has been given his way without the necessity for tampering with the Court—as they put it. The ones who've pulled out of the fight are making a lot of the fact Hughes will now have a five-to-four majority."

"I know," Francis said, and paused. "But Hughes isn't satisfied with that one-vote majority, of course."

"Nope. I don't know that I blame him completely, Francis." McAdam grinned again. "I hope I'm not treading on your propriety, Mr. Justice, by remarking that you fellows on the Court have everybody guessing."

Francis grinned back. "No, Chet. The Court is paying the price of having become a celebrity."

"Yup. Well, there was that switch of Bacon's in the Chicago case. That one really floored the President. And now there's that Atkinson free speech case coming up—that is, I suppose it's about due, and I'm not trying to pump you, Francis. But anyway, I see the pundits are worrying in print about that one. Whether Bacon will stick to his switch, that is, and uphold the government's refusal to let Atkinson speak in East Potomac Park. If he does—and I'm quoting the pundits—that'll give Hughes another victory he doesn't want just now."

"Yes." Francis could think of nothing to say. He did not blame McAdam, because he knew that in this particular aspect of the conversation McAdam was guileless. He was talking politics, not attempting to pump a member of the Supreme Court.

McAdam laughed. "Francis, I apologize. Dammit, I get to talking about that damned Court plan—it's all I think about these days —and I get careless. I wish to hell you'd forget you were a gentleman and tell me to shut my goddamned mouth."

That was just the trouble, Francis was thinking later, leaning back in his chair with his feet on his desk. He would like to have told McAdam to shut up, but it wouldn't have served any purpose. He not only had to think of the Atkinson case, whose papers were strewn all over the desk, but he had to think about politics. About McAdam's and the President's and Charlie Mayborn's kind of politics. And he didn't want to.

McAdam had assumed, as everybody had a right to assume from the record, that Bacon's vote to uphold would make it a five-to-four vote in the government's favor. Bacon, Robson, Mitchell, Whitfield—and Francis Dalton. McAdam and everybody else knew that Francis Dalton had voted consistently to uphold the government in such cases—because that was the way Francis Dalton felt about the issues involved. He had made it quite plain in his many opinions holding the interests of the state above those of the individual in cases involving the preservation of public order.

In McAdam's mind, and in the public's mind, the Atkinson case fell into that category.

But did it? Francis lowered his legs from the desk and stood up to stroll across to the window. He looked out without seeing what lay beyond the pane. It was no use asking himself that question again. The Atkinson case *did not* fall into that category, and Francis had known it almost from the moment he scanned the briefs weeks ago. Atkinson was a dangerous rat, the worst of the American breed of neo-Nazis, and almost surely he was bound to do something someday that would land him in a penitentiary. But unfortunately that was not the point at issue. The point was whether the government had had the right to refuse to issue him a permit to speak in East Potomac Park merely because his speech might cause a disturbance. Even allowing that *might* was not quite the right word, since Atkinson's speech *probably* would have caused a riot, the fact remained that the government had to be wrong in denying him a right to speak. Free speech was free speech, even for rats like Atkinson. Once Atkinson had turned free speech into dangerous license, Francis would be prepared to uphold any court which found him guilty of inciting to riot, but he could not deny him the right to speak in the first place on the chance—however great—that the speech would cause trouble.

It had all seemed so simple, those several weeks before. The government had missed on this one, and although Francis had understood, and sympathized with, what John Alden Hughes was trying to do, he had known that this was one case in which he could not see eye to eye with the President. It hadn't seemed to matter, then. From John Alden Hughes's viewpoint, the Court would be striking another blow against his doctrine of national discipline and perhaps he would be disappointed in the vote cast by his old friend and political ally, Francis Dalton. But at the time it had just been one of those things that happen; there had been other instances of disagreement between the President and himself, and both had accepted them as minor inevitabilities between men of sincerity and integrity. Indeed, Francis had given it very little thought; his instincts and his attitude toward the Constitution were conservative, but it had never occurred to him that his politics should affect his consideration of any point of law.

And now? "Goddammit." He said it aloud as he strode back to his desk and plumped himself down in the chair. The point at issue—the legal point—had not changed in the slightest degree; the government was in error in refusing Atkinson the permit to speak, and its action should be struck down. But now the political situation had changed—it now was to John Alden Hughes's advantage to have the Court decide against the government. Such an adverse decision, after a few weeks in which the Court seemed to be coming around to the administration's point of view, would give the President ammunition for his charge that the Court was determined to block his efforts to safeguard the national security. "See," the President could tell the nation in effect, "what did I tell you? Once again the Supreme Court is standing in our way." In particular, the President could and would use the decision to strengthen the spines of those legislators who had been wavering in their support of the Court plan on the grounds that the Court's recent favorable decisions and Feldman's resignation had made the Court bill unnecessary. "We can't trust this Court," he would tell them. "We need our kind of justices. We need my Court bill." And those men on the Hill, so susceptible not only to the Presidential charm but to polls that showed such strong support for the bill, would listen to him.

Well, and wasn't this what he, Francis Dalton, wanted? Francis swung his long legs onto the desk again, and closed his eyes, seeking to keep track of his conflicting thoughts. To be sure, it was what he wanted; he was in favor of the Court plan because the time had come for revamping the Court, for making it more nearly responsive to the era. It was not a question of the administration's managing the Court, but rather of changing the Court's complexion so that it would be refreshed and capable of considering its work in the light of the changes that had come over the country. So of course it was what he wanted. He wanted anything, anything legitimate, that would strengthen the President's hand. The case, then, should pose no dilemma for him. He was voting the way he felt, which was that the government was in the wrong. If his vote coincidentally helped to strengthen the President's hand, then all to the good. But it was not all to the good. That was the trouble.

It was, quite simply, a matter of facing the Charlie Mayborns of the world. Francis could not evade any longer looking at it that way. He would be voting his conscience and his knowledge of law and of the Constitution, but the Charlie Mayborns and the Harry Weisses and the Chet McAdams and perhaps even John Alden Hughes would not see it that way. They would applaud him and admire him and pat him on the back—for being a loyal party hack. They would see his vote not as a vote for what he thought was right but as a vote for what he knew was needed to help the President's Court plan.

He could hear Charlie Mayborn now: "Nice going, Francis." No, perhaps Charlie wouldn't say that. Perhaps he wouldn't say anything. But he would look; that would be enough. He would look at Francis Dalton in that comfortable, smug way of his, and he wouldn't have to say anything. Francis would get the message. To Charlie Mayborn, he would be just another of the boys who had delivered. The others wouldn't say anything, either, and their looks would not be as obvious as Charlie Mayborn's, but they would approve and they would be grateful. And in Congressional cloakrooms and at cocktail parties all over Washington, the word would be that Mr. Justice Dalton had found a way to help out his friend the President, and he had taken that way; he had made the switch so that John Alden Hughes would have another adverse decision to complain about. Mostly, the comments would be approving, for Washington enjoyed and condoned political maneuvers, but there would be those who wondered, who would say nothing, but who would shake their heads sadly.

He lowered his legs from the desk and picked up the majority opinion he had written, beautifully typed on Jane Swanson's electric machine—and still lying on his desk more than a week after Jane had laid it there. His majority opinion in the case of the United States of America versus Roger Atkinson, at least tentatively concurred in by Justices Hume, Feldman, Gillette and Baker. It should have gone downstairs to the printshop the day Jane Swanson delivered it to him; he shouldn't have had to think it over at all. But he had done little else for a week.

Feldman, as the senior justice on the majority, had assigned the opinion to him. The ironic touch? Did Feldman, in grim jest, consider it a kind of poetic justice that the conservative should be assigned the writing? No, Francis thought not. Feldman did not jest, even grimly; he was not that kind of man. Francis' arguments in conference had been telling, even more so than Hume's, and Feldman never insisted on writing an opinion when he was satisfied with another justice's verbal rendering of that opinion. No, the opinion had been assigned on Francis' merits; and anyway, Hume had written his share.

Hume had been carefully gracious. "It's good to have you on our side for a change, Mr. Justice," he'd said. "Your arguments were superb." None of them had seemed surprised at those arguments, not even the superficial Baker. Mitchell, in his rough Nevada way, had feigned hurt. "You not only deserted us, Francis," he said, "but you damned near convinced me." Bacon had said his piece and then retreated into silence, as he so often did these days. To Bacon, it was a question of the need for preserving national order in dangerous times weighed against individual rights, and he had used the obnoxious language in Atkinson's previous utterances to bolster his arguments.

"Here is a maniac who would bring Nazism back to life," Bacon pointed out. "Here is a man who has said, in other public speeches, 'There is only one thing to do with these niggers and their diseased minds and their filthy bodies and that is to hurl them all into the gas chambers.' Here is a man who appeals to what he calls 'fellow white Americans' to follow him into every Negro section in every city in America and put to the sword what he describes as the 'curse of America.' Gentlemen, I would point out that our police are quite capable of quelling riots started by such maniacs, but not the finest police force in the world is capable of preventing those riots from starting."

Francis had pointed out, briefly, that "Free speech is free speech. If we deny it in one case, however obnoxious the protagonist might be, we endanger the principle itself."

Bacon had sniffed. "Mr. Justice," he said, "every fact we have shows that Atkinson's presence on the platform would have caused a riot the police would have had to quell. The constitutional guarantees of free speech do not encompass an invitation to public disorder and violence."

Francis' insistence had been gentle. "Surely not," he said, "but Atkinson contends with validity that he could not be refused a permit to speak merely because of his past utterances and conduct. And, unfortunately, the government nowhere has entered a sufficiently strong denial that Atkinson was being deprived of his right of freedom of speech. It has not said, 'No, what we are doing is not an abridgment of freedom of speech,' and it has not offered what I would consider good and sufficient reasons why it believes it was doing something else, something vital to the public weal. The conclusion is obvious: Atkinson's right to speak was violated."

Now Francis riffled through the pages of the opinion. It was a good one. It was sound; there were no holes in it. He had found it proper to answer Frank Mitchell's complaint that Atkinson, in effect, was the kind of man no decent American could sympathize with, because it occurred to Francis that it was a thought held by many citizens. He had written, "It should be emphasized, at the risk of stating the obvious, that people seeking the protection of the Bill of Rights are often those ideologically unattractive to the majority of Americans, but the fact remains that it is people such as these who most often find themselves in trouble with the police and thus have need of the protection afforded by the Constitution to all."

He believed, too, that he had fairly and correctly interpreted Justice Holmes's statement that constitutional guarantees do not "protect a man from an injunction against uttering words that may have all the effect of force." To be sure, Atkinson's past words had had the effect of force, but none of his meetings prior to his application for a speaker's permit in East Potomac Park had resulted in more than violent heckling. Perhaps—probably—the East Potomac Park meeting would have caused a riot, but Francis could not go along with the argument that a man should be punished before the fact. Holmes was speaking of other cases; Francis had noted in his opinion that "there is no power in government under our Constitution to exercise prior restraint of the expression of views unless it is demonstrated on a record that such expression will immediately and irreparably create injury to the public weal."

It *was* a good opinion. Francis could not understand why Chief Justice Bacon had dissented. Bacon had always been almost as vigorous as Hume in his insistence on the so-called "absolutes" in the Bill of Rights, and his comments had always been caustic when Francis had dissented in previous cases obviously involving a clear and present danger to the nation. Previously, he had clashed repeatedly with Francis' viewpoint that individual rights might be abridged where the damage caused by the exercising of these rights would cause considerable injury to the public. Yet Francis did not agree for a minute with the whispered suggestions of Charlie Mayborn that Bacon was getting old and no longer cared to buck the prevailing sentiment in the country. Bacon would never be too old to buck anything or anybody. No, the only explanation—and even this seemed weak—was that Bacon had become troubled by the disturbances and rioting across the country and was now able to see a clear and present danger even when it did not exist, as in the Atkinson case.

He had to send the opinion down to the printers. It was ridiculous keeping it here on his desk while he played Hamlet. He must send it down. There was nothing else to do.

Francis got up and walked again to the window, noticing for the first time that Jane Swanson had put some kind of new plant on the sill. Yes, there *was* something else to do. He tried to push the thought away, to forget it had occurred to him, but it was there. It would not go away.

He *could* do something else. He could change his mind. It had been done before, if not often. Old Stubbs had once changed his mind when the majority opinion was already at the printers' and had gone along with the dissent. On an antitrust case. Stubbs had explained in his memoirs that he "just couldn't go along with those steel company lawyers."

He could change his mind. It seemed so simple, now, and it would solve his problem. He could join the dissent and then it would become the majority—and then there would be five votes to uphold the government against four opposed. He could change his mind and it would not cause a ripple outside the Court building; indeed, he would be applauded for his consistency because that was the way the public expected Francis Dalton to vote.

All he had to say was that he had been persuaded by the Chief Justice's arguments. Or by old Angus Whitfield's, or Henry Robson's. Not by Frank Mitchell's. Good, kind Frank Mitchell—he couldn't persuade anybody. But the others could—especially his old allies, Whitfield and Robson. He *belonged* with them. It was *unnatural* that he should vote with the other side. And that is what would cause the talk—the seeming *unnaturalness* of his vote. That is what would cause people to say he was doing it to give the President a helping hand.

He could change his mind; and that way he could show Charlie Mayborn he was not just another party hack, not just one of the boys who could be expected to deliver. Then he could face Charlie Mayborn and Chet McAdam and the others. It would be a defeat for them, because it would be still another decision upholding the President, when he so badly wanted the Court to resume its recalcitrance, but he would have their respect. They would know that he refused to go along on an adverse opinion merely to give the Court plan a shove. They wouldn't be able to gossip about him then.

He would have their respect—but, goddammit, what about his own self-respect? He slammed a fist down onto the windowsill. Well, he had his self-respect. *He* would know why he was doing it—if he did it. It was to save his reputation as a nonpolitical judge, and if in the process he lost a shred or two of his own liking for himself, that was not so important as the other. It was important that the country have respect for the Supreme Court; it was important to the government he served, to the state. He had to balance it carefully—the commonweal against the individual. And in this case the individual was himself, Francis Dalton, Associate Justice of the Supreme Court. And the individual didn't matter that much. Not when the reputation of a Supreme Court justice was involved.

He walked over to the desk and sat down to ring the buzzer for Jake Moriarty. It would take some work; they'd have to rattle their hocks. He smiled, and his finger lingered on its way to the buzzer button. Rattle your hocks. That's what Bea always said. A corn-fed Midwestern expression, she called it. God, he would like to talk to Bea. He missed her. He had been missing her too much lately. He reached for his phone and dialed for long distance and told the operator he wanted to speak to Miss Beatrice Hart at the GRamercy number he'd known by heart since the night he and Bea had met.

She wouldn't be home, he was thinking—when her voice came

over the line clearly and distinctly: "Yes, this is Miss Hart." And as he said hurriedly, "Hello, Bea, dear," he was thinking, she never asks who's calling.

"Francis, pet," she said. "You just had to call me, because I was sitting here wanting you to."

"I had to," Francis said. "I haven't heard your voice since last night."

"You lamb—you do say all the right things, Francis. All the nice things. And ghastly things are happening here, and I'd have had to call you and tell you if you hadn't called."

"Ghastly things?" Now what? Francis wondered, and rebuked himself for putting it that way. "Bea, what ghastly things?"

"Oh, Francis—it's such a nuisance to you. It's really only one ghastly thing, but I hate it so—happening to us."

"Bea dear, if it's happening to us, then I have to be in on it." Stop worrying yourself all the time, he told himself furiously. "What is it, Bea?"

"Francis, it's happened. That horrible Dolly Drake has us together in her column today—and not only that, she says we're concerned about Freddie's book."

Good God! Francis thought. That cheap, dirty little Dolly Drake. Goddamn her!

"Francis—are you there?" Beatrice's voice was edged with concern. "Darling—oh, what a shock for you!"

Francis found his voice. "Bea—it's all right. It was a shock, but I'm still here. Damn Dolly Drake to hell. Bea, how does she—link us?"

"Oh, you know, Francis—well, here it is: 'Stage Queen Beatrice Hart and Supreme Court Justice Francis Copley Dalton, Washington's most charming romantic twosome, are wringing each other's hands about the forthcoming book of brutally frank memoirs by Bea's second husband, the lady-killing Freddie Adams.' It's horrible."

Francis felt sick. Goddamn them all. Goddamn exhibitionistic show people and goddamn all those dirty little people around their fringes. They weren't content with gossiping about their own silly friends; they had to drag in Washington names for seasoning.

"It is horrible, Bea. It's damnable." He was so angry he

340

couldn't think of anything except that Dolly Drake had no business poking into the private affairs of a Supreme Court justice.

"Francis, I know." Now Beatrice's voice was low and tremulous, and hearing it, Francis was ashamed.

"Bea, I didn't mean it that way, dear." He did, but he didn't. It was hard for anybody else to understand, even Bea. "I'm not blaming you, dearest. It's just that I'm so goddamned furious at that Drake woman for sticking her nose into the government."

"I know, darling." Now she sounded hurried. "And I'm so worried—about you, Francis. It matters—so much to you. I know that."

"Yes, it matters." God, how it mattered. With John Alden Hughes and his friendly order warning him not to get hurt by it, and his unspoken *or else*. With everybody in Washington sitting in the stands to watch the fight over the Court plan, and with people like Frank Hoar ready to pounce on any little thing to help their cause. "It matters, Bea. You know how I feel."

"Of course I do." Still her voice was tremulous, almost hurt. "And I know I'm to blame."

Now he felt self-contempt rising in him. "Bea, don't say anything like that. It was a shock, and I'm taking some time to recover. But you're not to blame. Only Freddie is to blame."

"Francis, poor darling. You are so—decent. But if I hadn't married him . . ."

"Bea dear, we can't talk like that. That's silly and senseless. I've been—difficult, I know. But we can't undo things that have been done. I wish you'd never married him, but you did—and I knew it. I knew everything. And I fell in love with you. That's all we can say about it."

"Darling, thank you." How low her voice was. "But it's terrible, and I just wish—I can't help wishing—it had never happened. I'm so worried about you."

"Bea, I want you to love me enough to be worried about me. But the worrying alone won't help us. We've got to face it. I don't know what we can do about it—now."

"Francis, I do love you—and I wish I could think of something . . ."

"I'm afraid, Bea, there isn't anything that can be done, now."

"*Now*—yes. Now that I'm fighting Freddie." Her voice grew

firmer, its tone was almost detached. "Except that I could give in to him."

"No!" Francis' voice was like a shot. "Not now, Bea. Not ever, for that matter. We thought about that, and we decided we couldn't do it. No, you can't give in to him."

"No, I know I can't. I said it, I suggested it, but I couldn't have done it. I knew it when I was saying it—all I could do was hope you'd say no, too—as you did."

"Bea dear, I said no because it has to be no. We couldn't let him get away with his blackmail."

"No, darling, we can't. Oh, I'm so glad to hear you say that. We couldn't let him get away with it, because it wouldn't be right. I know you couldn't. You'll always do everything the right way— the way it has to be done."

Francis thought of the Atkinson case and told himself, Yes, I hope so. I hope I can do everything the right way.

"I hope so, Bea," he said. "I do hope so. And now, since there's nothing we can do immediately about it, let's not talk about it any more. Let's talk about us. Tell me about your dinner date with Jimmy Hughes."

They talked for a long time then, and when they had said goodbye and Francis had hung up, he leaned back in his chair and closed his eyes to think about her. She had said almost the same thing she had said the other night. Today she had said *You'll always do everything the right way*. The other night it had been *You'll always do the right thing according to the way you see it*. Suddenly he found himself thinking of Hume and seeing again the gentle justice's friendly face and hearing the words that expressed Hume's concern about another case before the Court. It was an unimportant case, but it was complicated by the thin line it drew between the government's interest and the interest of the individual involved. "It's hard these days," Hume had said. "I think it's harder these days than it's ever been to make this kind of decision. We are all concerned with the government's interest, because the government is all of us, and therefore its interest, in a sense, is ours. And we have the persuasive voice of our government, our friends in our government, wooing our support. In these days, a man has to ask himself: Is this what I think, or what someone else is thinking for me? And it's difficult; it's very difficult because what someone else is thinking for us—if that someone else speaks for our government—has the terrible validity of representing the interest of our government."

Is this what I think, or what someone else is thinking for me? That is the way Hume had put it. And Bea had said, *You'll always do the right thing according to the way you see it.* He leaned forward and put his hands on the desk, clasping and unclasping them. There was something that was more important than the little problem he had created for himself. Something that was more important than the Court plan or politics or being able to look the Charlie Mayborns of the world in the eye. He had seen that something important and he had written it that way, in the opinion which lay on the desk in front of him. He had seen the right way and he had written it down as he saw it, and then he had wavered because his thoughts had become involved with unimportant matters. There were only two important matters to consider. One was that Roger Atkinson, the Nazi, was an individual who was entitled to the protection of the Bill of Rights because the Bill of Rights said nothing about giving those rights only to those who deserved them. And the second important matter was that you had to *do the right thing according to the way you see it.* And, incidentally, to hell with Freddie Adams.

He had thought, earlier in the day, that it was necessary—to save his reputation, his name with the public—to switch to the Bacon side, so that people would not think he was voting politically to do a political favor for the President of the United States. It wasn't very clear to him then, but it was clear now. You didn't save your reputation by doing something you didn't believe in. You didn't preserve your public name by failing to do the right thing according to the way you saw it. There was only one way to do things, regardless of how it looked to the outside world, and that was to do it according to what you believed was right. The outside world didn't matter and neither, really, did the state—not in matters such as this. The state might wonder, but the state did not want a Supreme Court justice who cut corners, who voted against his conscience and against his understanding of the law merely to *look good*, merely to preserve an image. Not even to preserve an image the state, unknowingly, might prefer to have of him. You took the oath and that was that; you argued and you

343

voted in accordance with that oath. Goddamn the Charlie May-borns and all the rest; they made it so goddamned difficult. But they didn't matter, either. It was tough to realize what they would think, but on the Supreme Court they did not pay you for the political opinions people had of you. They paid you to do the right thing according to the way you saw it.

Damnation! The thought slipped cruelly into his mind like a knife, and it brought the actual physical pain of a swift cut. There was, still, Dolly Drake. He'd forgotten about that in the excitement of his thoughts—the thrill of his meeting of minds with Bea and with William Allen Hume on the Atkinson case. No, they did not pay you for the political opinions people had of you —but did they pay a Supreme Court justice to have his name linked with a juicy scandal told by a slimy little kiss-and-tell chorus boy? Francis writhed at the thought, and the thing in his throat almost became an audible moan. My God, but there would be hell to pay now; there would have to be. The press would be on him like a pack of wolves—polite wolves, in Washington, but with teeth just as sharp. He wouldn't be able to evade them—the hard-working wire-service men and the tough, tenacious women who regularly applied their sharp needles to a vague segment of Washington defined with self-conscious aggressiveness as "soci-ety." There would be the very hell to pay. Dolly Drake had no outlet in Washington, but she was in several hundred newspapers stretching all across the country, and her gossip would be read by millions. Frank Hoar would read it with a mental smacking of lips, and Claude Wilkins would make pious note of it, and all the other enemies of John Alden Hughes, whom he had been forced to make his enemies, would pounce upon it. And the President. What would he do? Once again, Francis recalled with pain that implied *or else*—that silent warning on John Alden Hughes's friendly face. Don't get hurt, he had said, and it was not advice; it was a warning.

Francis leaned back in his chair and let himself sigh. He closed his eyes to try to shut out the thoughts that came racing into his brain. Then he opened his eyes and thought: The hell with Dolly Drake, just now. There was too much else he had to do, too much to do *right*, according to the way he saw it.

344

His finger pressed the buzzer now, firmly, and he sat there smiling while he waited for Jake Moriarty.

When Jake walked in, he was glad to see him. Glad to see the coatless, rumpled figure, with its quizzical eyebrows and the horn-rimmed glasses pushed up into his hair and the shirt wrinkled over the pot belly.

"Yes, sir?" Jake's eyebrows were wondering about the smile on the boss's face.

Francis Dalton picked up the Atkinson opinion. "Jake, we'd better get this down to the printer. Everybody'll be wondering if I lost it."

"Yes, sir." Jake took the stapled pages from Francis' hand. "You did take a little longer than usual, Mr. Justice."

"Yes, I did, Jake." Francis stood up and put both hands behind his head and stretched. "It couldn't be helped though, Jake. I just finished my research."

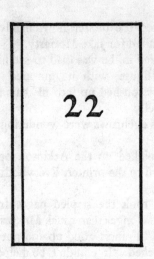

22

M r. Justice, I hate like hell to put this to you, but I have to—it's one of the things I do for a living." Jack Smalley's face was working with concern and his tone was genuinely apologetic.

"Jack, I understand." A Supreme Court justice was not often news, but when he was he was big news, and Francis knew that all over the country harassed men sitting at cluttered desks in newsrooms were demanding of the Jack Smalleys in their employ that they get something on the Justice Dalton-Beatrice Hart-Freddie Adams story.

"Hell, Mr. Justice, I don't suppose I would if I were in your shoes," the UPI man said. His body moved nervously as he perched on the edge of the green upholstered chair in Francis Dalton's living room. "I hated to barge in on you like this, practically at the crack of dawn, but I had to."

"Jack, it's all right." It was a small blessing that it should be Jack Smalley, whom he liked and respected. Francis picked up the coffeepot from the table in front of the sofa where he sat and filled Jack Smalley's cup. "Here, have some coffee while we trade nervousness, Jack."

Smalley sipped from his cup, then held it in front of his face, as though examining it. "It's good coffee," he said.

"It is," Francis said. "Mrs. Robinson is one of the few females who don't stint with the makings."

Smalley took another sip. "Well, sir, you know why I'm here. I have to ask you about that item in Dolly Drake's column."

"Yes?" Francis hated himself for being difficult, but he had to be careful, even with Jack Smalley.

"Well—what I have to ask you, Mr. Justice, is—are you and Miss Hart getting married? Or were you going to get married before Freddie Adams decided to write his book?"

Francis put his cup down on the table and wiped his lips with the napkin; little delaying actions, he told himself. But the question had been posed, and he'd have to face it.

"Jack, I have to tell you this, because it's the truth—even though it may seem vague, even though I may seem to be trying to evade the question." He picked up the cup again and took a large drink, gulping the black liquid. "I have to tell you, Jack, that Miss Hart's and my plans are indefinite, and that's all I can tell you."

"Yes, sir—thank you." Smalley was hurrying now. "That is, I mean—could Freddie Adams—uh, his plans—have anything to do with it? With your plans, I mean?"

Francis put down his cup and held up a hand. "Jack, I've told you all I can." He looked at Smalley and smiled. "But I'll add this, Jack—purely as an academic bonus: I don't think a person's plans, or two persons' plans, necessarily depend on what someone else does or doesn't do." There, by God, let 'em take that and chew on it—and you too, Frank Hoar.

Smalley stood up and reached for his hat. "All right, Mr. Justice. Thank you. Thank you for letting me in." He looked at his watch. "Holy Christ, it's not even eight o'clock yet! You sure must feel like murdering me."

Francis grinned. "No, not quite, Jack. I just wish you weren't so enterprising." He stood up and, with the expertness of political years, half walked, half guided Smalley to the door. "Sorry I couldn't do more for you, Jack."

Smalley smiled back. "That's all right, Mr. Justice—you did

pretty well." He turned to open the door, then turned back. "And good luck. Lots of luck."

"Thank you," Francis said. "Is there anybody who couldn't use some?"

Luck. I could use more than merely some, Francis was thinking as he distractedly glanced over the mail on his desk. He had made it to the office without any further intrusions on his Georgetown morning by the press, but they were after him in full cry. There they were on the desk, noted matter-of-factly on the little pink telephone slips. Eight in all, including two from New York, one from St. Louis and one from Los Angeles. He had returned the AP man's call as soon as he got to the office, to tell him the same things he had told Jack Smalley. But the rest—there was no point in getting involved. He pressed the buzzer on his desk and Jake Moriarty came in.

"Jake—Jake, you look pretty bloody sad."

Jake Moriarty shifted a foot. "I'm all right, sir. It's just too early, I guess." Then, in a blurting explosion, "This is a hell of a thing, Mr. Justice."

Francis managed a grin. "Yes, it is, Jake. A hell of a thing. But we'll just have to handle it. Don't let it get you down, Jake. I'm not going to let it get me down."

"That bitch Drake, goddamn her to hell." Jake's face was red with futile fury.

"Yes, I don't think she'll ever be my favorite journalist," Francis said. "But, Jake, to work. Look, get Helen Anderson on the phone and I'll talk to her. We won't bother with the rest."

"Why bother with Anderson?" Jake's tone was belligerent. "The hell with all of them."

"No, I'll talk to Helen. She's president of the Women's National Press Club, so I'll tell her what I told the AP and UPI and ask her to pass it on to her colleagues—that that's all there's going to be. Get her for me, Jake, and we'll have done with this."

After talking to Helen Anderson, Francis would have given anything to go home and go back to bed. He was bloody tired; this was a time when a man should be alone. But there was too much to be done—all the paper work on the desk, first, and then that helping hand he felt duty-bound to give John Alden Hughes in these last climactic hours of the Court fight. Hughes. It was surprising that he had not heard from the President—about Dolly Drake's little item. It was not only surprising; it was a little ominous. Mentally, Francis shook himself. That was nonsense, to think that way. If the President had something to say to him, he'd call up and say it—or call him over to say it to his face. It was pointless to conjure up thoughts of the President of the United States playing any kind of calculating game about an item in a gossip column. Still, it was surprising. And it was just as surprising that Frank Hoar—or, more probably, the fire-eating Bill Martin—had not ventured forth in print with a statement sorrowfully deploring the predicament the young Supreme Court justice found himself in.

"Mr. Justice." Jake stood in the open door. "Frank Hoar is on the line. Shall I shoo him away?"

Hoar. Well, here it comes, Francis thought. Speak of the devil. I'm sorry, Francis. By God, I'm sorry, Mr. Justice, but I just got to get out this statement. You understand. Thought you'd like to know about it in advance. By God, I'm sorry, Mr. Justice. You know that.

Francis said, "No, Jake, I'll take the call."

He picked up the phone as Jake was closing the door and waited for Hoar's voice.

"Hello—hello, Mr. Justice?" Hoar's voice was an abrasion.

"Yes—hello, Senator. Hello, Frank."

"Francis, glad I caught you." It was an excited voice, now.

"Nice to hear your voice, Frank."

"Francis, I'm not going to take up any of your time. And I'm not going to use a lot of pretty phrases. I'm just going to tell you this." Hoar's voice paused and he cleared his throat. "I saw that item in Dolly Drake's column, sir, and so did some of my colleagues. I've been on the phone with 'em all, and so has Claude Wilkins. It's made quite a stir." The voice paused again.

"Yes, Frank," Francis said. My God, he thought, spit it out. I'm a big boy now.

"Yes, Francis," Hoar said. "And I'll give you Frank Hoar's word—and Claude Wilkins's word, by God—that anybody on our side who tries to use that filthy little piece of gossip against you, or against John Alden Hughes, will be publicly disowned. That's all."

"Frank!" For a moment Francis was afraid Hoar was going to hang up.

"Yes, Francis." Now Hoar sounded tired.

"Frank, I don't know what to say." He didn't. How could men, politicians, behave like that—so well, so decently? "I don't know what to say, Frank, except that—well, you've just made the human race look pretty damned good."

"Yes, well . . ." Hoar sounded uncomfortable. "Well, hell, that's the way it is, Francis. And you can depend on it."

"I know I can, Frank." Astonished, Francis told himself: I may start crying any minute. "And, Frank—thank you. Thank you and yours."

"Yes, well, O.K. You're welcome, Francis. I'll see you around. Goodbye, sir."

"Goodbye, sir," Francis said, and he wondered why his eyes were dry.

If the fight for the Court plan could be won, it would be Chet McAdam who would win it; Francis knew that now as he observed the Senate Majority Leader in his fierce, last-ditch battle with the plan's enemies. Francis could not have blamed McAdam if he had deserted the fight after his rebuff by the President, but he recognized the motive behind McAdam's new ferocity in the hand-to-hand struggle on Capitol Hill. John Alden Hughes, in effect, had reneged on his promise to McAdam; the carrot was still there on the stick, but the President had added new conditions which McAdam must meet in order to enjoy that carrot. After his first disappointment, McAdam had accepted those conditions; he wanted a place on the Supreme Court, and, as a politician, he realized that as circumstances changed, the good politician changed with them and fought on—to get what he wanted. This was the newly aggressive Chet McAdam with whom Francis now found himself working. McAdam may have believed at first that the President would accept a compromise in the plan; now that that compromise had been rejected, he threw himself into the fight with renewed vigor because it was the only thing left for him to do.

There was one condition, however; McAdam had bluntly rejected the conspiratorial assistance of both Charlie Mayborn and

Harry Weiss and had demanded that the President work with him through Francis. "It's quite simple," Hughes told Francis. "Chet doesn't trust Mayborn and Weiss. Probably he no longer trusts me, either. And I can't blame him. But he does trust you, Francis. He told me, 'Francis Dalton is a man I can talk to.' That is quite a tribute, Francis; apparently it's more than Chet can say about me."

Francis had been moved by this gesture on McAdam's part, but deprecated it in his conversation with the President. "Of course, I've known Chet for a long time," he told Hughes. "And I suppose he feels I can take a detached view of things."

Hughes had grinned in a way that seemed painful. "Well, he should, Francis, he should. Especially after that Atkinson decision. I think it increased Chet's respect for your integrity." He put up his hand as Francis started to speak. "No, Francis, I'm not going to let you feel that you should discuss it with me; I just want to say that *I* never needed any reassurance. I know you pretty well."

Francis said, "Thank you, Mr. President—John. That makes me feel pretty good."

Hughes smiled, graciously this time. "You should always feel good, Francis. You're a man of conscience and rectitude. Oh, I suppose I'd use you more if you'd let me; a President has to use everybody he can lay his hands on to try to get the job done. But, Francis—I hope you recognize the fact that even a President of the United States can have the proper respect, and admiration, for integrity. Sometimes, in a lieutenant, it can be bothersome—sometimes it will stand in the way of some project that the President's own decency and integrity feel is necessary to the public weal. But—like Chet McAdam—I like people around me I can trust."

Francis could only smile back. "It was a pretty clear case, Mr. President. These days the public seems to make a great deal of Justice Holmes's initial ruling that speech might be limited when there is a 'clear and present danger.' But people seem to forget that Holmes himself soon became a dissenter to the application of that opinion. I believe we all have to go along with Holmes's clarification in 1919 in which he stated that speech could be restrained only where some emergency made it 'im-

351

mediately dangerous to leave the correction of evil counsels to time.' Even in this era, Atkinson's evil counsels can safely be left to time."

Hughes had disagreed with him, of course, but he had not pursued the point beyond remarking mildly that perhaps the White House was a better vantage point from which to detect clear and present danger; Francis felt one of his wonted throbs of sympathy for this young man beset by the problems of a turbulent era and so determined to solve them by vigorous action. Curiously, although the Atkinson decision had given the President new ammunition for his war against the Court, Hughes still could be displeased by the Court's overthrowing of the government's case. He would use the decision to help him push his Court plan, but he would never approve its principle. Francis knew what the President meant when he said the Atkinson decision had increased McAdam's respect for Francis' integrity; both Hughes and McAdam must have been aware of the debate that raged within him after Charlie Mayborn's sly suggestion that Francis could have given aid and comfort to the Court-packing cause by voting against the President in the Sons of Slaves case. Francis didn't know about Mayborn, but he knew both Hughes and McAdam recognized integrity when they encountered it. And yet, there was this Court-packing plan, and Francis was in it up to his neck. He wished he could be sure that his activities there were consistent with integrity. But there was so little time to give thought to one thing when thoughts of other things crowded into a man's brain.

Francis had waited stoically for the President to mention the Dolly Drake item, and he had not done so. He had not even displayed the trace of self-consciousness that would indicate it was on his mind. Francis thought of bringing it up, even of mentioning the call from Frank Hoar, but he rejected the idea. He had learned over the years that Hughes did not encourage the broaching of extraneous matters, particularly if they dealt with an unpleasant situation. No, he would remain silent unless or until the President brought it up. Then—then, having reached the bridge, he would cross it.

There was too much to do—even if the Court was in its winter recess and he had been relieved of the more formal chores of sitting four days a week and toiling through the suddenly interminable Friday conferences. Francis begrudged the time he spent on the Court plan, but there seemed no way out of it; the climax was upon them. Meanwhile, he had fallen behind in his own paper work, and now there were those overtures from Hoff. He had not spoken with Hoff himself, but Gleason's lawyer had kept the court clerk informed that he was rapidly completing his collection of "new material" in behalf of the convicted spy. If Hoff dumped this "new material" in Francis' lap, there would be nothing to do but review it and endure the agonizing ordeal of deciding whether there should be a stay of execution. It was nonsense to wish the whole Court was sitting; whatever Hoff had to offer, one justice could appraise it as expertly as the full bench, because it was that kind of case, a case in which only the submission of something spectacular could save him.

Once again, Claude Wilkins put his compromise proposition to the administration forces—but this time, privately to Chet McAdam, Wilkins argued that the Congress would be so relieved at escaping a desperate, all-out struggle that it would virtually assure passage and ratification. But now McAdam was as adamant as Hughes had been; the President had made it clear to him that there was no escape hatch if he wanted his place on the bench. "No, I won't go along, Claude," he told the Senator from Utah. "We don't want an amendment—we want our bill." But later he told Francis, "What can I do? All I want in this life is to be a member of the Supreme Court. People like Claude Wilkins want me to give it up now, when my big chance has come."

McAdam got his message across to his colleagues in the Senate, and the result was most gratifying to the Majority Leader. In his quiet conversations with an assortment of senators, Francis found them all furious with Hughes for refusing to pay his debt on time to McAdam, but it was clear that almost to a man they had braced themselves anew and were determined to push on in the fight for McAdam's sake. Pilney put it quite simply to Francis: "I'm only staying in this for Chet's sake." And the Senator from Nevada saw to it that the press was apprised of his thinking in an Associated Press story which told that "Senator Frederick C. Pilney of Nevada, President Pro Tem of the Senate, declared bluntly today that the Senate was united behind the President's Court plan 'because we're determined to do this last one thing for our friend, Chet McAdam.' "

Charlie Mayborn reported the President's reaction to this to Francis. "Hell, he doesn't care how he gets it as long as he gets it," the Attorney General remarked. "His pride would be hurt a hell of a lot more if he didn't get the bill." In the trenches of the opposition, Frank Hoar and Wilkins were properly concerned by this development, however, and Hoar persuaded Wilkins to approach McAdam on the compromise plan. "Well, we had to try," the Ohioan told Wilkins when Wilkins reported failure. "I don't like this goddamn old 'college try' business. The trouble with the Senate is that it's apt to get too sentimental about members of the club."

But McAdam refused to depend on sentiment; he whipped himself into new efforts in the home stretch. He found quiet counsel and some help in corralling the waverers from Vice-President Morgan and more grudging assistance from Pilney and from the irascible Alpheus Ward struggling with the calculated chaos the opposition had made of his Judiciary Committee hearings on the bill. But McAdam did most of the work himself, from early morning until late at night. Waverers who seemed ready for what the press called the "McAdam treatment" were led by the Majority Leader's assistants into McAdam's hideaway in the Capitol where McAdam conducted genial but persistent interviews in which he fought to get commitments. Francis listened in awe to McAdam's presentation of his case; he hammered away at the Gallup Poll's report of overwhelming public sentiment for the Court bill, and he reminded those of his colleagues coming up for re-election in the fall that they would have to give an account of themselves to this public at the polls. When Francis was not about, McAdam also hit hard at the Atkinson decision with the angry comment that those who believed the Court could be trusted now had been proved wrong. Nor did McAdam confine his burly activities to the waverers; he regularly phoned or invited in for "a little chat" most of the sure votes, because, as he explained to Francis, "Some of those boys are just looking for an excuse to run out—not on me but on the President. I've got to keep reminding them that I won't let them go."

Francis found much of this kind of sentiment among the senators he encountered. Hughes worried them by his apparent attempt to dominate the legislature. "Hell, I'm going along, but I don't care much for the situation," Paul Smart told Francis. "What I don't like about it is if the President wins this one, he'll be the big boss in this town. He'll have shown he can do anything he likes." But being from West Virginia, where urgent Federal aid was needed, Senator Smart had no choice. Francis discovered himself wishing he could avoid such encounters; these days he found them depressing, without quite knowing why.

Claude Wilkins put Paul Smart's sentiments into florid words for public consumption at both the committee hearings and on the floor of the Senate. Day after day, he dogged the President with his oratorical attacks, and his words were given the expected added weight by his position as an independent, which thus presumably left him clean of the partisan tar with which the opposition party had been brushed during the past campaign. Day after day, Wilkins reminded Hughes that "those of us who hold office in this government, however exalted or humble it may be, are creatures of the Constitution. To it we owe all our power and authority; without it we have nothing. I would remind those who seek to gain illegal power over other branches of the government that the three branches of our government were so constituted that the independent expression of honest difference could never be restrained, and no one branch could subjugate the others. That is the American system, and it is immeasurably more important than the passage of any legislation—any legislation at all."

Questioning an uncomfortable administration witness at the hearings, Wilkins embarrassed him by implying that he was part of a conspiracy to wreck the American system. While the witness grew red-faced, Wilkins poured out on him words that were almost accusations: "Today it may be the Court which is charged with forgetting its constitutional duties. Tomorrow it may be the Congress. Next week it may be the executive. Should we yield to temptation and punish the Court when we know we are creating a dangerous precedent, when we know we are clearing the path so that others, tomorrow, will inflict punishment on ourselves?"

Francis encountered Wilkins at the Cosmos Club that night

and congratulated him on his speech. "You really cowed that witness, Senator," Francis said. "I was almost frightened myself."

But Wilkins was not in a lighthearted mood. "Mr. Justice, you should be frightened," he said, lips pursed schoolteacher style. "In the condition the world is in now, we should not be thinking of enlarging the power of any one office, of any one person. There are enough dictatorships in the world."

"Oh, come now," Francis said. "Dictatorship is a hard word to use about John Alden Hughes."

"Perhaps, perhaps, Mr. Justice," Wilkins said. "Let us say merely that I declare for the continuance and perpetuation of government and rule by law, as distinguished from government and rule by men. I'm opposed to the reduction of the supremacy of law, because it means an increasing enlargement of the degree of personal government, and personal government means autocratic dominance."

It was useless to argue with him, Francis thought; Wilkins could not be made to see that if government was not strong enough to protect the individual, then the individual would be destroyed by those dictatorships abroad strong enough to take advantage of his lack of protection. Besides, Claude Wilkins was too irrevocably committed to his own speechmaking to care for the sound of another person's opinions.

Wilkins, thought Francis, was smug with the near certainty that the committee would vote down the President's bill, yet this did not worry either the President or Chet McAdam. "The committee was packed against us from the start," McAdam told Francis. "We never did have enough friends among that mixture of old fools and revolutionists." Nevertheless, the President was concerned about the publicity value of the committee's rejection of the bill, and he persuaded Francis to team up with Charlie Mayborn and write a minority report for submission when and if the committee said its official no. "It sure won't do any harm," Mayborn argued. "At least we'll be giving the newspaper readers something to ponder from our side of the fence. And we can't depend on old Alpheus Ward to write anything very ringing."

Francis was not happy about the assignment, yet he chided himself for his reluctance even as he entered a mild demurrer to the President's suggestion. He didn't know what was wrong with him lately; he seemed to have no stomach for the interminable maneuverings connected with the White House's stepped-up campaign, even though he succeeded in convincing himself almost daily that what Hughes was trying to do was basically correct. It was annoying, for that matter, that he should have to keep convincing himself. What he needed, Francis told himself, was a good rest. He hated the thought that there were times when his thinking seemed almost confused. It was not like him to give way to uncertainty and indecision. Almost angrily, Francis agreed to collaborate with Mayborn on the report; at least, he could curb some of Mayborn's instinctive hyperbole.

During those busy days Francis and Mayborn managed to squeeze in three long nights to work on the minority report. It consisted chiefly of the arguments presented to the committee by Mayborn, and they had Francis' to-the-point quality, dressed up in the more florid phrases of the Attorney General to give them public appeal. In the Court, Francis would never have cluttered up an opinion in such a fashion, but in the Court, he told himself, he was not selling anything; this report was designed to get through to the man in the street.

He and Mayborn dropped in on Alpheus Ward by appointment the day after Wilkins had charged on the Senate floor that John Alden Hughes "is callously seeking to evade the Constitution so as to deprive the people of their right to pass upon all amendments to the fundamental law." They found Ward half buried in his huge black leather swivel chair, a *Congressional Record* in his shaking hands.

Ward put down his *Record* and waved them to seats, his cranky face cracking and creaking in a smile that seemed perilously near a scowl.

"Afternoon, gentlemen," Ward said. "A man never gets any time to himself any more. But sit down, sit down."

Mayborn got to the point. "We're here to save you some work, Alpheus." He grinned. "We brought you a little present."

"What is it?" Ward's little eyes were beady and his voice breathed suspicion.

"Your report." Mayborn's voice was an unguent. "You know,

357

we talked about it the other day. Well, it's finished. Mr. Justice Dalton and I put the finishing touches to it last night." He dropped the stapled document on Ward's desk.

"Yes—yes, of course." Ward's words came hesitatingly, grudgingly. "We *talked* about it. That's all we did, Charlie. We just talked, is all." He leaned forward, beady eyes probing Mayborn's happy, political face. "What do you expect me to do with it, Charlie?"

"Do with it? Well, Alpheus, our understanding was that you'd use it, wasn't it? As a minority report?" Mayborn was the gentle mentor now, carefully reminding Ward of a gentleman's agreement.

"Use it?" Ward sat upright. "I never said we'd use it. Not as our report. Not verbatim." He turned his head and spat into a cuspidor at his feet. "I said we'd consider it and maybe incorporate some of your suggestions." His eyes were sly, now. "I said I'd be glad to look at it, Charlie."

Mayborn leaned forward in his chair. "Now, Alpheus, you know damn well that isn't what you said. I offered to write the report—with Francis—and you said go ahead, it was all right with you. That's why we put all that work into it, goddammit."

"Then that's a shame." Now Ward's voice rose to a quality almost of shrillness. "Then that's a goddamned shame, Charlie Mayborn. Because, by God, this committee is not going to let anybody else write its report, not while I'm chairman. If you think I'm going to go the rounds and ask any of my colleagues to sign this ersatz document of yours, you're nuttier'n a hoot owl in a full moon."

Francis stood up. "Alpheus, we wouldn't be here if that wasn't what we had understood," he said. "I'm sorry we misunderstood you, and we won't take any more of your time." He turned to Mayborn, an eyebrow up.

Ward seemed pleased with Francis' reaction. "Now, Mr. Justice, I'm not being ugly with you two. You know we're all in this together, all fighting for the same thing." And that was true, Francis reflected; for all his cussedness, Alpheus Ward was a sure vote.

"Of course I know that, Alpheus," Francis said. "It was just a

358

misunderstanding, that's all. But perhaps you will consider some of our arguments."

"Sure, sure I will," Ward said. He rose and leaned with both hands on his desk. "I sure as hell will, gentlemen. And thank you. Thank you kindly. We'll do all right, gentlemen, you'll see."

Outside, Mayborn was red-faced and his words sputtered. "We'll do all right," he mimicked Ward. "We'll do all right. The goddamned old fool. He'll screw it up if he can. Goddamn him to hell."

Francis was silent; it had occurred to him that with their dismissal by McAdam, both Mayborn and Harry Weiss had lost all their influence on Capitol Hill. Alpheus Ward, of course, rarely bothered to be polite to anyone, but until now even Alpheus had managed an air of cranky cooperation. It was a fact, of course, that McAdam's friends were irritated by the way McAdam was being harassed by the White House to go on with the job. Although Hughes had left the fight pretty much in his Majority Leader's hands, both Weiss and Mayborn had thought it wise to remind McAdam with irritating regularity that his place on the bench depended on his seeing the Court bill through to victory. McAdam writhed under these reminders, and discussed them bitterly with his friends; he never needed their help more than he did now, he emphasized.

Francis mentioned this goading process to the President, but Hughes was not concerned. "Francis, you are the diplomat of the team," he said. "Mayborn and Weiss are my gadflies. Sometimes perhaps they sting a little too hard, but I need them. I'm not going to interfere with their work. It's unpleasant, but in a fight like this you have to keep the heat on." Francis kept silent; he didn't trust his irritability.

It was true, too, of course, that a new situation had developed with the probability that the Senate Majority Leader's post would shortly be vacated, and this was helping to keep Alpheus Ward in line. Pilney and some others had been mentioned for the post, but it was Ward's opinion and that of the experts that, all things being equal, McAdam's mantle would fall on Alpheus's shoulders. Ward was troublesome, but he had always been an obedient lieutenant of the President, and there was every reason to believe that all he had to do was continue to go along on the Court bill to be assured of the leadership. Technically, of course, it was purely a Senate matter, but the man who got Hughes's nod would be in for the simple reason that few senators would vote against the choice of a popular President who could wreak horrible vengeance upon them in patronage matters.

Ward had put it bluntly to Hughes. "He told me, in effect, that he had always done my bidding and that if McAdam went to the Supreme Court he expected his reward," the President told Francis. "He's right, of course. He deserved the leadership. Ward may be a dreadful cold sore, but he cooperates. I'm sorry he didn't accept that report you and Charlie offered him, Francis, but I can't let it matter to me. Of all the candidates for Chet's job, Ward is the most dependable when the chips are down. And as Majority Leader he'll be trapped; he won't be able to get away with that preliminary bluster that's always so annoying. Alpheus Ward is the compleat pragmatist, Francis; I can handle him a lot easier than I've ever been able to handle Chet McAdam."

There was, immediately, another politician to handle. Paul Anderson had let it be bruited about that he was planning to walk out publicly on the Court plan. Ordinarily there would have been scant urgency about dealing with him, since the plan would not come before the House Judiciary Committee which he headed for some time, but at this point the President could not afford any defections at all among men whose names were widely known to the electorate. And Anderson, moving his hulk about Capitol Hill for whispered conversations in a corner here and a corner there, represented the Midwest and the troublesome farmers far more than did that area's members in the Senate. As Paul Anderson went, so might go the farmers, and there had already been too many signs of infidelity among that breed.

Francis, the detached diplomat, was set to work to keep Anderson in the fold, but he found Anderson amenable only to a point. "I won't say anything now," Anderson told him. "I want to watch how things develop, and besides, I'm worried about old Chet. But I never liked the Court plan; you know that. I don't see how I can go along unless some kind of compromise is worked out. My farmers don't like it, and they don't like some of the things Hughes is doing to them. I'll wait and see, Mr. Justice.

I won't interfere while the Senate is dealing with the bill, but that's all I can promise. There doesn't seem to be anything in it for my kind of people."

The President's smile was bleak when Francis reported on his interview. "We'll have to see," he said. "I believe Anderson is honestly concerned, but perhaps we can find something in it for him—and for his kind of people." And, Francis reflected rather sourly, Hughes seldom failed to "find something in it" for the people he needed.

The next day the Senate Judiciary Committee voted eleven to seven to report the Court bill unfavorably. In the majority report, written by Claude Wilkins, the opposition quoted George Washington, Thomas Jefferson, Andrew Jackson, Abraham Lincoln, Woodrow Wilson and even Franklin D. Roosevelt in support of its finding. It wound up the report with a segment of Washington's Farewell Address in which the first President warned that "the spirit of encroachment tends to consolidate the powers of all the departments in one, and thus to create, whatever the form of government, a real despotism."

In the Senate Press Gallery, Jack Smalley of UPI leafed through some documents in a briefcase and came up with a startling discovery. In voting down Franklin Roosevelt's Court bill in the thirties, the committee had used the identical quotation from the Washington address. The desk was interested, but not surprised. "Why not?" asked Ed McNally. "Senators today are just as lazy as they were in Roosevelt's time."

Francis didn't get a chance to talk to McAdam until lunchtime, when he returned to his office from downtown to find a message on his desk asking him to call the Majority Leader. His return call ultimately discovered McAdam in the Vice-President's office.

"Hello, Chet," Francis said. "I see Wilkins and Frank Hoar had their way with our committee."

McAdam's voice was hoarse but cheerful. "Oh—yes, that's pretty much the way we figured it, Francis. They did talk a little tougher in the majority report than I expected, though. I don't suppose it'll be pleasant reading for the President. I see old Frank Hoar in that crack about the bill being an insult to the free representatives of a free people."

"Yes, it's good high-sounding propaganda for their side," Francis said.

"Well, let 'em have their fun." McAdam sounded more than cheerful now. "We've been working over here while Wilkins and Hoar have been practicing their rhetoric. We had the last caucus today, Francis, and I wanted to pass the result on to you."

"Chet, it sounds almost like good news. Do you have a tally?"

"Yup, a final tally. It's not what I hoped for, but, by God, Francis, it will do on a day like this. Tom Morgan and I have been over it with a fine-tooth comb and we can't whittle it down any more. We figure on fifty-six votes sure for the bill."

"Fifty-six!" Francis wished he could feel more excited. Fifty-six sure votes meant fifty-six definite commitments from a Senate which had hemmed and hawed for long and exasperating weeks. "That is good news, Chet. And—you're *sure?*"

"Yes, Francis, I am. We'll start debate Monday. And, by God, I think we can make it—all the way. By God, Francis, the troops have come through for old Chet."

"Chet, congratulations. You deserve all the credit. You've done a terrific job. Terrific." Francis felt warmed by McAdam's exultant good cheer. "I suppose you've told the President." *Why* couldn't he share McAdam's delight?

"Yes, sir. Just left him. He feels pretty good, too."

He should, Francis thought. "I hope he congratulated you, too, Chet."

"Yes, he did." McAdam said it with a curious flatness. "Yes, he had a pat on the back for me." He paused. "You know, he's a hard man to please, Francis."

"Yes, I know," Francis said. Poor Chet, he thought.

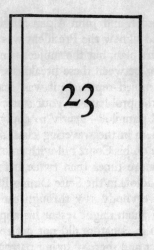

23

FRANCIS DALTON took the justices' private elevator this morning. He was still tired, after eight hours of sleep; the hugely attended Senatorial breakfast at the White House had left him as drained as though he had already done a day's work. He wished again he had been able to go South for a couple of weeks, as some of the other justices had done almost the moment the Court went into its winter recess. But his chores in behalf of the Court bill had cut severely into the time he could spend in his office; now he had to do his best to catch up with the routine. As he sat down heavily before his cluttered desk, he was exasperated to find a note informing him that Hoff had once again called the clerk of the Court. Instantly he reproached himself for his unfairness; he disliked Hoff personally and so he was in danger of judging Hoff's efforts in behalf of his wretched client on a personal basis. He would have to get at Hoff's brief and his bulging envelope of "new material" this morning; the execution was scheduled for Sing Sing at nine o'clock tonight. But first he just wanted to sit.

It had been, after all, a rather successful breakfast. Forty-three senators had shown up, their faces more or less dutiful in the presence of their leader, and John Alden Hughes had poured on the charm. Everybody knew the President was feeding his troops in behalf of his Court plan, but the subject was never mentioned. It had been too long between these breakfasts, the President had explained in a tone of self-reproach; it was time that they all had a long talk "about the problems of your states." That, of course, was the Presidential gimmick—gently to apply pressure on these senators, most of them in the wavering class, so that they would approach the debate on his Court bill with emotions so mixed that they would think more times than twice before sabotaging the bill. There were no idiots in the State Dining Room, and so Francis was sure that everybody saw through the President's tactic, but though some of them might resent his approach, none dared to challenge him on it. Senators did not get re-elected by antagonizing the President and thereby losing patronage for their constituents.

There was much to talk about on the subject of what Hughes called "the needs of your constituents." Judgeships, river dredgings, military installations, new defense plants, veterans' hospitals. A judgeship or two in hand, plus a new construction project paid for by Federal funds, would assure most of those senators of re-election even if they staged only token campaigns. The nation's security might be in the balance—and, to be sure, these toilers in the Senatorial vineyard would give that their strict attention at the proper time—but they would not be around to apply their wisdom unless they got something for the home folks.

It was more like a jovial family reunion, with John Alden Hughes ready and more or less willing—depending on future good behavior—to distribute presents to one and all. Everybody who wanted one had a whiskey sour to rid the system of cranky, early-morning thoughts, and by the time the silver coffeepots went around, there was a reasonably authentic air of good fellowship in the room.

To be sure, Handley of Minnesota could have that veterans' hospital—subject always, of course, to a check with Paul Anderson. The President suggested that Anderson might not see the importance of that hospital; perhaps Handley could have a chat with him. There was a flood control project for Hays of Connecticut, just to show that those who stood solidly for the plan received their rewards, but unfortunately there were "difficulties" about that harbor rehabilitation project for Massachusetts and Federal assistance for New Hampshire's textile mills. The President hoped those difficulties could be resolved in conversations between him and Massachusetts's Bailey and New Hampshire's Sanders—who had come out against the Court bill. After all, Hughes had been able to manage that Lake Michigan project for Childs of Illinois—whose vote was solid, thanks to pressure by Francis' friend, the financier Bob Estabrook. In short, the President suggested, all things were possible "if we can just get together on these things." He smiled around the table and added, rather soberly in that cheery atmosphere, "I'm sure we can, gentlemen. I'm sure we can."

Still, there had been no mention of the Court bill—with debate scheduled to open at ten o'clock that morning—until Francis found himself, as the breakfast was breaking up, with Julia Hughes. He had not seen the President's mother for several weeks; Julia Hughes had remained in Palm Springs since before the President's first speech except for one-day visits to the White House of which the press was not informed. As usual, the President's mother had insisted on keeping out of the limelight as much as possible; indeed, her voice had not been evident in the private councils since she had urged her son, in vain, not to make those early speeches. Francis knew it was not pique that had kept Julia Hughes out of it, because she had phoned Mayborn from Palm Springs to congratulate him on "winning the argument."

The President had introduced his mother to the table with the remark "Mother invited herself to this shindig so she could be with some old friends again," and Julia Hughes had stood for an instant, her white hair gleaming and that easy smile on her unlined face. She looked more like Jimmy than the President, but watching her, Francis realized that it was John who had inherited his mother's ease of manner and casual movements that bespoke instant friendliness without sacrificing any dignity.

"I thought John was very good," his mother said to Francis as the two lingered behind the general exodus into the foyer. "It's very difficult to cajole and at the same time remind your listeners that there is such a thing as retribution for the recalcitrant, but John carried it off."

"He's an artist in politics," Francis said. "He's one of the few who have made it an art."

"Yes." Julia Hughes seemed suddenly absent-minded. "I suppose it should be effective, but I don't know. They're a hard lot. John has made them pretty angry. You know I try not to interfere, but when John asked me, I told him it might be best to give Chet McAdam that vacancy on the Court. He'd have won himself a lot of friends that way."

"It was a difficult decision," Francis said, meaning it.

"Yes, it was. But John had to do it his way, Francis. You have to do things your way in this house. I don't mean to second-guess John. After all, McAdam is working harder than ever now. And I suppose that was the point of the whole thing."

"Yes, I suppose it was," Francis said.

Now Francis stretched his legs under his desk until the pleasant little pains came in his calves and thought: I need a vacation. He would have given anything to lie down on the sofa and take a long nap, but it was out of the question. It would take him several hours, at least, to go through the mass of material Hoff had brought him last night and which he had scarcely had time to glance over. The decision on a stay of execution was always a difficult one; now he was down to the wire, with Gleason scheduled to die before the day ended—and he was so tired.

The door opened a crack and Jake Moriarty's head appeared.

"It's Harry Weiss on the phone—I'm sorry, but I thought you might like to talk to him."

Francis sighed. These days he seldom *wanted* to talk to Harry Weiss, but Weiss was somebody you had to talk to; Harry didn't pick up the phone unless he had a message to transmit from the horse's mouth. "I'll take it, Jake." Ivory tower indeed!

"Good morning, Francis." Weiss's voice was unusually dulcet. "I hope I'm not disturbing you."

Not much, Francis thought. I'm just killing time trying to think about a man who's going to die in the electric chair tonight. "It's all right, Harry," Francis said. He did not quite succeed in keeping the weariness out of his voice.

"Francis, this is a personal call." Weiss did sound like a particularly unctuous undertaker. "I just wanted to check something out for the Boss."

"Oh." Then go ahead, Francis urged him silently; we all know the President isn't wondering about the state of my bowels. "Sure, Harry, check away."

"Francis, it's about the item in the papers—about you and Miss Hart."

"Yes?" Francis hoped he got the raised eyebrow into his tone. Damned if he'd help the man.

"I suppose you talked to UPI and AP," Weiss said, checking.

"Yes, I gave them both a statement," Francis said. Let Weiss dig, let him check.

"It says your plans—yours and Miss Hart's—are indefinite. And then there's something about not letting a third person influence you. Is that about what you told them, Francis?"

"It sounds like it, Harry. Why? Harry, are you calling at the President's request?"

"Well . . ." Weiss's voice had that careful quality that always crept into it when he was asked such a question. "Well, yes, Francis—in a way, I am."

"In a way—what does that mean, Harry?"

"Well"—Harry Weiss hated things to get sticky—"well, the fact is he asked about the Dolly Drake item the other day, and then he saw the stuff on the wires and he asked me about it again."

"Oh, and he told you to call me up and find out what I was getting mixed up in," Francis said. Now he let his voice be irritable. Goddamn all this crud.

"No—oh, no, Francis. The Boss was—concerned. He was concerned about you. He said something about he wondered how you were—oh, feeling, you know. He said he wondered if the wire services had got it straight. So I decided I'd call you."

You bet you did, Francis thought. You can recognize a Presidential order when you hear one—even when it's in double-talk. "All right, Harry. You've called me. The wire services got my statement straight. That's about the situation, Harry. O.K.?"

"Sure—O.K." Weiss's voice was hurrying. "Of course, Francis. I'm glad to hear it—that they got it straight, that is. But you know the Boss—he wouldn't want you to get into any kind of trouble. You know him; he'd like to help if he could."

"Yes, Harry. I understand. He told you he didn't want me to get into any trouble, did he?"

"Well—yes. I guess that's the gist of it. He's worried about you, Francis. Naturally. And said something about it would be too bad if you got into any trouble."

"Yes, I see." Francis somehow kept the anger out of his tone, the anger that was rising hot in him from deep inside his flesh. "All right, Harry. Please thank the President for—for being concerned about me. And tell him I'll try not to get into any trouble. O.K.?"

Harry Weiss sounded confused, almost defeated. "Sure. All right, Francis, I'll tell him. And sorry to bother you."

"That's all right, Harry. You didn't really." Not much, Francis thought, not so goddamned much. You could have been worse; you could have told me I had cancer. The fury was burning his flesh. "If that's all, I'll see you later." He hung up.

Or else. Don't get into any trouble, *or else.* The President hadn't said it that way; he hadn't said the *or else.* But it had been there. And now, in case Francis had missed the point the first time, John Alden Hughes had commissioned Harry Weiss to say it a little more clearly. *He said something about it would be too bad if you got into trouble.* Harry Weiss was a good man; he knew how to say things the President wanted said so that you got the point. It was one of Harry Weiss's many qualifications for the job he held—the job of keeping people in line for John Alden Hughes. Francis saw again the tabloid headline:

EX TO TELL ALL
ON JUSTICE'S GIRL

The anger wouldn't let him rest in his chair. Francis got up and marched across the room to the outer door, then marched back to the desk and stood there. By God, the pressure was on him. And why not? The pressure had been put on everybody else—on Chet McAdam and on all the senators who lived on patronage, on everybody a President had to use to get what he wanted. Why should he, Justice Francis Copley Dalton, escape it? He was in the Court fight. He had been lobbying for it. He was the dignity the President needed—the front man for the fight. And he had damned well better not lose that dignity. That is what the President had just told him, through Harry Weiss. He might have believed that his relationship with Bea was a personal affair, a private matter, but Hughes had reminded him that it was not. Hughes had reminded him that when a man is a Supreme Court justice—and, more important, a front man in a political campaign —his private affairs are a public matter. Francis Dalton's rectitude was a political weapon in the hands of the President; if a shadow were cast upon it, it became a political liability. And why not? Wasn't that the way he himself had always felt? Hadn't the highly moral Francis Dalton always insisted that the man in service to his government keep his personal life clean?

Francis sat down. Suddenly his thoughts were a muddle of confusion. The President had a right to be concerned about him and his troubles because Francis was a member of the President's staff in a battle he was determined to win. Francis had to acknowledge that. Not because he was Francis Dalton, but because he was a member of the team. Any President had the right to dictate his own standard of morality to any member of the team, so long as that person remained a member of the team. If a President was to get the things done that he believed had to be done, then those on his team had to behave themselves. They had to go along, in every way; they could not be a drag on his efforts.

It helped a little to close his eyes, Francis was thinking as he leaned back in the chair. No, he could not cavil at this point. They were all in it together, in the fight to change the Court, and the President had the right to demand that his team keep itself bright and shining for public consumption. Damn! Francis opened his eyes and leaned forward and smote the top of the desk with the flat of his hand. But, goddammit, what about Francis Dalton, human being? Didn't he matter at all? Didn't he and Bea matter? Must a justice of the Supreme Court of the United States relinquish his humanity? Must he forswear his human rights because he had sworn service to his government? Human rights. The term jerked at his mind, shaking up the jumble of thoughts that crowded it, and a sharp dagger of unease pricked at him. Human rights. Civil rights. He was dragging them into it now, now that he was *personally* concerned. Self-scorn seared him as he thought: *Now* you're thinking about human rights. Where is your wonted detachment *now*, where the cool academic premise that human rights are secondary to the rights and interests of the nation at large? Why are you so concerned, now, merely because the President of the United States has said: Don't get into any trouble, or else; get yourself out of that involvement with that actress lest you damage my Court plan. You are hurting now, Francis Dalton, because the President has exercised his prerogative of seeking to impose his will on you, personally, but you do not hurt when he attempts to impose his will on the Congress and on the Court through his Court-packing plan. You not only do not hurt, but you help the President all you can.

My God, Francis thought, I *am* seeing myself. At last. And what I am seeing is not pretty. I know now where those doubts of the past few weeks have come from. They have come from Francis Dalton, human being. And Francis Dalton, politician and lawyer, has always managed to sweep them under the rug, to pretend they were not there. And now I have come to the point where I must think about them seriously, where I must appraise them and sort them out, and set them each in its proper place—and there is no time for this job of thinking. Not yet; not until after Gleason. Not until I perform my official duty and sort out and appraise the facts and the arguments in the case of a human being named Harry Gleason. He looked at his watch and realized how late it was. God, he thought, I have got to straighten out that muddle in my brain that concerns me and Bea and the Court plan and John Alden Hughes. I owe it to myself to straighten it out, so I will know how I should think, so that I will be able to do the right thing as I see it. It's a debt I owe to myself and to Bea and to everyone who knows me, or thinks he knows me. But not now. I've got to sweep the doubts under the rug one last time while I consider the problem of Harry Gleason, spy. He opened the folder lying on the desk and took a deep breath, and he could feel his nose wrinkle with distaste as he perused the first typewritten words.

It was the typical spy case, but with sordid overtones. Francis accepted spying as a necessary evil of the era, and he could view with a certain equanimity and even, at times, admiration, the exploits of both the American and Soviet varieties of secret agent. But he found it impossible to stomach Harry Gleason, an American of what was known as a good family, an intellectual who had had all the so-called material advantages, and who had spied on his country for the Russians. If Gleason had been a Russian, or even, perhaps, the American son of Russian immigrants, Francis would have excused him on the ground of old-country loyalty, but the nation would be better off morally as well as on the basis of national security once Gleason was electrocuted.

Gleason had made such a point of serving the Soviet Union; that was what stirred Francis' ire and disgust. He had gone to Russia as a touring student to examine "Soviet culture," and he had remained to go into intensive training as a Soviet spy in his own country. On his return to the United States, he had been assigned to the odious chore of checking on the loyalty and reliability of American leaders of the underground Communist party. He had operated in the guise of a wealthy American political dilettante who apparently was willing to buy over any dissidents toying with the idea of defection. Testimony at his trial had shown that he had turned over to Moscow's secret executioners in America four of these would-be defectors; their bodies now lay in potter's fields in three American cities.

After these successes, Gleason had returned to Moscow, again as a tourist, and had undergone additional training in espionage. He had learned to encode and decode messages, to photograph documents, to fake documents like passports and Pentagon passes. Then, again, he had returned to his own country, this time as the commander-in-chief of Moscow's American spy apparatus.

It was incredible that Gleason should have been able to set himself up in a fashionable New York duplex apartment and go on living the life of the intellectual and playboy, but he had managed it for five long years. Five years of success in draining his native country of its defense secrets. To be sure, he had been ingenious. His arrangement of signals to his coconspirators smacked of his daily life—a torn matchbook on a table at the Stork Club; a penny placed atop the ledge of a booth in a Waldorf Astoria men's room; a scuff mark on the steps of the Metropolitan Museum of Art; a song sung by one of his *chanteuse* girl friends in an intimate cabaret in the East Fifties.

His guilt was plain; Francis was as sure of that as was possible. Gleason, of course, had maintained his innocence to the last, capering about the courtroom with playboylike posturings while his counsel kept hammering on the premise of mistaken identity.

But, after all, he had been identified by one of his own conspirators, who not only picked Gleason out of a lineup but provided the FBI with a bundle of documents for corroborating evidence. The old man, Burch, had taken the FBI to the "dead drops" the apparatus had used in Central Park and on the Brooklyn Bridge, and he had led them to the hiding place behind a panel in Gleason's apartment where Gleason kept the hollowed-out coins he used to transmit coded messages. Burch had opened those coins with a needle inserted in certain letters on their faces, and inside the FBI had found messages in code which Burch decoded for them from a master code.

It was poetic justice, or at least a neat piece of irony, that old Burch should have led the FBI to Gleason, for Burch had a personal interest in Gleason, the stool pigeon for Moscow. One of the four defectors on whom Gleason had informed had been named Wilson, but his real name was Burch and he was Burch's brother. Sometimes, Francis reflected, the spymasters of the world find themselves betrayed by a stooge who suddenly turns human being.

Truly, the FBI had done a magnificent job of tracking down Gleason—with that invaluable assist from the Central Intelligence Agency. For it was CIA that had had its eye on Burch for so long, its curiosity aroused by certain actions which seemed to imply that Burch could be had. Perhaps no one would ever know how the CIA agent got to Burch finally, but it was all there in the testimony—how Burch had suddenly blurted out what he knew to "an Embassy official" in Paris. From there the FBI could take over again and, by ceaseless surveillance and vigilance, finally pick out the man Burch knew only as "Richards" and who Burch believed lived in a small apartment in Brooklyn Heights. After that, identifying "Richards" as Gleason and moving in on him in his Manhattan apartment had been easy, and old Burch had gone over the paneled walls inch by inch until he suddenly pointed to a spot and said, "There—there is where you'll find the coins."

The trouble with the trial was that it had been surrounded by all the hysteria of those organizations which set themselves up as guardians of civil liberties. For some reason, Francis reflected, those organizations seldom troubled themselves with the poor

Skid Row derelict who had been framed by some graft-seeking cop, but could always be depended upon to come howling to the aid of the man charged with treason. There were, of course, more headlines to be earned along that path. At any rate, Gleason had had them all on his side, the professional sob sisters of Let's Be Palsy-Walsy With the Russians and the men of lofty rhetoric and scant logic who pictured themselves as the country's latter-day William Lloyd Garrisons and, besides, had little else to do.

Yet, though it took nearly three years, Gleason had been duly tried and convicted and sentenced to the electric chair. His appeals had been heard and denied, in an atmosphere of national stridency and of belligerent demands from women's rights organizations, clergymen and study groups that Gleason be freed forthwith and that the FBI be disbanded. Appeals had poured in from almost every country on the globe, and there had been riots in Paris, Calcutta and Rome, hunger strikes in London and Bombay, and carefully policed demonstrations in Moscow, Warsaw and Prague.

It is all here again, Francis noted, as he turned page after page in the Hoff exposition. It is all here, as if I had never read the transcripts of the trial and of the lost appeals, as if I had never even glanced at Hoff's brief, as if I had ignored the eight-column headlines that have shrieked from the newspapers' front pages for nearly three years. And yet, he thought, I have to go over it all. I have to read it all, lest there be something there I have missed on other days, in other readings.

It was true, of course, that both Appeals Court and the Supreme Court itself had rejected defense counsel's pleas that the FBI had broken the law in its investigation and in its presentation of the case at Gleason's trial. The Supreme Court decision against Gleason, in fact, had been a resounding eight-to-one, with only Hume expressing vaguely worded doubts. Surely, the nation had given Gleason every right he was entitled to; surely his case had had the benefit of the most careful scrutiny possible.

And yet was this, in fact, true? Francis stood up, a hand to his moist forehead, and walked over to examine absent-mindedly the portrait of Chief Justice Holmes. Suddenly, in exasperation, he knew that he could not answer that question with a yes. Not yet. Not until he had gone through that bulky document, not until his eyes had burned themselves out seeking the meaning of almost every word typed there. A man's life was at stake, and though it was a worthless life, its quality remained human. It was his job to do, and he had to do it alone. The application had been made to him, and he did not feel he could shift his individual responsibility to the Court. It was as simple as that.

Hoff's original application and his calls to the clerk had spoken of new evidence, new material purporting to prove FBI duplicity during investigation and trial. Francis distrusted Hoff; he distrusted the type of lawyer who, by his actions and words, rendered the suspicion that he was acting and talking for publicity's sake. But he could not condemn Gleason to death because Gleason's lawyer was personally obnoxious. He would have to stick at this job, wading through both the relevant and the irrelevant, working carefully, reading closely, lest he miss a fact or a point that could mean a reprieve for a man condemned to death. He would have to sit here all day because he had to do his duty by a convicted spy.

Francis walked back to his desk and sat down and picked up the heavy document and adjusted his eyes to its text. He did not look at the clock on his desk, but the thought came that in a prison on the Hudson River there were at that moment men tinkering with the controls of a squat and ugly wooden chair.

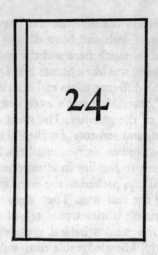

24

CHET McADAM'S LEGS ACHED with the tingling excitement of the occasion. As he stood in front of his desk on the left side of the Senate floor, he kept stretching them by rocking back and forth on toe and heel. Only a tiny corner of his mind attended the discussion brought on by Ralph Bailey's insignificant parliamentary inquiry. There would be nothing else to this day but debate on the Court plan, and although he would remain alert for noises in the wings, his concentration could not be wrenched from the point at issue. He had launched the debate, and when the Vice-President had finished explaining things to Bailey, the showdown battle would be on.

McAdam looked around him at the tasteless beige and red-streaked marble decor of the Senate chamber—tasteless and yet somehow representative of those who now filled the chamber: men mostly of good taste personally, each of whom could have given the chamber a flair if left alone to do the job, but whose ideas were distorted when mixed into a consensus. It was so often the way things happened in the Senate; compromise was necessary but the results it attained rarely achieved the elegant. Seldom did the Senate produce either a wholly good bill or a wholly bad bill, but almost always the bill that was possible. This chamber, with its cluttering of seals and busts of long-departed statesmen and lawgivers and its touch here and there denoting a brave attempt at the exquisite, was like a Senate bill. On the whole it was a fair example of the differing tastes and convictions of the nation.

It was a full house. McAdam's eyes roamed up and slowly made the rounds of the galleries. The usual delegation of diplomats was on hand, and senators' families—Helen was in her accustomed aisle seat, and as his eyes met hers, his wife winked and touched two fingers to her lips in affectionate salute. He looked up at the Press Gallery, packed to the point where reporters were standing all along the rear wall. They were on hand for the kill, too, and their running stories would tell of pitched battles won and lost and of the reasons behind these victories and defeats. They were, mostly, knowledgeable men and women who knew almost as much about the Senate as Chet McAdam did, and their news stories would be packed with expertise. It was not their fault that their stories would have to be incomplete. Their coverage was limited to what happened on the surface and to conversations with the principals in which inside information was carefully and strategically rationed. You did not lie to reporters; you merely left out certain facts which in cold print would do your side no good. And it was a good thing that was the way it was. Otherwise some reputations would suffer—John Alden Hughes's reputation for one, and Attorney General Charlie Mayborn's, and, probably, Chet McAdam's.

It was time. In the presiding chair, Tom Morgan had dotted the last "i" and crossed the last "t" for Ralph Bailey, and Bailey had lurched back into his seat. "Mr. President . . ." Chet McAdam began.

He began slowly and calmly, for he was determined to present the picture of a reasonable man reasoning with his peers. But the measured tones he affected in his first few sentences were inadequate to the task ahead; they could not contain the emotions and the pugnacity that churned and rose angrily within him. He felt his heavy body lurching impatiently as his words flowed out faster and as the rage born of frustration and long days of carefully restrained argument clawed its way into the open. He felt his heavy face grow heavier as his thick blood poured into it, giving it a feverish flush, and now he had to strike out at his enemies. He had to give the bit to his feelings and charge into battle.

He roared out his attack on the Supreme Court—"this little body of men who would frustrate the yearnings and ambitions of a great people." And, raising a clenched fist on high, "I ask you, Mr. President, what have we spawned in that little body of men across the street in their marble palace? Are we to stand by placidly, with cowardly mien and timorous trembling, while these willful and power-drunk men set themselves up as the ruling council of this blessed republic? Are we to stand by, shaking in our boots, while the Supreme Court takes it upon itself, not to interpret the law, but to make the law, and change the law, and manipulate the law according to its dangerously radical theories? Are we to stand by while those nine men, mouthing their lofty phrases and preening themselves in their robes, deliver our nation into domestic anarchy? Are we to stand by while those nine men then hand over this broken and disunited nation into the hands of the Communist slavemasters?"

From the galleries came a mass of sound that had the quality of a gigantic moan, and Tom Morgan permitted the sound to swell to its loudest before gaveling the room to order. Chet McAdam looked up at the galleries, his face angry and swollen, feeling the surging beat of blood at his temples.

"Where have we gone, Mr. President? What terrible path have we taken in this republic? What has happened to government of the people, and by the people and for the people? I ask you, Mr. President, is it government *by the people* when the nation is ruled by the Supreme Court? Is it government *of the people* when the Supreme Court says, 'We are the law'? Is it government *for the people* when the Supreme Court says, 'No, you may not do this, and no, you may not do that—to protect the people of the United States'?"

"Mr. President . . ." Claude Wilkins was on his feet, his face and figure prim, an arm extended languidly. "Mr. President . . . will the distinguished Majority Leader yield for a question?"

McAdam turned to Wilkins, his face bulging, his lips twisted into a snarl. He looked Wilkins up and down, silently, and as he did so he could hear his own breath issuing forth in little bursts.

"I yield," McAdam said shortly.

377

Claude Wilkins poked a thumb and forefinger at his blue polka-dot tie. "Mr. President, I may not have heard aright, and if so, I apologize for interrupting the distinguished Senator from New York. But may I ask, is it the speaker's assertion that the Congress has surrendered to the Supreme Court the responsibility of drafting the nation's laws?"

McAdam's upper lip rose in contempt. "I say to the distinguished Senator from Utah that that is exactly what I assert—to the shame of the republic!"

Wilkins smiled. "Then I say to the distinguished Majority Leader that I must be in a dream—for are we not, at this very moment, debating the enactment of a law? A law that will be passed or not passed by the Congress alone after a debate in which the Supreme Court will have no voice?"

"I have answered the Senator from Utah." McAdam's voice was flat and ugly. "Now, Mr. President, I shall continue . . ."

Now McAdam was warmed up to his task, and he plunged into it with a joyful fury. He lashed out at the opposition to the Court plan, and his mouth savored such words as "opportunists" and "devotees of defeat."

He sneered at his foes: "I find these men very much in evidence today, but, Mr. President, I would ask where were these men last November when an aroused and prosperous country trampled their standards into defeat? I will tell you where they were, Mr. President—they were skulking in their lairs, discredited and disowned by the electorate. The nation rejected their counsel last November. Can they possibly believe that now this same nation seeks their leadership? Oh, no, Mr. President, the nation has made it very plain what it thinks about the legislation we are now debating. It wants that legislation, Mr. President. It demands that legislation, Mr. President. And because my party believes in government *by* the people, the nation will get that legislation. And once again the calamity howlers and the soldiers of defeat will be discredited, disowned, rejected by the people."

"Mr. President . . ." This time it was Frank Hoar, his voice irascible, his face lined and tense. "Mr. President, will the Senator yield?"

McAdam made a point of not looking at Hoar. "I yield," he said, his tone dressed in a kind of contemptuous patience.

Hoar surveyed the galleries, his tongue tasting his lips daintily. "Mr. President, I always hesitate to interrupt the distinguished Majority Leader, for whom I have the highest respect and admiration. I realize, too, that the task set for him by the administration is a Herculean one, one to test the staunchest of partisans, and therefore I do not regard too harshly the boiling rhetoric and the desertion of logic which distinguish his remarks . . ."

McAdam's voice was like a whip. "I yielded for a question, Mr. President . . ."

"And I say to the distinguished Majority Leader that I am about to ask my question," Hoar put in hurriedly. "I hope I may remind the Majority Leader that the debate which just opened in this sacred chamber is an important one and that it may be prolonged; therefore I believe it would behoove us all to keep our patience and to make an attempt—make an attempt, I say—to keep a leash on emotions which only lead us into the tortuous paths of irrelevance . . ."

"The question! The question!" McAdam was roaring now. "Mr. President, I yielded for a question only. The distinguished Senator from Ohio is making a speech. I did not yield for a speech, but for a question . . ."

All over the chamber, senators raised a little storm of stage whispers, and in the galleries scores of feet shuffled and there were the sounds of moans and deprecatory little syllables. Above it came Frank Hoar's voice, cutting in on McAdam like a knife: "That question will be asked!"

"Then ask it!" McAdam thundered, forgetting in his rage the Senate rule prescribing use of the third person in communications on the floor.

The Vice-President's gavel pounded, but Hoar's voice came through again. "Mr. President, I confess I am sorely disturbed by this tumultuous turn of events, so early in the debate. I am sorry to see that the distinguished Majority Leader is letting his emotions take over. I really must offer a respectful suggestion . . ."

"Mr. President!" It was as if McAdam's big frame had been punctured by a sword thrust; his bellow was filled with both rage and pain. "Mr. President, I am not going to permit the Senator from Ohio to continue with his disgraceful performance. I raise a point of order, Mr. President. I remind the chair that a speaker need yield only for a question, and then only if he wishes to do so. I ask for prompt enforcement of that rule."

The look McAdam directed at Tom Morgan was glowering; his bottom lip outthrust belligerently. It was all arranged; he had talked it over with the Vice-President last night. Morgan could not mess it up.

Morgan's voice was gently sonorous. "The chair takes cognizance of the point of order raised by the Majority Leader. At this time I find it necessary to remind the Senate that the chair will rigorously enforce the rule which sets forth that a speaker may yield only for a question, and then only at his convenience."

Good boy, McAdam thought. Now twist it, Tom.

Morgan cleared his throat. "The chair would like to state further that it will strictly enforce the rule limiting senators to no more than two speeches on a bill in any day, and that the word 'day' in the rule will be interpreted to mean 'legislative day.' The chair does not have to remind the senators that a 'legislative day' is terminated only by formal adjournment of the Senate and thus, in effect, a 'legislative day' is not limited in length to the duration of a calendar day."

McAdam's insides surged with glee. As everybody knew, a legislative day could last for weeks, until the debate was concluded, and he would make this clear now.

"Mr. President," McAdam shouted, "I thank the chair for its ruling. And now I want to put the Senate on notice. Our legislative day will be a long one, gentlemen. For I tell you that there will be no adjournments, there will be nothing but recesses, until the debate is concluded."

All over the chamber, men jumped to their feet. At his desk, Frank Hoar stood, legs apart, shouting to be recognized, and Claude Wilkins was dancing up and down. But McAdam kept the floor in the midst of the hubbub.

"Mr. President," he roared, "I hope this chamber can be restored to order."

Morgan's gavel hammered away at the lectern, and in the galleries guards swept down menacingly on the restive and chattering visitors. Frank Hoar sat down, but Claude Wilkins's voice was almost a shriek: "Mr. President! Mr. President!"

McAdam glanced at Wilkins and then glanced away. "Mr.

President, I shall resume. Before I go back into the meat of the matter, however, I should like to say that I have been informed that the opponents of this bill have prepared a filibuster in a last, desperate attempt to defeat the people's wishes. I say to these desperate men—go ahead and filibuster. Go ahead and go through with your shameful plans. It will do you no good, for we have means to counter your obstructive tactics. I say to the Senate now: Those shameful tactics will not be tolerated."

The clatter resumed in the galleries, and suddenly a wild cry came piercing through the other noise: "Dictator! Dictator!" McAdam looked up to see an old man with a shaggy white mustache standing in the Visitors' Gallery, fist clenched at the end of an upraised arm. Even as he glanced up, McAdam saw a Senate guard plunge down into the crush of bodies and pluck the old man from his place and hustle him up the steps to the exit.

Tom Morgan's gavel beat its tattoo, and the Vice-President leaned forward, his face crimson.

"The chair cannot and will not tolerate disturbances in the galleries," he declared. "I would remind those in the galleries that they are present as guests of the Senate of the United States and that they may remain only so long as they behave in a manner befitting the dignity of the Senate. If the disturbances continue, the chair will be forced to empty the galleries."

McAdam turned to find Childs of Illinois pecking at his elbow, his stage whisper hoarse with excitement.

"Give 'em hell, Chet, give 'em hell."

McAdam's grin was ferocious. "That's what I intend to do, Harold. That's what I came up here for this morning."

"By God, Chet, you're putting on the performance of your life. I've never seen you any better."

"That's because I never felt better, Harold. This is one I intend to win."

Childs was beginning to move away again. "We're all with you, Chet." He stopped. "It's just too goddamn bad you have to work so hard for that guy in the White House."

McAdam looked down at Childs's cranky face. "He's the Boss, Harold." His words were short. "We're all in this together, but he's the Boss."

Childs's mouth seemed to grope for a smile but could manage

only a sneer. "Sure, sure. But he wouldn't get anywhere if he didn't have you, by God." He glided off.

Impatiently, McAdam resumed: "Mr. President . . ." But now he slowed his pace because he could afford to be more leisurely. He had won the first round with his insistence on strict enforcement of the rules, and now he was more relaxed. Hoar and Wilkins irritated him, but he had put them in their places for the moment. Now he could concentrate on his exposition of the Court plan, in all its simple attractiveness, and on the defense of the President who had led the party to such an overwhelming victory at the polls in November. He took an exultant delight in his carefully worded innuendoes, warning the faithful that if their faith wavered, the White House would punish their infidelity at the next election. McAdam was still worried about the waverers; they struck him as being too uneasy—he didn't like the look of their faces as they sat there in dutiful attendance on their leader's performance. Some of them undoubtedly would like to sneak off the reservation to dally with the Hoars and the Wilkinses. They had better be reminded of the necessity of staying in line.

As he put it aloud, "Our great party will see this legislation through to victory, as it has seen through to victory all the far-reaching and beneficent acts of legislation put forth by the administration in the last four years. We shall do it, because we are a united party—and we are a united party because there is no other way for a party to operate, no other way to get things done, no other way to assure the welfare of all members of the party in their individual struggles at the polls with the opposition." It was partisanship and politics-playing at its rawest, and McAdam did not care. He was standing on that floor to win, and you did not win in the Senate unless you went all out, unless you used all the weapons at your command, all the tricks learned in years of pursuing victory through gloomy back streets.

He spoke for three hours, and he enjoyed every minute of it. He toyed with Hoar and Wilkins and young Bill Martin as they sought to interrupt him for questions, brusquely rejecting every demand from Hoar and Wilkins, but once patronizingly permitting young Martin to put a query.

382

"Mr. President," Martin began in the shout he always used on the floor, "I should like to ask the distinguished Majority Leader if it is not a fact that a certain member of the Supreme Court has quoted the President of the United States as stating that he had to have a Supreme Court he could handle."

McAdam turned on Martin, his eyes hot with anger. "Mr. President, I shall reply to the junior Senator from Oklahoma that his sordid question does not deserve an answer, and I shall ask my colleagues if it is in keeping with the decorum of the Senate of the United States for a member of this house to deliver such innuendoes about our beloved President."

That was an uneasy moment; what Francis had said in a private talk during a party caucus was that the President wanted justices "who could be trusted." Goddamn those weak-kneed waverers, McAdam fumed; they were leaking all over the place.

At the end, McAdam turned over the floor to Hays of Connecticut, who owed the President everything for his re-election and who had developed into one of McAdam's most devout toilers in the legislative vineyard. Hays, who had been a boy orator and an Eagle Scout, was noted for his florid delivery, and McAdam paused on his way out to lunch to take in his opening. He found it in the Hays tradition.

Swaying slightly, the tall, slender Hays adjusted his horn-rimmed glasses and let fly: "The traitors are among us," he told the Senate quietly. "They move among us like thieves in the night, betraying the confidences of better men, selling out to the opposition, throwing their base ingratitude in the face of our great President. Their goal is political assassination plotted in the murky corners of their conspiratorial nights." His voice rose: "I accuse! I accuse! I accuse those men of plotting to sink the traitor's dagger into the back of John Alden Hughes!"

McAdam turned and strolled out into the cloakroom, to find the Vice-President suddenly at his side.

"The boy is in good form, Chet," Morgan said. He winked.

"Yes." McAdam grinned. "I think I heard that speech in Chicago, though."

"That's all right," Morgan said. "The public won't remember it."

They walked together to McAdam's hideaway office under the East Front of the Capitol, Morgan hurrying to keep up with the Majority Leader.

"You sure you want me for lunch, Chet?" asked the Vice-President. "Sure you wouldn't rather take a nap?"

"Nap! Hell, no! I can relax better talking to you, Tom. We'll just have a sandwich."

They sat together at McAdam's desk, eating their sandwiches —tomato and lettuce on toast—and saying little until they had taken their first sips of coffee.

Morgan put down his cup then, and grinned at McAdam. "I think you just might be making Hoar and Wilkins a mite nervous, Chet."

McAdam grinned back. "I figure on doing just that, Tom. They're pretty shrewd with their wheeling and dealing, but I don't believe they're as comfortable out there on the floor as they'd like to be."

"That was quite a performance, Chet. It's been a long time since I've heard one as good."

"I enjoyed it." McAdam took another sip of coffee, then put the cup down on his desk. "I've been aching to sound off after those long weeks of maneuvering. It does a man good."

"Yes, it seems to be doing you good, Chet. And I think you're getting the message across to certain members of the party who're coming up for re-election and will need some patronage."

McAdam's grin was cruel. "I hated to put it to them so bluntly, but, goddammit, you have to, Tom. I want those guys to trust me to reward or punish them. We've got to keep them in line."

"Well, you've made a good start, Chet. God all hemlock, you were like a bull out there. You're a new man when you're making a speech like that."

"That's a fact, Tom. I tell you, hard work never hurt anybody. It never hurt me. I eat well and I drink as much as I want, and so long as I get seven hours sleep I'm fine."

"Well, I sure envy you, Chet. If I ate half of what you stowed away, they'd be carting me off to Walter Reed Hospital."

McAdam looked at him. "You do look a little peaked, Tom. Why don't *you* take a nap? Hell, we can handle that bunch in there, today anyway."

Morgan sighed. "Nope. I'd like to, but I want to be in on the fun."

"Well, take it easy, Tom. This is going to be a long fight, and a tough one. Save your energy for the home stretch. We'll sure as hell need you then."

They strolled back to the floor together, exchanging meaningless chatter with the reporters en route, and when they got back to the floor Hays was still speaking—or rather, he had yielded for a question from Wilkins. As usual, the question was unimportant, but in the process of putting it, Wilkins managed to sneak in a remark about the dangers of centralizing the control of justice in Washington, and to wonder about the bill's effects on "the people's liberties." McAdam's face was solemn as he walked back to his desk, but inside he was smiling. Let 'em rave on, he told himself; we can handle them.

The excitement had returned to him, now that he was back on the front line. Hays was doing a good job; he was keeping the animals stirred up. McAdam felt his insides quivering with a kind of savage delight. Tom Morgan was right—he was a bull today.

Fred Pilney strolled over, one hand in his vest pocket. He took out a small square gold box and offered it to McAdam.

"Chet, why don't you take one of these?"

"Take one . . . ? What the hell is it?" McAdam whispered.

"They're for indigestion," Pilney said. "They're the only thing. I take one after every meal."

McAdam grinned at Pilney's face, sour with dyspepsia.

"Hell, Fred, I never had indigestion in my life. Give one to Tom Morgan; his stomach's always groaning."

Pilney seemed hurt. "It's just a precaution, Chet. Preventive medicine."

"Yeah." McAdam didn't want to talk about pills. "Hays doing all right?" he asked.

"Fine, I guess. I don't know where he gets those words of his, though. Ward's next, I reckon."

"Yes." McAdam looked around for Alpheus Ward and found him sitting upright in his chair, one hand cupped over an ear. "I suppose I'll have to stand still for some questioning first, though."

"Yes." Pilney's face was grim. "By God, when I speak, nobody's going to interrupt me. Goddamn hairsplitters."

"Right." Pilney was a bore, and McAdam suddenly found himself overcome with the desire to smoke a cigar. He stood up. "Hold the fort, Fred. I'm going to slip out for a minute or two and smoke an inch of cigar."

McAdam walked up the aisle, his step brisk, his face lined with good humor. He was having a hell of a good time and he was going to enjoy that cigar.

Francis Dalton tasted the nausea in his mouth as he leaned back in his chair to acknowledge, finally, what had to be done. It was a strange place he had come to, after the paths he had taken, after the goals he had sought. He had not intended to come to this place: to him it had never had the logic either of law or of the common-sense application of law. It was not the way he had ever viewed the law; it was so incompatible with his instinctive feeling for the law, with his previous instinctive knowledge of what was right and what was wrong. Distaste crept into him as there intruded the thought of what this would mean to the public outside. For a brief, unpleasant interlude, he would be a hero to the wrong people for the wrong reason; he writhed at the thought of their hands stretching out to touch him, to claim him for their side. He wanted nothing to do with them; they were alien to him and to everything he held to himself.

What had taken him to this place? Never before had he suggested in any way that he, a judge, knew best; indeed, he had always scoffed at those who believed there was a best to be known. There was a state to preserve, and he, as a servant of that state, was sworn to help preserve it. He had been proud of bearing the same honorable stigma which had been applied to Learned Hand, that he had been guilty of *il gran refuto*—an unwillingness to employ the power of his office to direct the application of law in the direction he thought wisest. He had never sat in judgment of the legislatures; that was the prerogative of the electorate. He did not see himself as a trustee, watching over the welfare of a citizenry seeking extralegal benefits from their fellow men. He had looked upon the Constitution coldly, and he had given each litigant his due under the rules currently existing. To him, the law had always been the law; it had never been what some judge, his emotions upset by circumstances, decided it was. He had paid his

386

obeisance to the Bill of Rights, but only when the employment of those rights wreaked no damage on the commonweal.

Yet, there was this miserable Gleason.

There was, unfortunately, this miserable Gleason. He should be dead. He should never have lived. But there he was, cowering in his death cell in Sing Sing. He was, perhaps, something less than a human being because of what he had done, but if you had to seek out the law and examine it, then he was as much a human being as Francis Dalton. He was a human being, an individual, and—worse—he was in trouble. He would not have come to Francis Dalton's personal attention otherwise. It was no good to call him names or to use his name as you would use profanity; his offenses against mankind were not the point at issue. The trouble he was in because of those offenses was the only thing that mattered.

Article V of the Bill of Rights did not make any exceptions. It said that no person shall be deprived of life, liberty, or property without due process of law. It did not say "except for the Gleasons of the world." There was no mention of regulation or restraint by the government in the Bill of Rights. There was no mention of exceptions. The Bill of Rights meant Gleason, as well as Dalton.

Francis stood up and picked up the stapled pages brought to him by the lawyer, Hoff. Here it all was, and how good was it? He didn't know. He really didn't know, and he couldn't know until he had had time to look into it. He had read it and he had digested it, fully. He knew what was in those stapled pages. What he didn't know was whether the intricate argument was supported by the thousands of pages of testimony and exhibits; it would take the rest of the day and most of the night to find out.

"It reads pretty phony." He remembered Jake Moriarty's words now, grasping at them for the reassurance he needed to throw the brief aside and forget it. He had asked Jake, "What do you think?" when Jake came in with coffee, and Jake had told him. Jake had read every word of it, too, before it came to his own eyes, and Jake was a good lawyer.

But the reassurance wouldn't come. That was Jake Moriarty's opinion; it was not Mr. Justice Francis Dalton's. To be sure, the material read pretty phony; there was even that dangerous glibness in it that shrieked of the carefully contrived. It was too pat, too well presented. And Hoff was no good. He was, obviously, a high-level shyster, a professional defender of men like Gleason for what he could get out of it in headlines and other notoriety. He could not trust Hoff. It was not logical to trust Hoff, to believe what he said and to reject what the FBI said. He had no illusions about the FBI's determination to win its cases, no matter what, but the FBI was not a liar. It might be a blunderer at times, but it was not a liar. And there was the rub. It did not look as if the FBI had blundered—but it might have. Hoff's presentation, in all its glibness, yet had a worrisome insistence; its argument left you wondering. Likewise, there was every reason to believe that the witness Burch was a good witness and true, but Hoff's argument did not so much dispute this as to suggest that in all his goodness, in all his trueness, Burch might have committed the human error of saying too much, of piling on evidence which could have been faulty atop evidence which was good enough.

Francis sat down and slumped in his chair and leaned back with his hands cradling the back of his head. He could not escape it—this was the way it had to be. The state was important; it had to be preserved. But its preservation had to be achieved within legal limits. It could not destroy an individual if the evidence calling for the destruction of that individual was in the least tainted. It could not destroy even an individual such as Gleason on those terms. It could not afford to do so and remain the kind of state to which free men could give their allegiance and their lives.

He enjoyed the luxury of leaning back; now he could enjoy a simple luxury, because out of the thoughts that had passed through his head in the last few hours there had come a kind of serenity, a relaxation of the tensions his doubts had imposed on his mind. He had believed that he would have to postpone sorting out his thoughts about his personal problems until he had disposed of the case of Harry Gleason, the spy. And now they were all sorted out; he had sorted them out without quite knowing it, that is, until a few minutes ago, when he had reached his decision on the Gleason case. And then he had realized, with a suddenness that was almost a physical shock, that he had also reached the decision on the case of Mr. Justice Dalton. In considering the case of the United States vs. Harry Gleason, he had also, subconsciously, considered the case of Francis Dalton, Supreme Court Justice and individual. And now, because he had discovered, late, a personal image of the kind of state he believed in, and realized what precautions must be taken to preserve that state so that it remained the servant of the individual—now he had found the personal serenity he had been seeking. He had many people to thank for helping him—Bea, bless her, and a judge named Hume and a politician named Frank Hoar, and a legal shyster named Hoff. For Hoff, after all, had provided the opportunity he needed to sort out his thoughts, to lay his doubts out in the open and examine them. In the case of Francis Dalton, there remained only the necessity of communicating his findings to the people who would be concerned with them. He would see to that as soon as he had finished with Harry Gleason. That would take time, a long nighttime, but he would get at it immediately. And when he had finished with that case, he could turn again to his own.

Hoff's "new material" was suspicious. Even its more solid points had that quality of glibness that raised the question of their authenticity. There was work to be done to explore those points, to make sure, to arrive at that point where he could either accept them or discard them. And in the meantime, he had to act—just in case. It didn't matter that the evidence was of the scantiest, and suspect as well. What mattered was that there was an individual involved—an individual named Gleason, but nevertheless a human being. A man could not be executed until the highest court seized this last chance to give serious consideration to his claims and prepare an opinion on those claims. He would work all night to give those claims the serious consideration of the Court, as represented by Francis Dalton. It was the only thing that could be done.

Francis looked at his watch. Three-thirty. The necessary calls should be made now. It would be indecent to wait any longer. He stretched an index finger to ring for Jake Moriarty, and the buzzer sounded.

Damn! He had told Miss Swanson he'd take no calls. But—it could be the White House.

"Yes," he said.

"Mr. Justice." Miss Swanson's voice was tremulous. "It's the Vice-President. He insists on talking to you. He says it's an emergency."

Tom Morgan. An emergency—but what? "Put him on," Francis said.

"Francis." Tom Morgan's voice was low.

"Yes, Tom, what is it? What's the matter, Tom?"

"Francis—Chet McAdam just dropped dead in the cloakroom." Francis gripped the phone, and his other hand clenched and unclenched swiftly.

"Chet McAdam—dead? Tom . . . ?"

"Yes, Francis, they're taking him out now. He just fell over, all of a sudden. He died immediately—at once. Helen is here—she's going out with the body."

"Chet McAdam—my God!" Francis held onto the edge of the desk with his free hand. "My God, Tom!"

"Yes, he went out to smoke a cigar and then he seemed to be dozing, the page said. Then he got up and he fell over onto the floor and there was blood streaming from his mouth and nose."

The details, Francis thought; Tom Morgan has to say something, so he is furnishing the details.

"Tom, thank you for calling," he said. "I'll do everything I can, of course. And you'll keep me in touch?"

"Yes." Morgan's voice was trembling now. "Yes, I'll keep you in touch, Francis. I thought I should call you."

"Thank you, Tom. Thank you. God, Tom, we've lost a great friend."

"Yes, we have," Tom Morgan said. "Yes, we have, goddammit." And he hung up.

Francis put the phone back on the hook and pressed the buzzer to call Jake Moriarty.

"Yes, sir?" Jake was in the doorway at once, shutting the door almost on his tail.

"Jake, you'll have to get busy. I want to put through a stay of execution for Gleason. Get things moving, immediately."

"Yes, sir." Jake moved back to the door, his hand reaching for the knob.

"And then come back as soon as you can, Jake. We've got a lot of work to do. And, Jake . . ."

"Yes, sir?"

"Jake, Chet McAdam has just dropped dead in the Senate cloakroom. Apparently of a stroke." Francis put up a hand as Jake started to speak. "We'll talk about it later, Jake, when you come back. After you put through that stay. Bring everything in here as soon as the stuff is ready for my signature."

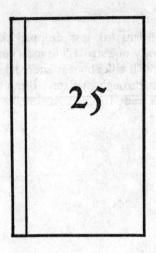

25

For a man who had snatched only an hour's nap on his office couch, Francis Dalton took considerable pride in the fact that physically he felt very well. He didn't believe he could say the same for Jake Moriarty. Before he left the office, he had had literally to lead Jake to the couch and lower him onto it. "Sleep until tomorrow, Jake," he'd told him. "I've called Miss Swanson and told her nobody is to come to the office today." Jake Moriarty could not have lasted long enough to be taken home; he was as comfortable as he could be with the blanket over him and Francis' old cashmere topcoat rolled up as a pillow. They had worked on the Hoff material all night—until five o'clock this morning. Then Francis had taken his brief nap while Jake put the papers in order, and when Jake woke him up, Francis was ready instantly for his final check of the papers; he had emerged from his deep sleep completely alert. He had called the White House as soon as it was decent to do so, and John Alden Hughes had said, "Yes, of course, Francis. Come over as soon as you can." So after a long shower and a quick shave, Francis was doing just that. He settled down comfortably on the seat of the cab. There was in him a vague, elusive sadness, yet he was content; he had done his job—

as it was prescribed in the rule book, and in his brain and his heart.

He was not even disturbed by the national hubbub it had caused. He glanced down at the Washington *Post* and *The New York Times* on the seat beside him, but he did not pick them up. DALTON HALTS GLEASON EXECUTION—FULL COURT TO ACT, said the *Post*. And the *Times:* DALTON STAYS EXECUTION OF SOVIET SPY—MOSCOW HAILS ELEVENTH HOUR ACT—CHIEF JUSTICE SUMMONS COURT.

The other headlines were still on Page One, too, at least in the *Post:* BEATRICE HART SILENT ON JUSTICE TROTH and PUBLISHER DEPLORES FUROR OVER ADAMS BOOK. Francis smiled; he didn't have time for bitterness. There was a publisher with a good press department—"deploring" the furor was as good a way as any to keep the furor in the headlines. Well, all that would have to wait until other things had been taken care of. There was the fact that Mr. Justice Dalton was not exactly a national hero this morning. First the Freddie Adams scandal, and now his stay of execution for Gleason. The President was probably waiting for him with a shotgun. And the Chief Justice would not be pinning any medals on him.

Yet Bacon had sounded surprisingly mild when he phoned at one o'clock in the morning from Tucson. The Chief Justice had even apologized for calling at "this unearthly hour." And then, "Of course, Mr. Justice, this has startled me. I am having the full Court summoned back to Washington immediately. We shall take up the case tomorrow morning."

Francis said, "Of course, Chief. I expected that."

"Yes." Bacon's tone gave the impression of uneasiness. "Mr. Justice, I hardly think you can expect your action to be upheld. The stay almost surely will be vacated."

It had been still too early for Francis to know, so he had said merely, "I did what I believed right, under the circumstances. Of course, I have complete trust in the Court."

But now he knew. He had done his homework—he and Jake Moriarty. He had given Gleason the whole night; he had checked and cross-checked every page of material on file in the case. He had *studied* Hoff's appeal. And his decision had come, clear-cut and unequivocal, the kind of decision about which he could say no other conclusion was possible.

Hoff's material *had* been bogus. It had been put together cleverly and it had been convincing, up to a point. But it had failed on every one of the major tests Francis had put it to. Not only was Gleason guilty, which was not the point, anyway—what mattered was that his trial had been conducted with the utmost fairness—but the FBI had *not* erred, even in the business of the wiretapping, and Burch's testimony was unassailable. It had taken all night to satisfy himself, but he was satisfied. The extraordinary sitting of the Court would be a brief formality; Francis would vote with the majority to vacate the stay.

Now he could reproach himself for his ugly shortness with Hoff when Hoff had found him with a midnight phone call. "God bless you, Mr. Justice," Hoff had said, and Francis had replied, "Don't blaspheme, Hoff"—and hung up. But Francis had wanted no blessing from anyone, least of all Hoff, for doing his duty. And he had been weary and irritable.

Francis glanced out the window of the cab, and found what he was looking for. The flags on the two Senate Office Buildings at half-staff for Chet McAdam. He looked back and to his left for the assurance that the Capitol's flag was also at half-staff. Curiously, it gave him comfort to see this last tribute to his friend. Poor Chet. The human sacrifice. The first sacrifice to John Alden Hughes's Court-packing plan.

The President's statement in the newspapers was a warm one, and Francis knew it was sincere. "Chester W. McAdam died in the performance of his duty. He died as a soldier, just as truly as men died on the Normandy beaches and at Valley Forge." That was true. And it was also true that, like some of those men on the Normandy beaches and at Valley Forge, Chet McAdam perhaps did not have to die. Francis had to say perhaps, because he did not know the answer to the question that had gnawed at him ever since Tom Morgan's voice told him of the collapse in the cloakroom. Chet McAdam had to fight, but did he have to die? Would he have died if the President had given him his reward on time? Francis did not know. Nobody really knew. Francis could grieve for his friend, but he could not indulge in a maudlin snap judgment condemning the President.

He picked up the *Post* with its headline MCADAM FALLS DEAD IN SENATE CLOAKROOM. Frank Hoar had said it for that bitter little body of men: "My friend Chet McAdam was murdered. He was struck down by the sword of another man's ambition, another man's greed for power." It was sad that Frank Hoar should have said such an ugly thing. And yet it was one way of putting it for those who could believe that Chet McAdam would be alive this morning if it had not been for the Court bill. Francis could not agree with Frank Hoar, but now he knew one thing. He knew that he, Mr. Justice Francis Dalton, had been wrong in the past. He would not accuse John Alden Hughes of murdering Chet McAdam, but he would forever— like a Monday morning quarterback—blame the President for not finding another way to get his job done when the question came up of what to do about Chet McAdam and his lifelong ambition. He would blame himself, too, for not seeing at the time that another way should have been found, because he realized, now, that he had been too careless in his consideration of the importance of the individual. The state, in the person of the President, had had a job to do, but in battling to do that job it had dealt with the lives of individuals. Chet McAdam was something far more important than the Majority Leader of the Senate; he was an individual, with an unalienable right to life, liberty and the pursuit of happiness. That right had been abridged by the President, with the condonation of Francis Dalton, among others. He would not judge John Alden Hughes, but from now on, on that point, he would disagree with him.

He owed Gleason thanks for helping him to see things as they had to be, as they were meant to be by the men who had sat in the humidity of that Philadelphia summer and written the rules in simple, easy-to-understand language. He owed Gleason thanks for making him see that there *were* absolutes in the Bill of Rights and that they could not be tampered with lest men die unjustly, or too soon, or without proper regard for the legal necessities. In the end, the decision had to be against Gleason, but that was unimportant. What was important was that Gleason's rights—the rights of the individual—had been protected. What was important, too, to Francis Dalton personally, was that he had been made to see that Chet McAdam's rights, and the rights of other individuals, had been abridged.

He felt an exultation intrude upon his sadness. He found himself exulting over a new truth within him: the truth that in a civilized republic man is responsible for his brother before he is responsible to the state. It was good, and cleansing, to see the truth that the man in government, whether he was sheriff, mayor, or Supreme Court justice, was there to protect man's rights, not to make man subject to the rights or the requirements of a well-ordered state. It excited him to know for the first time that in some cases the protection of a man's rights could and *should* cause temporary damage to the state. The Russians have a great deal, Francis reflected, but they do not have that.

The cab pulled into the southwest gate of the White House and rolled up the drive to the South Portico. "Jeez, that's the President there with his kid, ain't it?" the cab driver said.

John looked in the direction of the outthrown arm, and saw the President and little Bounce. They were standing in the Rose Garden, as though at attention. Francis paid the cab driver and got out and strolled over to the father and his son.

"Hello, Francis." The President turned, with a hand still resting lightly on Bounce's towhead. "We're having a funeral. Tweet is getting a military burial."

"Come see the grave—come and see it, Mr. Justice!" Bounce was bursting with excitement.

Francis joined them on the gravel path and shook hands with Bounce, who had leaped in front of his father, before exchanging a handclasp with the President.

"Who is Tweet?" Francis asked.

"He's my bird—he *was* my bird, my canary," Bounce said. "He died. We just buried him." He kicked at a toy cannon underfoot. "See, we gave him a salute. Eight guns. That's all the shells I had."

"That was a very nice tribute, Bounce," Francis said. "I'm sorry Tweet is dead, though."

"Yes." Bounce looked down at the little grave with its wooden cross. "He was a good bird. He had a bad stomach." A tear crept down through the freckles on his cheek. Bounce kept his head down. "I've got to go now, Mr. Justice. I have to go to school. Goodbye, sir." And he ran off.

"Poor little cuss," Hughes said. "He didn't want us to see him crying." He took Francis' arm. "Francis, let's go into the office. I've got some coffee in there."

They sat down in chairs on opposite sides of a coffee table under the portrait of George Washington, and the President poured the coffee from a silver urn.

"Well, Francis." Hughes's voice was tired. "You've stirred up the animals."

"Yes, I'm afraid I have, Mr. President. All for nothing, as it turns out."

"You mean . . . ?"

"Jake Moriarty and I worked all night on the Hoff stuff. It didn't hold up. There was no new argument that was at all supported. I'll vote to vacate the stay with the rest of them tomorrow."

"Well, now." The President looked hard at Francis. "And you stayed up all night—for nothing?"

"No, not for nothing. I didn't quite mean it that way." Francis' smile was wry. "I had to stay up—to find out. You see, I wasn't sure, and the only way to make sure was to give him a stay while I checked."

The President's sigh was huge, and two little vertical lines in his cheeks saddened his face. "Francis, this is—a surprise." He put down his cup. "Damn! I don't suppose I have to tell you that I was very unhappy at the stay. It seemed—frivolous."

"I'm sorry. All I can say is that it was not frivolous. There was doubt, not very reasonable doubt, but doubt. I had to make sure."

"Yes." The President picked up his cup and sipped from it slowly. "And of course it's raised hell all over the country. It hasn't—helped." A small smile formed on his lips. "And yet, I suppose I should congratulate you, Francis. I have to admit that what you did was in the tradition."

"Thank you, Mr. President. But I'm afraid I didn't think of it in that way. It just had to be done."

"I wonder." Hughes's smile departed. "I wonder if things have to be done—if they're injurious to the commonweal." He shook his head, as if trying to clear it. "Yes, I suppose they do. I suppose I can't expect the Supreme Court to make my problems its prime concern."

Francis' voice was soft. "Our function is a different one. We have to concern ourselves with other matters, even including the rights of an enemy spy." Self-consciously, he felt rising in him an irrelevant surge of affection for poor Baker, poor Baker with his faithless wife. Baker was a part of it, too; for better or for worse, the Bakers acted according to what they believed was right.

The President took another sip of his coffee. "But you didn't want to see me just to tell me this. And you could have called me—as I'm sure you would have."

"No, I didn't come here just for that, Mr. President. John—I would like to talk to you about something else." The *John* was necessary. He wanted this to be a talk between two friends.

"Of course, Francis." The President put down his cup and smiled. There was a wistfulness about him that Francis had not seen before. "You know that we've always been able to talk—about anything. It's something we've kept, through all the years, through all this."

"John, the best thing to do is tell you outright." Francis was eager to spill it all. "I want you to know that I can't go along with you any longer on the Court bill. I don't believe in it any longer."

The President's smile was gone. "Well—this is rather a surprise, Francis. I'll admit that." His mouth turned up, but the smile wouldn't come back. "But I don't punch my friends in the nose for that sort of thing. However, may I ask why?"

"Yes, sir, of course. It's so sudden, of course you have a right to be mystified. I don't quite know whether I'll be able to put it right, but it boils down to the fact that I've discovered the individual is more important than the state. And I don't believe the individual's rights can be protected properly if the Supreme Court is changed so that it reflects one man's point of view."

Francis paused to look at Hughes, and the President said, "Go on, Francis—I'm not going to interrupt."

"It boiled up in me while I was working on the Gleason case last night," Francis said. "It suddenly occurred to me that if we had all like-minded justices on the Court—justices who thought exactly as you did, or exactly as any other President did—then it might not be possible to grant a stay of execution to a man like Gleason. I knew that you had refused to grant clemency, and yet

398

there were reasons why I felt I should grant a stay. In the kind of Supreme Court you visualize, John, that might not have been possible."

He paused, but Hughes remained silent—and grim.

"I'm afraid we—all of us—have been trying to tamper with something of vital importance to our freedoms. We have been trying to achieve conformity in an area where conformity is a peril to the country. We have militated against the left, against the Communist menace which threatens our liberties. But the fact is that if we can curb the liberties of the left today, then at some later day we can do the same thing to the extreme right, or to the center, or to any other segment of opinion which at the moment happens to be unpopular.

"Your Court plan has been the climax of your struggle to reorganize a disorganized country, to protect it against its enemies both at home and abroad, to impose a national discipline that would strengthen the country, that would give it the national competence to resist its enemies. But in so doing, you have tried to whittle down the individual's basic liberties. You have done so in a good cause—in an attempt to save the country from Communism. I trust you implicitly, John—but I trust the Constitution more. If you could do this, John, so could some other President, a bad President who seized power and became a dictator. All this should have been plain to me from the beginning, but it wasn't. Perhaps it was the atmosphere in which I grew up, when everything was such a mess and I believed the American people were in need of some good old-fashioned Cromwellian discipline. Perhaps it was my early association with your conservative movement, when I discovered that all the decent people—or those I believed were decent—were on your side, while the other side had only the malcontents and the wild-eyed pinks. Perhaps it was just something chemical in me. At any rate, I realized last night that all along I had been rationalizing our right to tamper with the Constitution because *we* were all right, *we* were decent, *we* could be trusted."

Francis picked up his spoon from the saucer, then laid it down on the table. He had to say the rest.

"I was so wrong—and I believe you are wrong. What I believe now, what should always have been plain to me, is that no man can be trusted—*no man can be trusted to be a law unto himself,* even if his intentions are good. *No* man can be trusted. That is why we have the Constitution."

The President stood up and walked over to the French doors and looked out into the Rose Garden, then walked back to his chair and sat down. He took a cigarette from the box on the table and put it between his lips for a moment, but instead of lighting it, he put it down.

"A bad President," he said. "I see your point, Francis, but in one respect, at least, you're wrong. There's no such thing as a bad President, Francis. There couldn't be. The country wouldn't let any man be a bad President. Once he moves into this house, the country won't let him be the kind of man who could be a bad President. You couldn't know, because you've never been President, but that's the way it is. Thank God for it, too."

He picked up the silver table lighter and lit his cigarette. "But, of course, that's not really the point. The point is that you can't go along any longer, and you have come to me and told me so, honestly—and immediately. I do appreciate that."

Francis looked the President in the eye. "I had to tell you at once."

"Yes, you did. *You* did, because you are that kind of man. I'm not sure another man would have found it necessary."

"I'm sure any man would do the same thing."

"I'm not. Because, you see—you didn't have to. It wasn't necessary."

"Wasn't necessary? But why not, John?"

"Because, Francis, it doesn't matter any more."

The President stood up and walked over to his desk and leaned against it in the way Francis had seen him do so many times.

"The Court bill is dead."

"Dead! Dead? But the debate has just started."

"And it has just ended, Francis. It ended yesterday afternoon when Chet McAdam dropped dead in the cloakroom. When Chet McAdam died, the Court bill died with him."

"But—why? You've got the votes. McAdam totted them up for me. He was sure."

The President's voice was low, but its tone could not cloak the bitterness. "We *had* the votes, Francis. We—I—don't have them any longer. The boys have walked out on me."

Sympathy flooded up in Francis, inundating all the other feelings that had surged selfishly within him. "But this is pretty sudden, isn't it? Are you sure?"

The smile on the President's face was contrived and small. "Yes, I'm sure. I'm damned sure. It's all over now. I don't blame you, Francis. You've had your doubts all along; I saw that. I saw you struggling with them from the beginning, and I suppose I was pretty brutal about it. I wouldn't let you out from under— because I needed you. But those gentlemen on the Hill—I'm not sure I'll ever be able to understand them. They would have gone along, unwillingly, against their instincts, for the sake of their personal friendship with Chet McAdam. They were going along. We did have the votes. And now . . ." The little smile vanished and the hurt lines were creasing his forehead again. "It seems to me to be a hell of a way to legislate—with your glands."

Francis said slowly, "And now? How do you know for sure?"

"It's all there in the papers. I'm sure you saw Frank Hoar's statement."

"Oh—Hoar. That was too bad; I'm sure Frank will regret saying that. But . . ."

"Oh, Hoar doesn't matter, particularly. And the others aren't quite so ugly in their reactions. But they have reacted, Francis. The Speaker of the House called me last night, and so did Fred Pilney and Alpheus Ward and the Vice-President. They're cashing in their chips, Francis. They are not going along now with the Court bill. I didn't ask them why; I didn't have to. They are walking out because Chet McAdam is dead, and if they do not charge me with his murder, they at least hold me partly responsible. Anyway, the bill is dead."

"I'm sorry. I'm truly sorry."

"Thank you. I know you are. *You* are my friend, thank God. I don't have to apologize to anyone for what I have done in trying to put that Court bill across, and I know *you* wouldn't want me to apologize. I did what I believed had to be done. That is all a President can do. It's his responsibility, and he has to accept it. He can't do things the way somebody else wants them done, because that somebody else does not carry the responsibility."

He walked back to the chair and sat down. "But, Francis, what I wanted to explain to you—if you haven't already seen it—is how unnecessary it was for you to come here and tell me you could no longer support the bill. You didn't have to. You could have kept quiet and let me believe you were prepared to go along with me to the last—after all, it wasn't your fault the Senate decided to walk out on it."

Francis' reply was short. "I couldn't have done that."

Hughes looked at him and reached over and put his hand on Francis' arm.

"No, you couldn't have. Thank you for being that kind of man."

"John—thank you for saying that. I do appreciate it, more than you can know. But I don't want the atmosphere in this country to be such that you, the President of the United States, feel you should thank anyone for being honest, for doing what he believes is the right thing. And I can't help thinking that if such an atmosphere exists, people like me may be partially responsible."

"We all are, Francis. That's the tragedy of man's imperfection. Because certain things have to be done—or we believe, sincerely, that they have to be done—and because of *how* things sometimes have to be done in a system whose goodness does not always prohibit obstructionism—because of the state of the world—all of us find ourselves cutting corners here and there. And, unfortunately, reaching the point where we rationalize this corner-cutting, even argue in its favor. Since man is not yet among the angels, there doesn't seem to be any other way, Francis. Often, from where I sit, I'm convinced there is no other way. It may sound strange, but I have to do things those ways, or be unworthy of the responsibility given to me. I have to do my best for the majority, Francis, while regretting the broken bones among those in the minority."

Francis waited, to be sure the President had finished. "And there is where our basic disagreement has come. Of course you must act for the majority. Every President must, in his public worthiness. But don't you see—just as your function is to promote the welfare of the people as a whole, our function—the function of the courts—is to guard the welfare of the individual, of the minorities. Our function is to decide that any interference with the basic rights of the citizenry, as set forth by the Bill of Rights, is wrong. It is wrong. Period.

"The Atkinson case and the Gleason case have taught me something. Or rather, they have reminded me of some truths, some realities, some facts of life, I had carelessly overlooked. William Allen Hume is right—it is our duty to keep the Bill of Rights abreast of the times, to use the Bill of Rights to thwart every modern, streamlined effort that comes along with the intent of abridging man's rights. It's been a long time since Thomas Jefferson and Madison, and over those years man has come up with some clever ruses to deprive his fellows of their liberties. This man is refused his rights because he is a Communist, this man because he is a Nazi, this man because he is always calling strikes. The courts must use the Bill of Rights to confound the oppressors, by whatever political names they call themselves, no matter what the temporary damage to the republic.

"There has been much talk, especially here in the White House, that the Supreme Court is forever sticking its nose into matters that do not concern it. I now disagree. I believe it is time the Court acted to expand the area in which it exerts judicial influence. In the past, the Court has been too unwilling to intervene in so-called 'political questions.' Well, political questions, so-called, involve people, and where people are involved the Court also should involve itself. I go even further. It is now my conviction that the Court should watch over people who are likely to get into trouble for political reasons, and should stand between them and that impending trouble. A citizen should be protected from getting into trouble; by the time he is *in* trouble it often is too late to help him."

Francis leaned back in his chair and waved an arm self-deprecatingly. "I'm talking too much, John. I shouldn't have to make a speech."

The President's smile was a valid one, and his voice was soft. "Yes, I'm afraid you did have to make a speech, Francis. A man has to make a speech when he arrives at a new place in the road, as you have. And I know how to listen."

Francis looked at his friend and was warmed by what he saw.

403

Now was the time to pay the price. There were some debts he could not pay this good friend, but there was one decent thing he could do to help this man to whom he owed so much.

"John, there isn't much more, and I'll be brief. I'm resigning from the Court—and Bea and I are going to be married."

At first the President seemed not to have heard. He was gazing straight ahead. Then, in a sudden motion, he stood up and plunged both hands in his trouser pockets.

"You want to resign?" Hughes's voice was flat.

"Yes. It's what I have to do."

"What you have to do?" Francis had never heard the President's voice so low.

"Yes. It's—I owe you that." Francis hurried on now, anxious to be done with it. "I'm not resigning because of any ideological differences we may have. That would defeat the principle of the separation of powers. I'm resigning because of—because of Bea and me."

"What are you talking about?"

"It's quite simple. You have no right to dictate my principles, my political philosophy; I'm a member of an independent branch of the government. But you do have a perfect right to stand in judgment on my private life. You're the head of the government, and you have not only the right but the duty to insist that your appointees avoid public scandal. At first I was angry when Harry Weiss talked to me about it, but then I realized I had let myself in for all this, and that you had a right to be concerned. Worse than that, I dallied with Bea; in a sense, I held her at arm's length while I was pondering the unpleasant aspects of the situation—unpleasant, that is, to my position. We should have been married long ago."

Hughes walked over to the French doors and again stood there looking out at the grayness of the Rose Garden. Still with his back to the room, he said, "Francis, you're a damned fool."

He turned then, and put up a hand as Francis started to speak. "No, Francis, you don't really have any more to say. You've said enough. I suppose it's been my fault, the way I've poked into people's affairs, but I never dreamed you'd misunderstand. What's this about Harry Weiss?"

Francis was puzzled. "Why, he called me and said you were

concerned about me—about Bea and me. He said you didn't want me to get into any trouble. So I naturally assumed you were worried about a justice of the Supreme Court being mixed up in a scandal. It angered me at the time, but now I see you had a right to be concerned."

"My God!" Hughes walked back behind his desk and sat down. "This is ridiculous. Of course I was concerned about you. About *you*, Francis, not about a Supreme Court justice. I knew how damned moral you were, and I was afraid all that stuff in the gossip columns would hurt you, deeply—irreparably. My God, you did presume—you and your damned Irish-Catholic-Puritan guilty conscience. I had no intention of interfering in the relationship between you and Bea. I'd like to point out that I knew Bea before you did, and my only regret has been that she is not marrying my brother Jimmy instead of you."

Francis was standing now, emotions piling up inside, his lips dry, his mind a confusion of thoughts. "I don't understand."

"Dammit, Francis—what do you mean, you don't understand?" Hughes's exasperation seemed to be hurting his face. "I've just made my position crystal-clear. I was concerned about you and Bea because you were—are—friends of mine. I was concerned as I am concerned when one of Harry Weiss's children has scarlet fever. But I never intended to tell you because you were a member of the Supreme Court you could not marry the woman you loved." Hughes grinned. "Francis, you idiot, I am not the Church of England and you are not a poor, mixed-up young king. In this country, that sort of situation doesn't exist; it can't exist. I'm only the President of the United States, not the legally appointed guardian of my friends' private lives."

Through the warm excitement, the excited affection, that surged in him, Francis was trying to understand. "But I've always been led to believe . . ."

"Francis, you've always been led to believe certain things—by yourself. It was your own peculiarly rigid—and irrelevant—moral standards that led you to believe certain things." Hughes's smile widened. "Don't include me in on your Puritanism, young fellow."

Francis looked at the President, still trying to settle his thoughts, to winnow out the self-doubts. He wanted to cling to the good feeling Hughes's words had given him, but confusion was sowing suspicion in his mind: Dared he surrender himself to this good feeling, so suddenly?

"But, John—are you doing the right thing?" Francis had to be sure. He could not let his friend indulge himself in official carelessness for friendship's sake. "Are you doing the right thing? For the country? I came here to resign, because I felt I should. I still can't help believing it is the only way. It is all such a mess."

"Hell, yes, it's a mess, Francis." Hughes's voice was firm and his mouth was solemn again. "But that's your private affair. I expect you to sweat it out, like a man—and get married as soon as you can. You'll need Bea at your side to help you sweat it out. And as far as the country is concerned—well, I think the country can take care of itself in matters such as this. I believe the country, give or take a few sanctimonious old maids, eventually will conclude it's none of its business whom you marry, so long as the woman of your choice is not a convicted Soviet spy. I think you should have discovered long ago that the country as a whole consists of pretty decent citizens who are instinctively disinclined to stand in moral judgment of their fellow men. There is an inherent fairness in this land of ours that has enabled it to retain its national conscience while becoming the most powerful nation in the world. Because of that fairness, our people have not been corrupted by the power they wield."

"But, John, the people expect certain things in a Supreme Court justice." Exulting in his inner glow, Francis thought: but *I* must be fair, too.

"You are still confused. The country's stake in the matter is whether or not you are an honest judge, a man of principle. The country expects you to be that, and that's all. And if I'd ever had any doubts about that, Francis—which I haven't—you have made that clear to me today."

"Thank you, John." Now Francis could permit himself the smile he had been denying. So this *was* the way it was coming out. Now he could believe it, exulting in the belief. It was turning out all right, despite his fears. And yet, a new and separate good feeling rose in him. It was good that it was turning out this way, but it wouldn't have mattered if it hadn't, because he had known where he had to go.

He said, "Thank you again, John," and his grin grew wider and a little self-conscious. "I'm—rather embarrassed to say it, but I was sure you would demand my resignation, under the circumstances."

"Under the circumstances!" John Alden Hughes threw his head back, and there was nothing wrong with the famous Hughes laugh that filled the room. "Under the circumstances, indeed. Francis, the circumstances haven't changed a bit. You're the same man I appointed to the Supreme Court. Perhaps you're even a better man, even if I don't—and never will—agree with the premises you've just submitted to me. I appointed an honest man named Francis Dalton to the Supreme Court and I still have an honest man named Francis Dalton on that Court. You've insisted upon retaining your honesty, even despite my honestly unwitting attempts to tamper with it."

A grin spread over the President's face. "As a matter of fact, I do have a proposition to make to you, Mr. Justice. Even though I have new respect for you, I've still got *my* job to think about, and I'm damned if I like the idea of having still another justice I can't depend upon on that cantankerous Court. While you've been talking, Francis, I've been thinking some Machiavellian thoughts. You have to think those kind of thoughts in this office; it may not be pretty, but whenever something like this happens the President has to consider how it can be turned to his advantage, how it can be used to further the program *he* feels is necessary to the country's general welfare."

Hughes put up a hand to intercept the words he saw forming on Francis' lips. "No, let me finish. I *have* come up with something, Francis—a gimmick, if you will, that would permit me to turn this situation to some small advantage. It would help me if you did resign, Francis—not now, but in a few months' time—and then accept an appointment as head of the new Defense Mobilization Board. That way, I could appoint a man I could count on to the Court, and I'd still have the benefit of your services in an important job in which I am sure you would perform superbly. I have to offer this suggestion, Francis, because what I am trying to do here is more important than anything else."

Francis was surprised at the swiftness of his reply; his instincts were in full control now.

"John, I couldn't do that. I couldn't consider it. My answer has to be a flat no. I'll resign if you wish, but if I do the break will have to be clean. I would not . . . cooperate to deceive anyone."

The President sighed. "All right, I suppose I knew that would be your answer. But I had to try, because the President of the United States can't be a blasted Rover Boy. He has to look at things as I just did, in order to try to get the men he wants in the jobs where he wants them, to do the work he feels has to be done. But, perhaps unfortunately for the country, you're not the kind of man who'll play in my ball park, Francis. I regret it; at the same time I honor you for your integrity. I may be uneasy, from a political viewpoint, at having you remain on the Court, but I'm glad I can count you among my friends. Very well, Francis, you'll stay on the Court and I'll make do somehow because I'm not giving up. I can't give up. But . . . you're quite a man, sir."

Francis sensed a new calm coming over him. He could relax. He had done what he believed was right. And it had been right— in every way. "John, you've made me feel very good," he said. His voice was low in his new serenity.

"Thank God I have, Francis. That's the way you should feel." Hughes's nose wrinkled and his smile became wry. "Now I think we're both running out of words. It's been hard on both of us— all this sentiment."

Francis smiled. "Yes." Then, irrelevantly, "I suppose I'd better go home and get some sleep." *After I make that phone call,* he told himself.

"You certainly should." Hughes stuck out his hand and Francis took it, and the handclasp had its old firmness and warmth. "Thank you again. Go home and get some sleep and then later . . . Francis, would you do me a favor? Come over for dinner tomorrow night—you and Bea. There'll be just Liz and me."

"Yes, of course. Thanks, John—we'd like to."

"Good." The President of the United States put an arm around the justice of the Supreme Court and they walked together toward the door. "Let's say seven-thirty or so, Francis. It'll be—at last—like old times."

Francis Dalton walked out and down the wide corridor and through the West Wing foyer, and when the scattering of early-bird reporters clustered around him, he smiled at them and kept saying, "No comment, gentlemen." He liked reporters; it was too bad he couldn't tell them something. He decided he would walk down Pennsylvania Avenue to the drugstore at the corner of Seventeenth Street to make the call. He looked at his watch. It was only nine-thirty. Well, he would have to take a chance on waking her up.